Lyndon Johnson's Dual War

Kathleen J. Turner

Lyndon Johnson's Dual War

Vietnam and the Press

The University of Chicago Press
Chicago and London

Kathleen J. Turner is assistant professor of communication, University of Notre Dame.

The University of Chicago Press, Chicago 60637
The University of Chicago Press, Ltd., London
© 1985 by The University of Chicago
All rights reserved. Published 1985
Printed in the United States of America

94 93 92 91 90 89   5 4 3

Library of Congress Cataloging in Publication Data
Turner, Kathleen J., 1952–
   Lyndon Johnson's dual war.

   Bibliography: p.
   Includes index.
   1. Vietnamese Conflict, 1961–1975—Journalists.
2. Vietnamese Conflict, 1961–1975—United States.
3. Johnson, Lyndon B. (Lyndon Baines), 1908–1973.
4. Press and politics—United States.   5. United
States—Politics and government—1963–1969.   I. Title.
DS559.46.T87   1985   959.704′3   84-16389
ISBN 0-226-81731-8

Contents

Preface

This study examines the effect of presidential-press interactions on Lyndon B. Johnson's communication on Vietnam. It concerns three areas crucial to contemporary history: the presidency, the news media, and Vietnam. The study centers on the relationship of the three and on the relationships among interpersonal, public, and mediated communication. Through the examination of these complex interactions emerges evidence of the ways in which Johnson's relationship with the media influenced his Vietnam war rhetoric.

The study is subject to the flaws and frustrations of contemporary history. Although the wealth of resources at the Johnson Library inform the study, written documents will never provide historians with as much detail on the processes of decision-making, attitude change, and statement formulation as they would like. Johnson's reasons for deciding to give the Johns Hopkins speech, the details of his discussion with Walter Lippmann, and the role of various media accounts in motivating the delivery and content of that address, for example, are at best only suggested by historical materials. These inherent limitations are accentuated by restrictions that affect the availability of potentially relevant materials: the aides' files that might hold further information on the administration's actions remain largely unprocessed, and the National Security Files on Vietnam and on speeches are still heavily classified.

Moreover, to examine the possible effect of presidential-press interaction on Lyndon Johnson's Vietnam war rhetoric requires an exploration of numerous other concerns, important in understanding that potential relationship but not directly and specifically bearing on it. Thus, while the "credibility gap" charges came to center on Johnson's handling of the situation in Vietnam, their roots in Johnson's image as a master politician, in his surprisingly low budget in January of 1964, and in his denial of the stories about his fast driving cannot be ignored. The story of presidential-press interactions related to public statements on Vietnam thus follows a sometimes torturous route through the complexities of the presidency, the press, and Vietnam in all their aspects.

Even with these difficulties, however, the study clearly delineates the ways in which Johnson's perceptions of both individual members of the press and the role of media in society affected his planning, scheduling, and designing of public statements concerning America's role in Southeast Asia.

The study begins by setting the context for the research, examining in particular the rhetoric of limited war and presidential-press relations. As the chapter titles indicate, the study then proceeds chronologically, from a brief overview of Johnson's prepresidential years through the end of his tenure in office. At the outset the narrative delineates two essentially separate stories, one on Johnson's relationship with the press and the other on Johnson's handling of Vietnam. The two threads grow increasingly intertwined; by the end, they are virtually inseparable.

Chapter 5 differs in scope from the others in that it traces, in depth, the evolution of Johnson's address of April 7, 1965, at Johns Hopkins University. The chapter is intended to provide a detailed examination of the role of media-government interaction in the development and delivery of a major presidential message. To that end, the magnification of the microscope is doubled, illustrating the intricacies of presidential-press interactions more fully through a close analysis of this episode. Although it is not *the* watershed of Johnson's administration, the Johns Hopkins speech was selected for this magnified assessment because, coming at the midpoint of Johnson's tenure in office, its evolution indicates the ever-increasing intertwining of the LBJ-press and LBJ-Vietnam threads.

I am grateful to many people for their assistance in the preparation of this work. I cannot adequately express my appreciation to David M. Berg, professor of communication at Purdue University, who has influenced every page of this work. Two David Ross grants from the Purdue Research Foundation and a grant from the Lyndon Baines Johnson Foundation made research at the Johnson Library financially feasible. The archivists at the Johnson Library, especially Tina Lawson and Nancy Smith, provided the guidance that made research in the presidential papers an exciting and rewarding task. George Reedy, George Christian, James Reston, Walt W. Rostow, and Bob Hardesty were most generous with their time and recollections, and Liz Carpenter shared not only her wit and insight but also lunch at the Headliners Club in Austin.

Finally, very special thanks belong to my mother, one feisty, wonderful lady; to my dear husband Ray, who married me despite the rigors of this project and the differences in our politics; and to my cat Tigger, who has slept on it all.

1

Introduction

Lyndon Johnson never intended to become a wartime president. The wars that made Johnson's political blood course were those that attacked poverty, disease, ignorance, and bigotry, not those involving small but annoying countries in far corners of the world. He considered himself, both by training and by temperament, to be a man ideally suited to deal with the nation's domestic problems. As Johnson saw it, then, something akin to divine providence had thrust him into the White House at that very moment in history when the nation was ready to move, through bold and innovative advances in education and civil rights, to establish a Great Society.[1] By his own perception he was, quite simply, the right man in the right place at the right time.

Although the Johnson administration must be credited with significant pieces of social legislation, the president's dream of a Great Society was never to be fully realized. Despite his proclivity for domestic issues, Johnson found himself inextricably drawn, bit by bit, into increased military involvement in Vietnam. Unable to squelch the problem by a quick show of force, Johnson gradually committed an increasing number of American troops to the battle, redefined their advisory role as one of combat, and ordered massive bombing raids on North Vietnam. Well before he left office in January of 1969, the war in Vietnam had become both the president's and the nation's preoccupation.

As the nation's involvement in Southeast Asia increased, so too did Johnson's efforts to justify his policies to the American people. Initially Johnson fought against making the conflict into a front-page issue. Not until the Gulf of Tonkin incident, eight-and-one-half months into his presidency, did Johnson deliver his first major public statement to the American people specifically dealing with the situation in Vietnam. During the remaining four-and-one-half years he was in office, however, the president publicly addressed the problems of Vietnam in news conferences, remarks, and televised speeches on more than two hundred occasions.

However impressive the quantity of Johnson's Vietnam war rhetoric, its overall effectiveness was, of necessity, heavily dependent upon the media of mass communication. The vast majority of American citizens know of the policies, politics, and personalities of contemporary presidents only through mediated channels. Not oblivious of the degree to which the success of his communication on Vietnam was dependent upon media treatment, Lyndon Johnson called upon a variety of strategies in his interactions with the press as he sought to enhance his news coverage. Yet his efforts led to an antagonism on the part of many members of the media. It was this antagonism that, at least in part, ultimately led Lyndon Johnson to decide not to seek a second full term in office.

In light of the foregoing analysis, this study consists of a systematic and comprehensive investigation of the interaction between President Lyndon B. Johnson and the nation's press to determine how that interaction affected, and was affected by, the president's attempts to communicate with the public concerning the war in Vietnam. Key to its purpose is an understanding of the perceptions held by Johnson and by members of the media—of themselves, of each other, of the presidency, of the role of the press, of Vietnam—for it was on the basis of such perceptions that Johnson and members of the media interacted, and it was on the basis of that interaction that public statements were issued (or withheld) and news stories developed—and in turn further perceptions formed. The focus, then, is not on how the American public received Johnson's Vietnam rhetoric as transmitted and translated by the media, but rather on the ways in which the dynamics of the interactions between Johnson and the press affected Johnson's messages on Vietnam. The study traces relationships among interpersonal, public, and mediated communication in this context.

The purpose of the study is twofold. First, it delineates the ways in which Johnson's relationship with the media influenced his communication regarding Vietnam, illuminating a significant aspect of a critical era in history. In a larger sense, the study provides insight into the more general issues of the rhetoric of a limited war and the relationship between presidents and the media. Each of these issues will be examined in turn, as they illuminate Johnson, the press, and Vietnam.

The Rhetoric of Limited War

Regardless of their causes, American wars have always thrust upon the president heavy rhetorical responsibilities. War is an enterprise that involves "the direct or indirect participation of the entire community," not simply military personnel; it follows that, in A. A. DeWeerd's words, "there can be little effective progress toward mobilizing the physical and intellectual war potential of the nation until a large section of the public . . . [is] awakened to an interest in military matters and problems."[2]

The responsibility for awakening the public interest, as well as for providing a rationale sufficient to produce the necessary levels of support for a war effort, clearly belongs to the president. As commander in chief of the armed forces and as holder of the highest office in the land, American presidents traditionally have been able to base their appeals for support during wartime on widely accepted moral values. Thus, Americans in overwhelming numbers enthusiastically endorsed wars "to end all wars" and "to make the world safe for democracy." United States military involvement in Vietnam, however, posed more difficult problems of justification. Faced with a war lacking the apparent moral qualities of earlier armed conflicts, Presidents Kennedy, Johnson, and Nixon successively struggled to discover those arguments that would be sufficient to convince the public of the justification for America's presence in Vietnam.

By the time Lyndon Johnson succeeded to the presidency in 1963, the United States had been involved in the affairs of Southeast Asia for more than a decade. His approach to Vietnam during the first months after his abrupt assumption of the office was basically one of avoidance. He would not be the president to lose Vietnam, as he vowed early on; yet he preferred to forge ahead on domestic affairs. As military efforts expanded, however, Johnson found himself compelled to address the issue of America's role there with increasing frequency.

In doing so, however, Johnson had to strike a balance. On the one hand, Johnson was convinced that the lessons of history—Munich, the Second World War, the Korean conflict, and the Cuban missile crisis—all proved that unchecked aggression led only to wider conflict. "Aggression" served for Johnson as a devil term, rich in symbolic meaning, implying voracious, immoral greed and violence. By definition, then, aggression must be stopped, in Southeast Asia or wherever it occurred. Moreover, Johnson knew the traditional image of Democrats as being "soft on communism," a charge he abhorred.

On the other hand, Lyndon Johnson desperately wanted to avoid being pushed into a more feverish stance. He knew that Red China constituted a formidable external audience for his war policies, and he did not want to risk war with that Communist nation. Despite General Curtis LeMay's blithe recommendation to "nuke the

4

Chinks" to solve the problem, Johnson feared such catastrophic solutions and did not want to be backed into a position where that was even an option. He did not want to lose Vietnam, but he did not want to start World War III either.

Johnson thus confronted the dilemma of justifying a limited war, a dilemma that may be impossible for any president to resolve rhetorically. The destructive potential of available military technology demands, for both humane and political reasons, that the United States fight contemporary wars at less than its full capability. This limitation is of course in marked contrast to, for example, World War II, which constituted a total national military effort, made possible by a total rhetorical effort that convinced the public such action was necessitated by the moral principles involved—the defense of democracy and freedom. Such all-encompassing efforts are precluded in a nuclear age, for the president dares not risk (as Johnson dared not risk) the creation of a war fever that demands more aggressive action and that might ultimately lead to pressure to use nuclear weapons. The moral arguments traditionally employed to support American wars are thus inappropriate, and the political arguments that have supplanted them appear to be ineffective, lacking the same persuasive power and psychological impact. Deprived of the moral imperative of all-encompassing war efforts, a limited military involvement thus presents all the rhetorical hazards of a wartime situation—a perceived drain on the nation's resources, the loss of young lives, and policies subject to debate—without the rhetorical advantages of a fervent patriotic appeal with clear-cut heroes, villains, and victories. Unable to find convincing arguments to adequately support the war without endangering the country, the president—as Lyndon Johnson discovered—confronts growing opposition to his war policies.

The dilemma is only heightened by the power and prevalence of contemporary media: television brought the gore and violence of the Vietnam conflict into American living rooms night after night, juxtaposing plans for economic development of the Mekong Delta against pictures of defoliated jungles, and contrasting optimistic statements of progress with casualty rates superimposed on maps showing Viet Cong advances. During the Korean conflict television was in its infancy; only 2 percent of American homes owned a set in 1950, and newscasts were primitive, underfinanced, fifteen-minute operations. In contrast, Johnson faced Vietnam just as network news programs were expanded to half an hour, placing them at the fringe of prime time, expanding their news-gathering budgets, and increasing the need for news. Vietnam thus became our first television war.

Moreover, Vietnam was difficult for Americans to fathom, with its cultural, political, and historical contexts so different from Western tradition. Reporters thus encountered a full-blown version of the problem faced by most foreign reporters: having too much to cover while lacking the background on the country with which to do an adequate job. That the coverage concerned a guerrilla war, unlike the battles of World Wars I and II, further complicated the correspondents' task. In turn, media institutions perceived the average consumer of news to have only a limited interest in acquiring a more substantive knowledge of the situation. As a consequence, Michael Arlen observed, "sixty per cent of the people in this country right now know more about the 'weather picture' over major metropolitan areas than they could ever wish to know and a good deal less about Vietnam than might be useful."[3]

The conduct of a limited war is thus complicated in an age of television. Lacking clear-cut devil figures and front lines, such a conflict must be translated into palatable news packages night after night. As the Vietnam conflict ground on, the president's problems were exacerbated as the national press gravitated from an initial position of essential disinterest concerning Vietnam to one that was in large measure actively hostile to presidential policy. Walter Lippmann castigated Johnson for bombing North Vietnam at all, while Joseph Alsop hectored him for bombing only restricted targets. The disparate and conflicting views of the American public grew even more disparate and conflicting without rhetorical satisfaction of the issue. Providing rhetorical satisfaction proved all the more difficult because, although we tend to forget in light of the dissent of later years, Lyndon Johnson was acutely aware of the fact that he was being criticized not only for doing too much in Vietnam, but also for doing too little.

In the end, then, the opinion of the American public constituted what has been called "the essential domino" in the war. Johnson sought to, as he put it, "get our people to support us without having to be too provocative and warlike."[4] During two critical periods in the war—July of 1965, with the major increase in the number of American troops in Vietnam, and March of 1968, in the wake of the Tet offensive—Johnson considered declaring a state of national emergency, calling up the reserves, appearing before Congress to request special appropriations, and making an all-out public appeal to engender national support for his actions. Yet in each case, he felt the price of the flood of patriotism to support his policies was too high, so high that he had to risk not calling for it. He continued to hope to gain public support without having to be "too provocative and warlike." On those occasions when he did present major public justifications for the war, as in the Johns Hopkins and San Antonio addresses, the president abjured any new aspects of his handling of the conflict, emphasizing instead that he still followed the same policy and presented offers made "fifty times and more."

Yet the support that Johnson sought steadily eroded in the ambivalence of the limited-war rhetoric. Johnson's statements were neither sufficiently aggressive nor sufficiently conciliatory; his emphasis on consistency only exacerbated the sense of stalemate. The core of the problem, Halberstam noted, was that Johnson "could not unleash the dogs of war without creating dreams of victory."[5] Yet the victory did not come, and the essential domino fell. "Americans do not like long, inconclusive wars," reasoned one North Vietnamese official, "and this is going to be a long, inconclusive war. Thus we are sure to win in the end."[6] Ten years after he was relieved of his post in Vietnam, General William Westmoreland would concur: "In the final analysis," he decided, "we had the power but we didn't have the will." In his estimation, "we in this country cannot send men to the battlefield unless the public is going to be behind them. It is up to the politicians to ensure that such is the case."[7]

Lyndon Johnson, a consummate politician, could not find those arguments that would be sufficient to convince the public that America had to fight in Vietnam—and that it was equally imperative that America restrain herself in doing so. Even through 1967 and 1968, as his staff expressed growing concern over the restlessness and lack of a sense of purpose on the "home front," Johnson's public defense of his policies on Vietnam never appeared as a sustained, organized effort. Regardless of how strongly he felt America's obligation to support South Vietnam, he recognized that for the United States it was a limited war. In a nuclear age, in the face of Communist China and Russia, an all-out military effort accompanied by a government campaign to engender public support was not only inappropriate but dangerous. The result was a double bind: an inability to convince a large portion of the population that America was doing enough for Vietnam, coupled with an inability to convince another large element that America was not doing too much—ultimately leaving only a relative few who were not dissatisfied in some way with Johnson's conduct of the war. Given this understanding of the context in which he handled Vietnam, as George Herring points out, Johnson appears not so much the foolish or evil one as "a beleaguered executive attempting to maintain an established policy against an immediate threat in a situation where there was no attractive alternative."[8]

The dilemma is brought home by the fact that Eugene McCarthy gained greater support in the New Hampshire primaries of 1968 from those unhappy that Johnson had not taken a *harder* line in Vietnam than from those seeking a "softer" approach.[9] Given the constraints of the rhetoric of a limited war, it may not be possible to generate home-front support for military efforts of the sort that Westmoreland demanded. Johnson realized that the major question for the American public was the fundamental one: Why Vietnam? Yet he could not provide the simple, compelling answers they sought.

The Presidential-Press Relationship

A second area of focus in this study is the relationship between the president and the media. Although the interaction between government officials and members of the press has commonly been described as adversarial, significant elements of the relationship may be lost if it is not also viewed as symbiotic. As Michael Grossman and Frances Rourke point out, "the adversary concept provides no mechanism for understanding the enormous amount of cooperation and even collaboration that takes place between press . . . and government."[10] Government officials, particularly the president with his national constituency, must have the cooperation of the press if they are to effectively communicate with their publics. The press, on the other hand, needs government both to maintain its constitutional guarantee of freedom and as a source of information.

In spite of their mutual dependency, however, the major goals of government officials and members of the media are not only different, but antithetical. Each side seeks to maximize its ability "to select the items of information that will be defined as news and disclosed to the public."[11] Thus,

> executive officials seek to confine the choice as much as possible to items that will be favorable to them. Reporters, on the other hand, try to broaden the choice so that all potential items of news—both favorable and unfavorable—are included in the pool from which the selection of items to be published will be made.[12]

Because of their conflicting needs, therefore, each side attempts to structure the government-press interaction in ways that will allow one to exploit the weaknesses of the other and enhance its own

8

relative position. This blend of the symbiotic and the adversarial constitutes the relationship between the president and the media.

One of the president's chief advantages in his continuing power struggle with the press lies in the fact that his "activities sit so high on the media's agenda of subjects to cover."[13] Because of the public's fascination with news from the White House and because of the competitive nature of the news industry, media personnel have very little choice as to whether or not they will publish news of presidential activities. White House correspondent Sam Donaldson, for example, reports that "I have to argue not to be on the World News Tonight some nights 'cause I don't think I have the story, whereas many of my colleagues at ABC are desperately trying to get on."[14] Since the demand for such information is constant and, for the most part, exceeds the supply, the ability of the president to create situations that will dominate the headlines is much enhanced. Lyndon Johnson exploited this advantage of his position, for example, when in February 1966 he planned a meeting with South Vietnamese leaders in Hawaii which was calculated to overshadow the anticipated adverse publicity from William Fulbright's Senate hearings on Vietnam.

In addition, a president can wield a great deal of control over the access to information allowed correspondents, favoring those friendly to his administration and restricting those who have been critical. When William S. White, columnist and longtime friend of Johnson, traveled to Vietnam as a correspondent in early 1967, the president requested that General Westmoreland give him special attention as "an old and treasured friend of mine."[15] In contrast, Johnson refused an interview to Al Otten of the *Wall Street Journal* because he perceived the newpaper's reporting to be biased, and he would not allow Dan Rather to film staff members at work because he believed both Rather and CBS to be actively antagonistic to his administration. Johnson also utilized his ability to establish formats for press contacts in keeping with his preference for less formal communicative contexts. His "restless experimentalism about technique," to use Elmer Cornwell's phrase, resulted in everything from barbeque news conferences conducted from a bale of hay to background dinners with editors and publishers.[16]

Just as a president is able to turn the media's need for information to his own advantage, so too can the press exploit certain weaknesses of the government. Public officials, except in direct-communication situations, have long depended upon those who report the news to convey their message to the people. Even when a statement is available in full, as in a television broadcast, much of the public relies on media reports of the message for both its actual content and its implied meanings. While the press may have relatively little latitude in deciding whether or not to publicize news of the presidency, it has a great deal of flexibility in determining the manner in which the news will be presented. As Delmer Dunn verifies, the press has great "control over *how* these messages shall appear—that is, to what extent they will be conveyed with favorable symbols, how much space they will receive, and what sort of display they will be given."[17] Illustrating the point, Bill Moyers observes that "depending on who is looking and writing, the White House is brisk or brusque, assured or arrogant, casual or sloppy, frank or brutal, warm or corny, cautious or timid, compassionate or condescending, reserved or callous."[18] Although the selection of one set of these paired terms over the other could unquestionably have a profound influence on a reader's perception of the situation described, the basis for the selection of one term over the other may be largely subjective. The media's judgments of Johnson were based on three areas of consideration: personal, professional, and economic.

1. *Personal.* White House reporters felt, quite simply, that Johnson ought to recognize the fact that they were human beings with private lives and personal needs and to take this fact into consideration as much as possible when making his plans. Thus, their major objection to the frequent last-minute announcement of press conferences and travel plans was not so much that it hampered their professional duties (although it did that, too) as that it infringed on their personal lives, leaving them tied to the White House press room and unable to make plans of their own. It was an infringement that many reporters came to regard as the result of a pathological need for secrecy and a sadistic urge to punish the press corps, traits they extended to other aspects of Johnson's presidential performance—including the handling of Vietnam.

A second aspect of personal considerations is that of the interpersonal relations between the president and individual members of the media. As human beings rendering human judgments, correspondents, columnists, and commentators based their political assessments of the president in part on their personal assessments of Lyndon Johnson. Thus, when "several long-term correspondents at the White House" were asked why Lyndon Johnson was not receiving as favorable press treatment as that accorded John F. Kennedy, they replied: "Although Johnson has made even more of an effort than

Kennedy to cultivate and woo the press, most White House reporters don't care for him as a person. They liked Kennedy and enjoyed his company. Johnson hasn't won their affection."[19]

A third aspect of presidential-press interaction attributable at least in part to personal considerations arose from the fact that reporters often praised Johnson when government policies paralleled their own attitudes and opinions, and criticized him when they differed. The point at which personal opinions become professional political punditry is, of course, an ambiguous one. Nevertheless, Walter Lippmann's initial support of Johnson's presidency found its basis in the fact that the new chief executive was handling the office in a manner the columnist deemed appropriate, and his latter opposition to the war in Vietnam was rooted principally in his personal belief that Europe, not Asia, should be the focal point of American foreign policy. The administration, convinced that such personal attitudes formed the heart of political columns, thus invited Lippmann to preview Johnson's Johns Hopkins address and asked Joseph Alsop to report to the White House on his trip to Vietnam because it was "good public relations." As many members of the media gradually shifted their views from disinterest in Vietnam to opposition to Johnson's policies, however, William S. White would come to feel the personal animosity of his colleagues. "Every journalist I know who consistently supported Viet Nam was truly punished" by members of the press, he contended, especially in the East, while he knew "of nobody who was punished in the press because he was a dove."[20] These personal attitudes influenced jounalistic judgments, for White just as for Lippmann.

2. *Professional.* In addition to personal considerations, professional concerns formed a basis for media estimations of Johnson. These concerns included the technological and psychological demands of media newsgathering, to which the Johnson administration was expected to adjust.

At the most basic level, technological demands included what Bill Moyers termed the mechanics of press coverage, such as transportation, typewriters, hotel reservations, baggage handling, and telephone lines. Supplying these needs constituted a primary responsibility of the press office, selected and supported by the executive branch. The president's press secretary was thus largely responsible for the details of enabling the press corps to cover the president, a responsibility that members of the press corps regarded as their right, not their privilege. The extent to which the press corps felt this way is most easily illustrated by their reactions when they felt their rights were abrogated: press conferences conducted in the Oval Office, while walking around the South Lawn, or during barbecues at the LBJ ranch made it difficult for reporters to cover the president as they thought they were entitled to. Because impromptu news conferences caught correspondents off guard and prevented the attendance of specialized reporters who could ask more detailed questions, they were viewed negatively. The many unorthodox formats for these conferences precluded televised coverage, which left broadcasting representatives longing for the formal sessions of the Kennedy years. Reporters perceived Johnson's failure to adapt to these technological concerns as a failure to recognize their needs and thus accused the president of inhibiting the role of a free press in a democracy.

Professional concerns for newsgathering thus went beyond technological matters to conceptions of the role of the mass media in contemporary political life, conceptions the press corps felt Johnson not only did not share, but could not comprehend. To members of the media, the adversary relationship between press and president was both a natural and a necessary offshoot of their role as watchdogs for the American public. When they perceived Johnson to be attempting to set up "crony" relationships with them (such as during the flight back to Washington when he promised to make "big men" out of them if they would cooperate), and to be using them for his own purposes (such as his release of various budget figures), the press corps' assessment of Johnson's political savoir faire fell.

These professional judgments were then accentuated by the contrast between the press corps' conception of the presidency and their perceptions of Lyndon Johnson. The man's earthy language, robust stories, and attention to media accounts may have made him personally interesting, but on a professional level his attitude and behavior were judged to be unpresidential.

Professional concerns of the press corps thus ranged from the technological constraints of newsgathering to views of the presidency and the press, but the basic assumption by members of the media was that all of these concerns dealt with the right of the press to cover the presidency in an unimpeded manner, coupled with the expectation that a responsible government must cooperate.

3. *Economic.* Joining personal and professional criteria for judgments by the press were economic considerations. The Johnson administration was expected to cooperate in the profit-making concerns of the media institutions whose representatives were covering it; failure to do so evoked bitter complaints from those representatives which, when cast in economic terms, appeared to receive a

12

serious hearing by the president. George Reedy thus convinced John-son to drop the Saturday morning briefings as a staple in his news-conference diet by pointing out the cost to newspapers unprepared to handle unexpected news in their Sunday editions; George Christian gave serious attention to the White House Correspondents Associa-tion's complaint that their institutions' money would have been wasted had anything happened to Johnson in Austin while they were stranded in San Antonio. In both situations, the president's preroga-tives were considered secondary to the economic concerns of the media.

In viewing Lyndon Johnson's interaction with the press, then, both cooperative and competitive elements are apparent as each side sought to maximize its ability to define what would become news. Johnson continually sought to gain the understanding and support of the media, which he recognized as a prerequisite to reaching the American public as he wished. His strategies to enhance his press coverage thus influenced his rhetorical decisions throughout his presidency, including whether to issue public statements, how to schedule public statements, and what the content, organization, and language of public statements would be.

Given that members of the media ultimately serve as gatekeepers, Johnson was among those public officials who "may be willing," as Dunn suggests, "to alter the content of their messages to make sure that the message will appear. They may be willing to alter them even more in order to have them appear with prominent display."[21] This adaptation is most apparent in such specific instances as the evolu-tion of the Johns Hopkins address. Yet it is clear elsewhere as well, as when staff members tagged information as suitable for release from Austin on a slow news day and in the discussions of public opinion which often linked and frequently equated press attitudes with pub-lic attitudes.

Similarly, members of the media saw cooperation as an important element in their efforts to report the news. Philip Potter of the *Baltimore Sun* provided periodic assessments of Johnson's press rela-tions, and Charles Bailey of the *Minneapolis Star & Tribune* apolo-gized for not being available when the president asked to see him. Members of the White House press corps agreed not to write about the novelty of a news conference following a cabinet meeting in exchange for Johnson's holding one; when Tom Wicker of the *New York Times* unknowingly violated that agreement, they turned their anger on him, complaining that "Tom is screwing us up with the president." The relationship was not entirely symbiotic, however. Part of Lyndon Johnson's difficulty with the press resulted from his belief that it was the business of government to govern, and the business of the press to simply convey that governance to the people, preferably in a manner that would generate support for the president. Johnson's offer to make reporters "big men in their field" if they would provide favorable news coverage was entirely consistent with his belief that cooperation and compromise were beneficial, especially if they enabled him to reach his goals.

This concept of the role of media in the governing process was reinforced by Johnson's discomfort with the media, for his personal political style was not easily transferred to large groups and mediated channels. The effective one-on-one persuasion and legislative maneuvering that brought Johnson to power in the Senate had only partial success in the White House, and Johnson's inexperience in the role of public spokesman underscored his preference for interpersonal channels of communication which allowed him to "keep his options open." Whereas Johnson regarded the secrecy and maneuvers that accompanied such an approach not only as his right but as essential components of good government, members of the media viewed them as antithetical to the concept of democracy—a concept in which a free and active press serves a key role. Johnson, in turn, concurred with Edward P. Morgan's assessment that members of the media were prima donnas who not only expected to be informed of government actions but wanted to be consulted before decisions were made.

When journalists bridled at his approach, then, Johnson felt unappreciated, misunderstood, and betrayed. He found it difficult to, in Liz Carpenter's words, "forgive them their press passes."[22] In a fit of pique he would accuse columnists of turning against him on Vietnam because "they knew that no one receives a Pulitzer Prize these days by simply supporting the President."[23] He found it even harder to forgive them for the effects of this change of heart, not only on the American public but on members and associates of his administration as well. Johnson may well have been thinking of the media when he grimly quipped, "cast your bread upon the waters and the sharks will get it."[24]

The catch phrase of the Johnson administration was "the vantage point." Used as the title of the president's memoirs and found throughout the writings of his staff, the phrase signifies that the view

14

from the Oval Office is unlike that found anywhere else. Lyndon Johnson often wished that reporters understood that. Yet, as David Paletz and Robert Entman observe, "Presidents complaining about the press are like ships' captains objecting to the sea": they may not like the storms, but they could not be where they are without it.[25]

2

The Prepresidential Years

As with almost everything else about the man, accounts of Lyndon Johnson's youth and early political career are filled with well-honed tales and points of controversy. According to the family scrapbook, for example, his birth on August 27, 1908, inspired his paternal grandfather to ride through the countryside, telling neighbors and relatives that "a United States Senator was born today—my grandson." Although repeated in the glowing campaign biographies, this story is scoffed at by other accounts as the creative reconstruction of history by Johnson's mother, Rebekah Baines Johnson. Certainly Rebekah and Sam Ealy Johnson, Jr. had great ambitions for their firstborn. Both the Johnsons and the Baineses had achieved a degree of status and wealth only to lose it to the vagaries of the starkly beautiful but agriculturally exhausted terrain of the Texas Hill Country. The family fortunes of Rebekah and Sam fluctuated as well, as he tried his hand at such pursuits as real estate and farming.

Yet Sam Ealy Johnson's avocation was politics. Over the course of eighteen years, he was elected to five terms in the Texas legislature, filling the same seat that Lyndon's maternal grandfather had held after serving as Texas's secretary of state. As a legislator Sam encouraged his son's interest in politics, taking him on occasional trips to Austin and debating about populist philosophy and current events both in the state capital and at home. Three oft-repeated stories point to the ways Lyndon's father sought to encourage his son's political development: that the father used to wake his young son in the morning by shaking the boy's leg and saying, "Get up, Lyndon, every boy in town already has a thirty-minute head start on you"; that he told him, "if you couldn't come into a room full of people and tell right away who was for you and who was against you, you had no business in politics"; and that the older Johnson advised, "When you're talking you ain't learnin' nothin'." Young Lyndon thrived on these political activities.

Rebekah's admonitions on behalf of education met with a much less sympathetic reception. Although Lyndon was quick enough to perform well with relatively little effort in high school, he refused to go to college. His mother's reasoned arguments turned to desperate pleadings, which were then joined by his father's threats. Lyndon's reponse, around his sixteenth birthday, was to seek his fortune in California. Johnson's later accounts of this period of his life would be, in Merle Miller's phrase, "straight John Steinbeck."[1] The storyteller in him spun tales of hard times, scant food, menial labor for minimal pay, and hitchhiking the fourteen hundred miles back home. While he probably had some of these experiences, more careful examination reveals that he spent most of his time out west working in the law office of his cousin and that his return to Texas a year or so later was in the comfort of another relative's Buick.

Even after his adventures in California, however, Lyndon Johnson was not yet convinced of the need for an education. Such biographers as Doris Kearns and Robert Caro contend that the young man's resistance to college was in fact rebellion against his parents, in a combination of a desire to break free and a disenchantment with education's ability to improve either his parents' lot or his own. However, after a period of bone-jarring labor building roads out of the hard caliche soil all day joined by his mother's persistent entreaties at night, he finally gave in. In February of 1927, the man who would later hope to be remembered as "the education president" enrolled in Southwest Texas State Teachers College at San Marcos, some sixty miles from his home in Johnson City.

It was at San Marcos, as the school was generally known, that the faculties which were to serve Johnson through four decades of politics clearly emerged. Needing a job to stay in school, like most students at the college, Johnson worked his way from cleanup crew to janitor's assistant and finally to special assistant to the secretary in the president's office. His promotions came through concerted efforts paired with cultivating the interests of an acquaintance of his father's: Dr. Cecil Evans, president of San Marcos, who had an abiding fascination with politics. Johnson's familiarity with legislators and his eagerness to discuss legislation pleased and impressed the chief administrator, and the student soon convinced him that he needed a new office assistant in the person of Lyndon B. Johnson.

According to Evans's secretary,

> this was quite an honor; no student had ever held the job before.
> . . .People who entered the office got the impression that Lyndon
> Johnson was running things, and rumors circulated that visitors had
> to get Johnson's permission to see the president. Since there were
> no inter-departmental telephones on the campus, one of Johnson's

primary duties was to carry messages from the college president to various departments. In this capacity he became well-known to key faculty members and was looked upon as a representative of the administration.[2]

Johnson thus demonstrated his incipient political traits: he assessed and attended to the predilections of a person in a key position; he recognized the potential in a post central to the organization's communication channels; and he redefined a simple messenger service into a gatekeeping process for information and opinion, thereby creating a role of power and importance for himself. His power base was further extended when Evans took advantage of his political knowledge during trips to Austin for legislative committee meetings and debates, and for selected correspondence and reports.

In addition to the creation of this niche of significance for himself, Johnson's practical preparation at San Marcos included participating on the debate team and editing the school newspaper. Through these activities he became aware of the existence of a secret organization known as the Black Stars, a group of football players who constituted the social and political elite on the campus. Johnson joined with his nonathletic friends to form the rival White Stars, challenging the Black Stars's domination of student government, college publications, and social activities. Complete with vows of secrecy, a member selection system, and frequent meetings, the organization provided young Johnson with such skills as parliamentary manipulation which he would later hone to perfection. On one occasion, for example, the White Stars arranged to hold elections for class officers in reverse order, so that popular Black Star members, nominated first, would be elected to less significant posts such as cheerleader. The White Stars then faced little opposition to their choice for class president. Johnson also developed his skills in interpersonal politicking and accurate vote counting, winning at least one election because he knew where the swing votes lay, and through tireless buttonholing he got them.

Johnson's position as assistant to the president's secretary offered special opportunities as well. One student recalled that "he could tell when the White Stars gained control because suddenly they had all the inside jobs in offices and the library, and the Black Stars were working outside on the construction and painting crews."[3] Those inside jobs were not only more prestigious but also better paying, an especially important consideration for the financially strapped students at San Marcos. Even before the formation of the White Stars,

18

Johnson had used his position to promote his roommate from the cleanup crew to "inspector of buildings." Johnson was not only at the center of information, but influenced the distribution of resources as well.

While biographers concur that Johnson's years at San Marcos reveal early indications of his characteristics as president, the portraits of the politician as a young man are painted with a variety of palettes. Interviews conducted by William Pool, Emmie Craddock, and David Conrad, for example, depict an ambitious, energetic, persuasive, and likeable student who was viewed by instructors and classmates with a mixture of amazement and respect. These positive recollections contrast sharply with those gathered by Caro, where classmates portrayed Johnson as a despised blend of "bootlicker and bully" whose nickname of "Bull" Johnson reflected their perceptions of his inability to tell the truth.[4] This darker picture attributes Johnson's political successes as much to sneaky tactics and underhanded strategies as to successful persuasion and parliamentarianism. Undoubtedly a complete portrait of Lyndon Johnson requires a combination of the perspectives; someone of his enormous personality certainly engendered strong feelings across the board. Apparently he was better received by the administration and faculty than by his peers; Johnson's good friend, Bill Deason, recalled that "he was never popular with his fellow students. . . . They thought he was arrogant. They may have been jealous of him because he had so much energy and could accomplish so much."[5]

Undisputed is the fact that, when Johnson received his bachelor's degree from San Marcos in 1930, the classroom work for his history major and government minor had been far less important for his general education than his extracurricular activities. He had developed the ability to analyze both an organization and important figures within it, to acquire a post and expand its importance, and to marshall effective political strategies.

For a period of nine months during his college career, Johnson had taught at a Mexican-American school in Cotulla, Texas, to earn enough money to continue at San Marcos. Following graduation he found another job in education, this time teaching public speaking in the Houston high school where his uncle was principal. Yet his sights were set on politics. During his senior year at San Marcos, he had helped to organize Welly Hopkins's successful campaign for a seat in the Texas legislature. Hopkins identified Johnson as being "gifted with a very unusual ability to meet and greet the public,"[6] and in November of 1931 the grateful politician repaid the young man by recommending him as the private secretary to the newly elected Congressman Richard Kleberg.

Johnson jumped at the opportunity to become the adminstrative aide to a United States representative, especially when that representative was part owner of the huge King Ranch. Kleberg was also the archetype of conservative Texas wealth and a playboy of some repute. By early December, then, Lyndon Johnson found himself in Washington, D.C., in charge of the office of a man who much preferred golf, racehorses, and fighting cocks to almost anything associated with politics. At the age of twenty-three, Johnson plunged into the process of organizing and managing Kleberg's office and, to the extent that he could, Kleberg.

In setting up the office, Johnson followed the same procedure that he had at San Marcos: he analyzed the structure of the organization, got to know the people, learned of habits and traditions, and set priorities for accomplishing his goals. Maintaining a solid base with the constituents in the large, well-populated home district came first, in Johnson's mind; they elected members of Congress, and they could keep them there. In order to respond to their requests, he needed to know how to maneuver through the intricacies of the federal government's bureaucratic maze: how to untangle a snafu on a pension for one of the many veterans in the district or how to answer a question for the struggling farmers, hit even harder by the Great Depression. With a missionary's zeal Johnson threw himself into the task of getting answers for constituents' mail, dictating more than three hundred letters in one day.

Johnson expected no less zeal from his office help, which for some time consisted of Luther Jones and Gene Latimer, the two star debaters whom he had coached briefly in Houston and lured to Washington after their graduation. Later he supplemented his staff by handing out the patronage jobs that were at a congressional member's disposal, such as elevator operator and postal worker, only to those who would spend their evening hours in Kleberg's office, helping to answer the voluminous amounts of mail.

Johnson drove both himself and his people hard: eighteen hours a day, seven days a week, he expected top-notch performances. When he felt that they were letting him down, he ranted and raved, but his staff kept working. Again, interpretations of Johnson's actions and motivations differ. Some contend that his energy, insight, and enthusiasm kept staffers on, for they forgave tongue-lashings as a sign of high standards or a way of letting off steam. Miller, for example, quotes Jones's description of the long hours and his contention that "nobody minded. I mean, the atmosphere was full of challenge, and this guy's enthusiasm was just absolutely contagious.'" Others, notably Caro, argue that Johnson was driven by "the energy of a man fleeing from something dreadful," and that his loyal assistants reciprocated with a deeply engrained psychological need to be totally dominated—which he was delighted to fulfill. As evidence Caro points to his interview with Latimer, in which the former assistant attributed recurrent nervous breakdowns and alcoholism to the strains of his employment by Lyndon Johnson; yet Latimer returned to work for him again and again.[8] Johnson's manner of treating subordinates, in part formulated during this period in Kleberg's office, would become the subject of media controversy during his presidency, with each side argued vehemently.

One of the reasons Johnson needed a productive, smoothly functioning office was the amount of time he devoted to related activities outside of the office. These included regular trips back home to hear constituents' complaints and to educate them, especially after FDR's election in 1932, on ways to get the most from the government for themselves. It also meant cultivating contacts of all sorts to learn as much as possible about politics and politicians. Johnson gleaned information from everyone who might offer it, from a doorkeeper to another of his father's acquaintances, Sam Rayburn. A member of Congress since 1913, Rayburn knew the House, its participants, and its procedures. Over the years this wily Texan would provide valuable tutelage on these subjects to the son of the man with whom he had served in the Texas legislature.

Johnson also moved to revamp the "Little Congress." A club of legislative secretaries that was originally intended as a forum for debate and professional friendships, the Little Congress had gradually faded into a social gathering for a few oldtimers. Johnson decided that the organization's usefulness could be restored with him at the helm, so he marshalled other young congressional secretaries to overturn the seniority system, elect him as the youngest speaker, and revitalize the organization. In the process he also strengthened his ties with other congressional staffs, improved his opportunities for contacts with the prominent politicians now invited to address the group, and sharpened his parliamentary skills. Many of the oldtimers were embittered by Johnson's takeover and accused him of stealing the election through his liberal interpretation of the rules of membership. Yet Johnson maintained control, and under his management the debates and presentations of the Little Congress attracted the attention of both nationally known politicians and the media.

Johnson supplemented his Little Congress experience by accepting an additional job as doorkeeper, which included the relatively mundane task of notifying congressmen on the floor of visitors waiting in the lobby. Johnson, however, saw his new post as an opportunity to observe the speeches, the informal exchanges, the parliamentary maneuvering, and other fundamental daily functions of the legislature from the floor of the House itself. It also allowed scrutiny of the personalities involved in the legislative process.

Johnson's enthusiastic exploitation of all of the political opportunities the capital had to offer led an older congressional secretary to observe, "this skinny boy was as green as anybody could be, but within a few months he knew how to operate in Washington better than some who had been here for twenty years before him."[9] Johnson felt so confident in his job that press releases on benefits for the home district started appearing with his name before his employer's: "It was announced today by Lyndon B. Johnson, secretary to Congressman Kleberg . . . ."

After three-and-a-half years as secretary to Congressman Kleberg, Johnson decided it was time he had a top position of his own. In November of 1934, he had married Claudia Alta Taylor, now Lady Bird Johnson. In June of 1935, not yet twenty-seven years old, he moved his new bride back to Texas where he became the state director of the National Youth Administration, one of FDR's programs to employ young people during the depression. The post offered him the opportunity to help the youth with whom he empathized. It also allowed him to build on the political knowledge he had gained as Kleberg's secretary. First came the organization of his staff, many of them old friends. Then came the courting of contacts throughout the state, as Johnson built a base of support for himself as well as the NYA. The energetic leadership of this youngest of the NYA state directors drew praise from Eleanor Roosevelt, a particular advocate of this plan to employ and educate the young.

The experience of the NYA post encouraged Johnson to seek a seat in the House of Representatives, vacated by the death of James R. Buchanan in 1937. It would be a challenge. Eight others had entered the race, and at twenty-eight Johnson was by far the youngest candidate. Moreover, his work for Kleberg had spread his name through the old Fourteenth District rather than the new Tenth District whose votes he now sought; the districts had only Blanco County in common. Finally, while his NYA office had improved his visibility in some circles, it had not given him the widespread recognition granted to several of his opponents.

22

Nonetheless, Johnson wanted that congressional seat, and he went after it. He called on the political and fundraising acumen of Alvin Wirtz, former state senator and continuing political presence. He marshalled his loyal forces, including Deason and Latimer. Most important, he selected a strategy to distinguish himself from the passel of candidates, and then threw himself into making that distinction known. The strategy was all-out, unmitigated support for anything advocated by Roosevelt, including most especially FDR's controversial plan to pack the Supreme Court with liberal justices. "I personally don't think Lyndon gave two hoots in hell about the court plan," Luther Jones contended, but Johnson's stand drew publicity-laden fire from the others, publicity that was aided by the money and public relations talent brought in by Wirtz.[10]

Yet Johnson did not rely on publicity alone to get his message to the voters. In the Tenth District, towns were tiny and far apart, newspapers were an extravagance for most, and the lack of electricity in the vast rural areas meant the absence of radio. Lyndon Johnson set out to close the gap between himself and the front runners by closing the gap between himself and those widely spaced voters. As Caro describes in engrossing detail, Johnson embarked on a nonstop forty-two day campaign to reach the people, not only in the relatively large towns of three thousand but also in the most remote and isolated areas of the Texas Hill Country. In his cousin's words, "he went to the blackland belt, he went to the sandyland people—he went everywhere. He went to the people that no one had ever gone to. He went to the people on the forks of the creeks."[11] His unquenchably energetic outpouring of personal effort and activity was unmatched by any other candidate. Despite Johnson's spending the day of the special election in the hospital recovering from the removal of his appendix, it proved to be a good day for him: he managed to emerge with a victory.

The margin of the victory was narrow. Voter turnout for the special election was low, and the large cast of characters split the ballots nine ways. Although Johnson had three thousand votes more than the runner-up, he was sent to Congress by the votes of only 3 percent of the population of the Tenth District. Yet he went to Congress, and set about to become what Democratic politico Thomas Corcoran would describe as "the best Congressman for a district that *ever was*."[12]

He was off to a good start. The pro-FDR stand brought Johnson to the attention of the president, who appreciated his adamant support during a time of trial. Roosevelt met with the freshman representative while on vacation in Texas and the Gulf; he then arranged for

Johnson's appointment to the powerful Naval Affairs Committee—an unusually good assignment for a new member of Congress. He also put the young politician in touch with one of his key aides, Thomas Corcoran, better known as "Tommy the Cork." Corcoran, along with fellow New Dealers James H. Rowe and Abe Fortas, would prove to be valuable friends and allies not only during Johnson's years in Congress but also throughout his presidency.

As he had earlier, Johnson plunged wholeheartedly into Washington's political environment. The new representative courted his new friends and polished relationships with older ones, especially Sam Rayburn, who was first elected majority leader and then Speaker of the House. Johnson pushed his staff, which now included John Connally and Walter Jenkins, to keep in touch with the people back home. He increased his exceptional knowledge about the intricacies of the system and how to make it work for him.

As a consequence, Johnson succeeded in acquiring a phenomenal number of projects, programs, grants, and miscellaneous other services for his constituents. He snagged one of the first public housing projects for Austin; the others were in New York and New Orleans. He got public schools and libraries for the district. He had the agricultural regulations of several New Deal programs revised to benefit the farmers of the Hill Country. Through dogged persistence and a series of steps that included a conference with FDR, he brought electricity to the rural areas of the Hill Country and forever changed a way of life.[13] Johnson also gained approval for a number of water projects, including dams on the Colorado and Pedernales rivers, to provide power, irrigation, and flood control. His success in overcoming the legal entanglements involved in one project in particular, the Marshall Ford Dam, earned the representative the not inconsiderable financial support of its contractors, Herman and George Brown of Brown and Root.[14] By the end of the New Deal, Johnson had garnered some seventy million dollars' worth in federal projects for his district.[15]

While tending to business at home, Johnson also kept an eye on foreign affairs. A particular area of concern was Adolph Hitler's rise to power and its disturbing effects on Europe. In an attempt to keep the peace, British Prime Minister Neville Chamberlain met with the Nazi leader in Munich during September of 1938 and agreed to swap substantial portions of Czechoslovakia for Hitler's word that there would be no further war. When Hitler invaded the rest of Czechoslovakia and then Poland within a year, Munich became, for Lyndon Johnson and a generation of Americans, a symbol of appeasement and cowardly surrender that could never halt an aggressor. As Johnson would later characterize the brief period between Munich and the declaration of World War II, a state of peace may have existed, but "it was a weak-kneed peace, . . . propped up on fragile umbrellas of timid men who sought to buy security at the price of Democracy's soul." Given Ronnie Dugger's analysis, Johnson's Texas upbringing would have intensified his aversion to Munich, for the legend of the Alamo stressed standing firm and fighting for one's ideals, even to the point of death.[16] The alternative was to be a coward, a chicken, a timid man who made weak-kneed agreements. Munich and its aftermath would ever after play a central role in Johnson's conceptions of world affairs.

Although Johnson watched the events in Europe with interest, at heart he was a domestic politician. The struggle for power that most engaged him was in Washington, D.C. Unopposed in the 1938 and 1940 elections, Johnson could turn his attention elsewhere. The Democrats had lost more than eighty representatives' seats in the midterm election of 1938; and with FDR battling Wendell Willkie for an unprecedented third term, the elections of 1940 threatened to destroy the Democratic majority in the House. Representatives were hampered in their reelection efforts by the lack of an effective national organization: the Democratic National Committee devoted itself to the presidential race, and the Democratic Congressional Campaign Committee was poorly run, vastly underfunded, and ineffectual at best. Something had to be done, and Johnson convinced Rayburn and Roosevelt that despite his youth he should be given a crack at doing it.

In October of 1940, a scant three weeks before people went to the polls, Johnson started working as an informal adjunct to the campaign committee. The young congressman from Texas set out on his own: renting his own office and using his own staff, he raised his own money from his own sources and distributed the funds to candidates whom he had carefully identified as critically important. Contributions came from Brown and Root, from oil interests, from Corcoran's contacts in New York; money went out to beleaguered representatives all over the nation who had given up any hope of receiving aid from the party's national organizations. Speakers, endorsements, statistics, and other services followed the financial aid, to further assist in the campaigns. In each case, the provisions were carefully tailored to the needs of the candidate. And in each case, as he had in Kleberg's office, Johnson made certain that his name was out in front.

In return, Johnson asked the grateful candidates to supply information on political prospects in their districts through the last weeks of the election and on election day. As a consequence, he could provide FDR with up-to-date status reports not only on the congressional campaigns but also on the presidential race. Such accurate grassroots information was valuable at a time predating reliable public opinion polls.

Come time to tally the votes, Roosevelt had won and the Democrats had not lost sixty seats in the House but gained eight. Moreover, Lyndon Johnson had made his mark both on members of Congress and on the president, as well as once again expanding his network of contacts. His purpose in tackling the campaigns of others was not altruistic; as James Rowe acknowledged, "he was really trying to build a power base as a new congressman."[17] Although Caro contends that the resulting power "was simply the power of money," primarily siphoned from Herman Brown, it was really much more.[18] Wendell Willkie and the Republicans had far better funding, as Caro himself points out, and yet they lost. It was Johnson's astute assessment of which races were critical and why, his analysis of how his office could help, and his unstinting hard work that made the difference. Certainly the candidates would have floundered without money, but money alone, without Johnson's political acumen, would not have done the job for the party.

His success with the 1940 campaigns encouraged Johnson to seek a Senate seat in 1941 when Senator Morris Sheppard died. Johnson launched a well-organized, well-funded campaign, which went smoothly until the colorful governor, W. Lee O'Daniel, entered the race. Better known as "Pappy," O'Daniel got his start hawking flour over the radio, backed by a hillbilly band; upon entering the governor's race, he retained the hillbilly band and homespun twang for his political races. When the enormously popular Pappy entered the competition for the Senate's slot, Johnson had to run harder. He employed the aggressive hand-pumping of his first campaign and added full-scale extravaganzas of music, dancing, and speeches designed to counter the governor's tactics. The first returns showed that Johnson's plan had worked; he was ahead by some five thousand votes. Yet delayed returns and corrected totals chipped away at that lead until finally, three days after the election, O'Daniel had won by 1,311 votes. The congressman's staff urged him to contest the results, arguing that the massive last-minute changes clearly indicated a stolen election. Johnson decided to leave bad enough alone, some say because he felt the office would be cheapened if won by contest and some say because he knew that "adjustments" had been made in votes and contributions on both sides of the campaign.

26

The defeat, one of the few in Johnson's political career, sent him back to the House. There he remained, with the exception of a seven-month stint in the Navy following Pearl Harbor, until 1948. In that year, increasingly impatient with the slow pace and virtual anonymity of life in the House of Representatives, Johnson ran against former Texas governor Coke Stevenson for O'Daniel's seat in the Senate. Again Johnson campaigned full tilt, this time barnstorming the state in a helicopter christened the Johnson City Windmill. Like his earlier stand on Roosevelt's court plan, Johnson's novel mode of transportation attracted attention and publicity. Moreover, it enabled him to traverse his vast state quickly, visiting twenty to thirty towns a day, so that he could shake more hands and speak to more people.

The controversial results of the campaign almost seemed like a reverse replay of the 1941 election. More than a week after the ballots were cast, Johnson was declared the winner by a scant eighty-seven-vote margin. Stevenson's forces charged fraud in the election, eventually taking their challenge to the Supreme Court.[19] While Johnson won the decision, the narrow victory led a fellow senator to dub him "Landslide Lyndon"—a title that, much to Johnson's chagrin, stuck. Nonetheless, he was now a United States senator.

"Seldom," Evans and Novak observe, "has so colorful, so varied, and so exceptional a band of new Democratic Senators come into the Senate as the Democratic Class of '48."[20] Joining Johnson after the elections that kept Truman in the White House were Democrats Paul Douglas of Illinois, Hubert Humphrey of Minnesota, Robert S. Kerr of Oklahoma, Estes Kefauver of Tennessee, and Russell Long of Louisiana. Repeating patterns from his past, Lyndon Johnson proceeded immediately to inquire into the personalities and procedures, large and small, that governed the Senate. In the days when an informal union of senior Republicans and southern Democrats ruled that institution, Johnson saw that the recognition he sought must come through, or at least with, this conservative coalition. The young senator from Texas thus used his congressional experience in defense preparedness, gained on the House Naval Affairs Committee, to earn appointment to the Armed Services Committee—a group dominated by the Senate patriarch, Georgia's Richard B. Russell.

Observers often characterize Johnson's relationship with older established men as one of "professional son." The paternal attention and professional patronage bestowed in turn by Evans, Wirtz, and

Rayburn now came from the elder statesman from Georgia. Yet the younger politician did not enlist as an ever-obedient apprentice to the elder. While Johnson exhibited a deference to Russell and his colleagues, as he had to Rayburn, and eagerly sought access to and information from the senatorial power structure, he quietly stressed his independence. The "infinitely delicate" nature of what Evans and Novak term Johnson's "balancing act" is well illustrated by his approach to the southern caucus.[21] As a senator from Texas Johnson was expected to attend Russell's caucus meetings. The first weeks of his Senate career, however, brought no such attendance. Resisting formal membership in the southern caucus, Johnson later established an informal liaison with the group. With such moves, Johnson established the pattern that eventually brought him to power in the Senate: through flexibility, maintained largely by the avoidance of public commitment, and through the fostering of informal, interpersonal contacts, Johnson managed to accomplish most of his legislative and personal goals.

The balance of autonomy and alliance served Johnson well during his first years in the Senate. Much later, a fellow senator who became his vice president reflected:

> Johnson, as I recall him from the first days, was a political operator. Now I use the word "operator" not in a nefarious sense, but he understood the pieces; he understood the mechanism, and he always kept relationships that he could call on; his personal relationships were such that he could call on them if he needed them.[22]

The relationships Hubert Humphrey noted as so important to Johnson's success were called on in 1951, when Johnson sought the position of party whip. Despite the drain on his time, the reduced opportunity for contact with constituents, and the relative ineffectiveness of such elected posts when compared with the power exerted by the hoary clubs of the Senate, Johnson recognized the potential for personal advancement offered by the position of party whip. In fulfilling the whip's duties—to determine the positions of the party's senators on the myriad of legislation facing them, to assess the reasons for their positions, to inform the floor leader of their views, and to make sure the right senators were on the floor to vote at the right time—Johnson could establish contacts and acquire information to an extent denied the average senator.

And he did. Johnson haunted the cloakrooms, pored over legislation, and established contacts with other senators and their staffs. All the while he improved his knowledge and position, sharpening political skills by once again turning a previously little-used position into a post of information and potential power.

Building on the foundations he had established as party whip, Johnson moved to become the Democratic floor leader in 1953. The November elections of 1952 had placed Dwight D. Eisenhower in the White House and sent forty-eight Democrats, forty-seven Republicans, and one Independent—Wayne Morse of Oregon—to the Senate. When the Republicans gained the majority rule through the votes of the Independent and Vice-President Richard M. Nixon, Johnson recognized a difficult situation which nonetheless offered potential power to the Senate minority leader. With a Republican in the White House, Johnson felt that the position of floor leader would enable him to exert a significant influence over the policies and programs being developed while the Democratic party rebuilt itself. This position of strength was further accentuated by the Republicans' minimal margin of Senate control; the narrow coalition that voted for GOP rule could almost certainly be disrupted as key issues developed.

The new Senate minority leader moved carefully into this tenuous situation. He had already so effectively and forcefully lobbied his Democratic colleagues for the floor leadership that the liberal candidate's vote total was not even announced, to spare the other candidate his humiliation.[23] This election was especially important for its introduction of liberal Democratic senators, a relatively dissident crew, to Johnson's method of conducting political business, complete with accurate vote tallies and an ability to acquire votes. Johnson then proceeded to build on this show of solidarity by proposing changes in that most sacred cow of the Senate, the seniority system— a move that, at the very least, would appear questionable. How could Johnson build solidarity by assaulting tradition, especially a tradition held dear by members of his own party? As the new Democratic floor leader analyzed it, however, the seniority system was good for a few senators, but it was bad for the party. While the most senior legislators had three assignments, usually on prime committees, freshmen were relegated to one of the obscure committees—out of the center of Senate activity, out of the limelight, and out of the running for bringing government favors back to their home districts. As Johnson argued, young senators were like the Texas boy who complained that his brother "has been twowheres and I ain't been nowheres." Yet changing the system would require the cooperation of the elder statesmen; they must voluntarily relinquish one of their three major assignments so that the new people could be given one good committee. Johnson approached Richard Russell and his peers with the proposal. While Russell personally favored the idea, he was reluctant to get involved in any battle to change the system; however, his benign neutrality allowed Johnson's plan to pass unopposed.

In achieving this historic reform of the seniority system, Johnson solidified his ties with the Senate elders by consultation and refraint from attack, he attracted praise from the media for his progressive reforms, and he earned the gratitude of freshman senators. In addition, he had strengthened the post of Senate minority leader. Previously a nominal post lacking power and prestige, the floor leader now functioned as chief counselor and patron for freshman senators, advising them on committees to apply for and aiding them in the receipt of their choices. Just as Johnson had learned and used interpersonal communication channels to expand his post in the college president's office, he now expanded the power and influence of his Senate position by becoming a source of information, advice, and patronage.

Although now firmly established as a party spokesman, Johnson decided against using his position to attack the Republican administration. Aware of the great popularity of the new president and convinced of the need to maintain contacts on both of the almost evenly divided sides of the aisle, Johnson adopted what he termed "the politics of responsibility." In so doing, he rejected the sentiment previously expressed by Republican Senator Robert A. Taft, the majority leader, that "the business of the opposition is to oppose." Instead, he embraced a bipartisan spirit, characterizing himself as the beloved Eisenhower's primary supporter, as opposed to the dissident conservatives of the president's own party. George Reedy, staff assistant and press secretary to Johnson during periods of both his senatorial and presidential terms, summarized the resulting strategy:

> The formula was simple. It involved a careful analysis of the divisions within the two parties; a calculation of the most extreme Democratic objective that could be achieved on the basis of those divisions; the drafting of amendments calculated to unite the Democrats and divide the Republicans; and an obstinate refusal to fight for unattainable objectives.[24]

Johnson's carefully calculated and restrained position led him on one occasion to muse that "the President must wonder at times whether he could not do a better job for his country if he were not weighed down by the Republican Party."[25]

Johnson maintained this stance even after the 1954 elections re-

30

turned a Democratic majority to the Senate and made Lyndon John-son the youngest majority leader ever to serve either party. Unlike the many congressional leaders who embraced strong ideologies and vigorous legislative debate as ideals, Johnson's values lay in repre-sentative government, political compromise, and enacted legisla-tion. Raising issues simply to make a point publicly or simply to generate discussion in an area of concern was, in his view, just so much "rambling talk." As Johnson observed, "it is a politician's task to pass legislation, not to sit around saying principled things."[26] This philosophy, so basic to Johnson's approach to politics, led to the difficulties he encountered with the Democratic liberals in the Sen-ate throughout his tenure as floor leader: he could not understand what he regarded as their insistence on tilting at windmills.

Regarding the passage of legislation as his first duty, therefore, Johnson devised a method that enabled him to analyze the state of Senate legislation to a degree unequaled by his predecessors. This intensely personal system allowed the majority leader an unpre-cedented degree of control over the labyrinthian jungle of Senate politics.

The basis for Johnson's system was his pragmatic view of politics. In order to enact legislation, a politician needs votes; and Johnson's skill at taking accurate head counts in the nebulous maze of senato-rial bargaining and at marshalling his forces for bills large and small became legendary. As Senate majority leader, he expanded the posi-tion he had established while minority leader by acquiring control over the distribution of resources and increasing their value—and his. The assignment of office space, for example, had previously been a routine matter, based on seniority and carried out by the Senate Committee on Rules and Administration; Johnson transferred both the task and its potential for influence to the party leader's office. In the leader's role as chairman of the Democratic Policy Committee, Johnson also assumed responsibility for scheduling legislation on the floor. With timing frequently a key to the success of legislation, cooperation from the majority leader thus became even more crucial to many senators. In addition, Johnson's control of the Senate Demo-cratic Campaign Committee, like the counterpart for the House elections that Johnson aided so well in 1940, provided further oppor-tunity to know the political concerns of each senator and to be known, in return, as a valuable resource. The responsibility for these various tasks, some seemingly insignificant and others obviously integral to the functions of the legislative body, resulted in Johnson's personally knowing the purposes, procedures, traditions, and key figures of every political power center in Washington, and how he could make them work in his favor.

Johnson thus established contacts, extended favors, and built what some political analysts called "the Johnson Network": a system of senators upon whom the majority leader could usually rely, and who in turn found favor with him. Thus in 1957, for example, Johnson would retain funding for a land survey in Maine despite the battle over paring down Eisenhower's budget, because Senator Margaret Chase Smith had worked with the network before and Johnson knew he would need her votes in an upcoming legislative confrontation. Successful operation of this network demanded that Johnson keep track of its members and keep them informed of his expectations. For this he employed his large staff, his impressive system of contacts, and his own well-honed ability to elicit, store, and utilize all brands of politically useful information, from the work of legislative maneuvering to the latest cloakroom gossip. Key to this political intelligence system was the quick and resourceful Bobby Baker, the "ninety-seventh senator" who later faced charges of bribery and blackmail on Johnson's behalf. Baker provided invariably precise vote counts which enabled Johnson to assess a bill's chances of passing, the weak votes possibly open to change, and the areas in need of bolstering—all better than the opposition.

The intelligence system did not focus on head counts alone. Johnson also used it to learn of his colleagues' goals, gaffes, and grievances in all areas of their lives, keeping the information current and catalogued in his mind. Hubert Humphrey was later to marvel:

> He always knew all the little things that people did. I used to say he had his own private F.B.I. If you ever knew anybody, if you'd been out on a date, or if you'd had a drink, or if you'd attended a meeting, or if you'd danced with a gal at a night club, he knew it! It was just incredible![27]

Johnson wove this information about the habits, idiosyncracies, and values of those who peopled Capitol Hill into an intricate and all-embracing tapestry of interpersonal politics. When Johnson had first assumed the position of floor leader in 1953, the venerable Richard Russell observed that "he doesn't have the best mind on the Democratic side of the Senate; he isn't the best orator; he isn't the best parliamentarian. But he's the best combination of all those qualities."[28] Certainly Johnson was not the best orator or debater; he rarely spoke formally on the floor, and when he did he relied heavily on manuscripts. What Johnson *was* best at—left unsaid by Russell—was face-to-face politicking, based on a sound knowledge of the system, a thorough review of the legislation at hand, and an intimate understanding of the people whose votes he courted.

The "Johnson Treatment," as this approach came to be called, was at the heart of Johnson's political success. Evans and Novak captured the flavor of this unique, intense technique:

> The treatment could last ten minutes or four hours. It came, enveloping its target, at the LBJ Ranch swimming pool, in one of LBJ's offices, in the Senate cloakroom, on the floor of the Senate itself—wherever Johnson might find a fellow Senator within his reach. Its tone could be supplication, accusation, cajolery, exuberance, scorn, tears, complaints, the hint of threat. It was all of these together. It ran the gamut of human emotions. Its velocity was breathtaking, and it was all in one direction. Interjections from the target were rare. Johnson anticipated them before they could be spoken. He moved in close, his face a scant millimeter from his target, his eyes widening and narrowing, his eyebrows rising and falling. From his pockets poured clippings, memos, statistics. Mimicry, humor, and the genius of analogy made the Treatment an almost hypnotic experience and rendered the target stunned and helpless.[29]

What elevated Johnson's exhortations from petty armtwisting to virtuosity was his grasp of the available means of persuasion. Each appeal was precisely adapted to the individual target, from anecdotes and analogies to the particularities of delivery. Knowing the legislation, the political situation, and the people as he did, he could marshall his appeals—from compelling social issues to what Evans and Novak call "that unique brand of shameless Johnsonian flattery that hardened politicians often found irresistable"[30]—to garner votes and fulfill his legislative duties as he viewed them.

Given his philosophy of politics and his personal attributes, Johnson not surprisingly shifted the arena of Senate activity from the floor to the offices and cloakrooms. Johnson thrived on the techniques of consensus legislation, which demanded accurate vote tallies, ardent courting of essential borderline votes, and the avoidance of unnecessarily antagonizing opponents, who could prove to be valuable allies on another issue if not alienated by the bill at hand. To ensure the successful use of his intelligence system and personal politicking, however, Johnson needed maximum flexibility. He thus avoided speaking on the floor, not only because he disliked facing large audiences and feared a forensic trap, but also because public commitment on a topic limited his options in dealing with the diversity of opinions required to consolidate on various issues. Johnson sought a legislative system based on consultation, cooperation, and compromise, not discussion and debate; and he found his goals enhanced— and passage of legislation increased—when he knew the votes before he ever brought legislation to the floor.

The result was not universally applauded. Paul Douglas, the feisty, liberal Democratic senator from Illinois, saw it as a perversion of the legislative process:

> Under Johnson, the Senate functions like a Greek Tragedy: all the action takes place offstage, before the play begins. Nothing is left to open and spontaneous debate, nothing is left for the participants but the enactment of their prescribed roles.[31]

For Douglas, the majority leader's approach denied the opportunity to examine alternatives, explore ideologies, and challenge perspectives. Yet to Johnson, such complaints ignored the fundamental duty of a legislative body: to enact legislation, without squandering time and energy on "rambling talk" and impossible issues.

This insistence on flexibility and productivity affected Johnson's relationship with the press as well as his dealings with the Senate. Johnson regarded reporters and the mass media as potentially useful tools on certain occasions and as potential threats to his carefully constructed consensus legislation on others. Since his first year in the Senate he had favored with information those newspapers that supported his actions, and he had written letters of refutation to those that did not. Johnson did, however, have some sense of the role of mass media in relationships between the government and the public. In 1954, for example, as Senate minority leader, Johnson had insisted that the Army-McCarthy hearings be televised, convinced (and correctly so) that Senator Joseph McCarthy's anti-communist crusade would not be able to withstand the direct national exposure afforded by the young medium.

Nevertheless, a key element in Johnson's successful legislative formula was the secrecy that enabled him to bargain, barter, persuade, and maneuver majority votes. The Senate majority leader's relationship with the press was, therefore, a calculated one: Johnson refused to divulge his position on some questions and issued a smoke screen on others. He calculated stories for their ability to influence

34

senators on particular issues. He resented liberal Democrats who took party fights before the press, yet he used news leaks himself to head off opposition. And, when it was all over, Johnson typically called press conferences to exult in his Senate's accomplishments before reporters.

To understand how Johnson could survive politically with such a variety of approaches to media relations requires some insight into the environment in which the senatorial press corps works. As columnist Russell Baker has suggested in truthful jest, political correspondents reflect the beat to which they are assigned:

> The State Department reporter quickly learns to talk like a fuddy-duddy and look grave, important, and inscrutable. The Capitol Hill reporter eschews the raucous spirit of the White House and affects the hooded expression of the man privy to many important deals. Like the politicians he covers, he tends to garrulity, coarse jokes, and bourbon, and learns to hate reform. The Pentagon man always seems to have just come in off maneuvers.[32]

The Senate is a large and complex organization; a bewildering array of lawmakers, aides, committees, procedures, and issues thus face the reporters assigned to it. The press corps on the Hill is aided in gathering information by good relationships with senators and their staffs; in turn, reporters find it both advantageous and relatively easy to protect their sources in an arena in which the principals are at least officially coequal and in which the prominence of individuals fluctuates with sometimes rapidly changing conditions. A state of symbiosis thus exists between journalists and lawmakers, between valuable channels and valuable sources.

The Senate constituted an almost perfect environment in which Lyndon Johnson could exercise his theories of government-press relations. On the one hand, he was far from being the only source of information; when reporters found his news slow or nonexistent, they explored the many other sources available. On the other hand, as Senate majority leader, Johnson was in an ideal position, especially with Republican control of the executive branch, to command journalistic attention when he wanted it.

As one might expect, Johnson brought his personal style of politics to bear on reporters as well as senators. Columns perceived as negative rated a call to the writer, favorable editorials warranted a letter, and cooperative journalists were invited for drinks and discussions on upcoming issues. On occasion, he even resorted to the full "Treatment." Johnson's longtime secretary Willie Day Taylor tells of Mary McGrory's experience with the senator:

> Mary has always been a flaming liberal and still is. And she asked
> for an interview with him and was granted one. I saw her before
> she went in, I saw her when she came out. She was just floating on
> air: "Oh, that poor man; that poor wonderful man. I wish there was
> something I could do for him. Could I go out and bake some
> cookies or anything I could do?"[33]

With reporters as with senators, a knowledge of the person, an impassioned display of enthusiasm, and a heavy dose of flattery could be most persuasive.

As a persuasive tool, however, the Johnson Treatment had its limitations. In particular, it only worked with one or two people at a time. The anecdotes and assertions so persuasively adaptive in private contexts seemed blunt and heavy-handed in a public setting. While reporters and columnists were often entranced in their individual session with Johnson, they were less than flattered when he turned the Johnson Treatment on press conferences. What was amusing, intriguing, and convincing on a one-to-one basis, especially for Senate reporters accustomed to such cozy conferences, appeared blatantly manipulative in large groups. Sensitive to intimations of manipulation, particularly in group contexts, reporters resented not only Johnson's public attempts to dominate them but also his failure to understand the reason for their resentment. Johnson, sensing their annoyance, responded warily and defensively, puzzled by what he saw as the press's inconsistency. Yet these tensions were only occasional, for senatorial newsgathering norms stressed the individual interviews at which Johnson excelled rather than the press conferences less conducive to his approach.

Small, personal conferences thus suited Johnson's abilities far better than large, formal audiences, whether on the floor of the legislature or before the media, and the context of the Senate not only allowed but encouraged this. Johnson's strengths found the perfect forum in that institution—its organization, its procedures, its channels of communication, and its processes of influence. As majority leader, Johnson was in his element, a fact noted at the time by columnist Stewart Alsop:

> There is always something peculiarly satisfying about watching a
> genuine professional at work, whether on the baseball diamond or
> on the floor of the United States Senate. Anyone who wants to see
> in action the best professional Floor Leader of our time need only
> visit the Senate gallery at a tense legislative moment and keep his
> eyes on the tall, lanky, slow-moving form of the Majority Leader as
> he ambles about on the floor below.[34]

36

Johnson was indeed a professional, in the sense that he was consumed by politics—its issues, its personalities, its legislation, and its effects. His mind's eye always focused on the Capitol. He may have cringed at reports depicting him as a workaholic, but even Sam Rayburn is said to have breathed a sigh of relief when he heard that his protégé had bought a ranch and some cattle. "Thank the Lord," he mused, "Lyndon will have something to talk about now besides business."[35] Even a massive heart attack in 1955 scarcely slowed him down; within a few days his staff had established a satellite office at the hospital so that he could continue his duties as floor leader.[36]

Among other things, Johnson's heart attack demonstrated the devotion of what Stewart Alsop characterized as "the biggest, the most efficient, the most ruthlessly overworked and the most loyal staff in the history of the Senate."[37] Johnson's drive demanded similarly driven assistants, as it had throughout his career. Mary Rather, Johnson's personal secretary, recalled that "once in a while I'd look up from my typewriter and ask myself whether I would work this hard for anyone else, including myself. I decided I wouldn't."[38] Through enthusiasm or domination, Johnson kept them on.

With his aggressive behind-the-scenes style, his philosophy of political pragmatism, and the help of his doggedly devoted staff, Johnson had conquered the intricacies of the Senate and made them his own. The result was record amounts of legislation passed under Johnson's leadership. In the process, Johnson had also managed in less than a decade to transform the job of Senate majority leader from inglorious drudgery to power and prestige.

On the strength of his success in the Senate, Johnson decided to run for the 1960 Democratic presidential nomination. The operation was hamstrung from the very beginning, however, for the decision was not clear-cut. Here again, accounts differ. Such analysts as Evans and Novak contend that, despite Johnson's prowess in the Senate, he did not understand the procedures and mechanisms for attaining a presidential nomination. In contrast, George Reedy argues that Johnson knew full well what to do; he just didn't know whether he wanted to do it or not.[39]

Whether caused by ignorance, ambivalence, or some mixture of the two, Johnson wavered so long between entering the race and staying out of it that his campaign was badly damaged before it even got started. Then he attempted to limit leaks of his potential candidacy to Texas newspapers; when the story reached the front page of the *New York Times*, Johnson disliked the sense that the publicity, however accurate, had forced his hand. Moreover, reflecting his self-doubts and political vacillations, Johnson's campaign plans were at best ephemeral, at worst inept. The precise vote-counting ability that was a cornerstone of his legislative successes disintegrated in the new arena, for Johnson counted on the same senators and Democratic leaders who had formed his power base in Congress. Either he did not realize that convention delegates are much more likely to be committed to congressmen, governors, and state legislators than to senators, or he was hesitant to approach people he did not know. Time and again Johnson's forces were promised delegates, votes that simply could not be delivered. This string of faux pas led Kearns to characterize him as "the perpetual tourist in the alien land of national politics," while Walter Lippmann dismissed him as a serious contender on the basis that "he knows little of the outside world."[40]

Compounding the inadequacies of Johnson's own campaign was the host of competitors facing him: Adlai Stevenson, Stuart Symington, Hubert Humphrey, and John F. Kennedy were among those hoping the 1960 Democratic National Convention would be theirs. When Kennedy's superior organization captured the nomination on the first ballot, Johnson's inaugural presidential bid—characterized by many as a comedy of errors—came to an end.

When Johnson accepted Kennedy's offer to become the vice-presidential nominee, he started a journey that would take him along paths he had never envisioned. John Kennedy's defeat of Richard Nixon signalled the beginning of three of the most difficult years of Lyndon Johnson's political life. As vice-president, Johnson had traded the power and prestige of Senate leadership for the limbo traditionally associated with the second highest office of the land. He felt constrained to avoid embarrassing Kennedy; as a result, one journalist recalled, "he just wouldn't communicate. He was just closed-mouthed."[41]

Johnson tried for a time to maintain a position in the Senate as chairman of the Democratic caucus. When both senators and the press then criticized him for his "power grab" in straddling the executive and legislative branches, Johnson withdrew, painfully relinquishing the role he had played with such relish.

Johnson did not, however, languish in total oblivion. Kennedy dispatched him on a number of trips abroad, to serve as ambassador at large. In his three-year tenure as vice-president, Johnson visited thirty-three foreign countries. Evaluations of the success of Johnson's diplomatic ventures varied: while some praised his demeanor as encapsulating the humanity and friendliness of personal American diplomacy, others echoed the State Department official who murmured, "Like some wines, Lyndon Johnson does not travel well."[42]

The general public in the countries he visited responded with warmth and enthusiasm as Johnson discussed the new water supply system with the elders and waded into the crowds to shake hands. Elected officials and people seeking the development of rural areas found common ground with the tall Texas rancher, and Johnson in turn found an easy rapport with them. Yet the energetic "ambassador of good will" disliked the lectures on protocol and admonitions of restraint from the diplomats. His exuberant campaign-style motorcades and outgoing down-home approach with leaders startled and distressed some people, official and journalistic alike.

Illustrative of the different interpretations of Johnson's international diplomatic role is the "camel driver incident." Johnson had, according to one longtime aide, "a surprising ability to communicate with very poor peasants,"[43] and he enjoyed forays into poor and rural areas of the countries he visited to talk with the people there. One such expedition in Pakistan brought him to a camel driver. In the ensuing discussion, Johnson invited the Pakistani to visit him in the United States—an offer the man accepted. The trip turned out to be a success: the man was dignified, articulate, and witty, and the press coverage was amused, but generally favorable. Yet interpretations of Johnson's gesture differed: was it a generous, warmhearted offer demonstrating Johnson's humanity, or was it a crass, unthinking move with the potential to become an international incident?

Johnson's relations with the press were not enhanced by such differences of opinion. Stories leaked by disgruntled officials often depicted Johnson in an extremely negative light. While the journalists on Capitol Hill might not always have been enamored of Johnson, they rarely portrayed any senator badly, given the close, almost familial contact between congressional reporters and their sources. Yet the reporters who accompanied the vice-president on his round-the-world trips were strangers, unrestrained by such norms of coverage, generally unfamiliar with the powerfully persuasive private Johnson, and frequently unimpressed by the public Johnson they encountered. Johnson, in turn, retaliated with the suspicion and distrust he had displayed as Senate majority leader when his press conferences turned sour, now made bitter by his sense of being trapped in the vice-presidency. Thus, when Eric Sevareid, the CBS commentator, failed to appear at a press conference that the vice-president held in England, Johnson pulled the list of the forty-four invited correspondents from his pocket, "took out a fat dark pencil, circled Sevareid's name, and stuck it back in his pocket."[44]

Kennedy, however, could not have been overly worried about Johnson's actions or his press coverage, for the president continued to send him overseas on a total of eleven separate vice-presidential tours. Assignments ranged from representing the United States at the inauguration of Juan Bosch as the president of the Dominican Republic to a fact-finding tour of Southeast Asia in May of 1961. The latter journey provided Johnson with an especially significant exposure to an area with which he had had only limited contact. As Senate minority leader, he had been among the congressional leaders who believed allied support to be a prerequisite to consideration of Eisenhower's proposed intervention in 1954 to save French Indochina from the Communists. Even then, however, Vietnam was simply one of the great many nations to be dealt with by American foreign policy. The trip to Southeast Asia, however, gave Johnson a clearer sense of urgency about the area's problems, as his report to Kennedy upon his return indicates. He warned, with a curious mixture of caution and commitment, of serious difficulties in that region.[45] Johnson cited not only "the momentary threat of Communism itself," to which he felt United States leadership must respond, but also the dangers posed by "hunger, ignorance, poverty, and disease." The United States, Johnson concluded, might well have to face a "fundamental decision" regarding its role: "whether we are to attempt to meet the challenge of Communist expansion now in Southeast Asia by a major effort in support of the forces of freedom in the area or throw in the towel." His choice of language left little doubt as to his view on the matter; ironically, Johnson was discussing the issue that was to become the primary concern of his own presidency in an unexpectedly short time.

3

Transition to the Presidency,
November 1963 to Spring 1964

By his own account, Lyndon Baines Johnson had taken his oath as the thirty-sixth president of the United States "in a climate of national anguish."[1] His predecessor had been assassinated—in the vice-president's home state, to complicate matters—and the country's shock deepened when the accused murderer was in turn assassinated. The glamour, glory, and youth of Camelot had shattered, and Lyndon Johnson, who thrived on the exercise of power, found himself thrust to its pinnacle under dreadful circumstances.

Johnson's handling of the abrupt transition to power would later come under fire, but at the time his actions were praised as subdued and appropriate. On the advice of Attorney General Robert F. Kennedy, brother of the slain leader, Johnson took the oath of office while still in Dallas to emphasize the continuity of leadership. Although Johnson was later criticized for rushing to assume his new office before the slain president's body was cold, the man legally became president the moment Kennedy died—with or without the oath of office. Returning to Washington with his wife, Mrs. Kennedy, and the dead president, Johnson sought the advice of a range of people to help ease the abrupt transition. He consulted with congressional leaders, agency directors, and business figures, mixing these calls and visits with such messages as his expression of sympathy to Rose Kennedy, mother of the late president. He established a commission of respected citizens to thoroughly investigate the assassination and report its findings, and he sought the advice of such columnists as Joseph Alsop concerning the commission's constitution. He called on Kennedy's staff members, urging each to remain because, he said, he needed them more than Kennedy had—not only for information and advice, but as a symbol of continuity to restore the confidence of the shaken nation. In the face of Johnson's appeals not a single one of the major figures of the New Frontier left for three months, until Ted Sorensen resigned to write a history of the Kennedy administration. Others, notably Secretary of Defense Robert McNamara and Secretary of State Dean Rusk, stayed for as long as three years, truly becoming part of the Johnson administration.

At the end of that first dreadful day as president, Johnson assessed the situation. The final entry in the Daily Diary for November 22, 1963, reads:

> 1:00 A.M.—Pres. retired to his room—discussed w/Valenti, Moyers, & Cater in his room until 3:00 re-enacting the day's situation, talking about how the press and public [were] going to interpret his administration, and many different things.

Johnson did not forget the press during these first, stressful hours of his presidency; he was in fact concerned with their interpretations. Charles Roberts of *Newsweek*, one of the two reporters who returned from Dallas on Air Force One after Kennedy's death, recalled the new president's inquiries, as relayed continuously through aides, about whether the newsmen had received the information they needed. Once back in Washington, Johnson contacted a number of journalists, commentators, editors, and publishers, soliciting their views and their support. In addition, the new first family contacted the publisher of the *Washington Post*, a longtime friend. Liz Carpenter, Mrs. Johnson's press secretary and a special assistant to Johnson, reported to the president on November 23:

> Per your instructions, I have reached Kay Graham and she is coming to visit with Lady Bird at 4:00 P.M. today.
> She was deeply touched by your call and said, "Tell them both we will do anything we can."[2]

These early contacts with journalists and congressmen, friends and leaders, allies and staff members touched the multitude of bases that needed touching. Johnson combined these personal conferences with a message to Congress, televised nationwide. On Wednesday, November 27, Johnson told his hushed audience: "All that I have, I would have given gladly not to be standing here today."[3] Echoing John Kennedy's inaugural call, "let us begin," Johnson's exhortation rang out, "let us continue." The new president emphasized that Kennedy's memory deserved passage of key legislation, including the civil rights bill, which the administration had been unable to move through Congress. Embracing Kennedy's program as his own, underscoring his experience as a Senate leader, Johnson sought to forge shock and sorrow into progressive and positive action. Reaching the nation by addressing Congress, the political home he had known and loved, Johnson placed on their shoulders the burden of appropriate

42

action, not only to memorialize the dead president but also to vindicate the violence of his death.

Johnson received high praise for his restrained but assured performance during the early days of his administration. *Newsweek* described his first week as one "that inspired admiration in nearly
everyone who saw him or heard him—a week that demonstrated his
extraordinary firmness and self-confidence in taking hold of the
world's toughest job."[4] Walter Lippmann applauded Johnson's role as
a "bridge of unbridgeable chasms," healing the wounds of the nation.[5]

Yet such praise could not alter the difficulty of the situation.
Kennedy's death was violent, the transition abrupt, and the successor
a marked contrast to the creator of Camelot. A country intrigued
with the vitality and polish of the Kennedys found them replaced by a
6'4" Texan with large features and a drawl.

The contrast seemed especially marked to the many members of
the media, particularly those of the White House press corps, who
had thrived on the New Frontier. From columnist Joseph Alsop, who
helped write speeches, to the many who were simply great admirers
of Kennedy, journalists enjoyed the young president's tenure. Louis
Heren, correspondent from the London *Times*, mused that despite
the tensions, from the normal daily annoyances to the Bay of Pigs,
"the brief Kennedy years had been fun. . . . The assumption was that
the Johnson years would be dull: efficient, but dull."[6]

Yet it was not merely the anticipation of boredom which made the
press corps wary of the new president. Kennedy had engaged them;
Lyndon Johnson was a different breed. Philip Geyelin, editor of the
Washington Post's editorial page, reflected on Johnson's entry into
the presidency:

> It was his fate to be almost the antithesis of John F. Kennedy. . . .
> Johnson's initial image was a debit against his account. He was the
> cowboy who had rent the Taj Mahal with a rebel yell. He was the
> wheeler-dealer master parliamentarian, a caricature out of an Amer-
> ican Western, with an uncultivated accent and an often unintelli-
> gent turn of phrase. He was ungraceful and uninspiring. He was
> also Western rather than Eastern.[7]

Such images did not endear Johnson to journalists. The Texas background became a particularly raw point for both the president and the
press, breeding a suspicion and distrust based on regional differences
which, to each side, also implied stylistic and philosophical dichoto-

mies. Two years after leaving the presidency, Johnson traced his incompatibility with the press to these roots:

> One reason the country could not rally behind a Southern President, I was convinced, was that the metropolitan press of the Eastern seaboard would never permit it. My experience in office confirmed this reaction. I was not thinking just of the derisive articles about my style, my clothes, my manner, my accent, and my family—although I admit I received enough of that kind of treatment in my first few months as President to last a lifetime. I was also thinking of a more deep-seated and far-reaching attitude—a disdain for the South that seems to be woven into the fabric of Northern experience. . . . Perhaps it all stems from the deep-rooted bitterness engendered by civil strife over a hundred years ago, for emotional clichés outlast all others and the Southern cliché is perhaps the most emotional of all. . . . To my mind, these attitudes represent an automatic reflex, unconscious or deliberate, on the part of opinion molders of the North and East in the press and television.[8]

For the press's part, the *New York Times*'s Scotty Reston may protest that most of the well-known figures in the media are "small-town boys" by background and disposition;[9] yet most are also oriented toward the eastern-based style of the institutions in which they work. For all of Johnson's years on Capitol Hill, he had not relinquished his Texas roots; a career in Congress, with its constantly changing, nationally drawn components, encouraged this retention.

In the winter of 1963–64, however, such sentiments remained largely unspoken. Johnson embraced Kennedy's programs and worked to bolster his press relationships, but avoided the formal, televised press conferences at which Kennedy had excelled. In part, Johnson did not welcome the inevitable comparisons of the two men's styles which the press conferences would evoke; in part, Johnson simply was not comfortable in that format. The new president preferred more informal settings. So it was that a routine Saturday briefing with his press secretary turned, on the spur of the moment, into Johnson's first presidential press conference when he invited reporters to join him for coffee in the Oval Office. There they juggled cups, pens, and notebooks as Johnson discussed staff appointments, the budget, foreign affairs, and his first two weeks in office. With this spontaneous and unorthodox meeting Johnson indicated the direction his future interactions with the press would likely take.

"Reporters are hungry for news about you; they must produce

something," Nancy Dickerson told the president soon after he took office.[10] The NBC reporter and Johnson family friend advised him to organize his press operation quickly to properly feed that need for information. Drawing his organization primarily from press secretary Pierre Salinger, a Kennedy holdover, and George Reedy, who had been speech writer, press secretary, and adviser to Johnson since his Senate days, Johnson's press office thanked editors for favorable pieces, welcomed new members to the White House press corps, and passed journalists' requests for stories and photographs on to Johnson along with their recommendations.[11] Johnson himself joined in this process, as when he called Joseph Alsop to thank him for a supportive article.[12]

These letters, memoranda, and telephone conversations were often couched in terms that equated cooperation with friendship. To Johnson, this seemed natural: press friendship and press support went hand in hand. His power in the Senate had resulted from locating and using the sources of influence, intertwining knowledge of the individuals and issues with finely honed procedural skills; the Senate press corps had been one of those sources of influence utilized by Johnson. He approached the presidency in a similar manner, investigating options and opportunities. To his mind, the White House press corps resembled that of the Senate: as part of the "family," they could be relied upon to respond to appeals on behalf of the national welfare; as somewhat unreliable relatives, however, they sometimes needed additional appeals based on the self-benefits to be realized from cooperation.

Journalists' first exposure to this perspective came on January 5, 1964, on the flight returning to Washington after the president and his entourage spent the holidays at the LBJ ranch. Once in the air, Johnson wandered into the reporters' area and started chatting about their future relationship. Frank Cormier, the White House correspondent for United Press International who was aboard the flight, related part of the discussion:

> "I'm the only President you've got," Johnson told us, "and I intend to be President of all the people. I need your help. If I succeed, you succeed. We all succeed or fail together. With your help, I'll do the best job that's in me for our country. I don't want Jack Kennedy looking down at me from heaven and saying he picked the wrong Vice-President. But I can't do the job alone. I need your help."
>
> Leaning forward and speaking earnestly in a soft drawl, he promised we could become the best-informed reporters in Washington. . . .

But he made it clear he could wield a stick as well as a carrot, saying, "If you want to play it the other way, I know how to play it both ways, too, and I know how to cut off the flow of news except in handouts." But the carrot was predominant as he concluded:

"There's no reason why members of the White House press corps shouldn't be the best-informed, most-respected, highest-paid reporters in Washington. If you help me, I'll help you. I'll make you-all big men in your profession."[13]

Johnson's pleas for support and understanding in return for news and information implied a conception of press and government as cooperative enterprises in which the president's store of rewards and punishments provided extra incentive. To him, such a team effort seemed natural; it echoed the techniques that had served him so well in Congress. Yet the reporters on the flight were amazed, for such a view was antithetical to their own conceptions of the presidential-press relationship. To them, the two forces served not as a team but as adversaries facing off in sometimes compatible but often conflicting roles. The White House press corps in particular, unlike the more low-key Capitol Hill reporters, viewed themselves as Dan Rather would later describe: as "watchdogs, not attack dogs, on the one hand, and *certainly not lap dogs* on the other, but watchdogs" (emphasis added).[14] Johnson's proposal to form what Cormier characterized as "a mutual aid society" thus struck the journalists as at best naïve and at worst insulting and manipulative; the correspondents would have agreed with George Reedy's later assessment that Johnson and the reporters "were not even in the same physical dimension, let alone on the same wavelength."[15] Such interpretations both accentuated and were accentuated by views of the new president as a wheeling, dealing horse trader.

The suspicions held by members of the press were not lessened during this period by the administration's actual handling of stories. One of Johnson's earliest imbroglios with the press had its roots in his first press conference, the impromptu meeting over coffee on December 7, 1963. Asked about the fiscal 1965 budget, to be presented to the Congress that January, Johnson pointed out that President Kennedy's last budget of $98.8 billion would have to be increased. Talk had been that the figure would break the $100 billion mark, for the largest peacetime budget in the nation's history; Johnson indicated that it would likely be $102 or $103 billion. Over the next three weeks, figures fell in that range, until the correspondents' New Year's Eve party at Austin's Driskell Hotel: Johnson, who had stopped by for a drink and a chat, informed members of the group that the budget would be closer to $100 billion—far lower than any figures mentioned previously and sufficient to fuel stories on the president's energetic cost-cutting measures. When the actual budget was finally revealed in mid-January, however, Johnson had reduced the figures to $97.9 billion—not only lower than previous estimates, but also lower than Kennedy's last budget. Hugh Sidey, a *Time-Life* columnist, summarized press reactions:

> Newsmen were as astonished as others who watch the budget, which can't be too many. But LBJ, at least to some persons, looked like a fiscal wizard. The correspondents, however, who had been writing of his terrible anguish at getting the budget to near $100 billion were not so happy. They felt that they had been deceived, and they had. They felt that they had been made a part of some sort of game designed for the greater glory of Lyndon Johnson. They had. On the Hill, with his old journalistic pals, Johnson would have had no trouble. They would have chuckled and forgotten about it. But the White House is much different. . . .White House correspondents . . . resented the Johnson game.[16]

Perhaps this "fiscal wizardry" was not so much a matter of news grandstanding as one of making the bill more palatable to its political and economic foes by a dramatic demonstration of fiscal responsibility; the secrecy and surprise would then have been necessary elements to achieve the desired effect. Yet undoubtedly Johnson also wanted to attract media attention to his feat—"to show a little garter," as he liked to say. Moreover, regardless of Johnson's intentions, many members of the press interpreted his methods as his "most impressive technique—the one that has been defined as declaring that the brook is too broad for leaping, then leaping it."[17] Johnson would later acknowledge this interpretation by the media, telling NBC's Chet Huntley that the handling of his first budget formed the beginning of the "credibility gap."[18]

Nor was the brouhaha over the budget an isolated case. In December of 1963, Johnson contacted Princeton historian Eric Goldman to formulate and coordinate a group of the "best minds" in the country, providing ideas about problems, goals, and programs for the new administration. Johnson continually stressed that both this task group, focusing especially on domestic affairs, and Goldman's role were to be kept secret. As Goldman pointed out in his book, *The Tragedy of Lyndon Johnson*, such strict silence is difficult, particularly when working with people throughout the country in the president's name. On January 2, 1964, the *Washington Post* carried a front-page story announcing the intention of Arthur Schlesinger, Jr., to resign from the White House staff and the appointment of Gold-man as a replacement for the position commonly regarded as "resident intellectual." Johnson was disturbed, both by the story and by the comparison. According to Goldman, top presidential aide Walter Jenkins informed him tersely, "You are not the Johnson Arthur Schlesinger. Nobody is going to be the Johnson Arthur Schlesinger. Nobody is going to be the Johnson anything of Kennedy. *This is a different administration.*"[19]

Despite this story, Johnson continued to stress secrecy regarding both Goldman's role and that of the task group—so much so that members of the group asked if Johnson were ashamed of them, or planned simply to go through the motions of appealing to "intellectuals." When Joseph Alsop wrote a column pegging Goldman as the clear successor to Schlesinger, journalists pressed the White House for further details—and received evasive answers and what Goldman termed "the necessary weasels." In conforming to Johnson's dictum of secrecy, Goldman and press secretary Salinger found themselves presenting the historian "in the strange guise of unpaid, part-time 'idea man' collecting ideas on the street corner," rather than a man living in the capital, coordinating "an informal liaison with experts that was hardly unusual in the modern White House," and receiving a government per diem for his efforts. The secrecy Johnson had cherished as a means of flexibility in the Senate now garnered him the seeds of suspicion and distrust among the press.

Yet stories on the domestic-affairs group and Goldman's appointment had to take their place among the president's concerns. Of major importance in the early months of 1964 was the crisis in the Panama Canal Zone. Described by Evans and Novak as resembling "nothing so much as a bit of Kansas transplanted in the tropics,"[20] the zone was perceived by many Panamanians as an anachronistic oasis of prim progress nestled amidst the grimy destitution of that South American country. When local residents protested this situation, as they occasionally did, the United States granted minor concessions to avoid major confrontations over the treaty agreement as a whole. One such concession, granted by President Kennedy in 1962, provided for the American and Panamanian flags to fly side by side over the zone.

Undoubtedly the provision seemed simple enough at the time. Yet on January 7, 1964, high school students in the zone, with the heightened patriotism often displayed by U.S. nationals abroad, refused to equate the Stars and Stripes with the colors of Panama. The response from Panamanian students turned into a full-scale riot when adults joined in the fray. Panamanian President Robert I. Chiari, facing a national election that May, blamed communists for the uprising but cut off diplomatic relations with the United States and demanded renegotiation of the treaty as the only way to end violence.

Johnson faced an equally delicate situation: six weeks into his presidency, dealing with a region in which his predecessor's efforts had excelled, facing an election in November, and abhorrent of possible Republican accusations that the Democrats were "soft on communism," Lyndon Johnson confronted his first foreign crisis. Drawing from his Senate experiences, Johnson first tried some "telephone diplomacy," hoping the interpersonal contact between politicians would result in a mutually satisfactory solution. Yet when Johnson insisted on the restoration of order before any talks could even be considered, Chiari balked.

After five days of rioting, more than twenty deaths (including four American soldiers), and innumerable injuries, an uneasy quiet descended over the Canal Zone; but the two nations remained locked in a diplomatic standoff. Their differences were encapsulated in a seemingly trivial choice of words: Chiari, determined to present a firm front for his tiny nation, insisted that the countries agree to "negotiate" a new treaty, while Johnson, equally determined to represent America strongly, would consent only to "discuss" the terms of a new treaty. Assisted by negotiators from the Organization of American States, the conferences between Panama and the United States struggled along. The meetings were further hampered when Johnson rejected OAS proposals as inadequate remedies requiring disproportionate American commitments and used his remarks to the third anniversary celebration of the Alliance for Progress to tell members of the Pan American Union that the two countries had not yet had "a genuine meeting of the minds."[21]

On March 21, 1964, however, Johnson changed his stance. Ambling into another routine Saturday briefing with his press secretary, the president startled assembled reporters by reading a letter to the OAS president agreeing to "review" the treaty and areas of contention between the United States and Panama. Avoiding the disputed words "discuss" and "negotiate," praising Panama and Chiari, Johnson thus accepted an alternative suggested by the Panamanian president more than a week earlier. On April 3, 1964, an agreement was signed; even so, it could not erase the ludicrous sight of tiny Panama holding the world's policeman in a stalemate.

The Panama crisis had not broken until six weeks after Johnson came to office, and most other foreign affairs remained calm. This lull allowed the new president a breathing spell, especially welcome in that time of domestic confusion.

The opportunity to forget, even if only temporarily, matters of foreign affairs was especially welcome to a man like Lyndon Johnson. From the earliest beginnings of his career, the issues that warmed his political heart were domestic issues. Rural development, social security, unemployment, and education were the matters that had most deeply concerned him as far back as his days as Congressman Kleberg's secretary. Throughout the years this most political and pragmatic of politicians had evolved a messianic hope for enabling all Americans to share in America's bounty; now, although he regretted the tragedy that resulted in his opportunity, he was in a position to take significant steps toward the institution of his vision for the nation. One need look no further than Johnson's first State of the Union address, delivered January 8, 1964, to discern his priorities: it was the first such speech since World War II to stress, by placement and by language, domestic affairs.

Johnson's background in foreign relations lay primarily in his congressional committee work on military preparedness. The experience familiarized him with American defenses, other countries' military capacities, and people within the Pentagon; it also put him in a position to call hearings on America's poor showing in the "space race" when the Russians launched Sputnik in 1957. Yet this background in defense preparedness had not exposed him to the details of diplomacy, treaties, and similar areas of foreign relations; these he knew only insofar as was necessary for the passage of relevant legislation. As vice-president, Johnson sat in on a number of Kennedy's foreign-affairs meetings, but he rarely took an active role.

As a result, Johnson's approach to the realm of foreign affairs drew heavily on his Senate experiences and the recommendations of his advisers. He believed in the personal touch in international relations, feeling that a conference "eyeball to eyeball" gave him a better sense of world leaders and greater opportunity for finding a common ground. With elected officials he sensed the special commonality of accountability to constituents; with diplomats, most of whom were appointed, he was less comfortable.

Johnson's first opportunity as president to test his belief in face-to-face communication on an international scale came after Kennedy's funeral, when various foreign dignitaries came to pay their respects to the fallen leader and to assess his successor. Accounts indicate that reactions were mixed; some were impressed by his approach, some startled, and some put off. While Lady Bird insists that the story is apocryphal, journalists contend that Z. A. Bhutto found himself among those put off. According to their stories, Bhutto, the foreign minister of Pakistan, brashly criticized American foreign policy during their interview, and "Johnson dressed him down as he had reporters who had written stories displeasing him in his Majority Leader days."[22] Pointing out that Pakistan's increasing sympathy with Peking's policies over Washington's seemed inconsistent with his country's acceptance of a sizeable foreign-aid allotment from the United States, the new president left the volatile, vociferous Bhutto nearly speechless, not to mention the startled American officials who were present. Perhaps the incident never occurred, but this tale gained currency during the early months of the Johnson administration, indicative of the forceful, manipulative image the new president was acquiring among members of the press.

Whatever the press coverage, the international version of the Johnson Treatment was not always effective. It failed, for example, to thaw Charles de Gaulle's chilly attitude toward Franco-American relations, a reaction that first puzzled and then angered Johnson. In subsequent encounters with foreign leaders, the American chief of state found the same uneven reception: his relationship with West Germany's Chancellor Ludwig Erhard was excellent, while that with Sir Alec Douglas-Home of Britain was dismal. Johnson came to recognize the difficulty of transferring his fabled ability to understand, persuade, and control within the Senate environment to that of foreign relations: cultural differences often impeded that basic and essential understanding; even when they did not, the separation of personal relations from national interest tended to nullify the effects of such interpersonal interactions. Within a few months after assuming the presidency, Johnson had wearied of attempting the personal-political transferral that had come so naturally before.

One foreign-relations problem that confronted Johnson early in his administration, and never proved amenable to that personal touch, was that of Vietnam. Although the roots of United States involvement in Southeast Asia have been variously identified, the overall rationale is usually ascribed to the Truman Doctrine with its pledge to resist communist expansion generally, while the first specific act of commitment is identified as President Eisenhower's 1954 letter to South Vietnamese Premier Diem promising American support to "assist the government of Vietnam in developing and maintaining a strong, viable state capable of resisting attempted subversion, or aggression through military means."[23] Introducing what would later become a major justification for American military involvement in Southeast Asia, Eisenhower explained, "you have a row of dominoes set up, you knock over the first one and what will happen to the last one is a certainty that it will go over very quickly."[24]

The formation of SEATO (Southeast Asia Treaty Organization) in September of 1954, while not requiring an automatic rejoinder to any armed attack as the NATO treaty does, nonetheless codified America's intention to combat such communist expansion in that region.

Despite Eisenhower's articulation of the "domino theory," the problems of Vietnam remained largely obscured throughout his administration. Thus, when he stepped down, Eisenhower left the situation in Southeast Asia with nary a mention to the incoming chief executive, covering the subject neither in his outline of international situations nor during their briefings. Kennedy's reaction, once he learned more about the situation, was one of amazement: "'You know,' he said in disbelief to White House adviser Walt W. Rostow, 'Ike never briefed me about Vietnam.'"[25] Steps taken by the young president to discover the nature of affairs in that region included dispatching Vice-President Lyndon Johnson on what Kennedy called "a special fact-finding mission to Asia" only five months after assuming office.[26]

Johnson's report on his tour, as noted earlier, warned of the constancy of the communist effort, the instability of the Vietnamese government, the poverty of the people, and the need for a clear decision regarding the United States' role in the region. Concurring with Johnson's admonitions concerning the country's significant social and political problems, and accepting the basic thrust of the domino theory, Kennedy felt that communist encroachment into Southeast Asia needed a firm American response—especially in light of the Bay of Pigs fiasco, the blockade of Berlin, increasing instability in Laos, and Khrushchev's vow to support all "wars of national liberation" in Third World countries. Nevertheless, Kennedy was reluctant to commit combat troops to South Vietnam, choosing instead to continue Eisenhower's policy of providing economic and military assistance. In the process, however, he extended the nature and range of that assistance. The number of American advisers in Vietnam thus grew from several hundred when Kennedy assumed office to more than sixteen thousand at the time of his death less than three years later.[27] Moreover, the troops' role was redefined to include combat support missions as well as base-oriented training, which dramatically increased American casualty rates. Finally, covert intelligence operations were launched against the North Vietnamese.

Although he dramatically expanded the American role in the area, Kennedy paid relatively little attention to the problems of Vietnam. It was, as Louis Heren characterized it, "just one of those problems that face great nations which take upon themselves the responsibility of maintaining world peace."[28] Moreover, it was a problem that puzzled Kennedy, and he preferred to buy time with minimal actions that delayed any major decisions. By mid-1962, the Kennedy administration even felt generally optimistic about Vietnam, especially with the reported success of the strategic-hamlet program which gathered the rural populace into protected villages.

Yet the optimism was based on misinformation from the South Vietnamese army, the ARVN. The figures on the success of the strategic-hamlet program, for example, were liberally inflated by each level of reporting in order to impress superiors and retain American aid. Moreover, the statistics focused on such gross measures as the number of people entering these hamlets and the number of Viet Cong killed, with no effort to discover that the peasants deeply resented the coercive uprooting entailed in the program.

These difficulties in Vietnam forced their way into official American consciousness when the Diem regime was overthrown, just prior to the Kennedy assassination, apparently with both direct and indirect encouragement from various American officials. The small country's political situation worsened as the one unifying factor for the majority of the populace—hatred of Diem's corrupt and dictatorial regime—disappeared. Only then did the United States personnel discover the extent to which the GVN's reports were unreliable.

Never to be satisfactorily resolved is the question of what John Fitzgerald Kennedy would have done regarding Vietnam had he lived. Many writers, including David Halberstam, contend that the Kennedy people "knew the war was being lost, but they never got it down on paper or into their own statements."[29] Their perspective sees the young president as striving to extricate the United States from the morass; he certainly would not, they argue, have taken the precipitous steps of his successor. Yet conjuring up such historical hypotheticals constitutes a risky business. In an interview for the newly expanded half hour Huntley-Brinkley newscast just two-and-a-half months before his death, Kennedy stressed his belief in the domino theory, his conviction that Communist China posed a significant threat as "a powerful force," his fear of losing Vietnam as China had been lost before it, and his rejection of withdrawal as an option.[30] In the same interview, he acknowledged the troubling ambivalence of the situation, and it is certain that before his death he was troubled by the inability of American efforts to inject social, political, and military stability into the region. Judgments of his course of action had he lived are problematic.

Thrust into the tumultuous situation instead, with its rapid deterioration on all fronts, was Lyndon Johnson. Despite his earlier fact-finding trip to the area, Johnson cared even less than Kennedy for the problems of Vietnam. Between the traditionally left-handed approach taken by the United States to that part of the globe and Johnson's own proclivities toward domestic issues, he was not particularly interested in the foreign affairs of Southeast Asia. Yet Diem's overthrow and the ensuing chaos in South Vietnam demanded attention.

Two factors particularly influenced Johnson's response to Vietnam upon coming into office. One was the character of his personal involvement, forged from his vice-presidential trip to Southeast Asia. That trip had convinced him of the need for "a clear-cut and strong program of action" to resist the communist aggression he found there.[31] To understand his perceptions and the foreign policies that grew from them, one must realize that, as mentioned earlier, aggression functioned as a devil term of major proportions for Lyndon Johnson, who heard it resound with the lesson of Munich: when free nations fail to repel encroachment, they suffer a world war in consequence. William S. White, a journalist and close friend who talked with Johnson after his return, felt that the vice-president's trip resulted in "a major moral and emotional commitment by Johnson to this policy [of a continued American determination to resist aggression in Vietnam] before he became President."[32]

This commitment was intensified by the second factor: the nature of Johnson's succession to the presidency. As Kennedy's vice-president, he was, at least initially, placed in something of a caretaker role, obligated to follow through on the late president's programs and policies. On the issue of Vietnam, Johnson believed that obligation required a firm role, and he accepted that duty willingly and with conviction. Additionally, Johnson felt constrained to demonstrate to the world, allies and antagonists alike, that America's strength and responsibility were not lessened by its period of grief and self-searching. Thus it was that Johnson pledged himself to "seeing things through in Vietnam," first stated publicly in his message to Congress and the nation on November 27, 1963, when he assured his audience

54

that he would uphold American commitments "from South Vietnam to West Berlin."[33]

It was appropriate, then, that one of the new president's first conferences was with Ambassador Henry Cabot Lodge, who had flown in from Vietnam to confer with President Kennedy. Lodge reviewed the factors leading to the coup, the still-unstable political situation, and American military and economic programs, while John McCone, director of the Central Intelligence Agency, added his assessments. The result of the conference was a reassertion of the United States' general policy on Vietnam, including aspirations and dilemmas, obligations and misgivings. Even with the difficulties of policy, Johnson ordered an immediate halt to the internal squabbling among members of the U.S. Mission in Vietnam—the Defense Department, CIA, military officials, and others constituting the American contingent in that country. The dissension had complicated the American role in South Vietnamese political affairs, already bountifully complex, and increased confusion of ARVN military reporting, already abundantly confused. While these tensions in part reflected the ambiguities of American policy for that country, Johnson nonetheless demanded a coordinated effort by the U.S. Mission abroad.

The conference with these men was followed by discussions with Mike Mansfield, senator from Montana and majority leader since 1961. Their talks brought copies of Mansfield's correspondence on the subject with Kennedy, correspondence allegedly rejected by Kennedy for its pessimistic assessment.[34] Johnson also sought further information, announcing at his first press conference of December 7, 1963, that he had asked McNamara to go to Vietnam to appraise the American presence.

Upon his return, McNamara drafted a four-page memorandum to the president outlining his reactions. "The situation," the secretary of defense reported, "is very disturbing."[35] The new South Vietnamese government was "indecisive and drifting," so preoccupied with political matters that military operations suffered; the U.S. Mission "lacks leadership, has been poorly informed, and is not working to a common plan"; the Viet Cong controlled a number of key provinces; and infiltration from North Vietnam continued at a rapid rate. Neutralization of Vietnam, vociferously advocated by Charles de Gaulle, was opposed by the new government (like many American officials, they regarded it as tantamount to inviting a communist takeover); and McNamara noted that despite official statements of United States opposition to neutralization, "our attitude is somewhat suspect because of editorials by the *New York Times* and mention by Walter Lippmann and others." The government's formal policy was doubted, given the widely circulated media reports contradicting it; the *New York Times* accounts fostered fears difficult to quell with diplomatic reiterations.

While McNamara did not feel a substantial increase in American resources and personnel would be beneficial, clearly some steps had to be taken: "Current trends, unless reversed in the next 2–3 months, will lead to neutralization at best and more likely to a Communist-controlled state." He admitted that his evaluation might be "overly pessimistic," but felt close monitoring and careful cooperation were essential.

CIA Director John McCone concurred with McNamara's conclusions, telling the president that "there is no substantial difference between Secretary McNamara and myself except perhaps I feel a little less pessimistic than he. Nevertheless, . . . there are more reasons to be pessimistic than to be optimistic about prospects of our success in South Vietnam."[36]

Of particular concern to McNamara, McCone, and Johnson was what the secretary of defense termed "the grave reporting weakness" resulting from "our undue dependence on distorted Vietnamese reporting," which was more concerned with brownie points and Yankee bucks than with accuracy.[37] To resolve this reliance on unrealistically optimistic accounts, the United States established its own channels of intelligence and military reporting, and thus took another step toward Americanizing the war. The National Security Files on Viet Nam contain a number of the resulting CIA reports, entitled "The Situation in South Vietnam: Weekly Report of the Intelligence and Reporting Subcommittee of the Intraagency Vietnam Coordinating Committee."

McNamara's findings also encouraged the president to reiterate his support of Lodge's work as ambassador—by public statements of endorsement, by sending new personnel with whom Lodge could work more easily, and by instructing stateside agencies that Lodge's requests were to be given "highest priority" and a "prompt and sympathetic response."[38]

Despite these actions, Vietnam was far from uppermost in Johnson's mind. The new president was busy learning the intricacies of the executive branch, pushing for a tax bill and civil rights legislation, and mapping out programs for his administration that were based on, but extended beyond, Kennedy's plans. The problems and issues of Vietnam were primarily handled by others in his administration. Thus, when Mike Mansfield sent Johnson a mildly critical letter along with a copy of a strongly critical speech he had given, National Security Adviser McGeorge Bundy asked McNamara and Secretary of State Dean Rusk to draft refutations which Johnson "can review and then use with Senator Mansfield if he wishes."[39]

To the extent that the early Johnson administration was concerned with Vietnam at all, it did evidence a consistent awareness of problems resulting from media coverage of the area. Earlier, Kennedy had requested that the *New York Times* withdraw Halberstam from Saigon because his stories "raised doubts at home about the wisdom of American policy there";[40] by the time Johnson entered office, the adverse accounts were slowly increasing. McNamara's December report, for example, had pointed to the difficulty of American diplomatic efforts against neutralization in light of contradictory speculation by Walter Lippmann and the *New York Times*. Moreover, McNamara was not alone in his concern. After the military junta that had overthrown Diem on November 1 was itself replaced less than three months later by General Nguyen Khanh and a group of officers, White House aide Michael V. Forrestal informed Johnson that

> our major problem this morning appears to be with our own press. Scotty Reston has written in the "Times" [*New York Times*] that we are "actually on record as favoring the 'neutralization' of the whole country, North Vietnam as well as South." . . .
>
> The other press problems are the Lambert and Kiker stories in the "Tribune" [*New York Herald Tribune*] which are typical of the sour grapes attitude of that newspaper. I think you should probably have a meeting this afternoon of your principal advisors on the Vietnam situation. . . . This meeting should be on the record.[41]

While no such meeting appears in the Daily Diary, Forrestal's decision to include the suggestion indicates the seriousness with which the media accounts were regarded.

Meetings with advisers notwithstanding, the *New York Times's* editorializing on neutralization caused sufficient concern by April that Forrestal held a "rather lengthy conversation" with the *Times's* Robert Kleiman, urging him to see both the administration's position and the difficulties created by media contradiction thereof.[42] Other concerns over media reports on Southeast Asia arose during this period as well. A *Time* correspondent's questions suggesting that Johnson would delay any Vietnam decision pending the 1964 election, for example, indicated that undercurrents of dissension about administration policy within the Pentagon had created several news sources out of the disgruntled.[43] In another notable instance, Rusk cabled the American embassy in Saigon to discuss the implications of reports by the *New York Times, New York Herald Tribune, Washington Post, Washington Star, Chicago Daily News*, and the wire services—a list indicative of the White House's orientation toward the eastern media.[44] The stories, reported the secretary of state, "emphasize villagers killed and effects [of] bombing upon civilian population," including pictures of a " 'Vietnamese child' with napalm burns in the arms of father after GVN bombers attacked village." Rusk implied that embassy officials should be well prepared to handle the inquiries which would inevitably follow.

For the ambassador's part, Henry Cabot Lodge made it clear that he personally would maintain control of news dissemination when he instructed that Barry Zorthian, new director of the United States Information Agency in Vietnam, "should understand that he will not (repeat not) have responsibility for press relations (newspaper, magazine, television, radio) as I do this work myself."[45]

Yet government officials were not alone in their concern for the news operation in Vietnam. Reporters, perhaps for different reasons, were equally troubled. In a 1964 essay for the *Columbia Journalism Review*, Malcolm Browne discussed his dissatisfactions as an Associated Press correspondent in Saigon between 1961 and 1963, updating it with reports from fellow journalists still stationed there. Browne noted that the strict South Vietnamese policies on news handling frustrated correspondents, whose newsgathering efforts were further hampered by the American officials' reticence to risk "diplomatic friction with the Vietnamese government."[46] By July of 1964, the feud between journalists and officials was so intense that the Pentagon launched a $50,000 program to improve both press facilities and press relations in Vietnam—a move correspondents wryly dubbed Operation Candor.

Procedural obstacles constituted only a part of the problem of accurately reporting events from Vietnam. As Browne observed:

> Viet Nam does not lend itself well to numerical reporting, or even to the kind of simple, narrative statement required of the average newspaper lead. There are too many uncertainties, too many shades of gray, too many dangers of applying English-language clichés to a situation that cannot be described by clichés. . . .

58

> War reporting itself, for example, is technically fairly simple. Reporting a single clash with the number of casualties is not unlike reporting a sports event. By an adroit use of verbs, the writer can create an impact that comes close to reproducing reality.
>
> But in Viet Nam, the actual clashes are probably less important than the social upheaval of the nation. These are difficult to capture in words, and for a reader to digest.

The complexities of reporting the conflict in Vietnam corresponded to the difficulties of Americans trying to understand it, and more especially, to United States involvement there. Some government officials sensed this confusion. Henry Cabot Lodge, for example, concluded that the extent of the mail asking "why Viet-Nam is important, how we are doing, and what we should do in the future" indicated "a real demand for a 'full dress' presentation on what to you and me are obvious fundamentals."[47] As a consequence, Lodge drafted an essay for *Foreign Affairs* to present such an explanation to "columnists, editors, and so called 'opinion makers.' " In requesting comment and approval from Undersecretary of State W. Averell Harriman, Lodge argued that "undoubtedly, the most important single factor in the whole Viet-Nam problem is support from the American home front"; United States citizens needed to understand and support their country's role in the conflict. McGeorge Bundy sent a copy of Lodge's essay, which he called "fascinating," on to Johnson;[48] but despite Lodge's conviction that the story should be told, the essay he proposed never appeared in *Foreign Affairs*, and the available White House files do not reveal why.

Walt W. Rostow, chairman of the State Department's Policy Planning Council and Bundy's eventual successor as national security adviser, shared Lodge's concern regarding "the depth of the public confusion about both the U.S. stake in the outcome in Viet Nam and the character of the conflict."[49] Rostow traced this confusion in large part to "the reporting of the war," which

> tends to portray it as a vicious, indigenous civil war in which the United States has somehow become involved in ambiguous ways, there being little consciousness of the international background to the 1962 and 1954 Accords. It is easy in Washington to underestimate the cumulative effect of Halberstam's *New York Times* reporting, as well as recent *U.S. News and World Report* stories, statements in the Senate, etc.

Like Malcolm Browne, Rostow despaired of the media's attempts to encapsulate the war in their reports. Unlike Browne, Rostow believed that the difficulty could be easily remedied: the administration could easily rectify the misconceptions created by such media accounts, he concluded, "should more vigorous action be judged necessary." The White House would simply develop a campaign to reach "reporters, editors, publishers, Congressional leaders, and key citizens" with its information to "strengthen our hand in pursuing current lines of policy as well as laying a firmer base for action against the North, should that course be judged necessary at a later time."

Yet herein lay a key to Johnson's early approach to Vietnam: he did not want to take more vigorous action, either in Southeast Asia or, more especially, at home. That issue constituted a necessary commitment which seemed less of a nuisance when kept in low profile, and he intended it to remain that way. Misconceptions about America's role in Vietnam among the press and public proved annoying, but Johnson remained unconvinced that the misconceptions were widespread enough or significant enough to justify the effort of elaborate public clarification. While later observers have both directly and indirectly traced Johnson's reluctance about addressing the issue publicly to a compulsive secrecy and an inherently warlike nature, his concerns were much less Machiavellian than such charges imply. Certainly he was wary of turning a peripheral political issue into a central one, so soon after Kennedy's death and so close to a presidential election; mostly, however, he simply preferred to focus his attention on domestic affairs. Johnson was not suppressing a major issue in early 1964, for it had not yet become that. Vietnam simply did not consume a significant proportion of his time or energy at this stage; he assumed it was important enough to U.S. security to attend to, yet he also assumed that it required relatively little attention.

The president did continue to monitor the situation, requesting that McNamara and General Taylor return there during the second week of March 1964, to further assess the problem. They concluded that while the situation had deteriorated, increased American aid to build the South Vietnamese army and the long-hoped-for political stability might bring improvement. In his account of the National Security Council meeting held upon the return of McNamara and Taylor to the United States, Johnson related that the Joint Chiefs of Staff felt more drastic actions—including "immediate measures against the North"—were necessary.[50] However, South Vietnamese military weaknesses and the risk of involving the Russians and Chinese weighed against such a decision. Even when Hanoi increased its offensive in the summer of 1964, Johnson was reluctant to escalate the conflict. He would request an additional $125 million from Congress in increased aid for South Vietnam in May of 1964,[51] but the persistent belief that time and money would strengthen the South Vietnamese government, coupled with a steadfast resistance to the dangers of expanded military action, encouraged a continuation of current policies.

Shortly after Johnson had assumed the presidency, a column by Drew Pearson predicted that the new chief executive "would be sensitive in his press relations."[52] Pearson's use of the word "sensitive," in light of later developments, may seem ironic. The new president, however, was sensitive to the press in a number of the meanings of that term. As Senate majority leader, Johnson had for the most part shunned the spotlight of the news, preferring the freedom of obscurity. As president, Johnson would have liked to retain the flexibility of movement he enjoyed in the Senate, but after three long years in the shadows of the vice-presidency he also welcomed the attention traditionally the prerogative of America's chief executive. From the beginning of his administration, even in the austere months following the assassination, Johnson felt that he should dominate the news. Encouraged by longtime friend and supporter Jack Valenti, a Houston advertising and public relations specialist who thrived on the creation of pseudoevents, Johnson sought favorable press coverage as instrumental to the overall success of his administration.

An example of Johnson's desire for good coverage which had little authentication but wide circulation depicts the president calling top public-affairs specialists onto the Oval Office carpet just days before Christmas, chastising them because "you're not getting my picture on the front page the way you did Kennedy's."

The story may be apocryphal, but its point is not. On January 23, 1964, veteran Johnson aide Horace Busby sent the president an eight-page memorandum outlining twenty-one "creative and innovative image-broadening activities," which ranged from going to a variety of churches, to shifting several ambassadorial assignments in order "to divert columnists and State Department critics," to sponsoring a conference on the arts.[53] Of special interest are the suggestions designed to refute "political smears": photographs of the Johnsons reading in the White House living quarters, to counter the "widespread false impression that the President is not a reader"; pictures of Johnson strolling with his wife and bowling with his daughters, to combat the images of Johnson as a hard-driving political maneuverer with health problems from overwork; and visits with various intellectuals, for "if there is an important segment still withholding judgment on the President, it is the intellectual community—including the artistic community."

Reports that Johnson was not a reader rankled the White House staff for two reasons: the man read voraciously, and the charge was usually joined with a lament by the "intellectuals" for Kennedy's Camelot. Johnson did read enormous amounts of materials, but books did not tend to be among them. Illustrative was the experience of one journalist who asked several members of the staff what books Johnson had read recently. Eager to prove the stories of nonreading wrong, each thought a moment, and then announced with delight, "Barbara Ward's *The Rich Nations and the Poor Nations!*" As Liz Carpenter so wryly observes, the eradication of poverty, disease, and ignorance advocated in Ward's volume were indeed central to Johnson's goals, "but any self-respecting speechwriter was bound to be obliged to vary the words from time to time."[54] Busby apparently felt no such compunction, for his memorandum suggests that in the photograph Johnson "might be reading some such authentic personal favorite as Barbara Ward's 'Poor Nations, Rich Nations.' "

Busby's memorandum also contained a suggestion for image-broadening that must have made Johnson shudder:

> President's picture wearing cap, released together with background from Pierre Salinger that President thinks "every man ought to have and wear a cap." This would serve as a style-setting story with much friendly, good-feeling publicity. Also: very effective counter to present Eastern over-emphasis on the ten-and-five gallon hats.

Clearly, Busby's lengthy memorandum reflected Johnson's concern for his media image, a concern apparent in other ways as well. Just as he had tried the Johnson Treatment in the realm of foreign affairs, so too did he use it in his press relations. Identifying influential columnists, publishers, and reporters, Johnson courted them as he would senators or an important political interest group: he strove to be accessible to people on the *New York Times, Washington Post,* and *Baltimore Sun;* he invited the publishers, editor, and chief White House correspondent of the *New York Herald Tribune* for dinner; he sent his own plane to bring columnist Scotty Reston and his wife to the LBJ ranch for the holidays.[55] He also favored the regular White House press corps over roving reporters with casual chats as well as impromptu press conferences.

In spite of his efforts, Johnson's tactics irritated many members of the media. Lippmann and Reston were wary of Johnson's advances, while others resented what they perceived as his attempts to trade personal favors for favorable stories, as if the reporters were malleable, unconscionable hacks rather than trained professionals. The unannounced, unbroadcast press conferences which Johnson regarded as "flexible" and favorable for the regular White House correspondents annoyed those accustomed to the well-prepared, formal conferences at which John Kennedy had excelled. They fumed at a lack of preparation time, the restricted opportunity to call in experts in significant areas, and their inability to leave the White House for fear of missing some spontaneous presidential announcement. A letter to Johnson from Charles W. Bailey of the *Minneapolis Star & Tribune* illustrates a journalist's chagrin at missing an opportunity for an interview:

> My apologies for not being on hand when you were kind enough to offer to give me a few minutes. I had just left to walk back to my office to write a story about your tax bill speech. If you ever feel like giving me a second chance I'll sure try to be more available.[56]

To miss major press conferences because they were called under similarly impromptu conditions, as they often were, heightened reportorial chagrin into indignation.

Especially irritating to reporters were the Saturday morning press conferences. Johnson loved them for their potential to capture Sunday headlines, but journalists—especially those from newspapers—hated them for the difficulties they imposed on meeting deadlines, not to mention the inconveniences in their personal lives. Two months into the Johnson administration, reporters complained heartily about the "quickies," a complaint that in turn irritated the president. During a conference in the Oval Office on January 25, Johnson admonished:

> Don't run out of here if you have any questions you want to ask. Ask them. I will answer them. This is not a quickie news conference. I don't know what you would call a formal one. I guess I ought to wear a white tie. I came to work this morning and I didn't think it was formal; I just thought I was supposed to be here. And if you all are here, I will give you anything I know at any time . . . .
>   I never enjoy anything more than polite, courteous, fair, judicious reporters, and I think all of you qualify.[57]

Although many journalists interpreted Johnson's reaction as one of petulance over his inability to manipulate them, others sympathized with the president's position. Thus, ABC's Edward P. Morgan argued that

> the press itself is partly to blame for the president's communication problem. We Washington correspondents have been coddled and spoiled and we can be pouting primadonnas when we want to be. As one veteran put it, we like to fancy that the president will check with us not only before he makes a speech but before he makes a decision. And then we reserve the right to criticize both form and substance and compare them unfavorably with the way some previous president would have handled it.[58]

Yet members of the press were not alone in their discomfort with Johnson's approach. Rotund, gregarious Pierre Salinger had stayed with the new administration out of loyalty to Kennedy's programs, but the press secretary had never really been a part of the Johnson organization. From the beginning, George Reedy had performed many of the behind-the-scenes duties of press secretary, including such important functions as routing requests from reporters. In addition to his devotion to Kennedy, Salinger disliked Johnson's approach to the press, regretted his handling of the Panama crisis, and disagreed with his dismissal of the White House photographer.[59] On March 18, 1964, Salinger officially turned the job of press secretary over to Reedy, whose laconic style and close association with Johnson suited him for the position.

Yet Reedy was, by his own admission, reluctant to assume the post.[60] He anticipated difficulties between the president and the press and did not relish being caught in the middle. Johnson, the aide knew, faced all of the image problems to which Busby had earlier referred, plus others. When, for example, the president turned off many of the lights, both inside and outside of the White House, in an attempt to underscore the emphasis on economy in his dramatically low $97.9 billion budget, the press promptly dubbed him "Light Bulb" Johnson. This "cornball" depiction was further emphasized in the minds of some journalists as word circulated that Johnson distrusted the "Eastern liberal press" for its inability to understand and accept a president from Texas.

An early account of Johnson's antipathy toward the eastern press is provided by Eugene Patterson, then editor of the *Atlanta Constitution*. After a dinner at the home of *Manchester Guardian* correspondent Max Freedman, the president offered Patterson and his wife a ride back to their hotel. Once settled in the limousine, Johnson opened the conversation by predicting problems in the future relationship between himself and the press, predicated, he felt, on the "chasm" that separated a southern president from an eastern press. When Patterson demurred, Johnson said, "somberly,"

> You watch the *New York Times.* Whenever they take an editorial position, you'll see that same editorial position rolling across the country. Within two weeks, papers all over the country will be writing the same thing they do. And the *New York Times* doesn't like me.[61]

When Patterson protested that the *Times* had thus far been favorable, the president sighed, "Sure, as long as I do all right. But," he said, "you wait until I make one mistake." Although Patterson disagreed at the time, his assessment five years later had changed: "I think he reads the press pretty well."

Patterson was not alone in hearing of Johnson's unhappy predictions for his future with the press. After a conference with the president, James Reston called the veteran Democratic political adviser James Rowe because, as Rowe later wrote the president, the columnist was disturbed about "his talk with you about the Washington press. He feels you are wrong in your belief that the Washington press will be against you because you are a Southerner, and he asked me to talk to you about it if I agreed with him."[62] While Rowe said he "was sure the Northern Liberals felt that way about Southern Presidents," he was equally certain that a more important presidential concern was winning elections. Although Rowe would seem to be dismissing the importance of the press in the political process, he went on to warn Johnson to attend to Lippmann and Reston, as later discussions explore in further detail.

For whatever reason, Johnson continued battling image problems during the early spring of 1964. Two of the stories that appeared reinforced Johnson's reputation as a manipulative politician. The first concerned the Bobby Baker case, in which Johnson's former Senate aide was accused of mixing his official position with private business dealings. The testimony included charges that the life insurance agent through whom Baker had arranged a policy for Lyndon Johnson had been "encouraged" to show his appreciation by purchasing advertising from Lady Bird Johnson's television station in Austin and by sending the then majority leader a stereo for Christmas. When columnist Drew Pearson impugned the insurance man's testimony by using information provided by the FBI, the *New York Times* ran a front-page story attacking the White House for interfering in the case.[63]

The Baker story received further national exposure when the "Silent Witness" made the cover of *Time* magazine on March 6, 1964. On March 15, in the wake of this publicity, Johnson faced a question about his "protégé" and his "friend" during a nationally televised interview with network representatives. The president responded by saying that Bobby Baker was "no protégé of anyone; he was there before I came to the Senate for ten years, doing a job substantially the same as he is doing now; he was elected by all the Senators, appointed by no one."[64] Admitting only that Baker had been "an employee of mine," Johnson washed his hands of his former aide.

The first lady's television station, KTBC, also figured in the second story of the spring of 1964 that accentuated Johnson's image as manipulator. Two carefully documented articles by Louis M. Kohlmeier appeared in the March 23 and 24 issues of the *Wall Street Journal*, describing the acquisition and development of the Johnson family fortune. Built around the television station which Mrs. Johnson had purchased with her inheritance, the Johnson money grew through careful management of KTBC, favorable rulings by the Federal Communications Commission, and wise investment of the profits in Texas land. The clear implication of the *Journal* stories was that the key element in the station's success, the FCC approvals at auspicious times, had resulted from Johnson's political position and pressures he was able to exert.

In this case, Lady Bird Johnson's hard work and her economic and managerial acumen must not be underrated; her pride and interest in the station are abundantly clear in *A White House Diary*. Moreover, it is doubtful that Johnson exerted any overt pressure on the FCC for favorable rulings; he more likely regarded the approvals as the benefits of being an upstanding citizen, a government servant, and a wise business partner. Yet for those who saw Johnson as a master of political pressure and trade-off, the station's success was one more indication of Johnson's true nature.

Perhaps the key ingredient in Johnson's early presidential image crisis lay not in the early stories of Bobby Baker and the family fortune, but in one that appeared after the Easter holidays. Johnson, filled with the joy of spring and the exuberance of being president, had returned to his ranch for the weekend. Piling into his Lincoln Continental with four reporters, three of them female, Johnson embarked on one of his favorite ranch pastimes: a fast ride through the Texas countryside, revelling in his cattle, his land, and his friends. A beer in one hand, the steering wheel in the other, the president regaled his passengers with descriptions of the reproductive features of a prize bull, then peeled out at a rapid pace.

66

When the journalists, safely returned to the press corps fold, recounted their experiences, stories began to circulate. When later asked by a reporter about taking unnecessary risks by driving ninety miles an hour in a seventy-mile-per-hour zone, Johnson responded ingenuously, "I am unaware that I have ever driven past seventy."[65] The first speeding story was not then filed by one of reporters in the car, but by one of their attentive colleagues who listened to the accounts that evening in Austin's Headliners Club. As Cormier observes, that initial story was relatively mild, but it was sufficient "to move the episode out of the off-the-record category and send others scurrying after more vivid facts."[66]

The issue of the ranch tour did not really explode, however, until the following Monday, when the new *Time* magazine hit the stands. Its account of the "Texas joyride" opened:

> A cream-colored Lincoln Continental driven by the President of the U.S. flashed up a long Texas hill, swung into the left lane to pass two cars poking along under 85 m.p.h., and thundered on over the crest of the hill—squarely into the path of an upcoming car. The President charged on, his paper cup of Pearl beer within easy sipping distance. The other motorist veered off the paved surface to safety on the road's shoulder. Groaned a passenger in the President's car when the ride was over: "That's the closest John McCormack has come to the White House yet."[67]

Describing the reactions of the three newswomen, including "Hearst's pretty blonde Marianne Means," the story continued:

> As he drove, Johnson talked about his cattle, once plunged into what one startled newswoman called a "very graphic description of the sex life of a bull."
> . . . During the tour, Reporter Means, her baby-blue eyes fastened on Johnson, cooed: "Mr. President, you're fun."
> Through all the fun, the President sipped beer from his paper cup. Eventually he ran dry, refilled once from Marianne's supply, emptied his cup again, and took off at speeds up to 90 m.p.h. to get more. . . . Someone gasped at how fast Johnson was driving. Quickly, Lyndon took one hand from the wheel, removed his five-gallon hat and flopped it on the dashboard to cover the speedometer.

As a result of the publicity, ministers preached sermons on the evils of drink; editorials chided the highest officer in the land for breaking the speed limit and endangering others; a nation too close to one president's death shuddered at the prospect of another. With *Time*'s sanction, a story that might otherwise have remained a sidebar, cautiously couched as an unsubstantiated rumor, became hard news and stirred a host of other stories.

The story was certainly not one the Johnson staff would have wanted, especially in an election year. They feared that it might move beyond a depiction of Johnson as a crude and careless Texan to irrevocably crystallize the image of a reckless president, immeasurably harming his administration. Only George Reedy contended that the story was beneficial; he believed that the stories of a beer-drinking, fast-driving man who delighted the ladies created a macho image which aided the president incalculably—a view he could not convince the president to share.[68] Coming on the heels of the Baker case and the financial stories, the drinking-and-driving accounts caused Johnson to banish *Time* and the *New York Times* from presidential grace, to wait for the scant and grudgingly granted forgiveness that came only on rare occasions.

Beyond concern over the possible political ramifications, Johnson felt personally betrayed. He had invited reporters to the ranch for conversation, beer, and a bit of driving, and they had repaid his hospitality with bitterly mocking attacks. Reedy has suggested that Johnson would not have let down his guard with the reporters had they been male rather than female;[69] whatever the reason for his exuberance, the president regretted it now. When longtime friend and journalist William S. White discussed the incident with him, Johnson exclaimed, "But, Bill, you don't understand. They were my guests." White elaborated on the implications of such a view for presidential-press relationships:

> If reporters were with him personally in a context of that kind, he did think of them as his guests, and of course they didn't think of that at all. He had the old-fashioned idea if you have a man to your house to dinner, even if he's a press man, he doesn't go out later and say you were doing this, that, and the other. He could never grasp that people did this.[70]

Conversely, the "people" in the press corps could never grasp the idea that Johnson felt this way. While they welcomed the opportunity to be guests (even though most were at the same time suspicious of Johnson's intent), they never regarded their role as journalists to be excluded by their role as guests. Even off-the-record encounters were seen as indirect grist for the reporting mill.

Ironically, on the very day the damning *Time* story appeared, Jack Valenti sent a memorandum to aides Bill Moyers and Horace Busby instructing them on the need to scour the newspapers each day so they can "insert in the [*Congressional*] *Record* every favorable story—column—editorial appearing in the newspapers in this area—and around the country." Valenti divided ten newspapers among the three of them and assigned a fourth person to monitor the rest.[71]

Although the proposal was pure Valenti in style, it clearly suggested Johnson's determination to dominate the news as president—a goal Valenti embraced wholeheartedly. It also, however, pointed to a disagreement within the administration, reflecting a problem Johnson himself sensed regarding his approach to publicity. Evans and Novak identified it as the conflict between "the policy of Containment and the policy of Exposure."[72] While advocates of each approach concurred that the president should be in the news, and in a more favorable light than that cast during the early months of 1964, they disagreed on how to accomplish those goals. Valenti and the "exposure school" concocted meetings, trips, and appearances through which they hoped to reveal Johnson's natural exuberance to the American public. News-making ventures were thus greeted eagerly by this group.

In contrast, the "containment" advocates felt such exposure had to be carefully controlled. Goldman objected that such activities were all too often "transparently contrived; they overexposed the President, often in situations where he showed to little advantage; they encouraged an emphasis on sheer public relations, a kind of thinking toward which Lyndon Johnson was only too prone."[73] Instead of what Reedy derided as "this gimmicky form of public relations,"[74] the more conservative containment advocates recommended limited exposure, arguing that only by containing Johnson's exuberance and by restricting press access to him could the rash of negative stories be checked.

Johnson himself was ambivalent about the issue. While he revelled in the publicity, he detested criticism. Should he show his enjoyment of the pinnacle of power, or retreat into presidential dignity? His March and April coverage prompted him toward the latter. Thus, his first reaction to the beer-drinking and fast-driving stories—after fury—was to cease the casual drink-and-chat interaction with the press which had been standard up to that point. As spring continued, however, Johnson could not restrain himself. He joked about the joyrides: "Be careful on the roads. The country is full of crazy drivers." When he hoisted his beagle Him by the ears and editorials howled about cruelty to animals, he responded that the dog "doesn't yelp unless an AP photographer gets too close to him." In spite of all of his previous difficulties, just one hundred days after entering office the president's spirits were so high he lifted the embargo: on February 29, 1964, he provided the first formal, televised, Kennedy-style press conference of his administration and acquitted himself admirably.

Perhaps the clearest sign of Johnson's recovery from the earlier bad press and the strongest incentive for the exposure school came when Johnson's personal intervention headed off a potentially disastrous railroad strike. Delighted with his success, the president had to share his triumph with the nation via prime-time television. To do so, Johnson and the negotiators had to go to the WTOP television studios, because the time needed to set up equipment in the White House would delay the announcement beyond news time. Bundling the negotiators into cars to race through rush-hour traffic, Johnson appeared before the cameras as an energetic and creative emcee, even pulling out of his pocket a letter from a young girl, Cathy May Baker, who pleaded for a settlement so that her grandmother could attend her confirmation (never mind that the communion had already occurred, with the grandmother in attendance; did Johnson know?). The performance, argues Evans and Novak,

> was Johnson's presidential takeoff. Magically, the depressing self-analysis and image preoccupation of transition days were for the time being no longer relevant. By one positive act, Johnson had established a distinctive image for his administration. . . . The fact that he had triumphed immeasurably bolstered his confidence, further changing the tone of his presidency, which now became both resilient and resonant.[75]

In his ensuing enthusiasm, Johnson pushed for the completion of plans for permanent television facilities within the White House, complete with cameras kept in readiness around the clock. Such an installation would have made the frantic dash to the CBS building to announce the railroad settlement unnecessary; first proposed in January, the facilities seemed all the more desirable in April.[76] The president also accepted a proposal that he meet with the heads of the various Washington news bureaus to provide background information that would aid the general understanding and interpretive reporting efforts.[77]

Yet Johnson retained his wariness of the media. On May 19, 1964, Reedy sent Valenti a list of twenty correspondents, each assigned to one of six staff members.[78] Even though press relationships were now

70

relatively good, monitoring articles and providing encouragement for pro-administration interpretations, he reasoned, could only help the Johnson image.

By the spring of 1964, then, Lyndon Johnson had already experienced a honeymoon, a falling out, and a reconciliation with the press. All the while, the issue of Vietnam waited impatiently in the wings.

4

Increasing Complications, Spring 1964 to Winter 1964–65

As spring turned into the summer of 1964, Lyndon Johnson settled into the White House. In April his exuberance over warmer weather and the glories of the presidency had pulled him onto the Truman balcony, with poet Carl Sandburg at his side, to holler to reporters below: "Haaaalllllloooo down there, I've got Carl Sandburg with me!"[1] As the first lady described him, he was "exhilarated, on that Olympian peak."[2] Johnson revelled in the power and prestige of his office, which enabled him to tackle problems and power politics to an unprecedented extent. The scene on the White House balcony served as "his kind of paean to the Presidency" in those early months.[3]

Yet the ecstasy was not complete. Naggingly, quietly, insistently, Vietnam intruded. The chaos of South Vietnamese politics continued, contrary to the administration's hopes that the government would stabilize and assume a greater role in the conflict. For its part, North Vietnam added regular troops to its guerrilla units, preparing for more conventional warfare. Still seeking to resolve the conflict on a quieter level, the Johnson administration moved to institute "a wide variety of sabotage and psychological operations against North Vietnam" as recommended in McNamara's memorandum of December 21, 1963.[4] With a code name of Operation Plan 34-A, the program called for American advisers to supervise the South Vietnamese navy in conducting small-scale attacks on North Vietnamese coastal installations. In addition, a program known as DeSoto patrols assigned United States destroyers to the surveillance of North Vietnamese radar systems and naval operations. These covert actions were coupled with elaborate contingency planning for pressures against the North. Through the spring and summer of 1964, then, air strikes, clandestine operations, and plans for possible escalation increased. Even while pushing his staff to outline deterrent programs, Johnson resisted instituting them. Yet the very fact that such military efforts were outlined in detail made them clear alternatives, especially as the clandestine strikes went into effect.

These measured efforts, intended to provide the quiet show of force that the president hoped would demoralize the North Vietnamese while allowing the South to gain political stability, failed to accomplish either. By the summer of 1964 the problems in Southeast Asia proved to be a major preoccupation, while his wife fretted over that "poor, lonesome, beleaguered man."[5] Not even social engagements could bring Johnson respite: a dinner with Joseph Alsop brought the columnist's warning that if the president failed to commit more troops to Vietnam he would preside over America's first military defeat—a prospect Lyndon Johnson certainly did not savor. It was a cry of doom that Alsop had practiced, for in 1950 he had authored a three-part series for the *Saturday Evening Post* entitled "Why We Lost China," and the columnist had laid full blame on Truman and the State Department. As Halberstam observes, the former China staff officer based his conclusion on the assumption that China was ours—and, more specifically, the president's—to lose.[6] More recent forays to defend the Kennedy administration's policies on Vietnam had cemented Alsop's view of the importance of Southeast Asia to the United States' interests. At dinner with Johnson, then, Alsop used his interpretation of China to underscore his case for a stronger American role in Vietnam—perspectives that to Johnson were uncomfortably analogous.

Johnson was always highly conscious of those who, like Alsop, felt the United States should marshall its full military capability to rectify the situation; at the same time, he still sought to maintain Vietnam as a low-profile issue. On Vietnam, as with other issues, Johnson wanted to keep his options open. In May of 1964, William Bundy (McGeorge Bundy's brother and the assistant secretary of state for Far Eastern affairs) collaborated with Pentagon officials to outline one such option: a thirty-day scenario of escalated attacks, to culminate in the full-scale bombing of North Vietnam.[7] The program was never carried out as written, although it did foreshadow several future steps regarding Vietnam. The scenario started, for example, with a presidential speech requesting a joint resolution of Congress in support of the planned American actions. Members of the administration explored the feasibility of such a move; several on the staff conducted discreet investigations into potential congressional support while Cater urged Bundy to seek a vaguely worded but short-term resolution to clarify America's commitment during the election period.[8] Whatever form it might take, such a public congressional sanction was a critical first step in any course of action for Lyndon Johnson; as a politician reared on Capitol Hill, he was convinced that the root of Truman's problems in Korea lay in "his failure to ask Congress for an expression of its backing."[9]

Yet to request such a resolution meant turning Vietnam into a front-page, lead-headline issue, which Johnson did not want. Even a more general speech was too much at this stage, although several staff members perceived a need for the public articulation of the administration's efforts in Vietnam. In May of 1964, for example, Walt Rostow had pressed Rusk to address the need for "a low-key campaign of public information" on America's role in Southeast Asia, aimed in particular at key reporters, editors, and publishers, given "the depth of public confusion" as fostered by and reflected in media reports.[10] Douglass Cater shared Rostow's concern as he urged the president to develop "new projects of real or symbolic value . . . to affirm (a) our determination not to retreat from this area, [and] (b) our overriding interest in building peace rather than waging war."[11] Cater himself contributed to this effort, for on June 24, 1964, McGeorge Bundy sent to Johnson Cater's draft of "a possible speech on Southeast Asia to Congress," which the national security adviser described as "the best connected statement on the subject that has yet been done here."[12] Yet the president rejected Cater's draft, explaining, "We don't ask Congress to do anything—Why go before them unless you do?"[13] Still feeling Vietnam was best handled firmly but quietly and with restraint, Johnson was reluctant to translate plans for escalation into military action; he was even more reluctant to address Congress or the nation on the issue.

Nor was Johnson encouraged to provide further public clarification on his policy in Southeast Asia given media coverage of the statements he did offer. In June of 1964, for example, his remarks at the Swedish Day picnic in Minneapolis began with the biblical passage, "to everything there is a season, and a time to every purpose under heaven . . . a time of war and a time of peace."[14] Expressing his hope that the world was moving toward a time of peace, Johnson nonetheless cautioned:

> Today, as always, if a nation is to keep its freedom, it must be prepared to risk war. When necessary, we will take that risk. But as long as I am President, I will spare neither my office nor myself in the quest for peace.
> That peace is much more than the absence of war.

The remainder of the speech then delineated his conception of peace. Media accounts of these remarks concentrated not on this delineation of peace, however, but on the threat of war. The coverage of the

New York Times the following day was typical when it headlined: "Johnson Affirms US Would Fight to Protect Asia; President, in Minneapolis, Stresses Determination to 'Risk War' if Necessary." Obviously Johnson found such an emphasis to be misplaced, as a memorandum from White House aide Douglass Cater indicates. Cater, whose experience in journalism enhanced his role as informal press liaison, advised Johnson that

> quite clearly, the reporters played the "risk war" part of your Sunday's speech all out of context. The reason, I discover, lies in their frustration at previous backgrounders held by Rusk and others. The reporters complain that they are being victimized when officials talk tougher off-the-record than they do on the record. They were looking for an excuse to confirm previous stories.[15]

Johnson's handwritten response to Cater revealed little sympathy with the media's sense of righteous indignation and still less with their accusations of administrative inconsistency:

> Hope you explain to reporters that this week tough line and next week soft line is not adm. but reporters' conclusions. We are where we were Nov. 22.

Despite this annoyance with "reporters' conclusions," however, Johnson still felt that a full statement of the administration's position would only complicate the matter. A full public statement would focus attention on the area as one of concern; it would stir a flurry of congressional responses; it would trigger a flood of unsolicited advice from columnists. A presidential statement would also escalate the issue in the eyes of Communist China, and Johnson was keenly aware of the risks involved in such an escalation. So he continued to downplay Vietnam as a way of keeping his options open. He dealt with the conflicting demands of the rhetoric of limited war by avoiding public justifications while proceeding with the military preparations that he felt were necessary.

Clearly, this balancing act of firm restraint with quiet action created tension, a tension impinging on Johnson's joyous exercise of presidential power. The summer's tension brought with it a major political decision: should Johnson run for election in the 1964 presidential race? The pressures to run were considerable. If he stepped down at the end of thirteen months, his political career would be over at the age of fifty-six, and his presidential record would be one of a caretaker merely carrying on the Kennedy legacy. Johnson longed to be president in his own right, to forge a consensus government for the nation as he had for the Senate. So much beckoned to be accomplished, and he felt he was the one to do it. In describing his assumption of the presidency, Johnson related that he saw "three conditions coming together in historic harmony" at that point: "a recognition of need, a willingness to act, and someone to lead the effort."[16] To refuse the Democratic nomination in 1964 would be to eliminate that third essential element, condemning his visions of eradicating poverty and alleviating bigotry to remain just that—only visions. With more time he could move from enactor of the Kennedy legislation to creator of the Johnsonian Great Society. The potentialities enticed him.

Yet Johnson had doubts. A primary concern, as Lady Bird's diary continually indicates, was Vietnam.[17] What painful possibilities lay ahead? What actions might prove necessary?

In his memoirs, Johnson said nothing of the role of Vietnam in his indecision. Instead, he observed that "the Presidency of the United States was a prize with a heavy price," including "scathing attacks" on himself and his family that could only intensify during a political campaign. He felt that the antipathy of an eastern metropolitan press toward a southern president would not lessen these criticisms either. In addition, Johnson cited a concern for his health, a concern that he and his staff had sought to alleviate in the minds of the press and the public from his earliest days as president. In his memoirs, however, Johnson noted that his heart attack at age forty-six resulted in part from his heavy senatorial duties; his reelection decision came when he was nine years older, with even heavier presidential responsibilities.[18]

On May 14, 1964, Lady Bird outlined her evaluation of each course of action for her husband.[19] If Johnson did bow out of the race, she wrote, his motives would be questioned, the nation would feel "keen, even bitter disappointment," and his various Texas interests would be "chicken-feed compared to what you are used to." While he would have more time for his family, daughters Lynda and Luci would soon be on their own, and Lady Bird feared "seeing you semi-idle, frustrated, looking back at what you left." Among other results, she noted, "you may look around for a scape-goat. I do not want to be it."

On the other hand, Mrs. Johnson continued, if he ran he would "most probably be elected President." Criticisms and occasional bad decisions would be inevitable, and inevitably painful; and, she told her husband, "you may die earlier than you would otherwise." Assessing each alternative, she encouraged her husband to stay in, and then refuse reelection in 1968. By then, she felt, "the juices of life will be stilled enough to let you come home in relative peace and acceptance."

Yet Johnson remained undecided. As Lady Bird pondered, "he wishes there were some honorable way out of it. . . . And yet, caught on this pinpoint in history, what exit is there?"[20] In the meantime, members of the media stepped up their inquiries about his campaign plans. To many in the press corps, such as AP correspondent Frank Cormier, "Johnson's misgivings [about mounting a national campaign] were close to subliminal."[21] The man's activities could be (and were) interpreted as that special blend of the presidential and the political available to an incumbent. Viewed as an inherent politician, Johnson's protestations were interpreted as a ploy—one that was met with amusement and some irritation among the press. The correspondents pointed to the inconsistency in telling them he had not yet made up his mind, and then greeting a crowd in Detroit by recalling that old song, "Will You Love Me in November as You Do in May?"[22]

The president, in turn, resented such an interpretation. "I prefer to maintain as much flexibility as a man can until the moment a decision becomes final," he later explained. "Thus during that period, while I considered the question of whether or not to run for President, I foreclosed nothing. I took no action that would automatically trap me into a decision. I *did* keep all my options open" (emphasis Johnson's).[23] It only confirmed for Johnson the difficulty of working with "the metropolitan press of the Eastern seaboard" when the news media insisted that such flexibility, especially in light of his efforts on behalf of Kennedy's legislation, meant he was "racing hard to capture the Democratic nomination."[24]

Whether Johnson resented the media reports because they were true or because they misinterpreted his intentions is of only partial concern here, although it does seem clear both that Johnson was 99 percent certain to run for reelection and that he truly did want to "keep his options open." The episode's major importance, rather, lies in its illumination of differing perceptions as they influenced future presidential-press actions and interactions. Columnists and reporters perceived Johnson's statements as political maneuvers; whether they were intrigued, amused, or annoyed by the approach, their perceptions affected their interpretations of Johnson's presidency. The views particularly influenced columnists, for they cull stories, rumors, and nuances from their friends in the Washington press corps—interpretations that correspondents may discuss but do not use in their news reports. "Shop talk" thus becomes half-speculative, half-omniscient punditry. Moreover, these perceptions, especially as articulated in the columns, formed further pieces of the mosaic of the presidential-press relationship—important both for Johnson and for the media.[25]

While resisting questions on his campaign intentions, however, Johnson still sought favorable contacts with the press in an amazing variety of formats. Uncomfortable with the formality of televised press conferences, Johnson continued the more casual tone set by his first meeting with correspondents over coffee in the Oval Office. Barbeques at the ranch, tours of the White House living quarters, and long conversations with groups of three and four characterized the president's press contacts during this first year. Johnson is, as political scientist Elmer Cornwell observed, the only president who "tried seriously to turn the clock back to pre-Truman practices" of press conferences, seeking to reinstate the less formal approach adopted by Franklin Roosevelt.[26]

Yet he did so over growing protests from members of the media. Those in broadcasting objected that Johnson's formats gave unfair advantage to the print media, while the press corps generally continued to deride his impromptu conferences as "quickies." Without advance notice, the White House reporters increasingly complained, they could not call on their experts in such fields as foreign relations and finance to "come to the press conference prepared to ask detailed, incisive questions."[27] The more charitable reporters regretted the limitations placed on questions by their lack of background, while the more cynical muttered that that was exactly what Johnson wanted—broad questions that did not probe into his programs and policies too deeply. Limited training in specific areas was not all that curbed the questions of the White House regulars, they argued; the dependency on Johnson's good will for their information also inhibited the range and tone of inquiries. As George Reedy noted, the regular correspondents "recognize that their bread and butter is dependent upon the White House. If they're frozen out in the cold, they're really out of luck."[28]

Johnson's spontaneous news spirit irritated correspondents for another reason as well: because they never knew when the president might meander into the press quarters or beckon to a select group, they felt tied to the press operation. A casual stroll, a midday lunch with friends, or an early departure might well cost a reporter both a story and prestige in a competitive business—or even, some worried, a job. Constantly on edge from anticipating the possibilities, suffering from the press secretary's reluctance to declare a "news lid" in the

face of an unpredictable president, and knowing that Johnson's reticence to hold formal press conferences made the impromptu contacts
all the more precious, the lives of the White House regulars were not
eased by the Johnsonian philosophy of press relations.

For his part, Johnson felt that the correspondents' criticisms were
unjustified. He *was* available; the people in the media simply had to
recognize that as president *he* determined the timing and the setting
of that availability. As long as he saw the regular members of the
White House press corps on a reasonably frequent basis—a group
whom he felt "understood things better" than "the sort of hit-and-
run types"—Johnson felt reporters had no cause for complaint.[29]

Yet complain they did. As press secretary, George Reedy sought to
mollify the correspondents while supporting his employer. Pressured
to provide a press conference, Reedy urged Johnson to meet with a
group from the media; Johnson consistently refused. Finally, Reedy
suggested that the president stroll around the South Lawn with the
press corps, answering their questions as he walked. Johnson liked
the idea, "maybe because it was a little bit gimmicky," Reedy
speculated.[30]

Reedy's idea for a press conference solved one problem, but it
created another. Proposed as a one-time solution by a desperate press
secretary, the walking press conference turned into a regular feature
in the spring and summer of 1964—to the despair of the hammertoed
Reedy, the women correspondents in high heels, and the out-of-shape
press corps. Disgruntled reporters charged that the president would
meet the press only in formats that made it difficult for correspondents to adequately cover him—jostling in "walkathons," juggling
coffee cups, or wiping barbeque sauce from their fingers. The
peripetetic press conferences struck some reporters as fun but foolish, while in others they inspired "a maximum of confusion and a
minimum of benevolence toward Lyndon Johnson."[31] Correspondents struggled to keep up with the pace of the 6'4" president; they
struggled to hear what he was saying; and they struggled to catch
enough breath to ask a question while struggling to avoid entangling
themselves in the chain leashes of Johnson's beagles, which were
frequent companions on these talking tours.

Yet the format gave Johnson control over the situation, a control he
found both satisfying and comforting. Striding around the White
House grounds, muses Sidey, provided the man with a safety valve,
for

> the burdens of war, of death, of taxes, of disease, of hunger poured
> out of Lyndon Johnson. He didn't really ask for sympathy, but he

almost pleaded for understanding and sometimes he nearly demanded it ("There's only one President—like him or not") from that random band of reporters and White House staff members who trailed in his wake as he went around and around the macadam driveway, nose high in the fresh air, looking off down the South Lawn toward the Washington Monument and the Jefferson Memorial.[32]

Exercise, the safety valve of talk, and a captive audience—Johnson gained all three, while fulfilling his obligation to the press. The tours inspired Philip Potter of the *Baltimore Sun* to suggest that the press corps adopt an anthem: "He walks with us, and he talks with us, and he tells us we are his own."[33]

Not all of Johnson's press contacts consisted of these walkathons. The walks themselves often followed conferences in the Oval Office (although even there correspondents struggled to hear, jostled to see, and juggled to write). In addition, Johnson used his meetings with the bureau chiefs to provide background information, and he continued to meet with smaller groups of reporters. Yet even these earned him criticism: what Philip Geyelin termed the "private talkathons with newsmen" found Johnson talking most of the time, which correspondents said resulted in "too much to be digested either by the media which had to package it and send it over the wires or by the people themselves."[34] Whereas their earlier complaint had been one of inaccessibility and a lack of information, the press corps now objected to the overabundance of material; whether feast or famine, the amount of information impeded normal news-gathering techniques which in turn complicated the media's job.

Even with these more usual press contacts, however, Johnson continued to experiment with new formats. Special assistant Jack Valenti had suggested the Saturday morning press conferences, which Johnson loved for their ability to dominate the front pages on Sunday and reporters hated for their regular intrusion into the weekend. Reedy finally persuaded Johnson to drop them, using two arguments. First, he pointed out that the vast majority of any Sunday newspaper is printed on Thursday, so most were unprepared for the major, last-minute news coverage demanded by a Saturday morning presidential news conference. As a consequence, Johnson's Saturday forums could cost an additional $600,000 for a paper like the *New York Times*—a figure eliciting, as Reedy stressed to the president, "terrible howls" and little favor from editors and publishers.[35]

Reedy then researched media audiences to argue that the combination of radio, television, and morning and evening newspapers during the week reached an audience of one hundred and ten million, while Sunday morning circulation reached only fifty million—and eliminated most follow-up stories as well. Faced with these statistics, Johnson finally relinquished the Saturday morning conferences, leaving a relieved but aggrieved Reedy: "I had to do an awful lot of research, research which I shouldn't have had to do because what I had to do was to go out and get facts and demonstrate something that I already knew anyway."[36]

Reedy felt Johnson's press relations often suffered because the president's misconceptions were encouraged by the ideas of several advisers. "Jack Valenti, Bill Moyers . . . all of those people actually believe in this gimmicky form of press relations," contended Reedy, "and I don't."[37] Yet George Reedy, father of the walking press conference, devised another "gimmicky" brainchild out of his desperation to get the president to hold "a full-dress press conference."[38] On May 6, 1964, Johnson held a televised press conference before reporters and their families on the South Lawn of the White House. Complete with the Marine Band, cookies, punch, and beagles, the children's press conference was described by one correspondent as "a crossbreeding of sober news and Disneyland."[39] Johnson, relates Reedy, "enjoyed it hugely because of all the pictures with the kids, and it was really quite a gimmick. I enjoyed it hugely too because I was able to get one real honest-to-God televised press conference out of it."[40]

"I try to give you variety," Johnson told the press corps after the children's press conference.[41] The president did indeed give them that—so much so, reporters decided, that "in comparison, the Kennedy administration began to look very staid."[42] Johnson's love of making rapid choices affected even his travel plans, and members of the media did not care for the way this characteristic affected their news coverage. Decisions to spend a weekend at the ranch sometimes came on such short notice as to leave Lady Bird breathless and correspondents "without so much as a toothbrush" to take along.[43] In part, Johnson's decisions depended on his work; legislative progress, the length of meetings, or the state of a crisis affected his plans. Yet Johnson also loved spur-of-the-moment flexibility, being able to suggest a holiday in Texas to Mrs. Johnson as though he had just thought of the idea.

The correspondents found such flexibility only irritating. Even if an anticipated trip did not materialize, the media institutions had to pay for the airplanes that had been chartered for the press. When Johnson did dash off to the ranch for a respite, the correspondents' weekend plans were ruined, replaced with a weekend of hotel life and stalking an unpredictable president through the Hill Country. In one case they even commandeered a garbage truck as the only available means of transportation to the scene of a presidential speech. Struggling to adapt Washington clothes and thinking to the Texas climate and life-style, the reporters were usually housed in San Antonio or Austin, and "came to feel like shuttlecocks" as they bounced between their hotels and the ranch.[44]

Reedy, caught in the middle, resorted to the trick of offering "advice to prudent men" concerning possible travel plans; the device became a standing joke in his briefings. The press secretary found little help on the subject from the president, for according to Reedy, Johnson felt that such problems in arranging press coverage of his travels were of concern, but only to a small extent. "He thought," Reedy explained,

> and I was never able to disabuse him of this, that my whole
> strategy was to make the press happy by seeing that their bags were
> carried and that they had adequate airplane space and adequate
> hotel space—he thought I was pampering the press. I wasn't. I was
> just trying to set up rational procedures so that the press could
> cover him.[45]

Regarding such details as "pampering" rather than necessities, then, Johnson felt little responsibility to change his plans—or his announcement of them—accordingly. Moreover, Valenti observed, Johnson was "determined to prove that the press was not going to be allowed to lead him around by the nose."[46] In retrospect, Valenti traced the roots of the credibility gap to this tension over travel: "the disruption of a reporter's home life, the jostling of his rational good sense, [and] a president's vexing discomfort at revealing his schedule," the aide contended, provided the irritation and motivation to pursue less than flattering stories about Lyndon Johnson.[47] What reporters viewed as colossal presidential insensitivity did not inspire any great love and admiration for Lyndon Johnson.

As the capital turned into a summer steambath, Johnson frequently journeyed back to the ranch, often on short notice. In early August, however, a crisis kept him riveted to the White House. While on a DeSoto patrol in the Gulf of Tonkin, the USS *Maddox* was attacked by three North Vietnamese PT boats in the early morning hours of August 2, 1964. The *Maddox* returned their fire, sinking one vessel. After meeting with key advisers, Johnson ordered the patrol to continue with nominal naval and air reinforcements, staying farther from the mainland (and therefore deeper into international waters), but he did not order retaliatory action. The president's advisers felt confident that the reinforced patrol would not be raided, especially with the warning to the North Vietnamese that further attacks would elicit reprisals.[48]

On August 4, however, the *Maddox* and the supporting USS *C. Turner Joy* were again fired upon by North Vietnamese guns. Initial reports clearly stated that the two ships had been attacked, although later messages—garbled by bad weather and an inexperienced technician—confused the details of the attack. McNamara moved to clarify the situation, and Johnson quickly ordered a heavy air strike against torpedo bases and an oil depot in the North.[49] In the meantime, the president moved to avoid Truman's Korean mistake: he called the congressional leadership to the White House so that he could review the situation and lay the groundwork for gaining a congressional resolution of support. Such support was necessary, Johnson told the leadership, because he did not "want to go in unless Congress goes in with me."[50] As Schlesinger notes, Johnson's concern over congressional support was political, not constitutional; he had no doubt but that the legal authority for such retaliatory action lay squarely with the executive branch, but the ever politically minded president wanted legislative backing as well.[51] Presented with urgent reports on the situation, all sixteen congressional leaders—from Mike Mansfield and William Fulbright to House minority leader Charles Halleck of Indiana—endorsed Johnson's orders.[52]

Nor did Johnson neglect Barry Goldwater, the senator from Arizona whose nomination as the Republican candidate for president had come just two weeks earlier. Although Johnson clearly felt that the North Vietnamese attacks demanded retaliatory measures, Goldwater's candidacy may well have provided a subtle reinforcement for taking firm action, for the Republican's campaign centered on an aspect of the Democrats' image to which Johnson had been sensitive since his Senate days. Democrats, the president worried, labored under the public's conception of them as "soft on communism" and unwilling to forthrightly resist aggression; Johnson did not want to encourage that perception, especially in an election year.[53] Goldwater had fired up audiences for months by condemning the lack of a will to win against the communists—a lack endemic to the Democratic administration—as a sign of America's deteriorating moral fiber. Johnson's aides had taken note of his criticisms.[54] Regardless of any indecision about his own candidacy, Lyndon Johnson refused to relinquish all the flag-waving patriotism of military preparedness and national defense to the GOP. In that sense, the Gulf of Tonkin incident provided Johnson with an opportunity to couple firmness with restraint, countering charges of Democratic softness while implicitly questioning the Republican candidate's response in the same position. To acknowledge this is not to assert, as some later accounts have, that the Johnson administration forced or concocted the Gulf of Tonkin affair simply to allow a Democratic show of strength. Nor did it seize upon the slightest incident to launch into warfare on a wider scale, for the first attack on August 2 would have provided sufficient excuse. Even so, Johnson was not insensitive to the political ramifications of his actions.

Accordingly, when Johnson faced the television cameras at 11:36 that night of August 4, 1964, he stressed that the response to the "open aggression on the high seas against the United States of America" would be rapid and strong; even as he was speaking the planes flew north.[55] "The determination of all Americans," promised Johnson, "to carry out our full commitment to the people and to the government of South Viet-Nam will be redoubled by this outrage." Even so, Johnson noted, the American response was "limited and fitting. . . . We still seek no wider war."

The "Radio and Television Report to the American People Following Renewed Aggression in the Gulf of Tonkin" thus constituted Johnson's first major speech to the American public specifically dealing with the situation in Vietnam; it did not come until eight-and-one-half months after he had entered office. Designed as a specific response to a specific situation, the speech's primary goal was to engender congressional, and therefore public, support for his actions.

After the president's speech, then, the administration turned its attention to the passage of the resolution, which contained phrases echoing the resolution proposed that May by William Bundy. In later years this time would be regarded as a turning point in the war: the point at which the Johnson administration made a psychological commitment to increased American military involvement; the point at which the administration camouflaged the extent of America's current role in South Vietnam; and the point at which Congress authorized the president to "take all necessary measures to repel any armed attack against the forces of the United States and to prevent further aggression"[56]—an authorization that later proved to be the source of much friction with Congress. Publication of the top-secret Defense Department history of the United States role in Indochina, undertaken in 1967 and now commonly known as the Pentagon Papers, revealed that the Operation 34-A program entailed a number of South Vietnamese attacks on North Vietnam under American command—including raids on July 30 and August 3, 1964.[57] While the 34-A operations were ostensibly not related to the DeSoto patrols, the North Vietnamese quite likely viewed them as such, and seeing the *Maddox* patrol as an extension of attacks seventy miles down the coastline would have constituted the provocation that Johnson's congressional presentation and nationally televised speech contended was lacking in the Gulf of Tonkin attacks. Furthermore, during his testimony in closed sessions of the Senate and House Foreign Relations Committee, McNamara acknowledged the South Vietnamese 34-A operations generally, but the secretary of defense explicitly denied U.S. naval involvement in and knowledge of these actions, and he avoided specific reference to the July 30 and August 3 raids.

In his memoirs, Johnson refuted allegations "that our destroyers were supporting the South Vietnamese naval action. The fact is that our DeSoto commanders did not even know where or when the 34-A attacks would occur."[58] That the commanders of such DeSoto patrols as that of the *Maddox* did not know the details of the 34-A raids would not necessarily remove the patrols from a role of military support; but Johnson was evidently reluctant to allow any direct connection, either in 1964 or in his memoirs.

Yet these challenges to the administration's version of the situation did not come until later. The Southeast Asia Resolution (which as Johnson sternly noted was the correct title for what was "often miscalled the 'Gulf of Tonkin Resolution' ")[59] passed the House and Senate with only two dissenters—Senators Wayne Morse and Ernest Gruening, early members of the peace bloc. Later analyses of the discussion before the resolution's passage, such as that offered by Goldman, would characterize it as having "the weird quality of being thoroughly troubled while its result was preordained."[60] Yet concerns about the ambiguity of the resolution were quickly answered, either by the senators who raised them or by William Fulbright, who served as floor leader for the resolution in his capacity as chairman of the Senate Foreign Relations Committee. As George Reedy observed, the Congress faced a president's request for a statement of support following attempts to torpedo an American naval vessel. Those in Congress who "have since stated that had they known what was to follow, they would not have voted" in favor of the resolution were, in Reedy's assessment, engaging in "not only hindsight but nonsense."[61] Guenter Lewy notes that such misgivings (which one may extend to members of the media as well as legislators) surfaced "only when the price of halting this aggression had risen considerably and when a successful conclusion of the American intervention had become an increasingly distant 'light at the end of the tunnel.' "[62]

At the time, then, the Gulf of Tonkin resolution appeared to be a shrewd political act on Johnson's part, which bolstered him both against the Republican claims of softness in the upcoming campaign and against potential charges that he failed to consult Congress before acting. The president's "rapid response to North Vietnamese provocation in the Gulf of Tonkin," staff members reported, received "overwhelming support from the press, Congress, labor and veterans organizations."[63] From Harry Truman and the *Chicago Tribune* to Walter Lippmann and the AFL-CIO, diverse and prestigious facets of the American public seemed to approve of Johnson's course of action.

Later the press's performance during this critical period in American foreign policy would be challenged as too unquestioning. Six years after the Gulf of Tonkin, for example, the *Los Angeles Times*'s Jules Witcover complained that "when the Government reported in August, 1964, that two American destroyers had been attacked in the Gulf of Tonkin, . . . there was no sustained effort by the daily press in Washington to ferret out its veracity."[64] Aronson extended this criticism when he marvelled that reporters at McNamara's press conference on August 5

> refrained from asking any questions that might embarrass the government, although it must have seemed inconceivable to any thoughtful reporter that a few small North Vietnamese gunboats would seek out and challenge the battleships of the United States fleet, knowing that such an action would provoke immediate and massive retaliation.[65]

In light of the Panamanian incidents earlier that year, it may not have surprised the reporters after all.

Whatever the reporters' level of incredulity, few questions were raised in August of 1964. As the authors of the Pentagon Papers remark, the handling of the Gulf of Tonkin incident "marked the crossing of an important threshold in the war, and it was accomplished with virtually no domestic criticism, indeed, with an evident increase in public support for the Administration."[66]

With the resolution obtained and the situation in Vietnam resuming its previous troubled but lower-profile status, Johnson turned his attention to the domestic issue of August: the Democratic National Convention. While considering whether or not he should run, he also faced the question of an appropriate vice-presidential candidate, which was a choice of special importance in light of the previous transition of power. According to Johnson, exploring the vice-presidential possibilities was entirely consistent with his determination to "keep his options open." To members of the press and other analysts, however, it represented a variety of other aims. Not all of these goals were incompatible with Johnson's open options, but none of them were clearly included in what some observers saw as his ingenuous version of perpetual indecision. Johnson's sense of the dramatic, his love of secrecy and the resulting flexibility, his enjoyment of the power and publicity accompanying a portending decision—all have been presented, with the attribution of varying degrees of intentionality and deception, as reasons for Johnson's reticence in revealing his plans for himself and a potential second in command.

Johnson's approach generated a great deal of publicity as reporters and pundits analyzed a range of possible candidates. Johnson deprecated this flurry of punditry: "Speculating on the Democratic ticket for 1964, the press was not dogmatic about its choice of the Vice Presidential nominee."[67] One potential choice, however, proved bothersome to the Texan: Robert F. Kennedy, attorney general and brother of the slain president. Johnson himself acknowledged that their relationship had never been "overly warm. . . . Too much separated us—too much history, too many differences in temperament."[68]

Part of the history that separated them included the 1960 Democratic convention. After John Kennedy had approached Johnson to offer the vice-presidential post, the Massachusetts group heard angry protests from several liberal factions, including labor and civil rights leaders. Uncertain of the proportions to which the rebellion might grow before Kennedy presented his choice to the convention, the nominee dispatched his brother to the Texan's suite. Explanations of Kennedy's motivations for the errand differ. In what Theodore White calls a "superb account" by a key liaison between Johnson and Kennedy, Philip Graham contended that Kennedy wanted to see how tenaciously Johnson had accepted the earlier offer in case "corrective action" seemed necessary. In contrast, longtime Kennedy aides Ken O'Donnell and Dave Powers argued that Bobby was simply conveying Jack's offer of a release from the vice-presidential post in case Johnson did not want to confront the mounting opposition from the various groups. Similar discrepancies mark versions of events that followed. Graham related that the younger Kennedy was delayed en route and thus arrived after the presidential candidate had concluded that the protests could be easily handled, and after he had notified Johnson of his renewed commitment, but before Robert Kennedy learned of this. According to O'Donnell and Powers, however, Sam Rayburn as Johnson's representative completely misunderstood Bobby's mission and set off an unnecessary panic in the Texas crew. Although the reports of Johnson's reactions to the younger Kennedy's advances vary from mild suspicion to extreme bitterness, the episode had an undeniably detrimental effect on the relationship.[69] The feelings of the Johnson staff for the younger Kennedy were not eased at the convention when Johnson's aide, Jake Jacobsen, passed out glasses of water and Bobby tasted one before handing it on to his brother.[70] In addition, a number of Johnson's supporters, including Marvin Watson and John Connally, were quite bitterly opposed to Johnson taking the vice-presidential post under John Kennedy.

Nor was the relationship between Lyndon Johnson and Robert Kennedy enhanced by increasing speculation in 1963 that John Kennedy would drop Johnson as vice-president the next year so that he could put his brother on the ticket. Johnson's concern about the circulation, if not about the truth, of these stories may in part be measured by the fact that he opened his memoirs with a refutation of them. The first line of the book is from his conversation with Kennedy on the morning of the president's assassination, when Kennedy said, "We're going to carry two states next year if we don't carry any others: Massachusetts and Texas." The first four pages of The Vantage Point are devoted to Johnson's explicit discussion of Kennedy's assurances that he would remain on the ticket, and implicit references are scattered throughout the remainder of the first chapter. "Never once in those three years," Johnson contended, "did I have any reason to believe that John Kennedy looked upon me as a liability."[71]

Although Johnson did not mention Robert Kennedy's name at this point in his memoirs, his concern is evident; that concern had grown as Johnson's time of decision about his own course of action drew closer. Later, recounting the political concerns of that summer for biographer Doris Kearns, Johnson would recall that

> every day . . . as soon as I opened the papers or turned on the television, there was something about Bobby Kennedy; there was some person or group talking about what a great Vice President he'd make. Somehow it just didn't seem fair. I'd given three years of loyal service to Jack Kennedy. During all that time I'd willingly stayed in the background; I knew that it was his Presidency, not

mine. . . . And then Kennedy was killed and I became the custodian of his will. I became the President. But none of this seemed to register with Bobby Kennedy, who acted like *he* was the custodian of the Kennedy dream, some kind of rightful heir to the throne. It just didn't seem fair. I'd waited for my turn. Bobby should've waited for his. But he and the Kennedy people wanted it now. A tidal wave of letters and memos about how great a Vice President Bobby would be swept over me. But no matter what, I simply couldn't let it happen. With Bobby on the ticket, I'd never know if I could be elected on my own.[72]

The "tidal wave" supporting Robert Kennedy included, in February of 1964, the New Hampshire primary results: 29,300 write-in votes for Johnson as president, and 25,000 for Kennedy as vice-president. McDowell wryly notes that Kennedy's supporters "were left with the uneasy feeling that they probably had helped Mr. Johnson make up his mind about a running mate after all."[73]

Johnson was understandably unwilling to serve as a fill-in between the Kennedy presidencies or as a footnote to the "Kennedy dynasty"; other factors reinforced this reluctance. The president felt Robert Kennedy lacked, among other traits, experience, political maturity, a knowledge of Congress, and the necessary broad-mindedness to serve as second in command. In addition, political polls indicated that the attorney general's vigorous pursuit of civil rights and steel-price rollbacks had offended southerners and the business community, so his selection as a running mate would cut into Johnson's support from two constituencies he especially wanted to sweep. Together with the differences in temperament and history, these factors further lessened Kennedy's chances as Johnson's vice-presidential pick.

The major part of what came to be known as the "Bobby problem," then, was Johnson's concern for how best to implement the decision he had already reached. He did not want to antagonize unnecessarily the strong Kennedy faction of the Democratic party, nor to be seen as callously bypassing the embodiment of the Kennedy legend. At the same time, however, he did not want to risk the possibility of Robert Kennedy being nominated from the floor.

So it was that on July 29, 1964, Johnson called Kennedy into his office. Reports of the meeting generally concur with the memorandum that Johnson said he read to the attorney general, which cast the president's concern in terms of the Democrats' welfare rather than his own misgivings.[74] Johnson told him that "it would be unwise for our party in this election to select you as the vice presidential nominee," especially in light of Goldwater's candidacy. Lacking the necessary appeal in the Middle West and the border states, and engendering criticism in the South, Kennedy would not sufficiently help the Democratic ticket. Johnson praised the attorney general's contributions and offered his help in "furthering your career," including assignment to government positions; but he would not select Kennedy as his running mate.

Kennedy reportedly accepted this decision quietly. A problem arose, however, in making this decision public. Johnson hoped Kennedy would announce his noncandidacy himself and enlisted Bundy's aid as a Kennedy associate to encourage this; but Kennedy felt the president should announce his own decision. The standoff ended when Johnson appeared on television the day after the meeting to report that he would not consider *any* member of the Cabinet as a vice-presidential candidate, to insure their continued vigilance at their appointed posts.[75]

The move met mixed reactions among political observers and the press, ranging from admiration to bemusement and derision. McDowell, for example, described the approach as "wonderfully oblique," at least to non-Kennedy supporters.[76] Cormier, on the other hand, found it to be "a transparent maneuver to eliminate Robert Kennedy from contention without seeming to single him out."[77] Skepticism increased the next day in a background session when Johnson assured his audience that the blanket exclusion of Cabinet members was necessary because Secretary of State Dean Rusk and Secretary of Agriculture Orville Freeman each had strong home-state campaigns pushing for their candidacy. Evans and Novak scoffed that "this marked the first—and last—report of any such effort."[78]

The episode did not end there, however. On July 31, two days after his meeting with Kennedy, Johnson lunched at the White House with Edward Folliard of the *Washington Post*, Tom Wicker of the *New York Times*, and Douglas Kiker of the *New York Herald Tribune*. In the aftermath of resolving the Bobby problem, the president indulged in what Theodore H. White has characterized as "a raconteur's relish of, as well as the art for, a good anecdote."[79] All of Johnson's finest storytelling techniques—from mimicking Kennedy's "funny voice" to exaggerating a gulp at the news of the decision—painted a skillful picture of Johnson and a much less flattering one of the attorney general. For the first time since the assassination, Johnson gloated about a victory over the Kennedys with reporters present. When details of the Wednesday meeting, as colored by Johnson's recounting, inevitably broke into print over the weekend, Robert Kennedy was furious. Johnson's perceptions and handling of the Bobby problem had been influenced by his concern over press stories and media interpretations; even so, he could not resist exultation in front of the correspondents. If there had been any hope of a reconciliation of sentiments before the reports, it was certainly gone now. On September 3, a week after the Democratic convention, Kennedy resigned as attorney general to run for United States senator in New York.

With Robert Kennedy and the Cabinet officials removed from contention, speculation about Johnson's running mate continued. In that sense, the president's approach had what may have been one of its intended effects—to steal some of the dramatic thunder from the Republicans. A pro forma Democratic convention, nominating the incumbent and his choice as everyone had known would be the case all summer, would suffer in comparison to the excitement of the GOP—even if that excitement derived from an internicene warfare that almost destroyed the Republican party in the process. Johnson's love of surprise and drama could not give all the glory to the other side.

As the convention grew closer, Hubert Humphrey emerged more and more clearly as the probable vice-presidential choice. A fellow member of Johnson's freshman Senate class of 1948, the Minnesotan exhibited the necessary strength in the Middle West and a good knowledge of Congress; moreover, he was vociferously supportive of Johnson and suited the elaborate qualifications the president set forth as ideals for his second in command. In mid-August, for example, Humphrey had delivered a speech on Vietnam for which McNamara had provided assistance; Bundy reported on the address to Johnson, noting it had been given "pursuant to a request of yours some time back (but delayed by the Gulf of Tonkin affair)."[80] The memorandum may refer to a test of a potential vice-president or to aid for one already selected. Yet Johnson continued to play cat-and-mouse, heightening the suspense with references to such possible contenders as Eugene McCarthy, Thomas Dodd, and Mike Mansfield. The air of mystery, building as time grew short, increased the desirability of the prize as well as the power of the man bestowing it. It also increased media speculation and irritation.

On August 24, 1964, the Democratic National Convention opened in Atlantic City, and Lyndon Johnson still had not announced his choice for vice-president. As the convention began, McCarthy telegrammed Johnson that he was removing himself from consideration—from use, some would say, as a pawn in the president's game. Johnson called him to request that he reconsider, but the senator had already released the text of the telegram to the media and he demurred.

With time growing ever shorter and options narrowing, Johnson and his beagles led the press corps on what Rowland Sweeney of the *Chicago Sun-Times* called the "Death March."[81] Lap after quarter-mile lap in the oppressive ninety-degree August heat, the reporters struggled to hear Johnson hold forth on the latest polls, on his barber's views of America, and on the medical report clearing him for further political service. Lap after steaming lap, as some of the less hardy fell away, they strained to hear news of a vice-president. Finally Johnson ever so casually mentioned that he had summoned Dodd and Humphrey to the White House for their "advice" and "recommendations" on the post. Did that mean Humphrey was the one? pressed reporters. "How can I tell you something I haven't made up my mind about?," the president snapped back.[82]

At the end of a grueling ninety-minute, four-mile jaunt, several correspondents—including the AP's Frank Cormier—filed stories pinning Humphrey as the choice. Others, however, still puzzled over the news:

> Humphrey *and* Dodd to the White House? Dodd for Vice-President? Would Johnson do *that*? Incredible, thought the politicians. Impossible, thought the press. But with Johnson's insatiable appetite for the surprise, anything seemed possible.[83]

As a consequence, other reporters wrote that Dodd could well be the president's choice, and Cormier received a frantic phone call from his office reporting that "Dodd for Vice-President" signs lined the convention-hall paint shop: was Cormier *sure* he wanted to file his story pegging Humphrey? Cormier stood by his prediction, but such pressure may help to account for his bitterness about what he termed Johnson's "charade."[84] NBC newscaster Chet Huntley later defended Johnson against such charges, saying that "he was playing it very close to the vest and as we know now the decision was not made very far in advance of the convention. He was still sort of gravitating back and forth among about three different people."[85] Unfortunately, Huntley did not specify which three he was referring to or the basis on which "we know now" about the circumstances.

An undercurrent to the speculation about a vice-president was the question of the president's own political status. Just six days before the convention opened, Johnson had startled a press conference by saying that he would go to the convention on Thursday, August 27—*if* he went at all. Pressuring Johnson for a clearer statement of his plans only elicited presidential irritation and a promise to announce his plans "when we know definitely what we are going to do."[86] Pressuring Reedy brought similar responses, until the press secretary sighed, gazed out the window, and related: "I am a man who always looks forward to each fresh and inspiring experience of the day. I find I am always surprised by the delightfully unexpected."[87]

Johnson insisted that he remained undecided about accepting the nomination until August 25; his contention is supported by the first lady in her published diary, although her reference to this last-minute debate appears not as a regular entry but as an addendum recorded in "late August."[88] On the 25th, the second day of the convention, Johnson related that he drafted a statement refusing the nomination, citing the fear that he could not provide a "leadership about which there is no doubt and a voice that men of all parties, sections, and color can follow." A cynical view of this statement might view it as a memorandum for the record, drafted to later vindicate Johnson against stories accusing him of political charades; Johnson himself insisted that he was undecided. Whatever the motivation, Reedy and other staff members told Johnson that he simply could not withdraw at such a late date, especially given Goldwater as the opposition. Lady Bird sent a note chiding him for a decision that "would be *wrong* for your country"; she assured him that, despite recent articles which they viewed as unfavorable, she was "not afraid of *Time* or lies or losing money or defeat."[89]

The media, however, saw none of this indecision; instead, they saw a political maneuverer who loved surprises, prided himself on good timing, and wanted to orchestrate the convention to his own liking. He had already moved an emotional film on John F. Kennedy from the first day of the convention to the last; his refusal to announce campaign plans seemed to fit his scheme of orchestration. Even when he called reporters together after his conference with Dodd and Humphrey to announce that he would leave for Atlantic City that night— a day ahead of schedule—Johnson refused to name his choice. Johnson's love of secrecy as a dramatic element conflicted with his longing for the trust and good will of reporters, as his news conference of the day indicated:

Q: Privately, before you make any announcement in Atlantic City will you advise the person whom you will recommend to be your running mate?

A: I have not gone into that. I have not thought of it . . . . I don't know whether I can reach him.

Q: You don't know?[90]

While the transcript of the press conference cannot recapture the full flavor of the exchange, it does suggest the press corps' annoyance with the president's tactics as well as his determination to proceed as he saw fit.

According to several accounts, Johnson was so insistent on total secrecy about his choice that when James Rowe finally approached Humphrey to tell him of his selection the adviser commanded him to tell no one. No one? responded Humphrey. But my wife Muriel must know! Humphrey's embarrassment was shared by Rowe, who felt the emphasis on secrecy to be overextended; he finally agreed that telling Mrs. Humphrey was permissible, as long as no one else knew.

Yet even after ordering Humphrey to maintain total silence and dodging reporters' questions at the news conference, Johnson's enthusiasm overcame his evasion. As he boarded Air Force One with Dodd and Humphrey to fly to the convention, the president presented the senator from Minnesota to reporters as the next vice-president of the United States.

That evening Johnson faced a convention hall lined with billboards that illustrated the concerns of the Great Society; the billboards were substituted for the traditional bunting and portraits, at the recommendation of public relations specialists at Doyle Dane Bernbach, in order to downplay the president's wheeler-dealer image. Johnson wanted the culmination of the ensuing campaign to be a landslide victory, not merely a win. He longed to achieve, as he termed it, a "mandate for unity," not only to enable him to enact the Great Society legislation he envisioned but also to turn Kennedy's legacy into Johnson's accomplishment.[91] The stress Kearns places on Johnson's fear of losing elections sometimes appears to be a product of psychohistorical excess; but the man no doubt wondered whether the prize was worth the heavy price.[92] He also undoubtedly longed to make the presidency unmistakably his own.

The potential for a major victory was enhanced by the nature of Johnson's opposition. Goldwater, nominated with his battle cry that "extremism in pursuit of liberty is no vice," seemed a tailor-made foil to Johnson's consensus politics. Perhaps, as some political analysts have suggested, the Republicans saw 1964 as a wasted year for them given Johnson's success in carrying on the programs of the martyred Kennedy, and therefore pushed Goldwater's candidacy to purge the party of its right-wing extremists. That candidacy delighted the Democrats, for "having inherited the entire political center," Johnson crowed, he could forge that unity he wanted so.[93] Goldwater's opposition to Medicare, to the war on poverty, to federal civil rights legislation, and to federal aid to education contrasted sharply with

Johnson's Great Society; his harangues against "appeasing the communists" countered Johnson's stress on a strong but peaceful coexistence. When news stories reported that the president was "taking a jab at Goldwater," Reedy suggested that Johnson simply explain to the bureau chiefs, in a "completely good humored" manner, that "the practical impact of almost any statement that you make today *is* a jab at Goldwater simply because of his determination to oppose you at every step."[94] As Goldwater increasingly antagonized moderates and liberals even in his own party, Johnson increasingly relished the prospect of being "president of all the people," reconciling black and white, North and South, business and labor, rich and poor, for an era of unprecedented social progress.

In both domestic and foreign affairs, then, consensus confronted extremism. In the campaign confrontations on foreign affairs, however, Vietnam was not a major issue. Those 1964 clashes centered primarily on the larger context of the cold war, spiced by Goldwater's harshly aggressive imagery. Although the Republican's point was that he would make America strong enough to prevent World War III, his persistent use of such terms as "holocaust," "nuclear attacks," "atomic weapons," and "pushing the button" gave a warlike temper to his speeches.

Johnson, in turn, played on his opponent's aggressive tone in his own campaign speeches. Gesturing at an imaginary button connected to the nuclear weapons he conjured up, the president warned darkly of the pressures tied to the "hot line," the dismal consequences of a lack of restraint, and the weighty decision facing the voters. Johnson strove to avoid mentioning Goldwater by name, and he instructed his aides to do the same. The famous "daisy girl" television commercial, for example, contained no reference to Goldwater at all. It simply showed a picture of a child pulling petals from a daisy; as a grim voice counted down, it dissolved into a huge mushrooming cloud. The inference was clear, however, and the commercial evoked such strongly negative reactions that it was withdrawn after only one showing on September 7, 1964. Yet that single showing created such a powerful impression, solidifying Goldwater's quick-on-the-trigger, warmongering image, that Republicans later claimed that it played a major role in their candidate's defeat.

Johnson's efforts to avoid direct attacks in his speeches sometimes slipped in the exuberance of campaigning. On one such occasion, as he spoke to a United Steelworkers convention, he warned: "You know it takes a man who loves his country to build a house, instead of a raving, ranting demagogue who wants to tear one down."[95] Afterwards he called several correspondents together. As Cormier recalled the episode:

> "You-all notice that in the speech back there I didn't say anything mean about Goldwater," the President began. "I talked about 'ravin', rantin' demagogues,' *plural.* I wasn't referrin' to any single individual. I just thought you-all might have misunderstood."
>
> We did not argue with him. Instead, when we got back to the White House, we reported Johnson's claim to George Reedy, who went to the West Wing basement and listened to a tape recording of the speech. Reedy returned with a brief message: "He said 'demagogue.'"[96]

While Vietnam did not form a major campaign issue, Johnson echoed this view of Goldwater as impulsive and hotheaded when it did arise. Later these campaign statements would be flung back bitterly at the president, with charges that he had promised peace and instead brought greater war within three months of his election. Johnson's speeches did reveal his commitment to counter aggression, a key to his later policies. Like the Texas Ranger in his anecdotes, the president wanted the world to know that Americans "have the will and determination, and if they ever hit us it is not going to stop us—we are just going to keep coming."[97] Yet the overall context of the speeches stressed Johnson's concern for restraint in handling the situation in Vietnam. Johnson emphasized that he resisted "those who say that you ought to go north and drop bombs" as a solution to the problems in Vietnam.[98] Moreover, he repeatedly contended that "we are not about to send American boys nine or ten thousand miles away from home to do what Asian boys ought to be doing for themselves."[99]

Johnson would later argue that those who cast him as the "peace" candidate and then claimed betrayal "were not willing to hear anything they did not want to hear."[100] His insistence that Americans should not be sent to do the Asians' job, he explained,

> was answering those who proposed, or implied, that we should take charge of the war or carry out actions that would risk a war with Communist China. I did not mean that we were not going to do any fighting, for we had already lost a good many men in Vietnam. . . .We were not going to rush in and take over, but we were going to live up to the commitments we had made.[101]

"The American people knew what they were voting for in 1964," he contended.[102] To Johnson, the charges of deception arose from incomplete and unfair abbreviations of his remarks (an ironic echo of Goldwater's complaints), and the president did not want his election cheapened by charges that the public was confused on important issues.

During the campaign, however, Johnson's Vietnam stand drew no such fire. His handling of the Gulf of Tonkin incident did underscore the balance of firmness and restraint that he advocated; but Southeast Asia was not a major topic of the campaign.

Regardless of the issues involved, the fall of 1964 demonstrated "Lyndon Johnson's unadorned, unrestrained, unabashed joy in all-out campaigning."[103] Freed from the constraints of television, eased from the bonds of his office, the president flung himself into taking his message to the people and "pressing the flesh," as he termed it. On innumerable campaign trips, Johnson would seize the bullhorn and exhort the crowds to "come hear the speakin'"; when they did, he illustrated his visions of the Great Society with stories of his youth, and he encapsulated his image of American determination in anecdotes about the Texas Rangers. At the encouragement of aides, he adopted a looser, more informal style of presentation; the result, a Johnson Treatment writ large, was a huge success.[104]

Johnson exulted in the enthusiastic responses, often falling behind schedule as his impromptu remarks and handshaking expanded to match the warmth of the receptions. He drew the press into his ebullience as well. On his trip to New England in late September, the president instructed a CBS photographer to crouch at his feet in the bubble-topped limousine, filming Johnson against the background of a surging, shouting, wildly supportive crowd. At another stop he brought Frank Cormier of the AP and Marquis Childs of the *St. Louis Post-Dispatch* to the restraining fence against which the crowd was pressed. "You-all say I've got no charisma—that crowds don't respond to me like they did to Kennedy," Johnson challenged. "You fellows stay right here beside me and I'll show you that you're wrong!" A cheering pandemonium greeted him as he shook hands down the length of the fence.[105]

Such surgings into the crowd may have reassured Johnson and quieted unfavorable comparisons of public reactions, but they stimulated other news stories that questioned the wisdom of Johnson's exposure to a potential Dallas. Citing the report of the Warren Commission, which characterized unscheduled stops as unnecessarily dangerous and noted that the chief executive had to cooperate with measures taken for his safety, the news stories expressed concern for the risks he was taking. To Johnson, however, such protective measures isolated him from his people and deprived him of an essential contact. Moreover, he informed the correspondents, he was "just amazed that the press would point up these things as creating a problem," for the chief of the Secret Service assured him that impromptu stops provided an "element of surprise" that served as a deterrent to rather than a creator of risk.[106]

As the election drew nearer, the "pollarama," as some staff members termed it, showed Johnson's lead increasing. Still he did not pause. He ordered the leaking of a complimentary letter; he sent notes of gratitude to the various media people and organizations for their support and endorsements; he solicited their opinion of his speeches; he met with such visible groups as black publishers.[107] The campaign proceeded smoothly and joyfully for Johnson, promising to culminate in a landslide which might not be of quite the proportions of Roosevelt's in 1936, but which would still be massive enough to make history.

Then, in mid-October, a crisis with both personal and political implications struck. On October 14, reporters from the *Washington Star* discovered that Walter Jenkins had been arrested in a YMCA pay toilet the week before, on the charge of "disorderly conduct" for homosexual activity with a sixty-year-old resident of a nearby veterans' home. Walter Jenkins—Johnson's top aide, his devoted assistant for twenty-five years, his confidant, whose wife was close to Lady Bird and whose daughter was Luci's best friend—had been arrested on a morals charge. Moreover, the press discovered, Jenkins had been picked up from the same washroom on the same charge five years earlier.

Jenkins himself took the call from the *Star's* editor asking for confirmation of the story; he appealed to longtime Johnson friend Abe Fortas for advice. Fortas notified Johnson, then campaigning in New York City; it was the first news Johnson had of either arrest. Working with another faithful Johnson adviser, Clark Clifford, Fortas hospitalized Jenkins, obtained his resignation from the White House staff, and personally called on the editors of the three Washington newspapers to ask them not to publish the story, on the grounds that it was a personal tragedy with little political significance. That night, however, the news went out over the wires.[108]

Johnson was stunned and concerned. Jenkins was a man who for years had immersed himself totally in serving Lyndon Johnson; desperate to escape the unceasing toil, the episode was perhaps his way of "committing political suicide."[109] The morning after the story broke, Lady Bird Johnson issued a statement touching in its sorrow and sympathy: "My heart is aching today for someone who has reached the end point of exhaustion in dedicated service to his country."[110] The president himself, however, delayed any release. He first ordered the FBI to investigate any breach of national security that might have resulted (Hoover reported on October 22 that there had been none), and asked pollster Oliver Quayle to conduct an emergency survey to determine the story's political impact. On the evening of October 15, when Quayle reported no significant shift in public sentiment in the wake of the incident, Johnson issued a tribute to Jenkins's "personal dedication, devotion, and tireless labor," and expressed the "deepest compassion for him and for his wife and six children."[111]

The Jenkins story was soon driven off the front page by other news—the ouster of Khrushchev, the election of a Labour government in Britain, and the explosion of China's first nuclear bomb. Yet Johnson clearly felt stung by the affair, personally and politically. When Goldwater referred to "the interim President and his curious crew" as an example of moral laxity in Washington, the president responded by telling reporters that Eisenhower had had a similar problem. It was, as Reedy observed, "an extremely unfortunate remark":[112] it revived a problem that had largely subsided by that time; it opened Johnson to the charges of "dirty politics" which he had thus far avoided; it underscored the fact that few top Johnson aides had received an FBI clearance; and it ignored the fact that the individual in question was only considered, but not hired, by the Eisenhower administration. As a result, Reedy regretted, the comment created "some deep bitterness among certain members of the press who were highly sympathetic toward the president at that point," as they accused him of "shooting from the hip" to deliver an unfair and ill-founded attack.[113]

Despite Johnson's fears, the Jenkins story did little to harm his landslide. With 61 percent of the popular vote and 486 of the 538 electoral votes, Lyndon Baines Johnson swept into the White House on his own landslide on November 3, 1964. "It seems to me," he told a friend, "that I have spent my whole life getting ready for this moment."[114] The presidency was truly his, on the basis of an unmistakable vote. "For the first time in all my life I truly felt loved by the American people" he would recollect.[115] The presidency was no longer someone else's; it was completely his own. He had demonstrated his strength to everyone, including members of the media.

In analyzing the presidential term that followed that election, such observers as Arthur Schlesinger say Johnson's misinterpretation of the results as an unmitigated triumph caused him to feel free to pursue any course of action he chose, with disastrous results; Kearns and others contend that, while proud of his large majority, Johnson understood its ambiguous nature. For his part, Johnson would later insist that he "knew from the start that the '64 election had given me a loophole rather than a mandate and that I had to move quickly before my support disappeared."[116] Eager to institute as much Great Society legislation as possible before that majority evaporated, Johnson outlined an impressive program to present to Congress in January of 1965. He reminded his congressional liaison staff that sixteen million votes could quickly erode, through natural attrition and unfavorable events, to a scant eight million; he therefore wanted to get this legislation passed quickly.

Johnson wanted everything, including the mass media, to cooperate in the birth of the Great Society. To that end, Johnson pushed ahead with plans for a permanent White House television facility to provide the kind of immediate, flexible media access that he loved; the cameras would be at his disposal for live or taped coverage on five minutes' notice.[117] In addition, the president directed renewed attention to the question of improving his press relations. A spate of stories appearing shortly after the election sparked particular concern, for they suggested that Johnson was inexperienced in and inattentive to foreign policy matters. Aide and former journalist Douglass Cater, pointing in particular to two stories on Vietnam by columnist Joseph Kraft and *Washington Post* correspondent Chalmers Roberts, traced the problem to a need for "better visibility given to your [Johnson's] role within government itself. Otherwise, those with axes-to-grind are encouraged to circulate their own policies as official."[118] Johnson's first step, Cater implied, should be to clarify his leadership on foreign policy issues for his subordinates, who were obviously sources for these stories. In addition, recognizing that individuals within government would quickly go outside of official channels for a sympathetic ear (eagerly offered by the press) if they did not find the administration to be receptive, Cater proposed that a solution might be found in regular meetings of the National Security Council. These meetings, contended the aide, could serve as "a useful forum for holding systematic reviews," even though it might not always be "helpful to genuine decision-making." Not only would "all principal sources of advice—including, particularly, the Joint Chiefs"—be consulted, thus alleviating the problem of the press soliciting news "from any who feel neglected"; but, Cater suggested, such meetings might also reduce reporters' "excessive preoccupation with your 'decision' on Vietnam."

100

Johnson forwarded Cater's memorandum to George Reedy, who responded, "I agree with Cater. . . . I think it is an excellent idea."[119] In addition, press aide Perry Barber further explored Cater's suggestion after a discussion with Reedy. The advantage of regular NSC meetings, Barber concluded, was that "good foreign policy public relations work (from a White House standpoint) is to condition the press and, thereby, the public, to events far enough in advance that events do not take on major proportions just before or at the time they take place."[120] Publicizing NSC meetings, as well as announcing the president's appointments, would aid this "conditioning" of the regular press corps—and, through them, the columnists and the public at large—by partially filling "the void left by a paucity of visible foreign policy events involving the President." This systematic but low-key approach would thereby provide "the background that minimizes the importance of events at the time they occur," which in turn would lessen pressure on the White House to handle and explain these events.

Johnson's concern extended beyond news coverage of his foreign policy decisions; he also solicited advice on how to improve his relationship with the media in more general terms. In early December the president asked Philip Potter, chief of the *Baltimore Sun*'s Washington bureau, for his "thoughts on White House press relations."[121] Potter's three-page response began by stressing "the individualism of the men and women you will be dealing with"; attempting to please them all, he implied, would be as foolish as condemning all for the transgressions of a few. Potter's first suggestion for Johnson, then, "is for you to do what you can to curb sensitivity to press criticism and error. It will only give you ulcers."

Given that, Potter encouraged the president to "maintain credibility, by giving us the real news, but not trying to contrive or manufacture news when there is none." Without extending that comment directly, he suggested that the press secretary's briefings be routine, for clarification of statements and notification of "your plans for travel and the like," but "not primarily for news-making purposes."

Regarding Johnson himself, Potter hoped that he would "maintain as best time permits the accessibility of your early months in office." He suggested one or two formal press conferences a month, "announced far enough ahead so that those accredited to the White House, but who cannot stay there steadily [including those from the foreign press, smaller bureaus, and other Washington beats], can have at least an occasional opportunity to see you and put questions."

Beyond that, the correspondent felt Johnson's informal sessions were "extremely useful," providing a justifiable advantage to the White House regulars. Some of these formats had drawbacks, of which Potter felt the president should be aware: the walking conferences made it difficult to hear and take notes; the Saturday conferences created deadline problems for many correspondents; and the impromptu conferences, while offering "very welcome accessibility" to the president, "put a burden of constantly staying on hand on those assigned to the White House." Potter also returned to the question of travel plans: "Your transport staff, it scarcely needs saying, should be as alert as possible to providing the White House press with the logistics it needs to do its work." Having thus catalogued a number of the key press corps complaints, Potter brushed off the occasional "griping" as something that "should not disturb you. It's the kind of griping G.I.'s do about a good officer who makes them work, but whom they trust and respect."

These suggestions from the *Baltimore Sun*'s bureau chief were joined in mid-February by a trio of letters from the editor of the *Denver Post*, Palmer "Ep" Hoyt, also considered a friend of the White House.[122] The journalist focused on two specific aspects of Johnson's relations with the media: presidential news conferences and briefings by the press secretary. Like Potter, Hoyt urged Johnson to hold televised press conferences, announced in advance, on a regular basis. Surely, he mused, "you can work out a plan to give adequate notice without any loss of presidential prerogative." The editor reminded Johnson that "controlling the national consensus is not the same as controlling the legislative majority," and television allowed the direct contact with the people which was vital to presidential control. Hoyt assured the president that "you have been much more effective in the large press conferences than you realize, particularly when you are relaxed and in a non-irritated mood," but he warned that "the mounting barrage of criticism regarding press conferences . . . is coming from men most friendly to you, men like James Reston and Roscoe Drummond." Johnson needed, in Hoyt's view, to "take your case to the people regularly . . . before you become a victim of your understandable resentment toward the press for their attacks on you."

As for the press secretary's news briefings, the journalist found the key difficulty to lie in Reedy's failure to provide informative answers to reporters' questions. Hoyt passed on the press corps' view that Reedy was "able and dependable and quite up to meeting their needs if only he were given the necessary help and support from the President." Because that attitude harmed Johnson as much as Reedy, Hoyt recommended that both take steps to remedy the perception: the president by informing his press secretary more fully, including "some red meat to feed to the hounds each day"; and the press secretary by "doing a little more reportorial homework" to come prepared with details of interest to the press corps, and by avoiding the "don't know" phraseology which "feeds the 'secretive' image." Hoyt concluded by stressing the scope of his suggestions; "I have been discussing improvements in molehills rather than mountains," he wrote, but "if enough sand blows on the molehills they can become mountains." Yet even with Valenti to champion Hoyt's recommendations, Johnson immediately rejected the aide's proposal for a preannounced television conference the following week and undertook no major efforts to brief Reedy more thoroughly.

The two journalists' detailed recommendations were not the only ones to be made in December 1964 and January 1965, as Johnson thrived on planning *his* administration. Two assistants to Liz Carpenter, Dave Waters and Simone Poulain, suggested that Johnson permit the television networks to cover one of the walking press conferences, complete with the dogs, to "show the press and the public that you are still sustaining great vitality and energy" as a means of combatting rumors "that you are weak in the knees, [or] that you are on your last leg."[123] Carpenter, whose primary assignment as Lady Bird Johnson's press secretary was coupled with an appointment as executive assistant to the president, had earlier recommended Poulain as someone "who knows TV problems as well as anyone in government" and should therefore be utilized.[124] Apparently Johnson did not value her services as highly, for the suggestion was not adopted. Carpenter later mused that this idea, like many others on the topic of media performance, had been solicited in one of Johnson's ceaseless drives for self-improvement.[125] Yet the advice floundered in Johnson's enduring conflict over the media. He wanted to communicate successfully over television, and he wanted members of the media to love him and to treat him well; but he resented that *he* might have to accommodate *them*, especially since he was, as he often noted, "leader of the Western world." Consequently, as this episode illustrates, he seesawed back and forth between courtship and rejection, and between soliciting advice and ignoring it.

During the early months of his new administration, however, Johnson still actively sought recommendations. A month after his memorandum on foreign-affairs coverage, Cater sent Johnson a broader analysis of "handling the news during the year ahead."[126] He reiterated his earlier proposal to use National Security Council meetings to "reduce press speculation over crisis sessions" and to help plug news leaks; furthermore, he thought the Cabinet might be used the same way. In addition, Cater suggested that the weekly release of reports to the president on successful programs "will help to generate positive news," and he pointed to a report on Latin America that made the front page of the *New York Times* as an example. Soliciting departmental evaluations of important upcoming events offered another way to discover those stories that deserved White House attention—a practice to which Reedy later objected, on the grounds that if the White House did not know about a story in the first place, then it should not be the point of release.[127]

Echoing Potter, Cater continued his analysis by recommending that the president hold two televised press conferences a month, with at least a one-day notice. The aide anticipated Johnson's objections when he noted that "while the large televised conference should not become a compulsory institution (as it became during Kennedy's time), it does have advantages that are not possible with the impromptu press conference." The informal background meetings that Johnson enjoyed should be continued, as should the sessions with the bureau chiefs, which Cater termed "a great success." [128] The aide also concurred with Barber's suggestion that more of the president's daily appointments be placed on the record: "the rule should be that all visits are public unless you rule to the contrary," Cater advised. "Otherwise, there will be a tendency to let the rule of caution dictate secrecy. I don't believe it helps to release a schedule each day which conceals more than it reveals."

Finally, Cater urged Johnson to commit himself, at least in principle, to four television programs during the coming year. Three might be selected from network proposals; the fourth, he felt, should follow the discussion format of the "Conversation with the President," from March of 1964, in which three representatives of the media had met with Johnson.

Valenti assured Cater that the president was "quite pleased" with his suggestions; he then circulated the memorandum for further responses.[129] Carpenter and Bundy strongly endorsed regular televised press conferences; Carpenter advised Johnson to keep his answers short "to avoid accusations of 'filibuster,'" and to "provide one light, humorous, 'planted' question that provokes a nice, warm response." Each concurred with Cater's recommendations for television programs; Bundy could "see great value in a Great Society program, and

equal value in a foreign affairs review." Both also agreed that Johnson's public calendar should be enlarged; "so many more interesting
things happen in the President's day," Carpenter lamented, "than
show up on the released calendar." Bundy did take exception to
Cater's proposed National Security Council and Cabinet meetings,
for "neither organization is a good instrument of real work, and
make-work meetings will drive you crazy and be cancelled as often as
not." Bundy left unaddressed the question of whether such meetings
could actually be expected to stem the unflattering news stories,
especially if the meetings were frequently cancelled. For whatever
reason, Cater's recommendation on meetings was not instituted; for
example, NSC meetings dropped from twenty-four in 1964 to only
ten, all devoted to Vietnam, the following year.

Reedy's press operation was also subject to scrutiny during this
period of administrative assessment, with the press office receiving
criticism on two points: a lack of accessibility which encouraged
speculative stories, and "occasions when the left hand doesn't know
what the right hand is doing."[130] Reedy would have concurred with at
least the latter criticism, although he attributed the confusion to
Johnson's failure to keep him informed.[131] That this critique came
from an assistant to Bill Moyers presaged changes in the press secretary's office.

Even Mrs. Johnson joined in the recommendations for approaching
the question of press relations in the new year. For Christmas in 1964
she presented her husband with a framed quotation from Lincoln: "If
I were to return, much less answer, all the attacks made on me, this
shop might as well be closed for any other business."[132]

Despite these suggestions, however, Johnson continued to stock-
pile grievances with the press, and they with him. The correspondents rankled at what they perceived to be peevish, obsessive duplicity: insisting that he drank domestic bourbon rather than the
imported scotch he preferred; denying any intention of naming Texas
associate Marvin Watson to the White House staff, and then selecting
him as the new appointments secretary; suggesting that his State of
the Union address for 1965 would be a simple statement of political
principles which he might not even give in person, and then delivering fifty minutes of detailed legislative proposals before the first
prime-time audience to view such an address; proclaiming that
photographer Yoichi Okamoto worked at the White House only
temporarily when he put in more than forty hours a week until
Johnson left office;[133] demanding that stories obtained at the ranch in
Texas carry a Washington dateline, which the *New York Times*

refused to do; once again predicting that the budget would be more than one hundred billion dollars, and once again producing one below that mark.

These complaints were joined by others. In a background session Johnson told reporters to expect major changes in the "Little Cabinet," consisting of the second-in-line in each department, but no such shake-up occurred. In a move similar to his handling of the Bobby problem, Johnson hoped to eliminate the undersecretary of labor, who was strongly supported by the AFL-CIO, by threatening all sub-Cabinet posts; but labor pressure prevented his replacement and nullified Johnson's predictions. Then Johnson wanted a start-of-session meeting with congressional leaders kept secret, despite its routine nature; that effort drew a letter of protest from one reporter:

> It is the sort of unnecessary secrecy that can lead not only to confusion on our side of the closed doors, but also to innocent distortions. . . .
>
> What looks more like a crisis (if no indications otherwise are at hand) than a meeting of Democratic and Republican Congressional leaders with the President—unannounced, and for all we know, called on the spur of the moment? Especially if, for an hour or an hour and a half, the White House refuses to confirm what we already know—that it is going on—and to tell us the purpose.[134]

Yet Johnson resisted informing the press of his purposes. Briefly hospitalized with a bronchial infection following the inauguration, Johnson could not attend Winston Churchill's funeral. When reporters asked why he named Chief Justice Earl Warren and Dean Rusk to go to London rather than Hubert Humphrey, he offered no explanation. The reason for the president's decision was that he feared that his illness might be worse than the physicians officially reported and, in light of the cold the vice-president had as well, Johnson felt Humphrey should not be travelling out of the country. At the same time, he did not wish to create undue public concern about presidential health, especially so soon after Kennedy's assassination. In the absence of any official explanation, however, columnists speculated that the president intended the move to keep his subordinate in line. The interpretation stirred Johnson to sarcastic observations on the press's interest in "the protocol involved in connection with funerals," as he told a press conference he would "bear in mind in connection with any future funerals your very strong feelings in the matter and try to act in accordance with our national interest."[135] Johnson's public display of bitterness prompted

106

both Douglass Cater and Ep Hoyt to label his outburst counterproductive; as Hoyt told the president, "you yourself have observed that it is easier to tell a man to go to hell than to get him to go."[136] Columnist Art Buchwald's rationale for the incident was the only one to bring a smile to the White House: Hubert Humphrey could not go to the funeral because he simply could not look sad.[137]

These sorts of grievances accumulated to create a sense among journalists that Johnson was firmly committed to what Evans and Novak labeled "a pattern of secrecy and sometimes duplicity that might be called Government by Indirection."[138] They felt his obsession with secrecy even compelled the president to rescind an appointment to a post if the news were published prematurely. While Reedy contends that Johnson would never refuse an appointment because of publicity, he observes that the president would postpone it, which still created bad press coverage.[139] This approach did help solidify Johnson's control over the executive branch by stressing that he was in charge, but it also contributed to the view of Johnson as politically manipulative. By February of 1965, members of the media were so suspicious of Johnson's motivations that they ascribed purely political purposes to the White House Lincoln Luncheon—a function that Eric Goldman, not the president, had designed as a union of culture and consensus.[140]

Thus, even while he sought suggestions on how to better his press relations, the reciprocal antagonisms of Johnson and the press increased. In the meantime, White House staff members launched their own efforts to improve press coverage if not press relations. For example, Bill Moyers chided Stewart Alsop for his *Saturday Evening Post* essay entitled "Blandness in the White House": Why should "so many of Washington's finest in the press corps bestow so much virtue on conflict as an end unto itself?" Alsop responded that he did not praise the "journalist-vultures," but rather admired Johnson's expertise in avoiding political battles. The title of the piece, he noted, was provided by the editors over his protests. The following day, Moyers thanked the columnist "for your letter and your understanding. I guess we're closer together than I thought."[141]

Staff members not only chided columnists for stories they perceived to be negative ones; they also aided friendly journalists. When William S. White requested information for a column, he received Reedy's figures on press contacts as of February 4, 1965: thirty-seven on-the-record press conferences, ten off-the-record conferences with transcripts, ten walks with the press, and five evening meetings with

bureau chiefs. Reedy added that Johnson had held three press conferences since his election, met with three press pools during his recent
illness, and talked with a press pool on every plane trip.[142]

Johnson himself joined in this crusade, as he instructed the former
chief of protocol to "straighten *Newsweek* out on its article" regarding his resignation.[143] He also refused an appointment with Henry
Gemmell and Al Otten of the *Wall Street Journal* with a note to
Reedy: "I don't believe I've ever had a fair story in the W.J. I know
Otten can't be fair—why should I punish myself?" When Reedy
argued that "one of our problems with the *Wall Street Journal* has
been lack of personal contact," Johnson replied, "Why don't you have
the interview?"[144] Nor would Johnson approve a request from Dan
Rather to film several presidential assistants, informing Reedy:
"This man & CBS out to get us anyway Bill Paley can. Tell him you
have much more work than you can handle and these men are
workers not actors."[145]

When Cormier failed to receive a gold-filled LBJ tie clip as a campaign memento and Christmas gift, he concluded that the omission
was part of "the freeze" he received after filing stories favorable to the
Kennedys.[146] The presidential-press honeymoon was long over.

"One of the most undignified things that happens to a public
official these days," Lady Bird once mused, "is being made a bone of
contention by the press."[147] That indignity, along with the nagging
instability of Vietnam, joined to rob the first lady of any sense of
elation at gaining 61 percent of the vote that November. On November 1, 1964, Viet Cong had shelled the air base at Bien Hoa, killing
several Americans and destroying a number of planes. Despite strong
internal pressure, especially from Ambassador Maxwell D. Taylor
and the Joint Chiefs of Staff, Johnson refused to authorize retaliatory
raids. The Gulf of Tonkin in August had been one situation; two days
before an election against Barry Goldwater was another, particularly
in light of the continued weakness—both political and military—of
the South Vietnamese.

The turmoil in Vietnam did not cease after the election, nor did
Johnson's growing impatience with the stickiness of the situation. In
September, according to his memoirs, the president had challenged
his advisers on whether Vietnam was "worth all this effort," and each
assured him it was.[148] At the end of November, in a rambling press
conference at the ranch, Johnson had fumed when a reporter inquired
about possible expansion of the war:

108

I don't want to give you any particular guideposts as to your conduct in the matter. But when you crawl out on a limb, you always
have to find another one to crawl back on.

I have just been sitting here in this serene atmosphere of the
Pedernales for the last few days reading about the wars that you
have involved us in. . . . I would say, generally speaking, that some
people are speculating and taking positions that I would think are
somewhat premature.[149]

Clearly, Johnson did not want the press to pressure him on Southeast
Asia, either publicly or privately. Yet the pressure was on. On Christmas Eve 1964, a U.S. officers' billet in Saigon was the target; again
Johnson resisted demands for retaliation. Such resistance was difficult, given that Joseph Alsop's column of the preceding day had
given compelling—and personal—articulation to the insistence on
stronger American intervention:

There are plenty of discouraged Americans in Saigon who think the
President is consciously prepared to accept defeat here. They believe he cannot bring himself to take measures needed to avert defeat, and they therefore suspect that he is simply planning to wait
until the end comes and then to disclaim responsibility. But since
the President has the means to avert defeat he cannot disclaim responsibility. It will be his defeat as well as a defeat for the American people and for millions of unhappy Vietnamese. It does not
seem credible that Lyndon B. Johnson intends to accept and preside
over such a defeat. But the alternatives open to him are narrowing
very fast.[150]

Delivering publicly the warning he had given earlier at the private
dinner at the White House, Alsop again raised the spectre of Johnson's being "the first American President to lose a war." Johnson
dreaded such an outcome, so completely inconsistent with his values
and perceptions; he also recognized the powerful constituencies in
Congress, business, and the military—and in the press as well—
chafing for more dramatic and successful action in Southeast Asia.
Yet he feared that more pointed military measures would trigger a
war not only with North Vietnam but also with China, and he
certainly did not want to be the president who presided over the
beginning of World War III, with the all-too-possible nuclear destruction of the world which that threatened to bring. Johnson kept striving to find a way to keep the American commitment he perceived in
Vietnam quietly, strongly, and successfully, without relinquishing

South Vietnam to communism but also without bringing on a much wider war. It was not a task he relished.

As Johnson assessed his thirteen months as president at the end of 1964, then, he found good reason for optimism in both domestic and foreign affairs—until he reached Vietnam, to which he turned "with the exasperated voice of a man discussing an ugly, incurable disease."[151] On December 29, the president sent Bundy a set of letters and editorials declaring that South Vietnam needed a strong government to develop nationalism and self-sufficiency.[152] He agreed with their argument, Johnson told his adviser; "there must be some way for us to concentrate our energies, talents, and resources toward a possible solution, i.e., stabilizing their confidence."

Johnson echoed this forlorn touch of desperation the following week in a memorandum to McNamara, which was taken almost entirely from a memorandum he had received from Bundy. Enclosing a copy of a *U.S. News and World Report* article entitled, "Can U.S. Win in Vietnam?," the president urged the defense secretary to

> develop a new plan for volunteer fighting forces that would proceed with a minimum of overhead and a maximum of energy in direct contact with the Vietnamese at all levels.
>
> I constantly hear, re Vietnam, we have too much staff, too much administration, too much clerical work, too much reporting, too much rotation and not enough action. . . .
>
> I suspect you and Mac are right in opposing larger U.S. forces, but let's develop some alternatives.[153]

That the president of the United States, generally the key but off-stage presence of presidential archives, should write two memoranda within ten days may be taken as a sign of the tension Johnson felt regarding the situation. He desperately wanted, but could not conceive of a quick, respectable, reasonable solution.

By the end of January of 1965, Bundy and McNamara fully shared the president's concern about Vietnam, telling him they were "pretty well convinced that our current policy can lead only to disastrous defeat."[154] The deterioration of the South Vietnamese government and the gains made by the Viet Cong had convinced them that only two alternatives remained: to "use our military power in the Far East and to force a change of Communist policy," or to "deploy all our resources along a track of negotiation, aimed at salvaging what little can be preserved with no major addition to our present military risks." Such alternatives as neutralization and withdrawal had been deemed unacceptable long before. While they felt both military

110

power and negotiations should be pursued, the former seemed to be required. Dean Rusk hesitated to agree with them, they noted; he did not deny the gravity of the situation, but he insisted that "the consequences of both escalation and withdrawal are so bad that we simply must find a way of making our present policy work. This would be good," sighed Bundy, "if it was possible. Bob and I do not think it is."

Within a week, the "present policy" would undergo a major change.

5

The Evolution of the Johns Hopkins Address, April 7, 1965

The Johnson administration responded to the Gulf of Tonkin incident as though it were an isolated, not-to-be-repeated case. Seeking a congressional resolution of support, addressing the American people, ordering retaliatory air strikes—all were designed as specific responses to a specific incident. Later, the congressional resolution would be used to justify further American action; but in August of 1964, Johnson's approach showed his primary concern to be handling the crisis, obtaining congressional support, and moving on to the election and those cherished domestic dreams, rather than establishing long-term policies for Vietnam or engendering massive public support for an extended war effort.

So it was that Vietnam once again subsided from the forefront of the presidential consciousness. The issue, however, was not entirely dormant; such incidents as the Christmas Eve attack in Saigon resulted in an increasingly pessimistic prognosis for an early end to American involvement. Yet it was not until February 6, 1965, six months after the adoption of the Gulf of Tonkin resolution, that a major incident forced the attention of both Johnson and the public back to the situation in Vietnam. On that day, Viet Cong guerrillas attacked the U.S. officers' barracks at Pleiku, killing eight Americans and wounding more than one hundred. For the first time, United States soldiers were the primary rather than the secondary targets for mortar fire.

Johnson was furious. As noted earlier, the fact that he preferred to view Vietnam as a peripheral issue did not reflect either a lack of concern for the area or a lack of ego involvement in American policy there. The American casualties at Pleiku activated both concern and ego involvement, especially given that the U.S. forces in Vietnam were still assigned as military advisers for the South Vietnamese troops, not as combat personnel. That they should become objects of Viet Cong attacks angered Johnson, who stormed about the outrage at the emergency session of the National Security Council called that

February 6. Using the fighting imagery of the frontier, the president declared before the NSC that

> we have kept our gun over the mantel and our shells in the cupboard for a long time now, and what was the result? They are killing our men while they sleep in the night. I can't ask our American soldiers out there to fight with one hand tied behind their backs.[1]

Johnson did not address the fact that the United States had moved a mantel and cupboard within sight of the Viet Cong; if American forces were attacked, he believed, the country was compelled to respond. Within twelve hours of the raid at Pleiku, the president had ordered Operation Flaming Dart to execute retaliatory air strikes on military targets in North Vietnam. He also ordered the withdrawal of all American dependents from the South, a step contemplated two weeks earlier but not undertaken because of concern over "the very dangerous psychological problems in initiating this action" and over the resultant press coverage.[2]

Underscoring Johnson's sense of urgency were the reports from McGeorge Bundy, in Vietnam at the time of the Pleiku attack. After visiting the camp, Bundy developed a relatively impassioned thirteen-page assessment of the situation, warning that American investment and responsibility in the area were critical for both the United States and Southeast Asia. "The stakes in Vietnam are extremely high," cautioned the national security adviser: "the international prestige of the United States, and a substantial part of our influence, are directly at risk in Vietnam."[3] In light of the rapidly deteriorating situation there, Bundy pressed for more stringent measures than a single tit-for-tat retaliation. Instead, he urged the adoption of sustained reprisals, with which continuous air strikes against the North were based on "the whole Viet Cong campaign of violence and terror in the South." Initially such reprisals should be placed within the context of "those acts of relatively high visibility such as the Pleiku incident"; later, he suggested, a "weekly list of outrages in the South" would prove sufficient. Bundy noted that the risks would be considerable, including significant American air losses, an extensive air war against North Vietnam, and increased U.S. casualties which would be "more visible to American feelings" than those sustained in South Vietnam. Despite these costs, the adviser contended, the reprisals were necessary to counter "a widespread belief that we do not have the will and force and patience and determination to take the necessary action and stay the course. . . . Once such a policy is put in force, we shall be able to speak in Vietnam on many topics and in many ways, with growing force and effectiveness."

Halberstam has marvelled at Bundy's "rare emotional response" to his glimpse of the casualties and destruction at Pleiku;[4] the adviser's memorandum of February 7, with its sympathy for "the weary country" with grim prospects and its assertion of American prestige at stake, limns his strong reaction. For the moment, Johnson rejected Bundy's proposal for sustained reprisals; yet the president was also deeply affected by the thought of Americans being attacked. Subsequently he would describe his perspective to Doris Kearns: " 'Suddenly,' Johnson later said, 'I realized that doing nothing was more dangerous than doing something.' "[5] His statement reflects the same intensity as his "gun over the mantel" declaration, for he was galvanized by Pleiku. It was a time of growing commitment for the president.

Yet Johnson still sought to contain the conflict, militarily and politically, at home and abroad. Reedy and Bundy held a background briefing for the press on February 8, but the majority of information provided was classified and off the record.[6] Busby asked Bundy for a presidential statement on both foreign and domestic affairs to be released after the Cabinet meeting of February 11, for "obviously, the media will associate the Cabinet session with the Southeast Asia developments"; but no statement was released.[7] Rusk queried General Westmoreland about recently captured physical material which could serve in a "hard-hitting and convincing demonstration establishing history of DRV [North Vietnamese] involvement and direction of VC, . . . for use in possible national press or TV briefing"; but no public briefing of this kind was held.[8]

Predictably, this low public profile did not satisfy everyone in the administration. James L. Greenfield, the assistant secretary of state for public affairs, called for the release of more official information on two fronts.[9] First, he requested a public statement to reiterate America's stake in Vietnam. Greenfield acknowledged that the Geneva Accords and Eisenhower's commitments might be "old-hat, even boring stuff" for those in government, but he pointed out that "the rationale for our actions during the past few weeks was almost entirely dropped from most of the stories that appeared after the first day of bombings." He assumed that if the media forgot the administration's rationale, so would the public.

While this official restatement of the government's position was a necessary first step, Greenfield noted, "it will not, however, satisfy many of the questions being asked by the press. . . . Many of them are unanswerable." While these probes "reflect journalistic rather than public pressure" at the moment, the assistant secretary observed, they were "both legitimate and pressing." Moreover, the government's tendency "to brush aside the general public statement on the excuse that it cannot include all the details demanded by the press . . . is not valid." Both press and public should be provided with information, Greenfield argued, even if it could not be complete.

This information would of necessity be truncated, in part because members of the administration were debating how best to approach the problem itself. Westmoreland and the Joint Chiefs of Staff pushed for major troop deployments with authorization for combat, including aggressive search and destroy missions. Taylor, on the other hand, argued for a more concerted air war, with soldiers supporting South Vietnamese troops as they defended key enclaves. The president himself favored air strikes over ground forces, for they required fewer American military personnel, incurred fewer American casualties, and demonstrated American determination to break Hanoi's resolve. When the limited retaliation of Operation Flaming Dart drew not a decrease but an increase in the North's resolve to attack American forces, Johnson ordered Operation Rolling Thunder to embark on the sustained reprisals which Bundy had recommended earlier. The imagery of the code names contrasted as did the purpose of the missions: the former was primarily intended to score political and psychological victories against the North Vietnamese through directed strikes, while the latter was designed to destroy the North's military support for the conflict through more general bombing.

In addition to ordering these continuous air strikes, Johnson authorized the dispatch of two Marine Corps battalions, the first American ground combat units to enter Vietnam. They had been sent at Westmoreland's request, despite Taylor's "grave reservations as to the wisdom and necessity of so doing."[10] Despite Johnson's reticence to assign ground forces, he approved the deployment, apparently viewing it as another specific response to an isolated situation rather than a significant step toward increased involvement. While the marines were ordered to help protect the extensive American and South Vietnamese installations at Danang, they were also instructed not to engage in the daily battles against the Viet Cong. Theirs was to be a role of limited military support. As Lewy observes, "this major decision, a watershed in the history of the American involvement in Vietnam, was made without very much discussion and planning";[11]

the commitment of United States ground forces occurred almost as a footnote to decisions regarding the air war.

With this broadening of American actions in Vietnam, American casualties skyrocketed. So too did the questions and confusion about the nature, extent, and justification of that involvement. The air attacks on North Vietnam swelled the ranks of senators objecting to America's policy in Southeast Asia. Originally composed of Wayne Morse of Oregon and Ernest Gruening of Alaska, the only two members of Congress to vote against the Gulf of Tonkin resolution, the growing "peace bloc" in Johnson's old haunts proved doubly galling to the president, for members of his own party protested American involvement the most vociferously. Democrats Frank Church of Idaho, George McGovern of North Dakota, and Mike Mansfield of Montana joined the protesters.

Nor was criticism limited to the Senate. At 8:00 P.M. on March 24, 1965, students and faculty at the University of Michigan began a twelve-hour marathon: the first "teach-in" against the war. The format of lectures and seminars condemning various aspects of United States involvement in Vietnam proved so successful that a national teach-in was quickly scheduled for May 15 in Washington, D.C., complete with an "afternoon policy confrontation" between speakers for and against American policy. The *New York Times* granted authenticity when it carried a complete transcript of the proceedings.

Foreign criticism mounted as well. Charles de Gaulle, leader of a nation itself once driven out of Indochina, called for a new Geneva conference and a halt in the U.S. bombing of the North. The Pakistani foreign minister, Z. A. Bhutto, disregarded his earlier contact with Johnson to criticize the American reprisal policy. Visits to the United States by Pakistani and Indian officials, outspoken against the American policy in Vietnam, were then postponed because they coincided with complicated congressional debates over foreign aid; the incident gained additional publicity when news of the postponements was leaked to the foreign press before the foreign governments were all formally notified.

Attacks on United States policy in Vietnam were not limited to public forums. In a top secret memorandum to Bundy entitled "One Dove's Lament," James C. Thomson, Jr., argued that "in South Vietnam we have stepped into a gross overcommitment of national prestige and resources on political, military, and geographic terrain which should long ago have persuaded us to avoid such a

116

commitment."[12] That excessive involvement, Thomson continued, promised further dangers given the grave risks involved in sustained air reprisals against North Vietnam, especially in light of the United States' international interests. Thomson's disquiet about these worldwide risks extended to the domestic front as well, for he argued that the American public viewed the air strikes "as a desperation move" in substitution for political stability in Saigon. The aide held the administration responsible for this conception, which was stimulated by "the polarization of political and press opinion in the absence of a clear and comprehensive message from the top of the Government." To Thomson, "the much-abused gentlemen of the *New York Times* and several thoughtful members of the President's own party on the Hill" had the right idea: "The only rational alternative remains negotiation," a path to which the administration had thus far not devoted "any of the care and vigor given to target selection and the like." Johnson needed to speak out on Vietnam, contended the aide, but he should do so on the basis of a thorough reconsideration of the bombing policy adopted after Pleiku. The available White House files contain no response to Thomson's lament.

Despite these negative reactions, Johnson's Vietnam policies enjoyed substantial public support. A Gallup poll taken just after the Pleiku retaliation, for example, showed 67 percent approval for the action and 64 percent opposition to withdrawing; a poll published March 12, five weeks later, indicated 66 percent support for the continuation of present U.S. efforts in South Vietnam.

The spring of 1965 also brought forth a flood of cries from those who felt the United States should not only continue but increase its efforts in Southeast Asia. General Curtis LeMay's reported recommendation to "nuke the Chinks"—to drop nuclear bombs on Communist China—certainly constituted an extreme version of such sentiments; yet perceptions of American prestige being diminished by gadfly attacks created pressure to use greater force in response. Restricting the attacks to bridges, ammunition depots, and military bases, they argued, lacked the forcefulness to be gained by bombing cities as well. As one contended, "this is no time for another Munich."[13]

In ordering air strikes on North Vietnam, then, Johnson faced criticism for doing both too much and not enough. It was during this period, historian Eric Goldman points out, that the terms "hawk" and "dove" gained currency. Although, as Goldman observes, "they did as much to confuse as to classify," the labels and their growing

popularity did capture the spirit of two strong strains of public opinion on the issue.[14]

The news media reflected these polar positions as well. The *New
York Times* editorials grew more and more critical of the American
bombing policy, as they urged Johnson to accept de Gaulle's suggestions before it was too late. Critiques with such headlines as "Black
Day in Vietnam" offered the advice to which Thomson referred in his
"Dove's Lament" to Bundy. In contrast, columnist Joseph Alsop
rejected neutralization as selling out, and encouraged Johnson to
adopt a course of continued air strikes to demonstrate that "the
President now means business at last," rather than simply employing
"another fruitless one-shot stunt" like the Gulf of Tonkin reprisals.[15]
Meanwhile, columnist James Reston admitted that he might lack
sufficient information on the war to second-guess Johnson's decisions, but he argued that "the least the President can do is to go before
the country and explain his objectives," to still "the babble of influential voices in Washington" muttering along without guidance
from their leader.[16]

One commentator who continued to be of special interest to the
Johnson administration was columnist Walter Lippmann. Early in
Johnson's presidency, veteran Democratic political adviser James
Rowe had warned Johnson that the Washington press corps is

> worse than a wolf pack when it comes to attacking public officials.
> But they are like a bunch of sheep in their own profession and they
> will always follow the bellwether sheep. . . .
>
> The only two newspapermen practically all of them admire are
> Walter Lippmann and Scotty Reston. As long as those two are for
> Lyndon Johnson he will, on the whole, get a good press from the
> rest of them.
>
> You certainly have Lippmann and Reston in your pocket now. I
> hope you do not lose them.[17]

Johnson doubted, as he said both at the time and in his memoirs, that
a southern president could ever receive fair treatment from what he
called "the metropolitan press of the Eastern seaboard." Yet he knew
the "bellwether" columnists could be useful to him—particularly
Lippmann, who in one poll of the Washington press corps garnered an
exceptional 42 percent of the vote as the fairest and most reliable
columnist on the political scene.[18] Lippmann had been enthusiastically supportive of Johnson in the first year of his presidency, praising
his healing influence during a time of trial. Johnson had reciprocated
by awarding him the Presidential Medal of Freedom, the nation's

118

highest civilian honor, in September of 1964. Vietnam, however, brought an increasing sense of disillusionment to the columnist. The key to American foreign policy lay in Europe, Lippmann argued, not Asia. Moreover, in the wake of Johnson's reprisal policy, the columnist complained that even

> apart from the question of morality and the gigantic risks of esca-
> lating the war, there is no sufficient reason to think that the North-
> ern communists can be bombed into submission. . . .
>   For this country to [further] involve itself in such a war in Asia
> would be an act of supreme folly. . . . There is no tolerable alterna-
> tive except a negotiated truce.[19]

As the bombings of North Vietnam continued through the spring of 1965 and no truce appeared, Lippmann's disenchantment deepened, and his columns provided pungent quotations for members of the peace bloc.

The Johnson administration watched media coverage of Vietnam during this period, thanking editors for supportive pieces and refuting columns that alleged McNamara's opposition to the retaliatory strikes.[20] Referring to one article in the *Minneapolis Tribune*, Carl T. Rowan of the USIA mused to Johnson: "What a help it would be if we could get more of the columnists and editorial writers in the country to replace the emotional axe-grinding with this kind of constructive comment."[21]

Despite this "emotional axe-grinding," Johnson still resisted a major public policy statement on Vietnam. For two months follow-ing the Pleiku attacks, Johnson spoke with individuals and small groups about American goals in Southeast Asia, but public messages on Vietnam were limited to White House statements and remarks at press conferences. The president's comments at his news confer-ences of March 13, March 20, and April 1 all echoed the same posi-tion: while the real goal of the United States in Vietnam was peace, aggression had to be stopped—in other words, what the American policy had been all along. Reporters were not always receptive to this approach; a reiteration of previous statements seemed inadequate to them when a major program of reprisals had been started with little public clarification of its purposes. Feelings ran so high before John-son's March 13 news conference that Douglass Cater advised the president to hold the session in spacious quarters, for "it has been my observation that certain members of the press grow more arrogant and insolent in proportion to the crowdedness of the room in which a press conference is being held. They seem to feel a certain anonymity in numbers."[22] Perhaps, suggested Cater, the wide-open spaces of the East Room would mitigate the tension. Again, however, Johnson was not without support from certain quarters of the media. Ep Hoyt, for example, instructed Valenti to praise the president for his conference of March 20, in which "he did a great deal to clarify public opinion and consolidate the consensus."[23]

Against this background of conflicting pressures and criticism, Lyndon Johnson called for a speech on Vietnam.[24] Aides had compiled excerpts from major policy statements in preparation for such an address, but they had lain dormant in the files; staff members had outlined foreign affairs speeches, but Johnson had rejected them.[25] In late March of 1965, however, the president decided that it was time for a full-fledged public statement on American policy regarding Southeast Asia.

McGeorge Bundy outlined the original draft of the speech, which focused on the history of American commitments to the region and the continued refusal "to accept aggression as the price of lowered tension."[26] The United States wanted no wider war, Bundy insisted, but any settlement of the conflict demanded that "the aggression against the people and Government of South Vietnam" must stop. Such a settlement would allow the United States "to cooperate in Southeast Asia in regional development." Bundy concluded his draft with recommendations to include references to the South Vietnamese government throughout the speech, "so that this is not just a U.S. policy and a U.S. program," and to end the address "on the note of steadfastness for peace—with a reprise on our hope to do those things—and only those things—which are necessary to repel aggression and which give promise of a brighter future for all concerned."

The potential importance of this address, which as yet had no firm date or setting for delivery, soon became apparent to Johnson's aides. In a memorandum to Johnson, attached to a second draft of the statement, Bundy suggested that "this may well be the most important foreign policy speech you have yet planned."[27] Bundy, along with Secretary of State Dean Rusk and Secretary of Defense Robert McNamara, encouraged an emphasis on the history of American involvement in Vietnam, complete with quotations from John Kennedy to, as Bundy explained, "give us protection and encouragement with some of the 'liberals' who are falsely telling each other that your policy is different from his."

From Bundy the draft went to Richard Goodwin, the brash but bright speech writer whose eloquence as a ghostwriter for Kennedy had attracted Johnson to him. It was Goodwin who had captured

Johnson's domestic visions in the phrase, "the Great Society." Working with Valenti, Goodwin now produced a two-pronged plan after Johnson's own heart: a proposal to create a team of experts to design a food program for South Vietnam, paired with a plan to develop the Mekong River region, the latter to be seeded with a billion dollar contribution from the United States. The cultivation of the Mekong Delta, a concept long bandied about within the administration, found the ideal format for its emergence in this major policy speech.[28]

Johnson responded enthusiastically. Here was an approach he could endorse. He had believed since his vice-presidential trip that the enemies of Southeast Asia were not only communism but "hunger, ignorance, poverty, and disease," and this proposal melded that belief with Johnson's can-do spirit to address the problem. Now he could envision expanding his War on Poverty from the home front to the Third World region, thus battling those enemies common to all humanity.

Over the next week—the end of March and the beginning of April—Bundy, Goodwin, Valenti, and others pored over drafts of the speech, making changes that ranged from minute to massive. According to the notations on one draft, "the diplomats," who were presumably representatives from the State Department, preferred one passage to refer simply to "Vietnam" rather than to "Vietnam's steaming soil"; the latter, they felt, "sounds patronizing."[29] Sections on economic development and the food program were watered down, beefed up, removed, and replaced, depending on who was working on which draft at what time. Goodwin lamented the deletion of what he called "the nice words about the Chinese people,"[30] while Valenti substituted the word "purpose" for "policy" in one paragraph to, as he explained, "avoid nitpicks from the [military] commanders."[31]

As these revisions were being undertaken, Johnson tried out various passages on select audiences. Leaders of the liberal Americans for Democratic Action, for example, arrived at the White House to protest the bombing of North Vietnam. In the exchange that followed, Johnson provided a preview of the speech in which he emphasized the Mekong River development proposal. While several of the ADA members left the meeting as opposed as they had been previously, many of the leaders, according to observer Jack Valenti, received the speech enthusiastically—so enthusiastically, in fact, that Johnson kept the National Security Council waiting for half an hour as he savored their support.

Such positive reactions encouraged Johnson to go ahead with the delivery of the speech; the state of the war and public opinion in late

March and early April provided further incentive. On March 30, a Viet Cong suicide squad attacked the United States embassy in Saigon, killing two Americans and sparking new outcries; *Time's* next issue headlined, "Outrages Like This." Two days later, seventeen nonaligned nations appealed to the United States and two dozen other countries to begin peace negotiations without preconditions.[32] Members of the administration were, in the meantime, none too satisfied with the state of affairs in Vietnam. Westmoreland continued to press for further ground troops with expanded responsibilities. Taylor's disgruntlement with the deployment of marine battalions revealed itself in a background interview; the subsequent published reports led to a testy exchange of telegrams between the ambassador and the secretary of state.[33] McCone challenged the effectiveness of current air strikes; if combat soldiers were added, he insisted that an increased tempo of raids would be necessary.[34] Rusk disliked the idea of a ground war, yet he agreed that even the broader strikes of Rolling Thunder could not control the battles in the South. McNamara asked McNaughton to explore options, which he did on March 24 in an eight-page draft entitled "Proposed Course of Action re Vietnam."[35] McNaughton first assessed American aims:

> 70%—To avoid a humiliating US defeat (to our reputation as a guarantor).
> 20%—To keep SVN (and then adjacent) territory from Chinese hands.
> 10%—To permit the people of SVN to enjoy a better, freer way of life.
> ALSO—To emerge from crisis without unacceptable taint from methods used.
> NOT—To "help a friend," although it would be hard to stay in if asked out.

Given these goals, McNaughton contended, the critical question was this: "Can the situation inside SVN be bottomed out (a) without extreme measures against the DRV and/or (b) without deployment of large numbers of US (and other) combat troops inside SVN?" The answer, in McNaughton's judgment, was "perhaps, but probably no." With that assumption he outlined a program for American action in Vietnam; under the heading of "important miscellany," he noted the need for an information program to "preserve US public support." Throughout McNaughton's proposal, the preservation of American pride and prestige constituted the principal criterion.

McNamara took this evaluation to the National Security Council meetings that Johnson called on April 1 and 2.[36] Emerging from those debates was the grudging approval of an eighteen to twenty thousand man increase in the U.S. support forces in Vietnam. Johnson also agreed to allow more active use of the marines stationed there, authorizing them to search out Viet Cong and North Vietnamese forces rather than performing solely as stationary backup troops for South Vietnamese soldiers. They were still, however, to operate primarily from the key enclaves. For the first few months, in fact, the troops simply expanded the area of their patrols, without supporting ARVN offensive missions. As Lewy notes, this initially limited role enabled Johnson to assess the effectiveness of these forces without fully committing them to fight a guerrilla war;[37] even as he authorized more troops in an expanded role, the president proceeded with caution.

Part of that caution included the avoidance of premature publicity as he sought to evaluate the efficacy of the new measures. In the memorandum authorizing the troop increase and more active role, Johnson insisted that "these movements and changes should be understood as being gradual and wholly consistent with existing policy." While Johnson would later be charged with committing all manner of fraud and deception during this period, the man was convinced that the policy was in fact the same one; the decisions of early 1965 simply undertook new measures to achieve that policy. It was the salience, not the intensity of his commitment which had changed, and while the means grew more drastic, Johnson's ends were the same: to fight aggression and to keep America's word.

Understanding this perception can help explain if not justify Johnson's insistence, during his news conference in the midst of the NSC meetings, that "I know of no far-reaching strategy that is being suggested or promulgated" regarding Vietnam.[38] He was especially sensitive to press criticism about the war at this time, for just two days before he had seen a column by Joe Kraft from a French newspaper which had declared that American foreign policy was now based merely on presidential whim.[39] Johnson directed Cater to "send to Bundy & other decision-making [people] to read—'Judge not lest ye be judged.'" Bundy had already seen the column, "but," he told Cater, "I decided not to test the boss's blood pressure."

Despite such challenges to the boss's blood pressure, Johnson decided to proceed with the speech as a way to emphasize the continuity of his policy on Vietnam. By Friday, April 2, Johnson had told Bundy that he would take over the national security adviser's speaking engagement at Johns Hopkins University, scheduled for the following Monday, to deliver his address. Officially, the president would be accepting an open-ended invitation previously extended by the college's president, Milton Eisenhower.

That very afternoon, however, delivery of the address was threatened. Lester Pearson, the prime minister of Canada, had arranged to present a speech at Temple University on that date and to lunch with the president at Camp David the day after. Pearson's address in Philadelphia, however, advised Johnson to order a pause in the bombing of North Vietnam as a means of encouraging peace. Johnson was, as Valenti characterized him in his notes at the time, "incensed" by the man's gratuitous advice (particularly coming, as it did, one day before their conference), and he was "surly with Bundy" for recommending the meeting in the first place. Although tempted to cancel the meeting, the president received the prime minister anyway. Hugh Sidey describes their encounter:

> A miffed Johnson looked across at Pearson. "What would you do,"
> he asked Pearson, "disarm without them doing it?" Pearson
> answered, "Oh, no." And then Johnson bored in. "Well, why didn't
> you mention them in your speech?" Pearson was a more humble
> man throughout the meal.[40]

Still fuming, Johnson called off Monday's speech, leaving its time of delivery open. Yet when Monday arrived he had reconsidered, deciding to deliver the speech at Johns Hopkins on that Wednesday, April 7. Even that morning of April 5, however, Reedy would tell his briefing only that "the President may speak later this week on Vietnam," refusing to provide any further details.[41]

The speech writers continued to revise and polish the address. They inserted a carefully worded passage on "energetically" moving toward a peaceful settlement, thus responding to the appeal from the seventeen nations. In justifying the phrasing of the insertion, the writers' notation referred not to dangers of international misunderstanding, but to the fear that "without these paragraphs the speech might not strike the sophisticated correspondents as saying anything important."[42]

In further revisions, the American response to the peace appeal was then moved, for greater emphasis, from the middle of the speech to the introduction. It was replaced by a passage that, as it turned out, came to have special significance:

124

> We will never be second in the search for such a peaceful settlement in Viet-Nam. . . .
>
> We have stated this position over and over again, fifty times and more, to friend and foe alike. And we remain ready, with this purpose, for unconditional discussions.[43]

"Unconditional discussions." In and out of Congress, members of the peace bloc had been pressuring Johnson to proclaim his openness to negotiations, and the plea from the seventeen nations increased that pressure. Johnson had resisted such recommendations earlier, protesting that he *had* been publicly open to negotiations, but that Hanoi had responded only with further aggressive acts. Thus it was consistent with Johnson's perception of the situation when this "new" offer was cast as one made "fifty times and more," which "we remain" ready to make again. In addition, the offer was for unconditional discussions, not negotiations; echoing the disputation of semantics with Panama, the former promised only to talk, not necessarily to reach a settlement.

At this stage, four days before the scheduled delivery, preparations for the speech intensified. Valenti showed the address to Jack Horner of the *Washington Star* and Philip Potter, editor of the *Baltimore Sun*. Horner cautioned that Reedy should give the press background that would clarify Johnson's usage of "unconditional talks" (for example, whether that included a cease-fire); Valenti's notes indicate that other than that, the journalist felt the speech was "fine." Potter composed a passage which was used almost verbatim.[44] The first paragraph contradicted "those who say" that China is destined to dominate Southeast Asia, contending that "there is no end to that argument until all of the nations of Asia are swallowed up"—a version of the domino theory which implicitly extends to the United States as well. The second paragraph, paralleling American responsibility in Asia to that in Europe, noted that World War II was fought on both continents. "When it ended," Potter's passage contended, "we found ourselves with continued responsibility for the defense of freedom." The passage thus refuted arguments, like those of Lippmann, that contended the United States had no vital stake in that region. The politics of ghostwriting almost deleted these paragraphs; as Valenti's notes comment, "Goodwin took out Potter's revisions, but we [Valenti and Potter] put them back in."

In addition to Valenti's advance work, the president himself joined the round of previews, reading a draft to the *New York Times*'s Charles Mohr, AP correspondent Doug Cornell, and two other reporters the day before the speech.[45] Of greater significance, however, was Johnson's off-the-record meeting that day with columnist Walter Lippmann.[46] Both McGeorge Bundy and the president had lunched with Lippmann in mid-March, seeking to quiet his uneasiness, and they now saw the Johns Hopkins speech as an important opportunity to court him further. Thus the columnist was invited to the White House on the day before the address. In a memorandum to Johnson before the conference, McGeorge Bundy suggested that it would be

> perfectly proper to show the current draft of your speech to Walter Lippmann and get his opinion. A part of our purpose, after all, is to plug his guns, and he can tell us better than anyone to what degree we have done so.
>
> The only risk I see in this is that we want to be awfully careful that the language we finally use is not harder than what he sees, and for that reason it may be better to read to him from the speech and to slide gently past the words "unconditional discussions." While I recommend these words myself and believe that they put us in a strong, balanced position, there is no doubt that some commentators will think they are not so much a clarification as a softening of the position.[47]

Bundy's concern for perceptions of the "hardness" or "softness" of the administration's stand indicates his cognizance of the fine line they were walking: to be hard enough to reassure hawks that the United States would not shirk its responsibilities, and yet to be soft enough that doves knew of America's openness to and hope for a peaceful settlement. As Goldman indicated, the labels may confuse as well as classify: Lippmann, like substantial portions of the public at this stage, did not want to withdraw at any cost. At the same time, the commentator did not want further American personnel and financial aid committed to Vietnam; to Lippmann, a negotiated truce was the only tolerable solution.

Recognizing the complexity and command of the columnist's position, then, Bundy recommended that Johnson further explore Lippmann's views. In particular, the aide advised inquiries as to "why he is pushing so hard for the notion of a single Vietnam," for "if he is going to advise negotiations, it seems to me he ought to be telling us what he expects to get" from North Vietnam. Otherwise, the president might inquire whether negotiations are "his idea of a quiet way of giving it [Vietnam] to the Communists." Moreover, Bundy continued,

> you may also want to make it clear to Lippmann that when we say
> we are ready to talk, we do not at all mean that we are ready for a
> ceasefire. . . . Walter needs to understand this, and if he gets it
> straight from you, he is likely to be less objectionable about it.
> Under pressure he will admit that the Secretary of Defense is excel-
> lent, but he will still think him wrong. He has a useful tendency to
> think the President himself is right.

Unfortunately there is no way of knowing the extent to which Johnson slid "gently past the words 'unconditional discussions.'" Reedy
contended that the president, in his eagerness to persuade the columnist, never gave Lippmann a chance to talk and therefore never
found out whether he liked the speech or not; Johnson simply
assumed that since the columnist said nothing negative he must have
agreed. Lippmann's colleagues, however, paint a different picture;
both Hugh Sidey and Evans and Novak reported the journalist to be
well satisfied with the speech after his preview. Ronald Steel's
account reconciles the two versions, reporting that Lippmann had
listened to Johnson's "monologue" for more than an hour and then
met with Bundy for almost as long. It was the session with Bundy
which gave him hope that Johnson might announce not only unconditional discussions but also an unconditional cease-fire, contrary to
Bundy's memorandum.[48]

Johnson undertook the same sort of lobbying effort with senators,
conferring with Mike Mansfield and William Fulbright for ninety
minutes and with Gale McGee, Frank Church, and George
McGovern for half an hour. That members of the press were accorded
treatment similar to that given the congressional leaders is a sign of
the importance Johnson placed on their role as conveyors and interpreters of his remarks. It may also be indicative of the similarity he
perceived between the two groups—a perception that angered correspondents for what they saw as implications that they could be
maneuvered into performing as political partisans rather than as
"objective critics."

Revisions in the address continued as the date drew closer. At
Johnson's request, Valenti composed a passage about Johnson asking
himself, "every night before I turn out the lights to sleep," whether
he had done enough to bring peace to the world. The passage, withheld from the advance copy of the speech, was inserted only into the
teleprompter copy from which the president would read, presumably
to add a more spontaneous and heartfelt note to the address.[49]

Other problems still remained to be solved. State Department speech writers had continually deleted the specific reference to a billion dollar contribution to the development plan, complaining that "it was too specific and we didn't have a plan for using it."[50] Johnson, however, liked both the figure and his equally specific designation of Eugene Black to head the development team. Former president of the World Bank and a respected financial adviser, Black offered the hard-headed credentials that would, as Bundy suggested, "neutralize Fulbright" and other critics.[51] Called by Bundy on the very afternoon of the speech, Black protested that he simply did not have the time to undertake a new charge. But when Johnson got on the phone, the financier found that he could not refuse his president—especially an insistent president who promised him, as Valenti recollected, that "we'll give you a doctor and a nurse and a 707 but we need you now."[52] Valenti provided one final editing during which, according to his notes for the record, he "got it down to about 2700 words, but told the Pres it was only 2400 words," the length Johnson favored.

On the afternoon of the speech, the text was distributed to the White House press corps. In addition, McGeorge Bundy, Robert McNamara, and George Ball filmed capsule background statements on Vietnam to be televised as previews for the president's message; several correspondents, who found this to be a peculiar device for a presidential statement, christened these spots the "singing commercials."[53] In final preparation for this major address, Johnson informed Undersecretary of State George Ball that the White House, not the State Department, would release the reply to the seventeen nonaligned nations' appeal on Vietnam.[54]

On that Wednesday night of April 7, 1965, Lyndon Johnson faced more than a thousand faculty and students in Johns Hopkins University's Shriver Auditorium, an estimated sixty million television viewers throughout the country, and an international audience as well. He delivered, as several contemporary descriptions characterized it, a "carrot-and-stick" speech. The president opened on a note of international solidarity with a vague reference to America's "joining the seventeen nations" who sent their views to some two dozen countries.[55] His primary purpose, however, was to "review once again with my own people the views of the American Government" regarding Southeast Asia—not to issue a new policy, but to restate established goals. Those goals explained the current United States involvement in Vietnam: "We fight because we must fight if we are to live in a world where every country can shape its own destiny." The ultimate objectives were peace and freedom, but "the infirmities of man are such that force must often precede reason, and the waste of war, the works of peace."

The structure of the speech throughout reflects this progression from force to reason, war to peace, stick to carrot. First came the stick: North Vietnam, urged on by "the deepening shadow of Communist China," has "attacked the independent nation of South Viet-Nam. Its object is total conquest." Why should the United States care? Why, asked Johnson, are we in Vietnam? His answer was threefold. First, "we are there because we have a promise to keep," in the form of commitments made by "every American President" since 1954. Second, "we are also there to strengthen world order," reliant in part on the world's confidence in "the value of an American commitment and in the value of America's word." Without such confidence, only "increased unrest and instability, and even wider war," could result. Finally, "we are also there because there are great stakes in the balance. . . . The central lesson of our time is that the appetite of aggression is never satisfied"; repelling aggression "in Southeast Asia—as we did in Europe" is the only path to peace.[56]

The American people, Johnson continued, did not seek war, but they refused "to abandon this small and brave nation to its enemies, and to the terror that must follow," or to "withdraw, either openly or under the cloak of a meaningless agreement," as long as North Vietnam attacks the South. Thus when "attacks on South Viet-Nam were stepped up," the level of American response, including air attacks, increased. The response was both fitting and forced. Moreover, it was consistent with past American commitments: "This is not a change of purpose. It is a change in what we believe that purpose requires."[57]

In the meantime, Johnson asserted, "the only path for reasonable men is the path of peaceful settlement." To that end, "we remain ready," as we have stated "over and over again, fifty times and more," for "unconditional discussions."

At this point, Johnson's emphasis and imagery shifted to the carrot. The brutal, terrorist aggressors became "the people of North Viet-Nam," who "want what their neighbors also desire: food for their hunger; health for their bodies; a chance to learn; progress for their country; and an end to the bondage of material misery." Here Johnson outlined Southeast Asia's "cooperative effort for development," with its "billion dollar American investment." Open to all who would enter in a spirit of "peaceful cooperation," such a program could give the region all it could want: food, water, power, medicine, schools, and perhaps even peace.

"A dam built across a great river," "a rich harvest in a hungry land," and "the sight of healthy children in a classroom" are images of success, Johnson concluded; "the guns and the bombs, the rockets and the warships, are all symbols of human failure." It was the responsibility of "this generation of the world" to "prevail over the enemies within man, and over the natural enemies of all mankind."

To withstand aggression as commitments demanded, to be open for discussions without preconditions, and to begin a massive regional development plan that "would dwarf even our own TVA"— these three elements constituted "the Johns Hopkins doctrine," which Johnson articulated that April 7. Like a schoolmaster, Johnson instructed rather than exhorted. The history of American commitments, the wisdom of present retaliation, the promise of future peace—if America and the world simply understood the premises from which he operated, he firmly believed, then they could not help but be persuaded. Accordingly, he did not directly ask his audience for its support; it was simply expected. Nor did he label the regional development plan a "proposal"; it was "the first step" that these countries were expected to take. There is no indication, either in the speech or in the available White House files, that Johnson or anyone in his administration ever discussed the plan with anyone from Southeast Asia. It was an offer that, in Johnson's view, simply could not be refused.

Initial reports of reactions at home and abroad appeared to fulfill Bundy's early prediction that the Johns Hopkins address would be Johnson's "most important foreign policy speech." *Newsweek*'s account observed that "few U.S. foreign-policy declarations of recent years met with such an immediate and overwhelmingly favorable response. At home, the editorial reaction was little short of lyrical. . . . Abroad, the response to the speech was even more striking."[58] The *New York Times*'s previous editorial criticism turned into praise for "an American policy . . . in which the country can take pride," while the *Washington Post* admired Johnson's skillful brandishment of both the sword and the olive branch.[59] Columnist Joseph Alsop, who had felt that "overlong waiting" to explain his policy on Vietnam "had left the President in a position of weakness," termed the Johns Hopkins address "a great speech" that acquitted its speaker well.[60]

The mail pouring into the White House indicated that many of the American public's questions had been answered by the address. As a memorandum for the record reported, "President Johnson's speech at

Johns Hopkins brought a sharp reversal in the heavy flow of critical mail. Volume of mail on Vietnam slowed after the speech," from approximately 2,000 letters, 304 telegrams, and 208 postcards received in the four days before the speech to approximately 789 letters and 559 telegrams in the five days after delivery, down by almost half. Both letters and telegrams "shifted from 5 to 1 against the President to better than 4 to 1 in his favor."[61]

Reactions in Congress were predominantly supportive as well. Senator George Smathers of Florida liked "the glint of iron" alongside "the velvet in the speech," while Senators Church and McGovern, critics who had been invited to a preview on the day of the speech, praised Johnson's openness to negotiations and his emphasis on the "works of peace."[62] Church cancelled a Senate-floor assault on the president's foreign policy after hearing his address; McGovern had already cancelled a speech on Vietnam in deference to Johnson's presentation.[63] Senate majority leader Mike Mansfield, who had warned Johnson from the earliest days of his presidency against the dangers of American overcommitment to Southeast Asia, praised the speech as a "profoundly moving and constructive statement which reveals both the great strength of President Johnson's resolve and his deep concern for the welfare of all people."[64]

Yet even with these enthusiastic responses, the seeds of future dissent, to be nurtured by subsequent events, were apparent. Senators Morse and Gruening criticized Johnson's failure to recognize the conflict as a civil rather than an international war that bombing could not solve.[65] On the other side, Senate minority leader Everett Dirksen of Illinois, previously a strong supporter of Johnson's Vietnam policy, denounced the development proposal as an attempt to buy friendship and peace.[66] The glint of iron did not shine through sufficiently for the Republican; "is this," Dirksen cried, "another case of where the American trumpets sound retreat?"[67] Despite Johnson's efforts, the stick did not totally satisfy the hawks nor the carrot the doves.

More subtle signs of unrest could also be detected. On the day before the Johns Hopkins speech, the *New York Times* editorialized that "a major task for President Johnson" in his address

> is to explain to the American people and to the world the basic
> American contention that Vietnam is crucial to American security,
> to the freedom of all Southeast Asia, to small nations everywhere,
> and to the hopes of containing Communism in Asia and the Far
> East. It is important that he explain that the methods the United

States is employing to defend South Vietnam are the wisest and most effective. Some of the best authorities on Asia disagree on the point. So do some of the leading experts on world Communism.[68]

Yet the explanations of America's presence in Vietnam that Johnson then provided were to receive scant attention in the *New York Times's* front-page account of the speech.[69] Perhaps such justifications were considered "old hat" and thus not as newsworthy as Johnson's offer for unconditional discussions; perhaps they lacked the conflict basic to "news." Even the Southeast Asian development plan, newsworthy enough to gain part of the headline, received only a third of the column space devoted to the offer of unconditional discussions and the refusal to quit fighting. As a result, although the title of Johnson's address was "Peace Without Conquest," the *New York Times's* stress on the conflict between nations and the intrigue of possible discussions greatly muted the peaceful images. The *Times's* main account, written by one of the four correspondents who had attended the background session given by Johnson on the day of the speech, emphasized military concerns far more than did the speech itself, and the sidebars echoed this tone.

In addition to the *Times's* orientation toward "the stick," articles in both the *New York Times* and the *Washington Post* noted a disparity between recent administration declarations and the Johns Hopkins speech. Citing Johnson's offer of unconditional discussions, with his insistence that it was one made many times before, the *Times* story reported: "Government sources maintained, as did the President, that the offer to talk unconditionally was not 'a marked change in policy.' However, the emphasis had been on the futility of negotiations and there had been nothing like tonight's clear offer."[70]

The *Washington Post* devoted part of its front page to a news analysis headlined, "President's Use of 'Unconditional' in Speech Viewed as Significant."[71] While not calling Johnson and his staff liars, the articles nonetheless clearly cast doubt upon the strict reliability of the administration's version of past and present policy. The skepticism conveyed by this aspect of the *Times* and *Post* coverage was, perhaps, among those events that led to the first use of the term "credibility gap" in print within two months after the Johns Hopkins speech.

Other elements of dissatisfaction with Johnson's address among members of the media were more obvious. In his column on the speech, Walter Lippmann, whose approval Johnson had so courted and coveted, wrote that while the address did "in some measure correct some of the defects of the public relations of the Administration," it was nonetheless "certainly too little, perhaps because it is too late, to change the course of the war."[72] The opening paragraph of the column reflected his conference with Johnson as presaged in the memorandum from Bundy; for example, Lippmann cautioned that "there was no illusion that the Viet Cong and Hanoi would be willing to cease and desist, and it was no less evident that the President's offer of 'unconditional discussions' was not meant to bring about a cease fire." The failure to announce a cease-fire helps explain why Lippmann's reported support of the speech after his preview failed to appear in his column. The man who before Johns Hopkins had been puzzled as to "why the Administration persists in keeping its war aims uncertain" afterwards wondered why the administration bothered to articulate them now that it was too late. Within a month, Lippmann was warning that "the President is in grave trouble" on his Vietnam policy, and the sizable opposition was a fact "the Administration should put . . . in its pipe and smoke." Later, Lippmann would say more bluntly of Johnson: "He misled me."[73]

For his part, Johnson felt misled and betrayed by what he viewed as Lippmann's quicksand support. "I thought my speech in Baltimore would satisfy Lippmann," he said after the Johns Hopkins address. "I went over it with him, but I find out now about Mr. Lippmann and Martin Luther King and some others—old slow me just catches up with them, then they are gone ahead of me."[74] Bundy and other administration officials continued to encourage the columnist to accept the president's arguments, but Johnson's disillusionment with Lippmann soon turned to bitterness. Within a year staff members were preparing lengthy reports outlining the inconsistencies of Lippmann's views during his long career.[75]

At that moment, however, all of this bad news lay in the future. Lippmann's column was only a small annoyance amidst the general joy of stemming the tide of criticism and outlining constructive action for Southeast Asia. Lyndon Johnson was exultant over Vietnam that April night in 1965 when he made the Johns Hopkins speech. As Lady Bird recorded in her memoirs:

> I had the thrilling feeling that we have taken the initiative. We are beginning to really explain to the world about Vietnam, about what we can do, about the promise of this epoch in history—that we are on the move against the negation of war and communism. It was exciting. I felt as if the stalemate had had a firecracker put under it.[76]

Two years and many speeches after delivering his Johns Hopkins address, Lyndon Johnson would again face the camera to "speak . . . of peace in Vietnam and Southeast Asia." This time, however, he would also announce his decision not to seek reelection. The role of Lyndon Johnson's relationship with the press in that decision was foreshadowed during the evolution of the speech of April 7, 1965.

6

Growing Discontent,
1965–1966

Two weeks after Lyndon Johnson delivered his speech on Vietnam at Johns Hopkins University, Robert McNamara submitted a three-page memorandum arguing that "the North Vietnamese Government has had ample opportunity to negotiate a settlement with us," but had responded only with belligerence, terrorism, and further aggression.[1] Detailing Viet Cong and North Vietnamese attacks, along with the United States' lack of retaliation or, at most, "limited and fitting" responses, the secretary of defense rejected claims that a bombing pause was necessary to encourage North Vietnamese acceptance of the Johns Hopkins offer for discussions. Johnson and his administration had "been abundantly clear" in their willingness to open talks, McNamara argued; equally clear were the negative temper and meaning of North Vietnamese responses. McNamara thus believed that the bombing should be continued.

Speech writer Richard Goodwin, however, suggested an alternative reading of Hanoi's response to the Johns Hopkins offer for unconditional discussions.[2] Analyzing the speech broadcast from North Vietnam after Johnson's Baltimore address, Goodwin acknowledged that some of the points in that message were clearly unacceptable. At the same time, Goodwin posited, the response did not explicitly stipulate American acceptance of each point prior to opening talks. Perhaps they "were meant as a statement of ultimate objectives" and as a reassurance for the National Liberation Front, the speech writer suggested, not as preconditions designed to antagonize the United States. Such an interpretation would allow each side to discuss the other's position; "this does not mean we accept them [the points in Hanoi's message] as conditions or that we have changed our mind about the essentials of final settlement."

While Johnson instructed staff member Bill Moyers, with whom Goodwin worked, to see both Bundy and himself on the question, apparently nothing came of this alternative interpretation, for the White House Central Files Office noted that no other material related to that memorandum had been received by July 24, 1965. With no perceived response from Hanoi to the Johns Hopkins offer, the bombing continued.

Johnson's pursuit of any proposal on Vietnam in depth was sharply curtailed during this spring of 1965, for another part of the world commanded his attention. On April 24, 1965, fighting broke out in the conflict-ridden Dominican Republic and spread rapidly. Within four days, the American ambassador in Santo Domingo sent an urgent cable to the White House: the situation was "deteriorating rapidly. . . . Time has come to land the Marines. American lives are in danger. . . . If Washington wishes, they [American troops] can be landed for the purpose of protecting evacuation of American citizens. I recommend immediate landings."[3]

The president immediately dispatched several hundred marines, apprised the congressional leadership of his decision, and appeared on nationwide television to explain the need for the intervention. In his haste to address the country that evening, Johnson broke into primetime viewing before the networks could inform their audience that the programs were being interrupted for a message from the president. As Reedy mused, the television audience saw "Bonanza" dissolve into a Johnsonian tirade against trouble in some small island someplace.[4] Compounding the Keystone Cops flavor of the address, the president went on to deliver a speech flawed by hasty preparation and a teleprompter mistake that caused him to repeat one passage twice. Because Johnson seemed oblivious to these errors, recalled the AP's Frank Cormier, "I actually wondered for a horrified moment if the President's mind had snapped under the strain."[5]

Despite this lack of polish in his statement of April 28, initial reactions to the president's handling of the crisis were predominantly favorable. In its May 7 issue, for example, *Time* praised Johnson for acting "swiftly and with strength of purpose." Others, including *Newsweek*, preferred to withhold initial judgment, albeit with the acknowledgment that the president's decisions were made under trying circumstances. Yet some factions attacked the landing of American troops as a heavy-handed intervention in a civil conflict and a betrayal of Kennedy's achievements under Alliance for Progress. These critics, in particular the liberals, recalled the doubts about Johnson's lack of experience in foreign affairs which had been expressed since his first days in office. Now, they paired the Dominican Republic with Vietnam to cite the consequences of such presidential inexperience in the complicated ways of the diplomatic world.

Stung by these comments and concerned by further word from the ambassador that communist forces were infiltrating the disorganized rebel troops, Johnson faced the television cameras on April 30 for the second time in three days to again justify his actions. In this statement he coupled his initial argument that American lives were endangered with veiled references to "people trained outside the Dominican Republic [who] are seeking to gain control."[6] Four days later, still plagued by criticism, Johnson once again addressed the nation in a sharp, emotional defense of his decision to act against "a band of Communist conspirators."[7]

The president then called a Cabinet meeting, not for decision-making purposes but "to use . . . as a forum for release of appropriate statements" on both the Dominican Republic and Vietnam.[8] Johnson also spent hours in more direct contact with members of the press, trying to convince them of the wisdom of his actions. The twelve days after the outbreak of the crisis brought presidential conferences with twenty-nine correspondents in seventeen visits, and five walks around the South Lawn.[9] During these sessions, the ambassador's cable warning that "American lives are in danger" was transformed into "American blood will run in the streets"; Johnson also depicted the ambassador crouched beneath his desk with bullets flying past as he telephoned the president, and he portrayed rampaging Dominican soldiers beheading people at will. The correspondents found such accounts to be implausible. When the American embassy in Santo Domingo then released a list of fifty-four "Communists and Castroist" leaders among the rebels before Johnson could object, reporters protested that the list included known conservatives and young adolescents and that it was simply another weak attempt to justify the administration's overreaction. In the long run, the numbers game harmed Johnson far more than the embassy officials responsible for compiling the list.

In the aftermath of the Dominican Republic crisis, observers would debate the nature of Johnson's response: was it a valid interpretation of the ambassador's cable as a call to save Americans and prevent another Cuba, or was it a visceral reaction of jingoistic dimensions? Yet critics on both sides agreed that Johnson's subsequent justifications for the intervention, with wild stories and proliferating rationales, harmed him. As the president sought to convince the press and the public of the necessity of his actions, his flawed performances, emotionally developed defenses, and inconsistent reconstructions of events fostered an image of knee-jerk imperialism.

The negative interpretation appeared to be more prevalent among members of the media than among the public, however, for a Gallup poll taken in mid-May showed 76 percent approval of Johnson's sending troops into Santo Domingo. For its part, the administration took solace in the support of such figures as Arthur Krock and Scotty Reston, although the latter would soon be taken to task for "five assertions of 'fact'" that the government did not find to be factual.[10] The predominant attitude toward the media, however, was one of frustration, which led the White House to contemplate the development of a white paper "to make people aware of the damage done by irresponsible reporting in a time of crisis," using the "fragmentary accounts" and "obvious distortions" of the Dominican coverage as documentation.[11] While apparently no white paper was undertaken on the topic, the recommendation reflects the administration's sensitivity to the role of the media in foreign affairs.

The Dominican Republic intervention thus fueled further presidential image problems in the spring of 1965. The media's perceptions of Johnson's lack of restraint generalized into a view of Johnson as failing to grasp the intricacies of foreign affairs. Newsweek's May 31 article entitled "Lyndon Johnson's Time of Trial," for example, characterized the president as "touchy, bitter, and exasperated" about the complexities of foreign policy. These new tensions joined recurring problems as Johnson's relations with the press continued to grate. The president continued to make last-minute travel plans. He continued to lead the press around the south grounds, inundating them with talks as they strode through the Washington heat. He continued to use impromptu press conferences, despite increasingly pointed memoranda from his press secretary noting that while Johnson had held a few more conferences than his predecessor, all thirty-six of Kennedy's had been called with "adequate notice," compared with only eighteen of Johnson's forty-one.[12]

Certainly Johnson could not be accused of neglecting the press; he attended to the generation, dissemination, and assessment of the news regarding the White House. Following Cater's earlier suggestion, he convened a "news-producing Cabinet meeting" on several occasions throughout the spring to stimulate favorable coverage.[13] He assented to a post-cabinet news conference on the condition that reporters not mention the novelty of the forum, although the step backfired when Tom Wicker of the New York Times unknowingly violated that agreement born of presidential-press symbiosis. The already nervous White House regulars complained that "Tom is screwing us up with the President," but Johnson continued to stress "getting more play on what the Cabinet reports."[14]

Johnson then asked White House photographer Yoichi Okamoto to produce "a terrific picture each day for release," a request that Oka-moto challenged as unrealistic but that seemed only reasonable to the president of the United States.[15] The senator-cum-president also sought wider distribution of favorable editorials and columns by their insertion in the *Congressional Record*; one such effort, which included letters of appreciation to 111 friendly journalists, brought a fervent note of gratitude to the staff members responsible: "Wonderful thanks congratulations—Please thank all who helped you and please keep it up."[16] He strove to assist such favorites as Marianne Means by granting numerous interviews, inviting her to state affairs and to Camp David, encouraging the syndication of her column, and providing her with detailed information; as he once instructed Cater, "help her with any material you can give her on this subject—All Hearst papers are quite friendly as is she."[17]

In addition, the enthusiastic newsmaker invited the top brass of the Associated Press for an off-the-record luncheon to expose them to the presidential perspective on world news.[18] The president also assumed an aggressive stance regarding other media stalwarts: at Johnson's request, four aides were assigned to take "primary (but not exclusive) charge" of twenty-four columnists, plus NBC and CBS, which had both had half-hour news programs since 1963.[19] ABC, which would not expand its fifteen-minute news format for another year and a half, did not make the list of key commentators to be straightened out by the administration. Busby would warn that "we are unwisely neglectful of the non-name columnists and writers whose influence in Washington is nil, but whose influence and circulation off the Atlantic seaboard is substantial."[20] Yet while others on the staff agreed that life beyond the capital was important, the bellwether sheep of the press continued to be the focus of White House attention.

Yet most of the attention directed toward the media was defensive in nature. Jack Valenti provided refutations of reporters' criticisms for an article entitled "The President and the Press" and fulfilled a presidential request to underline unfavorable passages in a column in *Look*.[21] Bill Moyers chided Chuck Roberts for his *Newsweek* article on the president.[22] A twelve-page collection detailed editorial complaints about Kennedy's handling of news conferences.[23] Even when offering praise Johnson could not resist a jab about unfavorable coverage; in a letter to one reporter, for example, he intoned: "Unaccustomed as I am to being overwhelmed with applause for most of *Time* magazine accounts about me, I want to tell you how much I appreciated the fine article you did on my schooling."[24]

By the early summer of 1965, the administration was preoccupied with its "image crisis." Joining stories already in circulation were tales of the heavy work loads, excessively long hours, and abusive treatment endured by the Johnson staff; according to these accounts, the president's reported tendency to ridicule, deride, and haze his aides created problems in recruiting staff members. Johnson had in part anticipated this interpretation; when Marvin Watson told him that Charles Mohr of the *New York Times* wanted to do a story on the new staff members, the president's reluctance almost sighed through his handwritten response: "No good can come from it but I don't know how to avoid."[25]

In the wake of the derogatory articles that followed, Johnson's loyal assistants protested that the work load was part of the job, that his impatience with mistakes was a measure of a man's magnitude, that his anger was usually directed more at the situation than at a particular aide, and that at any rate he rarely got as upset as the accounts depicted. A former staff member rejected the *Newsweek* story which portrayed Johnson as greeting him with "Well, playboy, did you have a good time last night?"; according to him, "it never occurred. Moreover, in all the time I worked for President Johnson, I suffered but a single mild rebuke—much milder than the circumstances would have justified."[26] From his long-ago days as the assistant to Kleberg's congressional secretary, Gene Latimer wrote to assure Johnson that the view of him as cruel to his staff was unfair:

> When anyone discusses "alleged cruelty" to staff I hasten to set the record straight. I have yet to hear of another boss who would lend you his money, keep your accounts, pay your bills, trust you with his children, and generally supervise your well-being.
> Nor have I ever heard any other ex-employee say anything except that he loves you.[27]

As one aide later mused, "it was a master-servant relationship, but it did leave you with affection for your master." Almost two decades later Reedy would describe Johnson in more graphic terms: "He may have been a son of a bitch but he was a colossal son of a bitch."[28] The charges and countercharges about Johnson's treatment of his staff, reverberating from his first days in Washington, became fuel for the columnists now that he was in the White House.

No doubt Jack Valenti had these charges in mind as he addressed the Advertising Federation of America in Boston on June 28, 1965. "Thank the Good Lord," Valenti told his audience, that President Johnson had "extra glands . . . that give him energy that ordinary men simply don't have"; that Johnson was "a sensitive man, a cultivated

140

man, a warm-hearted man"; that he was "not fond of those who continually say yes to him."[29] Valenti confessed to his audience that "I sleep each night a little better, a little more confidently because Lyndon Johnson is my President. For I know he lives and thinks and works to make sure that for all Americans, and indeed the growing body of the free world, the morning shall always come."

Members of the press who had gathered cruelty-to-staff stories now hooted in derision at this almost euphoric paean to Lyndon Johnson, which was so inconsistent with their view of him. Both Valenti and the president puzzled that a man could not praise his employer; "perhaps I was a bit gaudy in my appraisal and approval," Valenti acknowledged, but to decry his speech as sycophantic was, the aide felt, excessive. After all, he contended, his passage on "sleeping better" had merely paralleled the preceding paragraph, in which he cited Winston Churchill's moving exhortation to the French during World War II, when the prime minister assured them that the free world would relieve them of their long night's duties: "'Sleep well, my Frenchmen, sleep well to gather strength for the morning, for the morning shall come.'"

Despite these protests, the more common reading of Valenti's speech found vivid expression in a classic Herblock editorial cartoon. Entitled "Happy Days on the Old Plantation," it depicted Johnson clutching a cat-o'-nine-tails as he walked away from his cringing, brutalized aides—including Jack Valenti. The lower caption read: "a sensitive man . . . a warm-hearted man . . . I sleep each night a little better, a little more confidently because Lyndon Johnson is my President." The cartoon did not go unnoticed; when the 1965 Medal of Freedom winners included Herb Block, Johnson complained: "Why should I go around honoring people who attack me?"[30]

The discrepancies between the administration's view of Johnson and the press's view of him compounded the media's disenchantment with his penchant for secrecy, his unorthodox approach to press conferences, and his resistance to prearranged travel plans. These grievances accumulated in the first half of 1965 until the term "credibility gap" finally made it into print. As with many phrases, the roots of the term are obscured, but Henry Trewhitt of the *Baltimore Sun* posits that the term first emerged in Saigon to describe the "Five O'Clock Follies," as the press briefings there were called. The phrase made it through the journalistic grapevine and was commonly used among White House correspondents for some time before it first hit the newspapers as the headline in the *New York Herald Tribune* of

May 23, 1965, over an article by David Wise.[31] Although it was not popularized publicly for another six months or so, the phrase signaled the growing acrimony that would come to characterize the relationship between Johnson and the media. Searching for a solution, the president replaced George Reedy as press secretary with Bill Moyers.

Reedy and the president had had, by Reedy's own account, a stormy relationship.[32] Press secretary and staff member from Johnson's Senate days, Reedy was intensely loyal to and protective of his boss; yet he disagreed with Johnson's view of press relations, and he contended that he was left uninformed on crucial matters. On one occasion, afraid that Reedy would learn of his plans and pressure him to release information, Johnson ordered the press secretary to spend the day fishing in the Chesapeake Bay.[33]

The gentle, hefty man with a mane of white hair was thus relieved of his press duties, by mutual agreement, to undergo a badly needed operation on his feet. The man who replaced him, Bill Moyers, was Reedy's antithesis in both appearance and personality. Intensely disliked by Reedy, but much admired by Johnson, the new press secretary was a Baptist minister and Texas journalist who combined youth, ambition, energy, and a love of politics to thrive as a member of Johnson's staff. The early months of 1965 saw a growing role for Moyers in the press operation, including primary responsibility for following up on columnists and a background meeting on the budget, which several newsmen praised as "first rate."[34]

Yet Moyers's accession to the press secretary's post on July 9, 1965, represented more than simply a change of personnel. In contrast to Reedy's increasingly peripheral position in the White House, Moyers assumed a central role of control. The "containment" advocates, ignored in Johnson's exultation in exposure after settling the railroad dispute in April of 1964, were once again being heard. Moyers, acting as interpreter, would see the press more; Johnson, stung by the criticism, would heed the advice of columnists Drew Pearson and William S. White: he allowed too much media access and, concommitantly, paid too much attention to news stories about himself.[35] As Pearson contended, one problem with reporters was that

these guys go out and blab. There is an old saying that intimacy breeds contempt. . . .

I have heard various newsmen who have seen the President talk privately not merely about what he said but about his mannerisms,

> his alleged Texas corn, his alleged determination to influence the press through these personal interviews. They consider him a little too eager, a little too friendly, a little too self-revealing.
>
> Most of these guys will not go out and write about what the President said because they recognize their seal of confidence. But they will go out and talk to their colleagues.

Sometimes those colleagues would incorporate the information in their columns, but in any event, the gossip fed derogatory perceptions of the president which could do nothing but harm his press coverage. An object lesson for Johnson, continued Pearson, could be found in Dwight D. Eisenhower's press relations. Although Ike was "the most do-nothing President we have had in years," his image remained high throughout his tenure in office, in part because his press secretary allowed only occasional access by reporters. Thus even though he was playing golf and bridge, the columnist observed, Eisenhower retained "the aura of mystery and importance" so essential for an appropriately presidential image.

Johnson's associates thus advised him to quit trying so hard to succeed in his relations with the media. As Evans and Novak concluded, in "trying to win the press, he was alienating the press";[36] perhaps the greater reserve that Pearson recommended would be beneficial.

But Lyndon Baines Johnson was not Dwight D. Eisenhower; a man who so thrived on people and politics could not withdraw from the press. The quintessential LBJ was irrepressible. In October of 1965, for example, Johnson entered Bethesda Naval Hospital for gallbladder surgery. Moyers briefed the correspondents, and "snowed them with details," as he reported to the president.[37] Some of those details, such as the color slides of the gallstone and gallbladder, struck the reporters as "guaranteed to upset the squeamish,"[38] but the endless flood of information, Moyers felt, would help settle the country's concern. The press secretary had urged Johnson to continue "letting us give the press everything possible in the way of information and doing everything reasonable to meet their mechanical needs and the bread and butter of their business."[39] On the latter issue, Moyers diplomatically explored the question that had given both his predecessor and the White House correspondents such fits:

> As for the details and the mechanics of press coverage, I know these must be irritating to you, Mr. President. They are to me. But they are 90% of the problem of press coverage. Because we gener-

ally do get fair treatment on straight news coverage of your activities, . . . it is to our interest to make that coverage possible.

Space, telephones, telexes, briefings, parking spaces—these are all as vital to that coverage as telephones and transportation are to the President. Advance notice of movement, lighting, advance texts— these are the little things that do improve your press relations. But they should not concern you; that is my lot to worry about and I always regret when you have to spend your energy and effort on them.

Even with all of Moyers's attention to "the details and the mechanics," however, Johnson himself added to the lore of his presidency when he raised his pajama top to, as *Time* sniffed, "let the whole world inspect the ugly twelve-inch seam in the flesh under his right rib cage"—a display of his scar duly captured by photographers and transmitted to the world by *Time*.[40]

Lyndon Johnson's difficulties with the press were exacerbated by growing foreign-affairs crises. The Dominican Republic intervention, occurring in the midst of a major drive for domestic legislation, aroused particular concern in light of American involvement in Vietnam. To have United States troops committed in two small countries halfway around the globe from each other sparked renewed debates as to the wisdom of Johnson's foreign policies. The administration sought comfort where it could; Valenti, for example, assured Johnson that "*Time* magazine is in thorough accord with your current foreign policy in the Dominican Republic and Viet Nam."[41] Yet the intervention elicited a wave of criticism, particularly among the liberals, and the attacks would have major repercussions. Senator J. William Fulbright, a friend of the president's and hitherto a reluctant critic of foreign policy in light of his support for the Great Society, bitterly challenged Johnson's course of action in the Dominican Republic as one based on misinformation. The tirade, coming without warning on the day after the Fulbrights had dined in the executive mansion, marked the breaking point in the relationship between the senator from Arkansas and the president; after that point, the senator felt free to lambast Johnson's policies in South Vietnam.

Fulbright did not stand alone; the teach-ins against the war gained popularity, with a national protest held in the capital in May and others scheduled from California to Maine. These early protests were brought sharply home to Johnson in June of 1965 when the White

House Festival of the Arts, first suggested by Eric Goldman as a springtime salute to culture, turned into a forum of opinion on foreign policy. In what Mooney terms a "tragically hilarious account," Goldman details how poet Robert Lowell's withdrawal from the festival because of his "dismay and distrust" at "the strangeness of the Administration's recent actions" snowballed when the news hit the front page of the *New York Times*.[42] Once the story broke, other writers and artists protested. Mrs. Johnson and her aides then sought to exclude anti-Vietnam representatives and to eliminate controversial readings, and Johnson himself threatened to cancel the entire affair.

The festival did go on, even with noticeably absent artists, occasionally strained presentations, an editor chastising those who attended as "turncoats," and an angry president. The *New York Times* praised the affair, stressing that "by tolerating dissent within its own precincts, the White House raised its own and the nation's stature. For here was proof that democracy could practice what it preached in its most distinguished citadel."[43] Despite such praise for open-mindedness, the episode left Johnson, as his wife described him, "dour and grim."[44] According to Goldman, "within earshot of the press LBJ declared, 'Some of them insult me by staying away and some of them insult me by coming.' Privately he added, 'Don't they know I'm the only President they've got and a war is on?'"[45]

A war was indeed on, and rapidly escalating. In April, just before the Johns Hopkins speech, Johnson had approved the troop increase and authorized the marines to take offensive action when necessary. May 1965 had brought a five-day bombing pause; as the president told Ambassador Taylor,

> my purpose in this plan is to begin to clear a path either toward restoration of peace or toward increased military action, depending upon the reaction of the Communists. We have amply demonstrated our determination and our commitment in the last two months, and I now wish to gain some flexibility.[46]

Yet the flexibility that Johnson sought was constrained both by the reaction of the communists and by his own determination and commitment. In the weeks following the bombing pause, the Viet Cong launched a heavy and steadily accelerating summer offensive. The massive losses sustained by the ARVN were joined by increased political instability when yet another coup toppled yet another South Vietnamese government on June 12. The American military command and the Joint Chiefs of Staff pointed to the chaos as proof of the need for the more major involvement that they had advocated all along, even though they knew their proposals would meet with civilian opposition. When Westmoreland pressed for assurances of flexibility in the assignment of troops, for example, Admiral Ulysses S. Grant Sharp advised that the general probably did have the authority to commit them as he proposed. At the same time, cautioned the commander in chief of the Pacific, "I'm sure you realize that there would be grave political implications involved if sizable U.S. forces are committed for the first time and suffer a defeat."[47] The question of committing American troops was sensitive enough without a defeat complicating the issue.

Johnson was still reluctant to move in major ground forces, but the summer offensive forced investigation of the implications of increased military action. He sought advice from Attorney General Nicholas Katzenbach as to "whether further Congressional approval is necessary or desirable in connection with proposed deployment and use of troops in South Vietnam"; Katzenbach's seven-page memorandum concluded that it was not, and a subsequent memorandum of law reiterated the president's authority to commit American troops to combat.[48] The query indicates the degree of pressure Johnson felt, for while he had long maintained that Truman's major mistake in Korea was the failure to get congressional approval, he was now returning for support to the Gulf of Tonkin resolution passed almost a year before.

Yet Johnson did not want to open the proverbial can of worms with Congress at precisely the time that key components of his Great Society legislation reached a critical stage on Capitol Hill. Medicare, civil rights, education, and voting rights legislation were among the abundance of bills picking their way through the intricate politics of Congress. As Larry Berman details, Johnson feared that his accession to the pressures from the military and a request for the legislators' support on Vietnam would have stirred resistance from liberal factions, which would then withdraw vital support of the Great Society proposals.[49] On the other hand, the Viet Cong's summer offensive, which succeeded in further routs of South Vietnamese troops, would alienate crucial conservative legislators if allowed to continue without a response. Johnson himself would have difficulty doing nothing, given his view of the costs of appeasing aggressors.

Finally, on July 26, 1965, Johnson accelerated the limited war by taking a major step which he felt could satisfy the conflicting forces: he approved the use of American ground forces in battle, separately or in conjunction with South Vietnamese troops, as Westmoreland saw fit. While it did not include the forty-four battalions for which the military had been pressing since early June, the measure did allow the first United States involvement in major ground combat action in Vietnam; it also granted Westmoreland a much freer hand in conducting the war.

These decisions were undertaken with an absolute minimum of public announcement, as befitted Johnson's careful balancing of a limited war. White House assessments of general public opinion during June indicated some unrest about policies regarding Southeast Asia, but for the most part it took the form of vague questioning. James L. Greenfield, the assistant secretary of state for public affairs, concluded that

> extensive press discussion of the increasing U.S. military role in South Vietnam shows widespread acceptance of current U.S. policy; at the same time, many editors ask for fuller information about the role of U.S. forces there, and for fuller discussion of this role by Congress and the public.[50]

Greenfield assumed in this memorandum that "American opinion" was synonymous with the opinions of editors and the press, but he conveyed no sense of urgency to provide fuller discussion and information.

In Saigon, Ambassador Taylor found correspondents to be more vigorous in their inquiries; questions about the possibility of American troops serving under Vietnamese command had intensified with the arrival of Australian troops. Taylor's response was to cable Rusk that it would be "highly desirable to undertake long-delayed backgrounder on command relationship in the next few days," for it was a subject "which could create difficulties in U.S. public opinion and which is drawing increased interest from correspondents here."[51]

The press office at the White House faced similar cross-examination by correspondents as word leaked out about the troop increase and change of mission authorized on April 1. The *New York Times*'s editorial for June 9 charged that "a program of weapons supply, training, and combat advice to South Vietnamese, initiated by Presidents Eisenhower and Kennedy, has now been transformed by President Johnson into an American war against Asians." Yet the White House simply issued a statement repeating that "there has been no change in the mission of United States ground combat units in Vietnam in recent days or weeks."[52]

The statement did not quiet the discontent to be found on Capitol Hill, where one representative friendly to the administration called to report "widened unrest among the Congressmen about the situation in Vietnam." Wayne Morse of course shared that discontent, and in June he tried a new approach to the issue by outlining a six-page assessment of American policies in Vietnam.[53] The senator based his analysis on the "essential" that the United States' foreign policies "should command widespread support and respect throughout the world and throughout the United States; this is not presently the case." Morse then stressed the consequences in the absence of this essential:

> It would be a very serious mistake to think the American people would support a stalemated ground war in Vietnam for a period long enough to force the Communists into negotiating. They refused to support that kind of war in Korea. It became a choice between going all out to win, or ending it on almost any terms.

Morse then suggested a one-month bombing pause coupled with an appeal by the United States to the United Nations. McGeorge Bundy was clearly impressed by this "tightly reasoned and complex" memorandum, telling the president that "if we answer it point by point at this stage, we will be almost sure to trip over ourselves as we make tactical decisions in the coming months." As a consequence, he recommended sending a "soft answer" which thanked the senator for his "thoughtful memorandum"; he did not recommend that any of Morse's suggestions be adopted.

A bombing pause was in fact considered during June, in part because as Bundy noted it would "meet one persistent demand of our domestic critics and waverers"; yet the adviser predicted that any halt would also "arouse strong criticism among domestic hardliners—particularly among Republicans who are looking for a way to make capital out of any signs of our softness in Vietnam."[54] In addition, Bundy warned, "if U.S. forces were to get hurt during a pause, we would be giving a dangerous opening for Mel Laird; people just would not understand it." Johnson still faced pressure from both hawks and doves.

Thus, in addition to military concerns about allowing Hanoi to regroup and about losing South Vietnamese confidence, domestic political concerns about waverers and hardliners were a key reason for the consideration and rejection of a bombing pause in June. Similar consideration was given to the provision of a public statement on American expansion in Southeast Asia. The National Security Council files contain an "Outline of Public Justification for Increased Military Support in Vietnam," in the face of what the author termed "legitimate public concern over this unhappy situation."[55] The document, whose authorship is uncertain, then refuted the common argument that Vietnam constituted an internal dispute by contending that "whatever elements of a civil war exist in SVN today are heavily outweighed by the attempt by NVN to overthrow the established government of SVN." Given that aggression, "the build-up of U.S. military forces is designed to accomplish two major objectives: (a) to choke off the flow of men and arms from NVN, . . . [and] (b) to demonstrate to the VC that they cannot achieve victory in the South." At this stage, the administration still sought to dissuade the North Vietnamese and Viet Cong from continued violent action; the American objective was not yet defined as achieving victory over the enemy.

This outline was joined by a memorandum from William Bundy in which he elaborated on a draft for a presidential message. Bundy echoed Johnson's sentiments exactly when he stated that "we want to depict the present decision not as a new and separate escalation decision by the U.S., but as the essential response to increased VC strength and DRV involvement"; at the same time, the speech must refute allegations that the North Vietnamese buildup occurred "only *after* our bombing of the North."[56] A second sensitive issue to be addressed was the state of the South Vietnamese army; while the ARVN was a weak and disorganized entity, Bundy noted, the administration had to combat the image of "defection in 'masses' depicted by Walter Lippmann." Once again the columnist figured in plans for a presidential statement.

Urging a less formal approach than these two outlines, Jack Valenti recommended that Johnson stage another nationally televised "Conversation with the President."[57] He acknowledged that "Vietnam is an ugly problem, but," the aide contended, "the President can handle this without trouble." Besides, the timing was perfect for an exploration of his "miracle session" of Congress, with its abundant domestic legislation. In addition, Valenti suggested, the ease with which Johnson would handle the questions would serve to "counter press spite about the President being querulous and prickly; showing him relaxed, confident, and human is the best antidote."

Yet despite these proposals and preparations, the televised appearance met the same fate as the bombing halt, for much the same reason: each would provide a public target for criticism. Johnson was convinced that his actions were consistent with American goals in Vietnam; he was also convinced that a public speech could only engender opposition. He did encourage Cater's proposal to develop "a distinguished group outside government to speak out in support of the Administration against both the appeasers and those who would take rash risks," and he approved of CBS's Frank Stanton as a member of that committee;[58] but he did not want to make a statement on the war himself.

Even with the greater military support provided by the president's decision of June 26, the situation in Vietnam continued to deteriorate rapidly as the summer offensive forced the ARVN to relinquish control of more and more land. Westmoreland's request for further troop deployments became increasingly pointed as his prognosis for South Vietnamese success grew increasingly pessimistic. Johnson did not want to lose Vietnam nor to place undue burdens on the American military there, but he could not undertake that final step toward full commitment without an intensive review of his options. As a consequence, McNamara once again visited the American mission in Vietnam, and Johnson once again huddled with his advisers. Throughout the third week of July, they debated the ramifications of the three courses of action that McNamara presented: to "cut our losses and withdraw," to "continue at about the present level," or to "expand promptly and substantially the U.S. military pressure" and presence.[59]

By the end of these concentrated sessions, Johnson had settled for the third option, which McNamara had recommended as "the course involving the best odds of the best outcome with the most acceptable cost to the United States." To put that course of action into effect, the president authorized the troop level to rise from 75,000 to 175,000 by October; he rejected the enclave strategy in favor of the more aggressive search-and-destroy policy; and he agreed to accelerate the bombing campaign against the North. Essentially, the administration abandoned the hope that American soldiers could simply reinforce the South Vietnamese, and the Americans took over the war.

These July days held more than military decisions, however, for the political aspects had to be addressed. Bundy had warned Johnson before the July sessions that "it is increasingly urgent that we get ahead with planning for public support," including the distinguished Citizens' Committee that Cater had suggested.[60] Dean Rusk voiced a similar admonition at the meeting of July 21, when he suggested that acceptance of McNamara's third option would make the rapid development of "a scenario for Congressional and public actions" desirable.[61] In fact, attention to public opinion permeated the discussions, as three of the six items on an agenda for the 2:30 meeting on July 22 indicates:

How big a change in policy is this and how do we explain it—in political and military terms? . . .

Is this policy justified in terms of Vietnam, Asia or U.S. national interest—or all three? . . .

What are our war aims? What is the answer to Walter Lippmann's question on this point?[62]

The administration still longed to silence Walter Lippmann.

Johnson agreed that public opinion was important; the primary question was how to best handle it. Should he declare a state of national emergency, call up the reserves, appear before Congress to request special appropriations, and make an all-out public appeal? While engendering a flood of patriotic support for war appealed to the president, such a stance would be costly, for it could introduce the conflict as a major issue before Congress, threaten both his domestic legislation and his public support, and risk a confrontation with China or Russia. The price of an aggressive approach seemed much too high. "I think we can get our people to support us," Johnson ventured, "without having to be too provocative and warlike."[63]

Once again, then, Johnson decided that public knowledge of his decisions was best broached left-handedly. He accepted Bundy's argument that he should deliver a complete message on the situation rather than "dribble out bits and pieces of this to the press or to publishers,"[64] but he insisted that the announcement need be neither exclusive nor in prime time. He thus scheduled its delivery for the beginning of a press conference starting at noon on Wednesday, July 28; although nationally televised, the format and the more limited weekday audience aided the aura of a low-key presentation. In addition, the news about troop deployments merely led the way for announcements that NBC's John Chancellor would now head the Voice of America and that longtime friend and attorney Abe Fortas was Johnson's choice for a Supreme Court justice.[65] Through timing and context, the president implied that his statement on Vietnam was not a major one.

Johnson had been grim and preoccupied as he wrestled with the problem of Vietnam; now, the decision reached, he seemed energized. Anticipating problems regarding foreign affairs and equally anticipating their solutions, the president grinned to an aide: "I'm like a jackrabbit hunkered up in a storm."[66] As Lady Bird observed, he had already practiced scheduling press conferences "as a countermove, a chess play, to Senator Fulbright's speech about Vietnam" and other critical events;[67] now he moved to solidify his position, primarily through personal contacts and behind-the-scenes direction. He ordered dissemination of his news conference in booklet form, under the title, "Toward Peace with Honor"; this was soon joined by a tract answering the question, "Why Vietnam?"[68] After the July 28 announcement he held an off-the-record meeting with Fulbright, a rare step in light of the senator's pungent and personal opposition.[69] He responded to Mansfield's misgivings by asking McNamara if a group of Democratic senators might be organized to drum up support, and he told Cater to "go full steam hurry!" on the citizens' committee to support the administration's position on Vietnam.[70] He charged ahead with the Asian Development Bank, which would form the financial cornerstone of the Mekong River development project, meeting with Eugene Black numerous times throughout the year and on one occasion sending the banker to chat with Fulbright.[71]

Yet even this flurry of activity could not still the growing misgivings. For example, the escalation of the war brought an escalation in both reportorial problems and protests as well. As American involvement increased, so too did journalists' complaints that officials in South Vietnam were not allowing them to "cover this war as they have covered past wars, governed by the yardstick of genuine security censorship, administered by the military which the public trust in these war situations."[72] In return, American officials in Vietnam complained that most of the correspondents "are strictly third class . . . [and] cover the war from the bars in Saigon," and further, that "a number of young wire service and network correspondents there are thoroughly sour and poisonous in their reporting."[73] These mutual perceptions of mistrust and unprofessionalism exacerbated one another; as a result, one aide concluded, "communication and sympathy between the press and the military is nil."[74]

The White House followed the results of this lack of sympathy among correspondents at home and abroad. McPherson reported that a Viet Cong representative brandished copies of Lippmann's columns as evidence that the war lacked widespread support in America, while Bundy announced that columnist Joseph Kraft constituted "an important source of infection" about the Viet Cong's role in negotiations, so he intended to "give him a dose of antibiotics."[75] Not all staff efforts to counsel the press met with Johnson's approval; when Cater summarized the grievances of Joe Alsop, "who, as usual, was content to let me do all the listening," the president demanded, "Why see him?"[76] Johnson preferred such positive and visible actions as leaking to the press a supportive letter from the wife of a soldier in Vietnam.[77]

While the print media received the predominant share of White

152

House attention, an incident on August 5, 1965, reaffirmed the necessity of attending to the broadcast media as well. On that date, the CBS evening news transmitted a report that would anger the White House, shock viewers, and demonstrate both the power and the impotence of a television war: American viewers watched their marines using cigarette lighters to set fire to a Vietnamese village. Morley Safer's commentary failed to inform the audience that this was the conclusion of an extended and vicious guerrilla battle resulting in numerous American casualties; as a consequence, the report portrayed the action as a flippant and wanton destruction of civilian lives by marines and their trivial Western technology. The story also set a tone that other correspondents would quickly echo.

Reports on the nightly newscasts soon extended to special documentaries.[78] As the war escalated, the news coverage grew, and so too did protests against the expanded American role in Vietnam. On occasion, Johnson met these with humor; for example, he greeted the White House Conference on Education by welcoming participants to "the first White House teach-in."[79] As summer turned to fall and college campuses once again teemed with activity, however, demonstrations increased and his sense of humor diminished. Protestors challenged the first family when they flew to New York to sign the immigration bill and greet the pope; two Reed College students who had been selected as Presidential Scholars circulated a petition attacking Johnson's Vietnam policy; and staff members warned of the potential for serious repercussions from the demonstrations.[80]

Johnson's supporters, however, encouraged him "not to worry about the anti-Vietnam demonstrations. I think," concluded E. Palmer Hoyt of the *Denver Post*, that they were "a big flop in the overall basis."[81] Douglass Cater offered further encouragement to the president, observing "an increasing frustration over press irresponsibility in publicizing prospective Vietnam negotiation maneuvers."[82] The president might even want, suggested the former journalist, "to propose a voluntary moratorium on publicity about peace maneuvers" to combat such irresponsibility.

While the president may well have been cnamored of Cater's suggestion, the proposal was unrealistic. So too was Hoyt's admonition to ignore the protestors. As more Viet Cong and North Vietnamese poured into the South, even greater deployments of American troops were authorized, and the already vociferous critics grew louder and more numerous. These protests encouraged reexamination of a suggestion offered by McNamara during the July deliberations: to authorize a prolonged pause in the air attacks against North Vietnam, in order to dramatically publicize the administration's efforts for peace, to allow Hanoi to open negotiations, and to prepare the way for the further troop increases that might be needed. As the defense secretary submitted at the end of November, first, "we must lay a foundation in the minds of the American public and in world opinion for [the potential for] such an enlarged phase of the war and second, we should give NVN a face-saving chance to stop the aggression." While Rusk assumed that no positive response would be forthcoming from Hanoi, he acknowledged the importance of the pause as a way to prepare public opinion for possible escalation. In a cable to Lodge at the embassy in Saigon, he asserted that "the prospect of large-scale reinforcement in men and defense budget increases of some twenty billions for the next eighteen month period requires solid preparation of the American public. A crucial element will be clear demonstration that we have explored fully every alternative but that aggressor has left us no choice."[83]

Johnson thus ordered the Christmas bombing pause to be extended. Even if the pause did not bring peace, it would help calm the cacaphony of voices crying for a show of good faith by the administration and prepare them for what might lie ahead.

The bombing pause and the new year provided a natural time for reassessment. An English journalist, evaluating the president's prospects in 1966, contended that "as his third year of office began, there seemed every reason to suppose, always granted that a way out of the Vietnam involvement could be found, that the world would increasingly find Lyndon Johnson a healing influence."[84] Yet Johnson feared that he would find no way out of the involvement, and the ramifications of being caught in that morass troubled him. At one point in January he turned grimly to his wife and sighed, "we've lost the steel fight; we may lose the war [as well]."[85]

Johnson had not yet ordered resumption of the attacks on North Vietnam when he stepped to the podium to deliver his State of the Union address for 1966, the first of his presidency to emphasize foreign affairs over domestic concerns.[86] Citing three hundred private efforts for peace in the previous year alone, as well as the bombing halt and the renewed efforts to open talks, Johnson reported that "so far, we have received no response to prove either success or failure." The United States would continue to seek a peaceful settlement, the president stated; but this action would not include "abandoning South Vietnam to its attackers and to certain conquest," for "a just nation cannot leave to the cruelties of its enemies a people who have

154

staked their lives and independence on America's solemn pledge—a pledge which has grown through the commitments of three American Presidents."

Yet Johnson's justifications did not engender a groundswell of approval on that night of January 12. "The audience was cold and lethargic," the first lady worried; "I watched in vain for approval from old friends." Aching with the sense of separation from the forum in which her husband had excelled, she speculated, "maybe we are in a trough of a wave; erosion and frustrations have set in and now is the time for just dogged toughness."[87]

Johnson would need a healthy dose of that dogged toughness in 1966, for the war in Vietnam proved to be a Gordian knot. When the bombing pause stretched to thirty-seven days and still produced no hope for the opening of discussions, the air raids against North Vietnam resumed on January 31. The ground war provided little encouragement either. Unaccustomed to guerrilla warfare, the American troops broadcast their movements with massive preparations, took the same villages several times over as the "front line" ceaselessly undulated, and grew frustrated in the face of an evasive enemy that could select battle sites of its own choosing. As the North Vietnamese funneled more troops and equipment to the South, Westmoreland requested further deployments, which in turn were met with increased commitments from Hanoi and the Viet Cong. The quick and decisive end to the war with which the military had justified the July 1965 troop increases seemed as elusive as ever.

Even more elusive was a consensus in press, public, Congress, and the military that Johnson's chosen course on the war was the correct one. Members within each key audience displayed diametrically opposed and deeply held views on Vietnam. Leslie Gelb and Richard Betts's description of the resulting pressures would strike a responsive chord in Johnson's heart: the various groups "tried to keep the President's feet to the fire and had several other pots boiling for him no matter which way he jumped." Mulling over a conflict that seemed too much for some, not enough for others, and simply bewildering to most, the president worried, "are we getting it across to the world?"[88] The answer from many quarters was negative. *Time*, for example, was a magazine whose editors were so supportive of Johnson's war policies that correspondents' dismal accounts from Vietnam were transformed into glowing reports of progress; nonetheless, it complained that

> thus far, pacifist demonstrators, antiwar columnists, and dissident Democratic Congressmen have made their case far more per-

suasively and specifically than has the Administration. In large part, this is due to Johnson's reluctance to spell out the potential costs and dangers of the war. . . . If the President is to retain the nation's considerable support for the war, some such acknowledgment may well prove necessary.[89]

Like Reston's confusion over the administration's silence in the face of "the babble of voices" following Pleiku, *Time* grew impatient for Johnson to beat the drums and call forth a wartime spirit. For his part, Reston still did not doubt the president's sincerity in seeking "peace and freedom and a negotiated settlement in Vietnam," but his doubts about Johnson's policies grew ever more vociferous. The columnist contended that while American military efforts could probably vanquish from the South the North Vietnamese and Viet Cong, "it is highly unlikely that this will produce either domestic order in Saigon or an acquiescent Communist order in Hanoi and Peking." Moreover, he questioned whether this would justify the loss of lives. Johnson's mistake, according to Reston, lay in "applying the do or die sentiments of the Alamo (which, after all, was not a glorious success) to one of Walt W. Rostow's latest theories."[90] Like Walter Lippmann, Scotty Reston was no longer in Johnson's pocket.

Nor were the dissident Democratic congressmen of *Time's* account in Johnson's pocket, as they heightened the pressure for White House justifications. At the end of January, Fulbright opened hearings before the Senate Foreign Relations Committee which were nationally televised. Putting the administration's Vietnam policy on trial, Fulbright sought to take his protestations to the public. The move marked the rising dissent among members of Congress, as the peace bloc which began with Morse and Gruening swelled to include such senators as Vance Hartke of Indiana, an old protégé of the president's. The hearings also brought the first public breach between Johnson and Bobby Kennedy, when the senator from New York suggested that a new coalition government that included the Viet Cong be established in South Vietnam—a recommendation Hubert Humphrey compared to "putting foxes in the hen house."

Angry as Johnson was at what he viewed as gratuitous and unpatriotic dissent, he was perhaps cut most deeply by the criticisms of his old friends and colleagues on the Hill. In his memoirs the president noted that Fulbright and Morse "gave their advice and consent to SEATO" when the treaty came before the Senate in 1955. "I have little understanding," he scolded, "for those who talk and vote one way, and after having given our nation's pledge, act another; for those who stand firm when the sun is shining, but run for cover when a storm breaks." While mutual friends undertook several quiet efforts to effect a reconciliation between Johnson and Fulbright, neither side could be appeased.[91]

Determined to uphold America's pledge even in a storm, the president sent Rusk and Taylor to testify before the Senate panel, armed with a three-quarter-inch-thick collection of materials on the Gulf of Tonkin debates which included Fulbright's remarks as floor manager for the resolution.[92] Johnson also sought to divert attention from the hearings with his own actions; confident that major news coverage would follow the chief executive, he flew to Honolulu for a conference with South Vietnamese leaders and General Westmoreland. To underscore the theme of economic development for Southeast Asia, so fervently articulated in the Johns Hopkins address, Orville Freeman and John Gardner accompanied the president in their capacities as secretary of agriculture and secretary of health, education, and welfare. Their presence, like the billion dollar plan of the Johns Hopkins speech, not only signified a field of central concern to Johnson, but also functioned as an implicit public appeal to direct attention to peace in the face of growing discontent over conflict.

Even with these flourishes, the trip was characterized as a major blunder by critical observers. Hastily conceived and haphazardly organized, Johnson's efforts to emphasize economic development and allied support in Southeast Asia were overshadowed by stories criticizing the conference as a transparently obvious strategem to steal headlines from the Senate proceedings.

In a limited sense, the Fulbright hearings were also unsuccessful, for the move to rescind the Gulf of Tonkin resolution was defeated by 92 to 5; the senator's work on its behalf just a year-and-a-half before undoubtedly hurt these efforts. Yet the 1966 hearings helped to legitimize criticism of Johnson's war policies; they publicized the resentment of those senators who saw Johnson use earlier congressional support to justify pursuits they now strongly opposed, and they sharpened the dichotomy between those who demanded an immediate reduction of American involvement in Vietnam and those who sought immediate victories. While Fulbright noted defensively that the committee did not create the divisiveness nor could it control the extent of the news coverage, the decision to admit television cameras undoubtedly heightened the effects of the hearings.[93]

Presidential trips alone could not counter these more far-reaching results of the televised hearings, as several staff members recognized. The challenge called for a more direct response. George Reedy, back in the White House following his surgery, echoed Greenfield's contentions after Pleiku when he suggested that the administration had "been arguing the Vietnamese War at the wrong level. We have been assuming that the American people know a lot of things that they simply don't know and have presented some arguments which are really too sophisticated for the audience."[94] The administration's response to the unrest should not be complex, Reedy contended; it should instead address "some rather simple questions which can be answered easily," such as "how we had gotten into Viet Nam in the first place." The aide further recommended that a key for the success of such efforts lay in reaching influential editors, for explaining the fundamentals of United States policy to these important gatekeepers of information and opinion was an essential step which had not thus far been accomplished.

In response to the discontent crystallized by the Senate hearings, then, the White House accelerated its efforts to reach the press and the public with its message. Bundy and Humphrey, for example, were dispatched to defend the president on "Meet the Press"—a special assignment for the national security adviser, who after five years in the position had submitted his resignation to become the president of the Ford Foundation as of February 28. Johnson then asked Rusk to lunch with publisher John Knight, who was "whacking us each day on Vietnam," to help him see the wisdom of administration policy.[95] McPherson tried to stimulate favorable coverage by marshalling a committee of legal experts to defend "The Lawfulness of the United States Presence and Activities in Vietnam" against well-publicized claims of illegality by another group of lawyers, but the effort failed when the major media ignored the resulting brief. "It is hard," McPherson complained, "to generate interest in a 'pro' position" regarding the war.[96]

These measures reflected Johnson's growing absorption in the war. Vietnam constituted "about two-thirds of what we talk about these days," Mrs. Johnson observed in February.[97] Slowly, grimly, Johnson turned from the revels of power and the visions of domestic richness to the demands of being a wartime president, demands made all the more distressing by the constraints of a limited war. His popularity falling as distress over the lack of progress in Vietnam spread, Johnson "hunkered up" against the hailstorm and turned the White House machinery to defending his policies on Vietnam. As spring reached the Potomac and talk turned to the upcoming congressional races, the president seemed ready to abandon his cautious stance in favor of a khaki election, complete with an energetic, old-fashioned patriotic appeal on behalf of those boys in Vietnam.

158

Adding to the president's new aggressiveness in handling the public presentation of the war was the appointment in mid-April of Robert Kintner as a special assistant and secretary to the Cabinet. Under those ambiguous titles Kintner, the former president of NBC, served as an administrative coordinator of sorts and as a general adviser and liaison for press relations. A strong advocate of what he called "missionary work" among outspoken and influential critics of the president, including Reston, Kraft, and Evans and Novak, the new staff member argued that "if you spend time with people who are opposed to your policies without being too rough on them, you can over a period of time make some—but not all—changes in their attitude."[98]

Kintner launched with gusto into his campaign to convert the disbelievers. He chastised his former network for its snide tone regarding the president and for its airing of sensational stories rather than political news on Vietnam; all it took, he told Johnson, was "just a conversation between the head of NBC News and the person who gave him his job."[99] He urged media outlets to carry the story of Viet Cong guerrillas murdering women and children "just as they carried pictures of the shooting of the surrendering 'struggler' by a South Vietnamese officer," and he talked with Reston to persuade him to produce a column "rather friendly to the Administration."[100] When a luncheon discussion with Joseph Alsop revealed the columnist's concern that Johnson was angry with him, the aide provided the attention and reassurance necessary for Alsop to produce "extremely pro-Administration [columns] on foreign policy"; it was an episode that would be repeated in the future.[101] Kintner even convinced Johnson to see Rowland Evans off the record, acknowledging that the writer was "pugnacious, quite unfriendly, extremely talkative in private conversation, [and] has given the President, and certain members of the President's staff, an unfair beating"; still, Kintner argued, he was an effective, influential columnist who was widely read, especially in Washington and New York.[102] The meeting with the president, Kintner ventured, "could alter, at least temporarily, his attitude," so Johnson agreed to meet with him.

What Kintner termed his "missionary work" on behalf of the administration's Vietnam policies was not always successful, however. Shortly after coming to the White House, the staff member discovered that Johnson was angry with Katherine Graham, publisher of the *Washington Post* and *Newsweek*, and had excluded her from state functions for almost eighteen months. Eager to bring about a reconciliation, Kintner and Moyers visited Graham to tell her what Graham termed an "extraordinary story": that Johnson

> thought I had "called in my editors and told them that he was trying to buy me with dinners and that they shouldn't pay any attention to this."
>
> So I was absolutely baffled because I wouldn't "call in my editors." I mean, it isn't the way one operates, nor would I have thought anybody could buy anybody with dinners.[103]

At Kintner's insistence, Graham penned a note to Johnson, saying that two mutual friends had told her that the Washington grapevine had "carried back to you something I was supposed to have said about a year and a half ago. I was both sad and baffled at how such an erroneous report *could* have been invented" (emphasis Graham's).[104] If she had done such a thing, she assured Johnson, it "would have been pompous, stupid and rude," but she had not. "There are so many worries on your shoulders that I hesitate to bother you about this nonsense," Graham concluded, but "I just decided there was too much in our past to have such a horrid misapprehension lying around. Phil would not have liked it."

At the White House, Kintner drafted a response for Johnson that assured Graham that Johnson was "glad that this report is not true," a passage the president crossed out as he noted, "I believe and really know this is true therefore I can't say this."[105] Kintner ghosted, "Being human and engaged in a gigantic task, I naturally try to combat certain untruths that are published and certain inaccurate interpretations, for the single purpose of more correctly informing the public"; Johnson underlined "untruths" and scribbled in the margin, "appear almost daily in your paper." The president would not be reconciled. The Kintner draft was replaced with a version by Moyers, which Graham described as "frosty":

> I was, of course, happy to hear from you in your letter of May 16. The spirit in which it was written is most welcome. Mrs. Johnson and I are fond of you, as we were of Phil; he is still very sorely missed by those of us who knew him so well.
>
> There is so much said and written that is untrue that to try to deal with it would be an endless task. Contrary to what some of your columnist friends seem to feel, I let most of it pass. But I do feel obligated to try to combat certain untruths that take on larger proportions than others. I owe that to the Office, not to mention

160

my family. A great deal of gossip and opinion winds up in print, often under the guise of fact. A great deal more makes the cocktail circuit. It is always good to expose it as such when possible.[106]

The president changed "combat" to "correct," added the phrase "and that should be the duty and privilege of both of us" at the end, and signed under the closing of "sincerely" in contrast to Graham's "devotedly." Johnson "was not very forgiving," the publisher concluded.

Johnson may not have been forgiving, but he was adamant about correcting what he considered to be the untruths of the media. Charges that he could not recruit a distinguished staff brought forth rosters of the Phi Beta Kappa and Rhodes scholars serving under his administration and orders to place a story on the quality of his appointments in *Look* or the *New York Times Magazine*.[107] An article by James Deakin of the *St. Louis Post-Dispatch* and a panel on National Educational Television stimulated lengthy memoranda refuting their charges of a credibility gap point by point.[108] When Kintner, carefully avoiding any distinctions on the basis of adequate notice or walks on the South Lawn, reported that Johnson had held seventy-six press conferences as compared with Kennedy's sixty-six in their first 1,095 days in office, the president contrasted the statistics with reports of his inaccessibility and ordered Kintner to "see that AP & UP 'Smitty' get this & ask for *justice* only."[109] Those journalists whom the White House found to be annoying, such as Lippmann, Reston, and Peter Lisagor of the *Chicago Daily News*, would be scratched from a social function, to be replaced by William S. White, Joseph Alsop, and Marianne Means.[110] Furthermore, Lippmann served as the focus for a flood of memoranda by the administration during 1966; the year began with a refutation of his columns calling for retreat from Vietnam, proceeded to several memoranda now withdrawn from the White House files for security reasons, and culminated with "the Walter Lippmann project," which a file memorandum characterized as "a documentation illustrating the continuities and character of Walter Lippmann's opposition, constructed of capsule descriptions of his opposition to four Administrations on ten major issues."[111]

These attacks on media misconceptions were coupled with debates over presidential style before the cameras. The old bugaboo of televised, announced-in-advance news conferences remained; the president's conduct of the question and answer sessions pleased neither broadcast nor print media, eliciting a formal protest from CBS News and a vehement attack by Rowland Evans on an educational network show.[112] In the face of this criticism, Kintner urged Johnson to air more advance-notice sessions, for two reasons. Not only did the impromptu conferences, with all their difficulties, render reporters "less sympathetic to the person holding the conference," but, Kintner contended, the more formal format allowed the president to "get directly to the public with his own words."[113]

Johnson liked the concept of going directly to the people, but televised press conferences, and even televised speeches, did not strike him as "direct." The medium as intermediary irritated him, creating a tension shared by his wife: "At 3:30," she wrote, "I watched one of his confrontations, a televised press conference, the sort of thing you must steel yourself to go through, almost as you would to face a firing squad. I watched it on TV in my bedroom, every nerve aquiver with sympathy."[114] Lady Bird's discussions of these sessions are replete with the terminology of war, an analogy that Johnson himself found apt.

Others also sensed Johnson's discomfort with television and sought to help. A public relations man who claimed to have "given more thought than anyone else, over many years, to making more effective political uses of TV," sent long letters urging the president to update and animate his style before the cameras.[115] Reporter Jack Gould, fresh from an interview with Johnson, accosted Kintner to demand, "Why doesn't the President appear on television the same way he talked to me—the President is so gracious, affable, and well-informed. If he would use this 'style' on television, he would get a terrific public response."[116] Even Johnson's speech writers acknowledged that "neither his personality nor his true concerns are being projected adequately in his formal appearances," although they did praise his performance when the president focused not on the teleprompter and the camera but on the audience to which he spoke.[117]

Yet for Johnson, formal television appearances demanded formal presentations. In the latter half of 1966, several members of his staff concluded that the solution lay elsewhere. Taking a cue from George Gallup's view that "inaction hurts a President more than anything else," they proposed that Johnson adopt an energetic, highly visible stance to maintain the aggressive, tough image that was his strength.[118] This stance would pull news coverage to him on his own terms, playing to the vigorous sincerity of his natural style and delivery without boxing him in with formal televised performances.

By mid-1966, Johnson was eager for a more aggressive approach, especially on the topic of Vietnam. Spring brought congressional approval of the cornerstone for his Johns Hopkins dream, the Asian Development Bank; Johnson signed the bill on the very day that it was passed. Yet the spring had also brought new political crises to Saigon, resulting in Buddhist self-immolations which provided riveting television footage for the States. With these new instabilities and the stalemated guerrilla war came further troop increases and changes in the air war which were both militarily and politically dangerous. At the insistence of the Joint Chiefs of Staff and Walt Rostow, the new national security adviser, Johnson authorized raids on Hanoi and on North Vietnamese fuel depots. The CIA contended that such raids would not yield significant military gains, but Rostow cited the effectiveness of attacks on Germany's petroleum supplies during World War II, a compelling precedent for Johnson. Moreover, the president was stung by stories, leaked by disgruntled members of the Joint Chiefs, reporting that the war was not being prosecuted with sufficient vigor. The bombing of the fuel depots constituted a major policy debate during the spring of 1966 and a difficult decision for Johnson, whose daughter Luci took him to a Catholic church with "little monks" to pray for guidance. Dissatisfaction with the lack of progress in the conflict finally led Johnson to authorize the raids under carefully constructed guidelines beginning at the end of June.

As was the case with the 1965 troop increases, reaching the decision freed the president from his grim ambivalence. He was ready to defend his policies with energy and conviction. Combining this resolution with his aides' recommendations, then, Johnson embarked on a vigorous tour of the Midwest, defending American involvement in Vietnam before heartland audiences in Des Moines and Omaha. He intended to place his case before the American people, without the interferences of the media. As he hit the campaign trail to scour support for Democratic candidates, he incorporated a line of argument suggested by Jack Valenti. In analyzing the fall congressional elections and their implications of support for the president, the aide posited that

> the Viet Cong is watching the elections in November. If the President suffers defeat, they will *not* agree to peace talks for they will believe the country has deserted the President.
>
> If, however, the President wins in November, they will agree to sit down and talk for it would be clear the country is with the President.[119]

This interpretation was "a valid and sensible line," Valenti argued, "that ought to [be] fed to the writers" in the media, "for it would, by inference, uneasily mark those who voted against the President as wanting the war to continue, and aiding the VC through false, but nonetheless apparently accurate reading of the American mood."

Johnson agreed. As he toured the country stumping for Democrats, he reminded the audiences that few commentators had chastised the North Vietnamese for bombing hospitals with American soldiers; both their troops and their president, Johnson implied, deserved better support.

The enthusiastic responses from the local audiences rejuvenated the president. The desire to marshall the sort of grassroots support that Johnson sensed on his tour led him to reach out to small-town America even from the White House. Johnson received the suggestion from Daniel J. Dwyer, the general manager of the Port Jervis, New York, *Union-Gazette*, who wrote to request an interview with the president for his newspaper—circulation 4,500. He argued that

> the people of small-town America are not nearly as critical of the President's policies as might seem to be reflected by the questions asked at the televised press conferences. For example, the theme of our Veteran's Day program last year was "Support the Boys In Viet Nam," and it was the most successful one in more than a decade.[120]

Granting him an interview, Dwyer suggested, would help rectify "a somewhat distorted image [given by the Washington press corps] of just what questions are on the average American's mind." Dwyer thus echoed an observation by Louis Heren of the *Times* of London: the quiet support of the war from the Culpeper, Virginias, of the nation never attracted the attention of television cameras or the *New York Times*.[121]

Johnson's staff liked the idea, especially because, as Moyers told the president,

> they supported you strongly in 1964 and still do. And Dwyer feels that it is papers like his and towns like his who give you real support in your Vietnam policy.
>
> His story would be a good one. And we can move it nationally [over the wire services]. And it would be a unique grass-roots opinion from Washington.[122]

Johnson accepted the interview, delighting the Port Jervis journalists, the White House staff, and the president himself.

Yet circumventing television and the Washington press with campaign tours and small-town newspapers still only reached a small proportion of the American public. They left untouched such people

164

as those Harry McPherson met on his vacation, who complained that the president hadn't explained why America was involved in Vietnam. When the aide pursued the subject, his New England companions admitted that the administration had indeed given many speeches on the issue, but the official explanations rang hollow:

> They simply cannot believe we are there to "defend the freedom of South Vietnam." Why should we pick *that* place, to defend the freedom of *those* people? We don't defend the freedom of every country around the world just because some other country tries to take it away from them. . . . They wished the President would put the whole thing in the simplest terms of *Realpolitik*: we are there to fight China. She is trying to take Asia . . . so we are involved in an elemental, if dangerous, power struggle; that is acceptable, we are a power; to hell with "fighting for freedom" and "self-determination."[123]

They found the administration's altruistic justifications for American involvement to be specious; as a result, McPherson concluded, "it is an extremely unpopular war." The support of these middle- and upper-middle-class Americans was vital, the aide noted, "and we don't have much of it right now."

Valenti shared McPherson's concern over the lack of public support, worrying that even "people who are disposed to be favorable to the President simply can't understand why Vietnam is so important to us."[124] Valenti laid primary blame on television for the public's failure to comprehend the administration's policy. As he reasoned, "this is the first war totally covered by TV, and the vexing reality that TV sees only the American war, and not the Viet Cong war, is hurting us not only in this country but abroad." This one-sided view from the networks had been exacerbated by Johnson's reluctance to marshall a flood of patriotic militarism among the public, and the aggressiveness of the campaign tours did not really alter the situation. While his speeches demanded greater support for his policies and his troops, they did not address a more fundamental problem. As noted by one former aide, departed from the White House but still in close contact with Johnson: "until the home front, as it used to be called, is given a role, however small—until the people have a sense of participation and sacrifice—confusion will increase, frustration will spread, irritation will rise hazardously."[125] Neither Johnson's transitory campaign tours nor his rhetoric of limited war was sufficient to solve the problem. The United States was engaged in military conflict, but hadn't declared war; American boys were dying, but we wouldn't bomb civilian targets; there was a wartime economy, but little austerity or sacrifice was required. It simply didn't make sense to a growing proportion of the population.

The resulting confusion, frustration, and irritation over Vietnam began to take its toll on Johnson's beloved Great Society. Wayne Morse fought the administration's proposed education legislation as a way to protest its foreign policy, telling the Senate subcommittee that he intended "to place the responsibility for the Vietnam war where it belongs—on the doorstep of the White House."[126] For his part, the president came to be preoccupied with the war. He had to be warned away from including a passage on Southeast Asia in a proposed speech to the National Conference on Higher Education; as Cater cautioned, "I hope we will not steal the news play from the educational content" with the insertion of foreign affairs.[127] Involvement in that small country around the globe corroded Johnson's domestic visions, blocking his legislation and consuming his attention. By early fall, HEW Secretary John Gardner would warn that "the domestic program has lost its momentum," and the administration desperately needed to generate a new spirit for the attainment of the Great Society.[128] Almost alone in his optimism, economist Walter Heller outlined the need to prepare for economic prosperity after Vietnam. Although economic adviser Gardner Ackley suggested that the public announcement of such plans would "tend to reassure those who fear the problems that peace would bring," McPherson's handwritten note to Joe Califano at the bottom of Heller's letter conveyed his weariness on the subject: "I expect Walter Heller's memo will be met by thunderous silence. Maybe I am timid, but I rather hope it will. Oh what a long war this looks like."[129]

Johnson was coming to share this mournfulness by the fall of 1966. As more military decisions faced him, just before critical midterm congressional elections, the president felt intensified pressure to justify his war policies. He thus continued his peripetetic defense of the war with a tour of six countries in seventeen days. Officially, the cornerstone of this October trip was the Manila conference, which served as a meeting with the leaders of South Vietnam, South Korea, Australia, New Zealand, Thailand, and the Philippines. Designed to show a common front with the United States in its goals in Southeast Asia, the conference issued a statement entitled "Goals of Freedom," a communiqué promising the withdrawal of all allied troops as soon as the aggression from the North ceased, and a "Declaration of Peace and Progress in Asia and the Pacific." The American president was especially pleased with the third document, which in effect articulated the "Johnson Doctrine": "opposition to aggression; war against poverty, illiteracy, and disease; economic, social, and cultural cooperation on a regional basis; [and] searching for reconciliation and peace."[130]

Unofficially, the temper at Manila was neither positive nor conciliatory. The president met with Westmoreland to discuss the general's request for massive troop increases and for even wider bombing strikes, but Johnson was less than enthusiastic about the continual demand for resources which provided such meager results. He was coming to share McNamara's disenchantment with the war, for the secretary of defense had grown pessimistic about any chances for success. The bombing of the fuel depots had inflicted only minor damage in Hanoi, McNamara discovered, for the North Vietnamese quickly dispersed the storage areas for their petroleum. The South Vietnamese were no closer to achieving political stability than the North Vietnamese were to surrendering the fight, as the secretary found when he visited Saigon prior to the Manila conference, and yet these were two primary goals of the American intervention. An aborted assassination attempt against McNamara brought home the chaotic nature of the situation, and he now argued against increasing the commitment. Westmoreland's requests thus faced stern opposition from both McNamara and Johnson.

Yet these decisions were behind the scenes; the president still intended to utilize the trip as a productive forum for his policies. Johnson devoted a good deal of effort to giving correspondents "a proper slant on the trip," complete with special arrangements for network coverage and briefings for the White House correspondents, the bureau chiefs, the three news magazines' reporters, Cronkite, and Huntley and Brinkley.[131] He was rewarded with thorough coverage of the warm receptions in Australia and elsewhere, which delighted his staff; they were especially pleased with the president's surprise visit to the troops in Vietnam, which stimulated what Kintner called a "very moving special on NBC."[132] Johnson did encounter some antiwar demonstrators, described by Moyers as "quite profane and vulgar"; for the most part, however, the trip pleased the president.[133] In Australia he invited reporters to come in out of the cold weather and have a drink with him; in New Zealand he called to the CBS camera crew to ride in his limousine for good shots of the wildly surging, wholly supportive crowd that was cheering him. Exuberant over the response, Johnson once again felt friendly toward the media.

The president's enthusiasm carried him away in South Korea, however, where his empathy with the soldiers and his deeply felt commitment to fight aggression spilled forth as he addressed the American troops: his great-grandfather, the president said, had died at the Alamo. A check with the Texas Historical Society showed that no Johnson, no Baines, and no other forebear of Lyndon Baines Johnson's had been at the fabled stand to the death. The press office's explanation that a great-uncle had been killed in the battle of San Jacinto came too late to halt the new ripple of derision.

The mythical grandfather at the Alamo was joined by not-so-mythical campaign plans on that same overseas trip. On the journey, Bill Moyers told reporters that the president's schedule upon his return would include a large number of appearances as part of the congressional campaigns back home. Johnson, irritated at Moyers's early release of plans he did not yet want made public, strenuously denied that he had ever seriously considered such a tour. Asked if he had called off his plans to campaign, Johnson told a press conference that "we don't have any plans so when you don't have plans you don't cancel plans. The people of this country ought to know that all these cancelled plans primarily involve the imagination of people who phrase sentences and write columns, and have to report what they hope or what they imagine."[134] Members of the media were thus accused of fabricating their stories, when they had obtained their information from the president's own press office.

Johnson's denial startled press secretary Moyers, red-faced from briefing the reporters about plans the president said did not exist. It startled staff members Tom Johnson and DeVier Pierson, who were in the process of doing advance work for the trip.[135] It also surprised such politicians as Chicago's Mayor Richard Daley and Montana's Senator Mike Mansfield, who had announced the local arrangements that were being made for the president's visits. As Hal Cooper of the AP reported, "leading Democrats from coast to coast busied themselves today unplanning plans for unplanned campaign visits by President Johnson."[136]

The stories of the unplanned campaign plans and the longed-for heroic great-grandfather further fueled the issue of a credibility gap just at a time when Johnson felt his activity was overcoming that epithet. When *Newsweek* printed an article by Chuck Roberts detailing charges of presidential lies and deception, including the above episodes, Johnson angrily ordered his staff members to provide him with "a report which takes apart" the article; and Katherine Graham, who had made a brief reappearance on the White House social scene following Kintner's attempt at reconciliation, was once again banished from Johnson's circle.[137]

168

Nor was *Newsweek* alone as a presidential target. A Reston column on Johnson's domestic policies stirred the president to order an aide to call the columnist and "really eat him up. Tell him he's being dishonest and untruthful."[138] By the end of November, when Kintner requested the president's approval of his plans to speak to the International Radio and Television Executives Society to "urge a greater sense of public responsibility by broadcasters," Johnson's dark pencil scrawled underneath: "particularly on accuracy—They have very poor record and when Frank McGee is wrong the Pres of network ought to give up up *hell* [sic]!"[139]

In Johnson's pique about his public image, particularly on Vietnam, he confronted his speech writers as well. Rambling and copious notes from a meeting of eleven speech writers with Kintner and the president convey Johnson's frustration with public sentiments regarding Southeast Asia.[140] According to these notes, which the author refrained from editing in order "to preserve the full flavor" of the session, Johnson chastised the writers for penning speeches on Vietnam which "did not communicate his goals." He ordered two improvements in his addresses: "(1) 'Sex 'em up more' [and] (2) 'Make them Presidential.' " During one period when Johnson had left the room, one writer observed that "sexing them up" was precisely the problem, for the president's demand for a good "news lead" in every speech was impossible to fulfill. Upon Johnson's return, he himself articulated the desire for newsworthy gems in every address, but the notes do not indicate that anyone raised the same objection with him. In fact, few objections were raised by any of the speech writers as the president embarked on a lengthy discussion of the administration's goals in Vietnam to illustrate his requests. Johnson stressed that the speeches had to be

> simple enough, sharp enough to get the message across. . . . What did we want to achieve in Viet-Nam? What did we want for Asia?
>   We want "Territorial Integrity." We are against "Aggression." We want "Growth," "Security," "Plenty," "Peace."
>   We want to be able to communicate these goals as FDR did his "Four Freedoms"—sharply, succinctly, memorably.

The three-hour meeting thus turned from a discussion of the president's speeches per se to Johnson's explorations of that search for peace, plenty, and progress in Southeast Asia, goals that appeared ever more elusive.

As 1966 drew to a close, then, Johnson's dissatisfactions were intense. A cartoon by David Levine depicted a mournful president raising his shirt to show a gallbladder scar in the shape of Vietnam, while a play entitled *MacBird* depicted Johnson as Macbeth, John Kennedy as the murdered king, and Bobby Kennedy as the kinsman determined to reclaim the throne. The attacks took their toll on the man. He told Valenti that he would step down from the presidency then if he could, and he drew solace from assurances that he was the target of far more vindictive blame than he deserved.[141] When 1967 arrived, the White House staff would lack Valenti, Bundy, Busby, and Reedy, all longtime Johnson aides; within a month Moyers would leave as well, stung by the furor over campaign plans. Sadly, Johnson recognized that his dreams of the Great Society were mired in a tar baby of a war. Lady Bird lamented that even "the merry mood of Christmas . . . is dissipating under the onslaught of hostile press stories," accounts she found so ugly that "you can feel [them] in your bones."[142]

Lyndon Johnson had become a wartime president, and he did not like it.

7

Intensified Opposition, 1967

The grim sense of siege that had settled over the White House toward the end of 1966 carried into the early months of 1967. "Now is indeed 'the Valley of the Black Pig,'" Lady Bird Johnson sighed in one January diary entry. "A miasma of trouble hangs over everything."[1] The despondency primarily resulted from struggling to reconcile Vietnam with the budget as Johnson sought to provide the nation with both guns and butter. A difficult proposition at best, the president's efforts were further complicated by the nature of the war. As the first lady worried, "the temperament of our people [regarding Vietnam] seems to be, 'you must either get excited, get passionate, fight it [and] get it over with, or we must pull out.' It is unbelievably hard to fight a limited war."[2]

Yet in January of 1967, Lyndon Baines Johnson was determined to do just that. His State of the Union address in 1965 had introduced the Great Society proposals, but in his 1966 message domestic matters had relinquished their priority to foreign affairs. For the 1967 report the president concentrated on combining the two, stressing his belief that the country would be able "to meet our commitments at home and abroad—to continue to build a better America—and to reaffirm this nation's allegiance to freedom."[3] Johnson acknowledged that it was difficult to "fight a war of limited objectives over a period of time," on the one hand acting "with restraint when the temptation to 'get it over with' is inviting but dangerous" and on the other accepting "the necessity of choosing 'a great evil in order to ward off a greater.'" Even recognizing these difficulties, however, Johnson insisted that "with your understanding, I would hope your confidence, and your support, we are going to persist—and we are going to succeed."

The decision to aggressively defend the feasibility of his foreign and domestic pursuits broke the sense of gloom that had gripped Johnson earlier. The weekend before the delivery of the speech, Dan Rather of CBS characterized the president's mood as "buoyant":

He is relaxed and smiling. The bearishness that marked his weeks at the ranch during the holidays is gone. . . .

[With his State of the Union message,] he will submit a budget of about 135 billion dollars with a call to Congress, and the American people, to prove to the world that the country can win the war in Vietnam while building the Great Society.[4]

Johnson was convinced that, with a bit of financial tinkering and a dash of vigorous campaigning, both foreign and domestic needs could be met; his annual report to Congress and the nation provided the forum from which to proclaim that conviction and gather support.

While Mrs. Johnson worried that the congressional audience for the address was "cold" and lacking "the jovial camaraderie of most years,"[5] the president's staff members found generally enthusiastic responses when they polled members of the media, despite some complaints about the length of the message. Correspondents were especially pleased with the shift in focus; Cater, for example, reported that Mike McManus of *Time* was "extremely enthusiastic" about Johnson's "clear signal that the Great Society programs are going on," and the *Washington Post*'s Gerald Grant was "very much satisfied by the emphasis you gave to domestic programs."[6]

Encouraged by the reactions to this stance, Johnson decided to again try the person-to-person politicking at which he excelled in a new effort for peace: he wrote a letter to Ho Chi Minh, suggesting that previous efforts to open discussions may have been hampered by the distortion or misinterpretation of indirect communication.[7] It was time, Johnson suggested, for the two countries "to arrange for direct talks between trusted representatives in a secure setting and away from the glare of publicity." As soon as Johnson was certain that "infiltration into South Vietnam by land and by sea has stopped," he told the leader of North Vietnam, he would order a halt in the bombing and in further U.S. troop increases: "these acts of restraint on both sides would, I believe, make it possible for us to conduct serious and private discussions leading toward an early peace."

Ho Chi Minh replied that no talks could begin unless the United States would "stop the bombing, definitively and unconditionally, and all other acts of war against the Democratic Republic of Vietnam, withdraw from South Vietnam all its troops and those of its satellites, recognize the National Liberation Front of South Vietnam, and allow the people of Vietnam to settle their problems by themselves." Johnson concluded that "his answer prescribed the surrender of the South," under terms unacceptable to the United States.

Johnson was thus sensitive to charges that he had ignored or re-buffed all possibilities to open peace talks with Hanoi when stories circulated that Robert Kennedy had returned from Europe with a "peace feeler." While accounts of the episode are both garbled and piecemeal, apparently Kennedy's meeting with a top member of the French Foreign Office included discussion of a three-stage plan to open negotiations which reportedly paralleled earlier suggestions by Hanoi. The exact nature and importance of the discussion was con-fused by the language barrier (Kennedy did not speak French), the diplomatic caution of the French in discussing contacts with Hanoi, and the uncertainty as to whether the discussion constituted "a 'message,' or a 'signal,' or a 'feeler,' or merely a Gallic fantasy."[8] As rumors and news accounts circulated, however, Johnson took notice in light of both the subject and the individual involved. In February of 1967, then, Robert F. Kennedy was summoned to the White House to talk with the president about the reported peace feeler.

Johnson had long been irritated with *Newsweek* for its "Periscope" section, which he contended was a "whisper zone" of ill-founded rumor,[9] but he was furious with Kay Graham's publication when it then reported that his meeting with Kennedy had been stormy. The accounts did not heap praise on the senator from New York, depict-ing him as a naïve and somewhat bumbling innocent who "missed the point of the overture when he first heard it" and then handled the delicate situation poorly.[10] Yet *Newsweek* also reported that "the President roundly denounced Kennedy for leaking the story of the peace proposal and jeopardizing delicate U.S. negotiations, " and that staff member Walt Rostow left the meeting shaking his head and saying "it was rough. . . . It was very rough."[11] The stories prompted a presidential denial and a meeting of Rostow with Graham to insist on retraction of the story; when the publisher refused to oblige, her tenure in the doghouse lengthened. To further stir up the president's choler concerning the episode, *Newsweek*'s story found its way into accounts by the *Washington Post, Time*, Evans and Novak, and others, which led to a flurry of memoranda, letters, and meetings as staff members sought to calm the waters. "It is so difficult," com-plained Kintner, "to catch up with misleading impressions."[12]

Other journalistic coverage of the war attracted the president's wrath during the early months of 1967 as well. One target was Harrison Salisbury of the *New York Times*, who returned from six-teen days in Hanoi with reports that American bombs had inflicted civilian damage, despite government claims that the targets were exclusively military. Salisbury's dramatic adventure behind the lines drew a good deal of criticism from fellow journalists; William Randolph Hearst, Jr., for example, compared him to Tokyo Rose, while Chalmers Roberts of the *Washington Post* branded him "Ho's chosen instrument." Yet others, including the editors of the *Columbia Journalism Review*, applauded Salisbury's efforts to broaden Americans' perceptions of the war; Walter Lippmann praised his series as bringing "great honor to the profession of journalism with singular service to his country."[13]

The controversy over Salisbury's journey added to growing public unrest over the war. It also pressed correspondents to address the inadequacy of standard wartime reporting procedures to convey the intricacies of a limited conflict occurring in another culture. As a professor of sociology and journalism observed, "traditional methods of journalism are unable to cope effectively with a situation such as the one now existing in Southeast Asia."[14] The 1966 Senate hearings had not only legitimized disagreement with the administration's policies; they had also spurred the Washington press corps to probe further into details and discrepancies regarding the conflict. Roberts might condemn Salisbury's trip as the work of a traitor; columnist William S. White might continue to flail against Johnson's critics as "a little band of willful men, of so-called elite thinkers" filled with "intolerable self-willed dissent"; but the Senate hearings and the journalist's Hanoi journey had, to use Salisbury's phrase, broken "the pattern of acceptability" for coverage of the conflict in Vietnam.[15] Government versions of progress in Southeast Asia were no longer considered adequate by reporters.

The depression that Lady Bird Johnson had sensed in the early part of 1967 grew not only from the pressure of Vietnam but also from a changing of the White House guard, and the rumors and stories accompanying the changes. Bundy had gone to the Ford Foundation, Reedy to the Struthers Research Corporation, Busby to practice law, and the ever-present, effervescent Valenti to head the Motion Picture Association.

The departure of these longtime and well-trusted aides received a capstone, however, when Bill Moyers left, stung in the aftermath of the aborted campaign tour of late 1966. Ambitious, dynamic, identified by some as a surrogate son for the president, Moyers traded the West Wing for *Newsday* offices on February 1, 1967, amid stories that his departure left an irreplaceable void in the staff. Whether Moyers was a petty and deceptive man, as his predecessor as press secretary maintained, or a talented man who was "one of the two or three most valuable people the President had," as his successor posited, he clearly had been a highly influential staff member who had combined the position of press secretary with that of presidential confidant and valued staff member.[16] It was a combination that pleased the press corps, especially after Reedy's difficulties in obtaining information, but one that ultimately annoyed a president who wanted to be both the controller and the focal point of White House news.

The departure of Moyers heightened the already strong and sharply divided assessments of him. While Jack Valenti praised Moyers as "highly talented," "highly effective," and "superb in his job," other co-workers charged him with a variety of unprofessional behaviors.[17] One, for example, told of the eager aide circulating among correspondents during a folk-rock concert at the White House to mock Johnson for making feeble and ill-informed efforts to identify with the young. This perceived derision of his boss to better his own image angered Johnson's supporters, from veteran personal secretary Willie Day Taylor to aide Ernest Goldstein to journalist William S. White, as they directly and indirectly accused Moyers of fostering the credibility gap.[18] They traced stories of Johnson's cruelty to his staff back to the young aide; they contrasted *Time*'s favorable cover story on the press secretary with its attacks on his employer; and they compared the president's popularity under Reedy's guidance (77 percent the highest approval, 64 percent the lowest approval, and 70 percent the average approval) with that under Moyers (66 percent highest, 44 percent lowest, and 56 percent average).[19]

For the president's partisans, then, Moyers's ambitions had created the credibility gap. While one can argue the extent to which the press secretary deserved responsibility, Johnson placed full blame on his former confidant; by the end of his presidency his bitterness toward the former aide had grown to such an extent that a concerned acquaintance wrote the next press secretary, George Christian, to ask him to "urge Himself to lay off Moyers in his little backgrounders."[20] The breach between these two intense men was never healed.

When the low-key Christian first succeeded Moyers as press secretary, then, he stepped into the aftermath of a relationship turned rancorous. The situation was aggravated by new stories on the administration's difficulties in attracting and retaining good staff members. A cartoon in the *Los Angeles Times*, for example, depicted a White House bulletin board papered with notices of farewell parties, while the accompanying column by Charles Bartlett traced "the demoralization of his government" to Johnson's "petty vindictiveness, which seeps out of the White House, curls its way through the corridors of the bureaucracy and the salons of Georgetown, and settles upon the city like a dank, uncomfortable chill." Johnson's pique at these characterizations led him to deny information for two stories to Robert Donovan, the chief Washington correspondent for the Los Angeles paper. Despite Kintner's endorsement of Donovan as "an excellent reporter," Johnson refused to respond to either request because "I don't trust him or the *Times*."[21]

The aides who remained in the White House countered the image of their eminent dispensability with tables that showed that eighteen staff members had accumulated a total of 161 years with Johnson since his days as vice-president—a statistic they said should assure Johnson of "the loyalty and devotion of these people for you . . . [and] how low turnover on your staff really is."[22] They also used their contacts with such media people as Evans and Novak, Sidey, and Cassie Mackin to insist on the abundance of "bright young men" around the White House.[23] Other efforts to quell the negative view of Johnson's staff were undertaken as well. Cater encouraged Marvin Watson, the president's appointments secretary, to see James Reston in order to combat the image of himself as "a mysterious, inaccessible figure" who served as a persnickety detective and hatchet man for Johnson.[24] Cater saw this villainous image as yet another unfair and detrimental characterization of the administration by the media.

Christian therefore had his work cut out for him when he assumed Moyers's post. Primary methods of dealing with the pressures of his new duties were to maintain a low profile and to double-check information before releasing it. These practices earned him the nickname "Ol' Blabbermouth" among the White House press corps, but he also gained the respect and confidence of the correspondents, several of whom praised him as Johnson's best press secretary.[25] George Reedy's prediction held true: the new press secretary's "qualities of honesty and integrity" would prove far more beneficial to Johnson than a slick "overglamourization of the press office."[26]

In addition to maintaining this low but reliable profile, Christian also reinstated the practice, abandoned under Moyers, of asking staff members to submit reports of their contacts with the press which indicated the correspondent's name, organization, and topics of discussion. Such reports, the press office explained, enabled the president "to know what the press is saying"; they also helped the press office and the special assistants to maintain consistency in their remarks to reporters.[27] Clearly Christian intended to tighten the press

176

operation; as he observed of the new responsibilities he faced, there had been

> a good bit of loose talk, a good many problems created by people other than the press secretary . . . talking pretty loosely around reporters, which sometimes caused the President grief. It is also the type thing that creates credibility problems, because the reporter thinks he is getting correct information from somebody in the press office when actually he is not. . . . Then when something does develop in the opposite way there is a tendency to blame the President for it.[28]

Christian thus agreed with Johnson's top aides that "the best answer to 'credibility' was in the day-to-day operations of the Press Office," and the calm, good-humored attorney from Texas was determined to alleviate the difficulties of loose talk through quiet yet firm control over White House contacts with the media.[29] For Johnson, the new appointment marked another attempt to bolster his press relations and his popularity by instituting a new press secretary and trying to change his tone.

Clearly the president was disturbed by the increasingly shrill chorus crying "credibility gap," and he charged his staff to continue their defense against the charges. The memoranda refuting various articles and television programs on the subject were joined in early 1967 by a twenty-page paper detailing the "presidential credibility gaps" of Roosevelt, Truman, Eisenhower, and Kennedy. Written by aide Fred Panzer at Johnson's request, the extensive document contended that the only difference between the press problems of these four presidents and those of Johnson was that the once blatant charges of lying had now been replaced by a pervasive "smear technique" that "attempts to cloud all Presidential acts and statements."[30]

Yet lengthy memoranda within the White House could not quell the growing disenchantment with the Johnson administration's approach to public information. Even longtime Johnson supporter Philip Potter authored a front-page story on the credibility gap for the *Baltimore Sun*, citing the president's penchant for secrecy and control of information regarding travel plans, nominations, budgets, and Vietnam. While Potter's essay detailed complaints about Johnson in each of these areas, it was often sympathetic toward him as it contended that "one of the ablest Presidents this country has produced would be a better one if he would stop getting wounded every time a reporter or an editorial writer takes issue with him on some point."[31] Potter implied that Johnson's sensitivity to any criticism had aided the perceptions of a credibility gap.

Far less sympathetic in tone was Pauline Fredericks's broadcast for the "Today Show" on February 8, 1967. In it the United Nations correspondent for NBC charged that the president's talk of seeking peace in Vietnam was contradicted by the administration's continued refusal, since 1965, to open negotiations. The escalated bombing, she argued, proved an actual unwillingness to talk despite Johnson's public statements.[32]

Fredericks's broadcast signalled an intensification of the charges against Johnson, which increasingly focused on his handling of the war in Vietnam. When Johnsonian nemesis Walter Lippmann penned a two-part series devoted to the credibility gap, the columnist's list of grievances largely ignored the issues addressed by Potter, concentrating instead on deceptions regarding Southeast Asia.[33] The columns joined a speech in which Lippmann counseled journalists, "'Put not your trust in princes,'" especially those "misled by false historical analogies . . . [and] dangerous illusions of omnipotence" resulting in a "180-degree turn away" from the campaign promises of 1964.[34] The columnist's advice held a touch of irony coming from one who had trusted and then felt betrayed. A reluctance to reveal travel plans and budgets had sown the seeds of media dissatisfaction; Johnson's approach to the war in Vietnam reaped the harvest of bitterness, and the White House files gained the burgeoning category labeled "Credibility Gap."[35]

Initially the president's response to these intensified attacks was to remain silent, as part of the new posture he assumed after Christian became press secretary. This stance drew inquiries from the media about Johnson's new "air of humility" and complaints about the lack of news in the president's few sessions with reporters.[36] In late February of 1967, however, Johnson again decided to accelerate his public defense of his policies in Vietnam. He gave reporters a rousing articulation of his position in a press conference on February 27, which elicited a range of supportive comments from correspondents relieved by the long-awaited surge of material for stories, by the adaptation to the needs of print rather than broadcast media, and by the president's devotion of the conference to their questions without any preliminary statements of his own.[37] Johnson then submitted to a televised news conference on March 9; he was so conscientiously understated in outlining the bombing pauses and offers to start discussions on Vietnam which had received no response that Lady Bird "marveled that he could be so restrained—so bland, dignified, calm, even perhaps a little *too* slow" (emphasis hers).[38]

In addition to these news conferences to defend his policies in Southeast Asia, Johnson utilized one of his favorite techniques to attract news: travel. Within a week of his televised conference he journeyed to Nashville to address the Tennessee legislature, which had passed a resolution of support for his policy in Southeast Asia; his speech stressed that "reciprocity must be the fundamental principle of any reduction in hostilities. The United States cannot and will not reduce its activities unless and until there is some reduction on the other side."[39] This intention to stand firm until North Vietnam demonstrated its willingness to act in good faith was reiterated at the end of March, when Johnson flew to Guam to meet with leaders from Saigon. Afterwards the president announced that South Vietnamese troops would assume an increasing amount of military responsibility, that plans for the economic development of the area were explored, and that the United States would continue its supportive role until all aggression ceased.[40]

True, perhaps, to Gallup's notion that "inaction hurts a President more than anything else," especially if the president is mindful of the kind of activity he chooses to replace it, Johnson's efforts for justification joined the reorganized press operations to yield a new supportiveness among members of the Washington press corps. Kintner had advised Johnson that

> a Presidential appearance should be "an event"—"an event" if it is
> an address, in a major setting very carefully prepared, . . . "an
> event" if you have a televised press conference whereby you act
> very courteous[ly] to your questioners, show your knowledge of the
> government without notes and whereby even to the most vicious
> questions you respond with a degree of humor and kindness which
> the public likes. In my judgment, the tougher the question and the
> greater the charity used by the President in answering, the greater
> is the sympathy from the television watchers.[41]

In part due to these "measured appearances" which underscored his presidential position, in part to what Reedy termed "the traditional American sense of fair play" reacting to previous heavy criticism, comments and columns favorable to Johnson appeared with greater frequency in the early spring of 1967.[42] Eric Sevareid declared that the root of current presidential-press tensions could be found in the press's inability to understand Johnson's caution and his "master personality."[43] Then Howard K. Smith, who had earlier charged that "the 'Credibility Gap' cliché lacks substance," attacked Lippmann's columns as "not ringing true" and criticized media coverage of Johnson in general. Smith's support earned presidential approval for "all reasonable cooperation" of the White House staff with his proposed book on the administration, which Cater suggested "cannot help but be quite favorable in its treatment."[44]

The print media echoed these assessments; the journal *Report* published an editorial that favored the administration's position on the credibility gap, and the *Washington Star* dismissed that "imprecise and undefined phrase" as the result of either "inconsequential nit-picking, or matters of security in which, sometimes, something less then the full truth is in the national interest."[45]

Nor were these supportive statements limited to published accounts. At the Pennsylvania State University, an international panel of journalists contended that the American press did not appreciate the fact that it had "the best relations with government officials of any nation in the world."[46] Later that spring, even while acknowledging that Johnson's sensitivity to criticism often led to reactions that held "all the charm of a bull in an electric fence," Merriman Smith nonetheless lamented to his colleagues at a UPI breakfast that "President Johnson these days is the object of some of the worst vilification—even obscenity—that I've seen or heard in more than 25 years on the White House assignment."[47] His defense of the president was particularly poignant in light of the fact that his son had been killed in Vietnam a year earlier.

The public statements of support by journalists were coupled with a renewed hope among the White House press corps that fences could be mended. A number of correspondents told staff members that occasional disagreements did not mitigate their overall support for the president, and they expressed hope for increased understanding on both sides. One group approvingly noted Johnson's comment that he wanted to go to Texas for the weekend "if possible"—a tactic that let reporters know he was thinking of it without giving them "the idea that the President's mind is made up, [but] he is just letting them dangle."[48] Perhaps Reedy's advice made sense to Johnson when he counseled the president to establish regular procedures concerning travel, briefings, and news conferences because "newspapermen are much more conservative in their personal habits than they will admit even to themselves. Therefore, variations in routine and unexpected

happenings give them the impression of trickery and create an attitude of disbelief."[49] Predictability bred reassurance; notice forestalled
suspicion.

Efforts to effect a rapprochement thus came from both president
and press. Against this background, Kintner assured Johnson that "a
different image of the President, and a more effective one, has been
created."[50] Lady Bird concurred, sensing that "there is a slight lifting
of the clouds, an occasional ray of sunshine. Things *are* getting
better."[51] Even Rowland Evans, reported Kintner, could be counted
among those who wanted "to look at the President as an innovator
and administrator, and to forget whatever personal feelings there may
be"; perhaps Johnson should take advantage of this period by meeting
off the record with "certain key columnists including those who have
been unfriendly to the President" to improve his position. Among
those appearing on Kintner's list were Joseph Alsop, Robert Novak,
James Reston, Walter Cronkite, Chet Huntley, David Brinkley, and
Kay Graham. Although Johnson did not have professional conferences with any of them, Reston, Cronkite, Brinkley, and Graham
were all invited to the White House for social occasions within a
month.[52]

During this period of hope, Johnson addressed a White House
Correspondents Association dinner with remarks reflecting a willingness to poke fun at past tensions. First he assessed the AP's Frank
Cormier, being installed as the new head of the WHCA, as "real
presidential timber: larger than life, thin-skinned, and full of surprises." Then, for stories on Cormier's tenure, Johnson turned to
"notes" that he claimed to have discovered in the White House press
room, which he indirectly attributed to Lippmann. According to
Johnson, the jottings included these evaluations:

> Unpredictable President Frank Cormier canceled a long-standing
> dentist's appointment this morning. When questioned, Cormier re-
> torted that a President . . . receives many invitations to visit den-
> tists' offices but does not always go. . . .
>
> It's too bad President Cormier doesn't come across to the Amer-
> ican people the way he does face to face. He isn't really a wheeler-
> dealer at all, he only does the right things in the wrong way.[53]

While Johnson's remarks might be perceived as either good-humored
fun or sour grapes, Cormier allowed the more charitable reading in
his account, reflecting the greater optimism of the period.[54]

This era of better feeling, however, was soon to end. When Jack

Valenti passed Merriman Smith outside the Treasury building a few weeks after the UPI speech and offered his congratulations on a fine address, the correspondent snapped sharply at the former aide. In a later letter, Smith explained that after receiving brutal mail and the disdain of many colleagues for his comments on Johnson, he had

> picked up a transcript of the President's remarks to the White House Fellows in which he sympathized with those who would chloroform reporters. He also spoke in the same transcript of reporters who would rather "drink the hemlock" than accept the truth of some of his statistics.[55]

In those remarks, Johnson had recounted the story of a speech in the early 1900s, in which Sir William Osler said that if one subtracted "the work of the men above forty," the world would still have "the effective, moving, vitalizing work" of the most productive twenty-five- to forty-year-olds.[56] A Baltimore newspaper headlined its account, "Osler Recommends Chloroform at 60"; the president commented that "if Dr. Osler, upon reading that, was tempted to chloroform a reporter, I think he could have been forgiven. That was not the first time, nor the last, that a public figure has felt that urge." Johnson's views distressed Smith, as he told Valenti, for after censuring the sort of ugly viciousness to which he felt the president was being unfairly subjected, the correspondent found Johnson returning attacks in kind.

Within a week the White House correspondents as a whole were angry; they felt that Johnson had reverted to his old form. The president had debated over whether to attend Expo 67 in Canada; its emphasis on technological progress appealed to him. Yet if he went he would need to meet with Prime Minister Lester Pearson, who had urged him to stop the bombing just before his Johns Hopkins speech two years earlier, and he might well face anti-Vietnam demonstrators. Moreover, the situation in the Mideast was volatile, and while Johnson needed to be available if war broke out he did not want to create diplomatic problems with a public announcement of his concerns. Thus, Johnson decided to leave for the exposition at the last minute. The journalists, Christian reported, were furious: "they just resented being treated that cavalierly. They thought we should have warned them."[57] The hope that correspondents had taken from Johnson's earlier cautious phrasing about a possible trip to Texas now dissolved into anger once again.

On the same day in May that the president left for Canada, the *New*

182

York Times's Max Frankel, newly assigned to the White House beat, wrote Christian despairing of the antagonisms that he saw such interactions fueling:

> It is most painful for me to see my President being cut up, with deep bitterness, a bitterness that arises not from policy or principle but from the smallest problems of logistics and communication.
>
> I think I speak objectively when I say that all hands, from the President on down, are contributing to this bitterness. As a result, much too much attention is wasted or lavished on the most petty aspects of policy and personality. . . .
>
> I want this Administration to be judged, for good or ill, on things that really count.
>
> Why on earth must we all punish each other so strenuously on things that don't?[58]

When the press secretary passed this on to the president several days later, Johnson noted: "I agree—Let's get his views." Yet whether anything ever came of it is unclear.

The summer of 1967 turned out to be a long and difficult one for Lyndon Johnson after the hopefulness of the spring; press antagonisms were only part of his problems. Disenchantment intensified as the war dragged on; 65 percent of a Gallup-poll sample complained that the Johnson administration was not "telling the public all they should know about the Vietnam war." As the president observed in his memoirs, the factions demanding accelerated action against the North may not have been as publicly vocal as those who wanted immediate withdrawal from Vietnam, but they were just as insistent—and, to Johnson's way of thinking, even more powerful. Such senators as John Stennis, Strom Thurmond, and Harry Byrd, from their positions on the powerful Senate Preparedness Subcommittee on which Johnson himself had served, proclaimed the need for more aggressive military action; the president knew the potent political forces concentrated there. Lady Bird would point out more than a decade later that her husband's major pressure "was not from the left but from the right—people demanding that we get this thing over with by dropping the deadliest of bombs."[59]

In part to counter this pressure, General Westmoreland had been brought home in that spring flurry of justificatory activity designed to coax hawks and doves to reason together. In addition to his appearances before Congress and the Associated Press Managing Editors Convention, he met with Johnson on April 27 to press his request for 200,000 more troops. The conference brought few good tidings to the president, who questioned the ramifications of troop increases. "When we add divisions," queried Johnson, "can't the enemy add divisions? If so, where does it all end?" Westmoreland replied that a reciprocal increase would be likely, although the North Vietnamese and Viet Cong would face some difficulties in supporting a large deployment. The president, concerned about Chinese intervention, asked, "At what point does the enemy ask for volunteers?" The only response: "That," said Westmoreland, "is a good question."[60] It was not an answer designed to reassure Johnson.

The general's request sparked a new controversy within the administration. The Joint Chiefs of Staff endorsed not only the troop increases but also an expanded air war and contingency plans for ground action in Laos, Cambodia, and North Vietnam. In contrast, McNamara opposed the escalation, especially of the air war: "There continues to be no sign," he argued, "that the bombing has reduced Hanoi's will to resist or her ability to ship the necessary supplies south." Lacking any evidence that the air strikes were weakening either the spirit or the effort of North Vietnam, McNamara reasoned that

> we should not bomb for punitive reasons if it serves no other purpose—especially if analysis shows that the actions may be counterproductive. It costs American lives; it creates a backfire of revulsion and opposition by killing civilians; it creates serious risks; it may harden the enemy.[61]

Doubting the utility of the very strategies he had advocated, the secretary of defense worried that "there appears to be no attractive course of action for the United States concerning Vietnam."

McNamara's reservations about the effectiveness of escalation gained support from former National Security Adviser Bundy, who wrote to the White House to urge that "as a matter of high national policy there should be a publicly stated ceiling to the level of American participation in Vietnam, as long as there is no further marked escalation on the enemy side." He concluded that neither troop increases nor expanded bombing promised to be productive; and moreover, he contended that "uncertainty about the future size of the war is now having destructive effects on the national will" in the United States. Each factor alone constituted sufficient justification to deny further expansion of the war; together, Bundy argued, they demonstrated the military's proposals to be "both unproductive and unwise."[62]

Johnson, caught in the midst of these strongly contradictory rec-

184

ommendations, once again dispatched McNamara to survey the situation firsthand. Members of the press questioned whether this July trip to Vietnam served as an ex post facto justification for troop increases already planned but not yet announced.[63] While Rostow vehemently denied this interpretation, the meetings upon McNamara's return settled upon a troop increase of 45,000—a figure that was higher than the 30,000 ceiling that the secretary of defense had proposed in May but lower than the 80,000 men that General Westmoreland had requested to provide the "minimum essential force." In his memoirs Johnson quotes McNamara as reporting "complete accord" among himself, Westmoreland, and Wheeler on the troop levels; but it was undoubtedly a tenuous accord given the disparity of the views involved.[64] It was during this tumultuous summer of 1967 that McNamara commissioned the massive top-secret history of American policy concerning Vietnam which was to gain national attention as the Pentagon Papers.

Johnson himself was preoccupied during this period with two other major foreign-relations developments: the Six Day War in the Mideast and a well-publicized summit meeting with Soviet Premier Alexei Kosygin in Glassboro, New Jersey. The conference, diplomatically located halfway between New York and Washington, aided Johnson's ratings in the public opinion polls; so did the birth of his first grandson, Patrick Lyndon Nugent. Press aide Tom Johnson would bemoan the departure of the youngest member of the White House clan, observing that "he was a good story every day with all the riots and the war—he was a big help."[65] His grandfather needed all the help he could get, for the upswing in the ratings was short-lived. By mid-August the Gallup poll showed that the president's approval rating had sunk to a scant 39 percent, the lowest of his tenure in office.

Yet Johnson dug in further. He was a man who focused on projects, and as the war encroached ever more on his pursuit of the Great Society, Johnson accelerated his efforts to convince the doubters and silence the critics. Johnson carried his message to a variety of audiences; sessions on training and education projects turned into monologues on Vietnam, just as speech-writers' conferences had been transmuted earlier. A chance meeting could turn into a presidential rebuke for one's opposition, as illustrated by one well-polished story. Seeing Senator Frank Church of Idaho, the account related, Johnson put an arm around his shoulder:

> "Frank," he said, "that speech yo' made up wasn't one bit helpful."

"I'm sorry, Mr. President, the headlines exaggerated what I said."

"The headlines were all Ah read, Frank, and they're all the people read."

"But I didn't go any further than Walter Lippmann."

"Well, Frank," he said, "the next time you need money to build a dam in your state, you better go to Mr. Lippmann."[66]

While the story is probably apocryphal, it does capture Johnson's fervor.

The president also pushed ahead in his efforts to gain further funding for the Asian Development Bank, proposed in his Johns Hopkins speech two years earlier and approved by Congress with limited financial support a year later. To that end, he consulted with Eugene Black and members of the Treasury and State departments; he sought information on the foreign and domestic implications of the bill from Walt Rostow; and he pressured his congressional liaisons for accurate voting tallies on the proposed measure. The president also met personally on two occasions with "legislators who would be in a position to help the bill," which faced stiff opposition from members of the Senate Foreign Relations Committee and others. While Johnson sent a special message to Congress requesting these additional appropriations, he did so primarily to reassure the other countries involved in funding the project of his good faith, for he neither expected nor received enactment of the legislation.[67]

The Asian Development Bank Bill was just one victim of congressional malaise about the war. Although Johnson later characterized the dissent as "nothing but a lot of sound and poppycock stimulated by the personal needs of William Fulbright," the legislative unrest over Vietnam had played its role in the stagnation of Great Society programs.[68] The president thus found it doubly insulting when in August the senator from Arkansas contrasted the expenditures for Vietnam with the need for a program at home to eliminate rats. American involvement in the "unnecessary and immoral war," Fulbright argued, was morally, psychologically, and economically incompatible with the goals of the Great Society.[69]

Underscoring the relationship between the administration's domestic and foreign difficulties, the senator's "sound and poppycock" struck home. Johnson quickly dispatched staff member Fred Panzer to locate Fulbright's critiques of President Roosevelt; he found relatively little but concluded that "even as a freshman Congressman, Fulbright had little patience for anyone or anything that frustrates his vision of how U.S. foreign affairs should be handled."[70] Johnson's memoirs detail his campaign on behalf of the Rat Extermination and Control Act from its defeat in the House on July 20, 1967, to its passage in September, although the senator's name is not mentioned. The first lady's response to Fulbright's comparison, however, was more direct:

> I think the most frustrated I've been lately is reading a speech that Senator Fulbright made in which he indicated that the country is damned because we are spending so much in Vietnam instead of spending it here to take care of the poor and underprivileged—this from a man who has never voted for any Civil Rights measure and who even voted against Medicare in 1964. It will be sheer luxury someday to *talk* instead of *act*.[71]

There may be, she concluded, "enough right in our midst—whiners, self-doubters, gloom spreaders, who *can* beat us." Her husband clearly shared her view. Speaking to a convention of Jaycees in Baltimore, Johnson rejected the speech on poverty which his writers handed to him in order to ad-lib an attack on "the cussers and doubters" who would jeopardize the American position abroad.[72] Once again, the domestic concerns about which Johnson cared so passionately took a back seat to the defense of the war with which he did not want to deal.

Counted among those doubters and gloom spreaders, in Johnson's tally, were members of the media. He complained to the Jaycees' convention that "our newspapers and our TV programs and our radio commentators [have] informed us fully about the protesters and the 'peaceniks' who invaded the Pentagon" and marched in the streets, yet ignored the "10,000 young Americans" who enlisted during a single week. "Unfortunately," Johnson concluded, "a student carrying a sign or a protester wearing a beard, or an attention-seeker burning a draft card in front of a camera can get more attention—and more billing—than all 10,000 of these volunteers."

It was true that among many journalists, support for the war had declined and then turned sour as public sentiment changed. Previously supportive correspondents, including Forrest Boyd of the Mutual Broadcasting System, now felt that "the war is going nowhere"; the staunchly conservative *U.S. News and World Report* engaged in what Christian termed "sniping" at the president; and NBC aired a highly critical report from Vietnam depicting demoralized troops fighting with M-16s that often jammed.[73] When Joseph Alsop dropped out of the New York newspaper market, Johnson found himself with "no strong columnist support except for Drew Pearson in New York City itself on the Vietnam operation," and no hope of finding outlets for supportive writers like Marianne Means and William S. White.[74] Then *Newsweek* followed criticism of National Security Adviser Walt Rostow with a cover story that declared Lyndon Johnson to be "the first President in U.S. history to be beset simultaneously with a major war abroad and a major rebellion at home." Staff members refuted many of *Newsweek*'s statements, but concluded that several weary and disenchanted people within the administration were in fact leaking material and negative comments to the media.[75]

These sources within the White House fed such journalists as correspondent James Deakin of the *St. Louis Post-Dispatch*. Never an admirer of the president, he accelerated his attacks with an article in the August issue of *Esquire* entitled "The Dark Side of L.B.J." Deakin derided the president's "pose of humility" regarding opposition to his position on Vietnam. Johnson, the writer said, often talked of

> the right to dissent from his Vietnam policy. This . . . homily takes an invariable form. Everybody has the right to disagree. It is part of our God-given freedom. Go ahead, criticize me. It's okay. I can bear it. (A brave little smile.) That's what your President is paid for. (And remember, I'm the only President you've got.)[76]

"As a grey deceiver," Deakin concluded, "President Johnson has virtuoso range, from the minutiae of family history to the number of American troops in Vietnam and their mission."

Perceptions of Johnson's duplicity on the former topic annoyed journalists, but on the latter they found it unforgiveable. In an article in the *New Yorker*, Richard Rovere contended that Johnson had gotten himself into an untenable position with his handling of Vietnam.[77] The journalist recounted a specific instance to illustrate his point. According to Rovere, George Christian had learned that a television correspondent, dubbed "Network" in the article, planned a story on the administration's intentions to develop an electronic anti-infiltration barrier in Vietnam. The press secretary, contended Rovere, summoned "Network" to his office, demanded to know what story he had taped, and after checking with the president gave him a vigorous categorical denial that the government had any such intention. When McNamara announced plans to develop such a barrier just days later, the article suggested, "Network" felt he had been the foolish dupe of another Johnsonian credibility gap. The moral of the story, Rovere concluded, was that "no other President has ever had to live in an atmosphere so heavy with distrust and disbelief as Lyndon Johnson." The key to that distrust and disbelief was his handling of Vietnam, "an undeclared and an unpopular war . . . waged without the advantages of patriotic fervor." Such was the fate of a limited war.

Christian later asserted that the "barrier" episode was a classic case of a lack of communication within government which led to contradictory versions being released.[78] On the day that Christian had talked with "Network" (Dan Rather of CBS), the press secretary, in a routine memorandum to the president that also summarized other press contacts of the day, had reported Rather's intention to prepare such a story. Christian gave the Rather conference no special attention in his report; he simply noted that "after reasoning with him, he said he would scrub the piece." Christian, who recollected that he had responded to Rather's inquiry rather than summoning him as Rovere depicted it, indicated that he knew of no such barrier decision at the time. During his meeting with Rather, the press secretary said, he left briefly to double-check his story with a Defense Department spokesman who urged caution but who also confirmed that no new decision had been made. When McNamara had decided to proceed with barrier research and "to go ahead with a brief announcement to cut off further speculation" by the press, the defense secretary had not informed the White House since it did not involve a decision there. It was an action that ultimately, Christian acknowledged, "was going to leave me with a credibility gap."

It did. Despite a lengthy letter to Rovere explaining the episode from his perspective, Christian could not withdraw the story from print; it thus joined the other stories about Johnson's deception and strong-armed tactics.[79] Moreover, its moral remained: Johnson faced a press and public doubtful of his word on Vietnam.

Clearly Johnson was eager for both the press and the public to support his policies for Southeast Asia. After an embattled summer, he saw the South Vietnamese elections of September 3, 1967, as a forum to stress the progress made toward political stability and thus toward military independence. The panel of twenty-two American observers included legislators, clergymen, scholars, and four representatives of the news media: Eugene C. Patterson, editor of the *Atlanta Constitution*; John S. Knight, president of Knight Newspapers; Donald H. McGannon, president of the Westinghouse Broadcasting Company; and Stanford Smith, general manager of the American Newspaper Publishers Association.

The president met with the group upon their return to hear their reactions, before a number of reporters. Patterson, a supporter of the war at the time, recalled that the way Johnson set the scene, "it was a performance, not a report."[80] Calling on such friends and supporters as Governor Richard J. Hughes of New Jersey and Archbishop Robert E. Lucey of San Antonio, the president established a pattern of positive response before the correspondents. Patterson termed the proceedings "more or less a love feast," by which Johnson "was cutting himself off from what could have been some valuable reports." When the Atlanta editor was called upon, he suggested that the glowing praise of democracy amidst battle had neglected to place the elections within their context, including the fact that the current South Vietnamese government had barred several popular candidates from even entering the race. The president, Patterson recalled,

> had been taking notes with [a] pencil and he looked up at each person as he spoke, . . . and looked steadily at him and nodded and listened to the encouraging talk. But when I put the sour note into it, he looked quickly from his pad and glared at me with obvious anger as if I were doing an unfair thing. Then he put his head back down, [and] wrote studiedly with his pencil without looking at me again.

Given these perceptions of the briefing, Patterson was no doubt bemused by Johnson's account of the scene in his memoirs, in which the president listed the comments of six people praising the election as "a noble political exercise for self-enhancement and self-determination," and then concluded: "And so it went, as one after another of the observers expressed his views and reported on the things he had seen and learned."[81]

To Eric Sevareid, the importance of the South Vietnamese election lay in "the fact that it was held at all, not the degree of irregularities." Yet it also underscored the complexity of our involvement in a conflict out of the ken of American experience and values. As Sevareid noted,

> We believe that armies fight, governments govern, economic systems function, citizens are public spirited. We intervened massively in a country where none of this pertained. The overall reason we have suffered so much failure is that on every level—political, military, economic, psychological—Vietnam was in a state of anarchy.
>
> This is also why Vietnam represents a considerable failure of American journalism. It is not that our reporters are less able than they used to be, any more than our military men, diplomats or economists are less able; all are probably *more* able than in past wars. It is simply that the human mind cannot assemble so many disparate factors into a coherent pattern.[82]

American journalists could not clarify a pattern they could not discern; the difficulty of combining war reports with social and cultural analysis, identified by Malcolm Browne in 1964, remained.

Despite the president's efforts to reassure the American public that his Vietnam policies were justifiable, staff members increasingly sensed that, as press aide Tom Johnson concluded, "the administration is not getting its story out about Vietnam."[83] As a result, "the American people and the American press are skeptical, cynical, and—more often than not—uninformed." Aide Johnson and his colleague Kintner cited casualty reports, concern over possible troop increases, the belief that the war caused higher prices and higher taxes, poor daily public-information practices in Saigon, and a lack of coordination among the governmental information staff as sources of the problem. Their brainstorming spawned a variety of suggestions: "a spectacular domestic action" to offset war concerns; a Vietnam Information Coordinating Group to provide "a coherent, effective government information flow" and to anticipate weaknesses and potential trouble spots; the encouragement of favorable spokespeople to be available for television interviews and for speeches in Congress and elsewhere; and even the development of "a group of people to plant items, articles, etc., favorable to the President." Kintner reluctantly rejected the final idea as too dangerous and too expensive, given that most public relations firms "are wedded to Republican interests or charge too much."[84]

Elaborating on the need "to make satisfactory interviewees available" for the media, staff member Peter Benchley underscored the calls for better communication on the war with a report about television newscasts which he had monitored at Christian's request.[85] The aide concluded that CBS and NBC in particular "did little to balance their broadcasts," regardless of whether the attacks on Johnson's policies came from hawks or from doves. It was up to the administration to make the networks aware of congressional leaders and others who could speak on its behalf so that the White House received fair coverage.

Getting fair coverage concerned both staff members and friends of the administration, who found a marked contrast between the Johnson they knew and the Johnson of the press. Described by one university president as the difference between "a strong, decisive leader [and] . . . a man overtaken by events," the disparity was attributed to the media's "filtering" process.[86] The observer found the root of the problem in Vietnam, which had taken on "the dismal spectacle of a giant helplessly entrapped by a pigmy." The American people did not cotton to an image of themselves as stymied by a Third World nation, and the situation in Vietnam seemed like an all-too-elongated Panama Canal crisis.

Congressional members were well aware of this frustration, which in part explained the absence of pro-administration statements on the nightly news. Senator Joe Tydings of Maryland explained the problem to McPherson in terms the president could understand all too well. In the past a supporter of Johnson's Vietnam policies, Tydings now found the issue to be "a political albatross": the North Vietnamese

> aren't going to quit because we bomb them, and the South Vietnamese are still miles away from running an adequate show in the South. . . . People are so frustrated and negative in Maryland that any reasonably good Republican could clobber me this year and probably next. . . . Every political advisor I have says the only way I can save myself is by attacking the President. I won't do that, but it's going to be tough.[87]

McPherson, whose own disquiet about Vietnam had been intensified by his trip there in May, concluded his report of the remarks of Tydings by saying that "Birch Bayh, Fred Harris, Ed Muskie, and Phil Hart all have the same story to tell about their states. It is Vietnam, Vietnam." Johnson met with these senators in the weeks following, but he could see the ominous potential of this political reading: it presaged an evaporation of visible support on the war, the possible defeat of congressional allies for his foreign and domestic legislation, and a difficult campaign for the president himself. At the same time, when the Senate Preparedness Subcommittee opened hearings to investigate the effectiveness of the air war, Johnson knew that such key members as Stennis, Byrd, and Thurmond opposed the limitations on the bombing. In the opinion of the Pentagon Papers' authors, it was "surely no coincidence" that Johnson expanded armed reconnaissance and named sixteen new targets on the opening day of the hearings.[88] It was, as McPherson admitted to John Fischer of *Harper's*, "a hell of a dilemma."[89]

Few would argue that it was a dilemma; the question was how best to handle it. John P. Roche, a professor of politics at Brandeis University who followed Eric Goldman as Johnson's "intellectual in residence," believed that the best defense was a good offense. He sent the president a copy of a letter that Abraham Lincoln had sent to "a group of peaceniks," as Roche phrased it, for by analogy it countered recent criticism of Johnson "for suggesting that dissent on the war plays into the hands of Ho Chi Minh."[90] Prompted by Lincoln's letter, Roche argued that Johnson should not be accused of "wishing to suppress dissent" when he was simply "pointing out the natural and logical consequences of action," contrary to the interpretations of Deakin and other journalists.

While Roche assured Johnson of his propriety in chastising dissenters, others continued the search for a way to make America understand the need for a limited war in Vietnam. Early in the year Democratic adviser James Rowe had recommended that Johnson establish "a new program of explanations about why we are in Vietnam—based on self-interest and long-term security and not on legalistic grounds."[91] The moral obligations of international affairs held little sway with the public, Rowe implied; they must see how the conflict affects their own interests. The confidant of FDR and Truman counseled the president to help citizens comprehend two aspects about Vietnam:

> He should . . . attempt to get the people to accept some measures
> of progress in the war other than lines on a map—the traditional
> way they have been taught to measure progress or retreat in World
> Wars I and II, and Korea. He should also get across to the people
> the concept of the will to fight—that so long as the enemy in
> Southeast Asia believes there is the slightest chance that we will
> tire of the war and pull out, he will hang on. The problem is to
> convince the enemy that not only the President, but the American
> people also will stay and fight.

The concept of progress in a guerrilla war and the power of a determination to fight were in Rowe's eyes critical to the public's understanding of the administration's policies; the absence of such understanding constituted a major obstacle for the president.

Johnson's reaction to Rowe's memorandum is unrecorded, but the emphasis which the veteran politician placed on arguments of self-interest resurfaced eight months later in a form that captured the president's attention. Harry McPherson summarized for Johnson a conversation that he had with Albert Carr, an economist under Truman who had defended the president's policies in well-placed letters to the editor. McPherson recounted Carr's assessment of the problem: "people still can't get it deeply in their bones that we *ought* to be in Vietnam."[92] They couldn't conceive of "a ragtag revolutionary like Ho" attacking the West Coast; claims of defending democracy were inconsistent with the perception of South Vietnam as "a semi-country run by a junta of generals"; and the domino theory seemed farfetched. These standard explanations did not seem to justify American involvement to the public, but Carr proposed one that he believed would: that communist domination of Southeast Asia, close on the heels of the fall of South Vietnam, would strain Japanese and British economies, potentially leading to wars that would involve China, Russia, and the United States. In other words, the Carr-McPherson case outlined, "we are fighting a small war to keep from fighting a Third World War."

McPherson strongly endorsed Carr's proposal, and in his memorandum to the president he countered the objection he knew would come to Johnson's mind first:

> I know it seems we have used a million words to explain our presence there. But an awful lot of people—I would say over half the people—don't feel secure in the answers they have been given. . . .
> If it takes a task force to write such speeches [as Carr proposed], perhaps we should get started now. The theme should not be more "defending freedom" for a "little country that only wants to chart its own course." That, to an increasing number of people, is not worth 500,000 Americans, thousands of casualties, and $25 billion annually. A straight argument that our vital interests are involved, and why, might turn a lot of opinions around.

The "straight argument" that McPherson recommended was one of prevention: "we are fighting a small war to keep from fighting a Third World War." Only by showing that national interests were at stake in Vietnam could the administration build an effective case. In other words, McPherson advised a shift from an argument from justice to an argument from expediency: it wasn't that we *ought* to fight but that we *had* to fight in Vietnam.

Johnson agreed that the prevention of another world war constituted a powerful rationale for his policies; it was precisely that threat that had led to the peculiar fight-it-but-not-with-all-you've-got stance of limited war. Upon reading McPherson's memorandum, he responded, "I agree. Everybody should work full time the next few days."

"The next few days" turned into a month as various staff members contributed to the development of this new line of argument. During that month a battle for dominant rationales ensued. As McPherson pushed for a new argument from expediency, Rostow held out for the argument from justice. For example, Rostow provided two compilations of comments, one taken from statements by Asian leaders in support of the United States presence in Vietnam and the other from

John F. Kennedy's statements on Southeast Asia.[93] The latter, noted the national security adviser, would assure his successor that no "objective person can read this record without knowing that President Kennedy would have seen this through whatever the cost." Highlighting "the most significant passages" in yellow, with "red markings for items particularly quotable," Rostow reported that the basic elements of Kennedy's position were all consistent with the policy of the Johnson administration: "his explicit linkage of the commitment in Viet Nam to the SEATO Treaty; his flat acceptance of the domino theory in Southeast Asia; . . . his recurring linkage of Viet Nam to Berlin; and the general theme that the fate of our own liberty was involved in Viet Nam."

Rostow's use of such phrases as "seeing it through whatever the cost" indicated that the adviser did not altogether concur with McPherson's recommendations about the public's misgivings. Yet each of the two staff members had presented what the president felt to be a reasonable view. The development of this key address thus became the testing ground within the White House over public handling of the topic of Vietnam.

In a typically Johnsonian speech-writing procedure, McPherson worked on one draft of the speech while Rostow joined efforts with three other staff members on another; then they exchanged drafts. Reiterating his belief that "our own security . . . is the only justification people will buy now," McPherson criticized the Rostow version for its reliance on ambiguous rationales.[94] To warn vaguely of the danger that "the structure of order" might "erode" without American support was, the aide argued, insufficient: "I don't think people care much about structures of order eroding. I think they care about whether they will get into a big war later if they don't do something about a small war now."[95] Rostow's response to McPherson's critique is unrecorded in the available files.

Johnson had to decide which arguments to advance once he elected to use as his forum an address to the National Legislative Conference in San Antonio on September 29. Eventually Johnson chose to keep his options open by incorporating both the Rostow and the McPherson rationales to articulate what would become known as the San Antonio formula, presented one month after the Carr-McPherson proposal.

At the last minute the president also chose to allow live broadcasts of the speech. The address had not been planned as a televised message; even as late as the day before the speech, McPherson provided the president with drafts that had alternative introductions, depending on whether or not "you go on nationwide TV."[96] In fact, the decision to broadcast came so late that only NBC carried the address live, with the lack of forewarning causing uncharacteristically poor coverage for the president. Yet Johnson responded to what Lady Bird termed a "chorus these days, 'You've got to keep telling the people— go on TV'": he turned the San Antonio presentation into his first televised statement on Vietnam since the remarks he had recorded for broadcast after the Manila conference eleven months earlier.[97]

With this decision came a new phase in the president's approach to justifying the war in Vietnam. In the San Antonio speech, he preserved his Johns Hopkins formulation of United States involvement as the defense of Vietnamese freedom in the face of Northern aggression, but he incorporated a new emphasis on American security as the primary reason for that presence in Southeast Asia. "The key to all that we have done," Johnson advised in San Antonio, "is really our own security."[98] America's reaction to turmoil in other lands could not rest on a determination of its effect on "the immediate victim" alone, but on the risk it poses "to the United States of America and to the peace and security of the entire world of which we are a very vital part." The Johns Hopkins speech, in April of 1965, had presented Americans and Asians who were "dying for a world where each people may choose its own path to change." In contrast, September of 1967 found the United States battling the spread of communism throughout Vietnam, Laos, Thailand, Burma, and Indonesia to prevent the domino effect from bringing communism—and a third world war—to the United States.

On that September night, Johnson acknowledged that many people had "passionate convictions about the wisest course for our nation to follow," and that this included "many sincere and patriotic Americans who harbor doubts about sustaining the commitment that three Presidents and a half a million of our young men have made." This constituted an acknowledgment of doubt that Rostow's group had deleted from one draft of the speech but that McPherson contended was "the most obvious political truth about the situation" and could not be avoided. Even so, the acknowledgment retains Rostow's kind of emphasis on the commitment that had been made. Yet, Johnson insisted in the address, there had been "progress in the war itself, steady progress considering the war that we are fighting; rather dramatic progress considering the situation that actually prevailed when we sent our troops there in 1965." The qualification placed on the kind of progress that had been achieved was another item deleted by Rostow and his associates; it was restored when

McPherson warned that to claim "dramatic progress [alone] . . . will certainly make headlines and get us into a shooting match with correspondents out of Vietnam. Maybe we can win it," McPherson said darkly. "I hope we can."[99] The admonition sealed the passage's fate; as with the Johns Hopkins speech, a concern about media reactions influenced the language and tone of the address.

Given this progress, Johnson set forth the San Antonio formula:

> As we have told Hanoi time and time again, the heart of the matter is really this: The United States is willing to stop all aerial and naval bombardment of North Vietnam when this will lead promptly to productive discussions. We, of course, assume that while discussions proceed, North Vietnam would not take advantage of the bombing cessation or limitation.
>
> But Hanoi has not accepted any of these proposals.
>
> So it is by Hanoi's choice—and not ours, and not the rest of the world's—that the war continues.

Despite the speech's claim that the proposal had been made "time and time again," the San Antonio formula contained new elements. As Johnson himself later observed, it did not demand restricted North Vietnamese military action as a prerequisite to a bombing halt, nor did it ask for cessation of the action during such a pause, as his February letter to Ho Chi Minh had. Rather, "all we asked was that a cessation of bombing would lead promptly to peace talks and that those talks would be 'productive.'"[100]

In light of both this willingness to open discussions and this political and military progress in South Vietnam, why would the North Vietnamese persist in their war efforts? It was, Johnson informed his audience, because "they still hope that the people of the United States will not see this struggle through to the very end." Following Rowe's prescription concerning "the will to fight," however, the president assured them that

> I think they are wrong. I think it is the common failing of totalitarian regimes that they cannot really understand the nature of our democracy:
>   —They mistake dissent for disloyalty.
>   —They mistake restlessness for a rejection of policy.
>   —They mistake a few committees for a country.
>   —They misjudge individual speeches for public policy.

Johnson stressed that it was thus imperative, especially for those "brave men" in Vietnam who were "willing to risk their lives for their nation's security," that Americans recognize that

> we must not mislead the enemy. Let him not think that debate and dissent will produce wavering and withdrawal. For I can assure you they won't. Let him not think that protests will produce surrender. Because they won't. Let him not think that he will wait us out. For he won't.

Implicitly, then, the president informed his country that the only way to get Hanoi to the negotiating table was to unite behind the administration and their men in Vietnam. Following Roche's advice, Johnson decided to delineate the "natural and logical consequences" of dissent; following McPherson's, he made the primary consequence a threat to national security. While he clearly distinguished dissent from disloyalty in one section, the overall temper of the address strongly linked the two. Thus once again Johnson struggled to find an effective way to explain Vietnam and to forge a consensus out of the disparate viewpoints that existed even within his own administration. Like the Johns Hopkins speech, the San Antonio address tried to incorporate something to please everyone. As the skirmishes in the development of the address and the various strategies of appeal in the final speech would indicate, Johnson was himself still searching for the right combination of arguments—South Vietnamese liberty, national security, patriotic loyalty—to justify the limited war.

Responses to the San Antonio speech were what Horace Busby, out of the White House but still in touch with Johnson, characterized as "a curiously affirmative reaction: 'curious' in that I have encountered little negative reaction, even from hostile quarters, but, rather, comments crediting the President with 'sincerity.' "[101] Staff member Ernest Goldstein, in reporting the assessment of his brother at Yale, confirmed that "in the academic community the doves had an affirmative reaction to your speech."[102] Some disagreement remained, certainly, but there was "no question concerning your great sincerity and dedication. In every sense the speech came through very directly from you to each viewer. It was, in my opinion, a first-rate use of television." Goldstein did not mention the limited live coverage.

These reports reassured Johnson, who told a news conference the day after his speech that "I tried to discuss the general Government policy and to explain to all the people some of the things that I felt had not gotten through to them."[103] Several members of the media felt that Johnson met with some success in that goal; *Time*, for example, praised the address as "a hard-hitting speech, briskly delivered without any overtones of Johnson's weary-preacher style."[104] In two cases media support for the San Antonio address drew the direct attention of the president: Ralph McHugh's column for the Copley press led Watson to view the bureau chief as "worth cultivating," which Johnson did by ordering him "to be invited to some White House functions"; and the *Washington Star*'s editorial spurred Johnson to write a letter of appreciation and to inquire of his staff, "Could we know all the Star staff better—Horner is a model of accuracy and good judgment and I think it would be helpful for us to know more about each other."[105]

In addition to the positive media responses, the American ambassador to England told Johnson's staff that he felt the speech was "one of the very best he had done," and two-thirds of the people sending telegrams to the White House expressed approval.[106] A couple in Aldan, Pennsylvania, wired the president, "God Bless You—Keep up the good work," while A. G. Magee of Charleston, West Virginia, told him, "I support your Vietnam policy 100 percent."[107]

Yet among the responses coming to the Oval Office was a telegram from Joseph Rous of Illinois, who scolded: "Fool me once, shame on you. Fool me twice, shame on me." Rous's sentiments joined those of Kenneth Hines of New York, who wired: "Yak yak yak yak yak yak yak yak yak yak yak yak yak yak yak."

Such reactions were not limited to telegrams. The former speech writer who had coined the phrase "the Great Society" was not convinced by the speech, either; Richard Goodwin assumed an increasingly vociferous stance against Johnson's policies that fall.[108] Nor was *Life* magazine convinced, as it adopted a new editorial position that set White House aides to yearning for the strong support of the war expressed by publisher Henry Luce just a year earlier.[109]

In the months after the San Antonio speech, antiwar demonstrations continued. The capital saw major rallies in October, with signs saying "Hitler is Alive—in the White House," buttons demanding "Sterilize LBJ—no more ugly children," and posters asking "Lee Harvey Oswald, where are you now that we need you?" Protesters at Williams College walked out as Lady Bird Johnson opened the Center for Environmental Studies, and dissenters picketed her visit to the Yale Political Union. Their actions left the first lady regretful that she had served as "their bait" to "provide a vehicle for the dissenters, who were a minority, to mount a platform, to get inches in the paper and minutes on the television screen that they would not have gotten without me."[110]

The president himself encountered some of this discontent when, in anticipation of Johnson's attendance at Sunday services, the Reverend Cotesworth Pinckney Lewis turned his sermon at the old Bruton Parish Episcopal Church of Williamsburg into an exploration of Vietnam. "There is a rather general consensus that something is wrong in Vietnam," the minister intoned; "we wonder if some logical straightforward explanation might be given? . . . While pledging our loyalty, we humbly ask: 'Why?' " The Reverend Lewis denied any intention to criticize Johnson as he distributed copies of the sermon to the press; the first lady restricted her remarks to "wonderful choir"; and the president, who shook hands briefly with the minister, later declared, "Greater love hath no man than that he goes to the Episcopal Church with his wife!"[111]

As Johnson encountered increasing opposition to his policies on Vietnam, as he saw its effects on his family, as he saw a pall settle over his Great Society, his thoughts turned increasingly to the question of running again in 1968. His staff and political advisers provided a steady stream of assessments on the next elections. Even though McPherson had already warned of the senators' sense of the war as a political albatross, Rowe disputed the thesis that the 1966 vote indicated diminished support for either the administration or Vietnam. The ever-aggressive Roche urged the president to "build an effective national political organization" and to "forget (not *forgive*) the whole Kennedy caper," while he advised other aides to prepare rapid, pungent replies to Republican attacks: "to hell with statistics and detail; sock them in the *cohones* with choice *ad hominem* barbs."[112] Kintner had already advised the retention of Doyle Dane Bernbach as an agency that could handle Johnson's advertising account "enthusiastically, confidentially, and well," while Mary Wells should not be approached "because of past leaks" concerning her role as "image-maker" for the 1964 campaign.[113]

Always a man who preferred to keep his options open, Johnson's knowledge of the physical strain of the office and his awareness of the lack of consensus in the nation made the choice of stepping down an enticing one. As his wife observed, "it would be so easy, so tempting, to—as I have heard him say—let the armchair critics save each other, announce now he is not going to be a candidate, draw a circle for our energies, our brains, our hours, around our family, our business, our personal friends, and have fun in what is left to us of our life."[114] Yet resolving the problems, proving his critics wrong, and refusing to relinquish his duties in a time of trial beckoned strongly to the politician who prided himself on being a "can-do" man, one who turned ideals into realities and upheld his pledges. The fall of 1967 was filled with lengthy discussions debating the merits of each course of action with his wife, with friend and Texas governor John Connally, with physician Jim Cain, with lawyer and associate Abe Fortas, with press secretary George Christian and others.

The debate of the man who cherished consensus was sharpened by the country's political climate, as he sensed "a tidal wave of stories, murmurs, whispers, that create distrust, frustration, and uncertainty . . . and has borne pernicious fruit."[115] The tone of coverage had indeed grown more strident as fall turned into the winter of 1967. Two reporters, William McGaffin and Erwin Knoll, published an article headlining "The White House Lies"; various publications pointed to the "widening" credibility gap; and "two angry professors," spurred on by the media's phrase and their accounts of deception, marketed a credibility-gap game, complete with "a Citizens' playing deck and an Administration pack of lies, 4 liberty-bell counters, 90 truth trophies, dice, rules, and a colorful game board," all for only $5.95.[116]

Journalists received more grist for the media mill with highly visible and vocal attacks on Johnson's handling of Vietnam. Reviving the "peace feeler" furor from earlier in the year, Bobby Kennedy contended that in their February 9 meeting Johnson had tensely asserted that the war would be won in six months; Kennedy went on to charge that the administration had ignored opportunities that winter to open the negotiations which would have brought about an end to the conflict. The charge gained both ink and airtime, as well as an indignant call to refute the story from Rostow to Marquis Childs of the *St. Louis Post-Dispatch*.[117] Yet Richard Goodwin echoed the accusation on television when he appeared on the premier segment of "Face to Face," hosted by Evans and Novak; the former speech writer claimed that "the Administration has failed to take advantage from 1964 until this winter of three or four major opportunities for negotiation."[118]

The White House tackled these charges. The credibility gap received the close attention of Goldstein, Panzer, and Christian, who outlined a forty-two-page refutation of the accusations. Conceiving of the document as the basis for "a long article authored by a prominent public figure and published in a major magazine," its authors urged immediate action: "unless checked now, the Credibility Gap will be a major campaign issue."[119] Will Sparks then added a fifteen-page rebuttal of McGaffin and Knoll's article. Roche supplemented these highly confidential efforts with the suggestion that Cyrus Vance, deputy secretary of defense, represent the administration on a National Educational Television panel about the credibility gap. The aide contended that Vance would be especially good because of his knowledge of Vietnam, and "this is a battle we have to fight with the first team."[120]

In the meantime, the aides comforted themselves with the reassurance that not everyone perceived such a gap, even if their compatriots were English rather than American, and they assured the president that he was not the only politician with a gap.[121] McPherson told of Kennedy's efforts to achieve commonality with his New York audiences as he campaigned for senator, which sometimes moved him to renounce his Massachusetts birthplace by declaring, "I was born here." "What's worse," McPherson asked his employer, "a great-grandfather who didn't fight at the Alamo, or a Senatorial candidate who wasn't born where he said he was?"

The Alamo remark still had the potential to harm Johnson's credibility, as Goldstein insisted when he discovered the proposal to exclude the reference from the official presidential-papers version of the remarks at Camp Stanley. To delete the well-publicized misstatement, warned the aide, would only "reopen the entire affair and provide further ammunition for those who would argue that we are rewriting history."[122] He predicted that the ensuing controversy would prove especially harmful in the next campaign. His admonition was heeded, for the Camp Stanley comments appear in full. Rather than the footnote which Goldstein had suggested saying that Johnson's great-uncle had fought at San Jacinto, the item ends with an editorial remark that is unobtrusive except for its inconsistency with other notations in the president's *Public Papers*: it offered the information that Johnson "spoke extemporaneously" and that the item was taken from "the text released by the Office of the White House Press Secretary, Seoul, Korea." Both serve as implicit explanations for the president's fervor regarding his family at the Alamo.

In addition to marshalling these counterattacks concerning the credibility gap, the administration sought to encourage wide distribution of its message using a variety of channels. Aides "discreetly" gave documents on the Viet Cong to Joseph Alsop, who responded with seven columns echoing the San Antonio depiction of American progress which would continue "provided the home front does not fail the U.S. soldiers in the line at the very moment when the first great favorable turning point has . . . been reached."[123] They gloated over a *Look* essay by Edwin O. Reishhauser which supported

American involvement in the war; it was proclaimed to be "good stuff—from the right source: a Kennedy-type intellectual, a man of peace, an Asian expert."[124] Staff members also explored proposals for television exposure, including a public-broadcasting program by Ed Morgan with Humphrey or Bundy as "an Administration spokesman who would set forth our attitude to the war and the public impatience with the war," and a monthly report on Vietnam featuring Johnson, Bunker, and Westmoreland.[125] The final suggestion, McPherson told the president, would " 'de-politicize' your reports on Vietnam—to make you more of a commander-in-chief, and less of a beleaguered political figure trying to defend what is happening." While those involved were enthusiastic, a lack of network interest apparently killed the idea.

In addition to encouraging these supportive statements, the White House also countered versions of the war and the political scene that they found unacceptable. Several of these forays, such as the challenges of public opinion polls, were directed from the Oval Office. On the president's orders, Panzer ghosted five letters to enable unnamed others to complain about Gallup's proposed pairings for the 1968 Republican ticket; he backgrounded journalists on the proper interpretation of Gallup and Harris poll results, as Johnson requested; he called Gallup on the use of month-old statistics; and he pointed out that basic contradictions in the tallies demonstrated that "it is difficult for them to tell a complicated story of how the public feels" about Vietnam.[126] In Panzer's analysis, a poll said little when it showed that 63 percent favored a continuation of the bombing until North Vietnam agreed to negotiate, and yet 58 percent of the sample disapproved of Johnson's handling of the war: "in other words, a majority disapproves of the very same policy it approves." The aide's interpretation of the contradiction was that "while people favor bombing versus stopping the bombing, they just don't like the war"; he promised the president that he would contact Gallup and Harris to discuss the matter.

Johnson directed Panzer to defuse the polls; he asked Rostow to go after critics of the war. One result was a half-inch-thick document entitled, "A Response to Senator Case's Attack on the Administration's Handling of Vietnam," as a reply to charges from the Republican from New Jersey.[127] Another Rostow effort was an exchange of letters with *Newsweek* about a story with a dismal portrayal of the South Vietnamese army. In mid-October, Kay Graham wrote to Rostow that her White House correspondent, Chalmers Roberts, had reported the president's charge that "*Newsweek* editors had distorted the story in our October eighth issue about the quality of the ARVN—according to our Saigon bureau." She enclosed a cable from her Saigon correspondents saying that the story not only was correct but "could have been much tougher" if space constraints had not dictated shortening the article. Rostow then sent the cable to Johnson, asking permission to show Graham a government evaluation of the ARVN's improvement which Rostow termed "quite a contrast to the shallow journalism of *Newsweek*." Permission granted, Rostow then sent the document to Graham, observing that "the simple fact is the report from two responsible officials in Saigon has them [the two *Newsweek* correspondents] saying something different from what they say to you."[128]

Johnson was, as Lady Bird observed one evening, "in a fighting mood."[129] He encouraged Panzer to elaborate on his idea for "a pause in the bombing of the President," first suggested in a writers' meeting and then developed into a speech at Johnson's request.[130] The campaign would begin with the bipartisan support already expressed by Democrat Claude Pepper and Republican Robert Taft on the floor of the House; this would be combined with support from such groups as labor unions, the National Association of Manufacturers, the U.S. Chamber of Commerce, the American Legion, and the Committee for Responsible Patriotism. The demonstrators' chants of "Hey, hey, LBJ, how many kids did you kill today?" would joust with such slogans as "Halt the howling—for 30 days" and "Don't let our vocal chords work for the Viet Cong." While Panzer admitted that some of the slogans sounded "wild," he argued: "so do the opposition's."

As Johnson directed these efforts, his spirit of political activity was rejuvenated. He was further encouraged by his session on November 1 with the "Wise Men," an informal advisory group of former high government advisers and officials, who assessed the military situation in Vietnam to be generally satisfactory. Their key concern lay in the realm of public opinion: the administration needed a better program to ensure public appreciation of American goals and successes. His own fighting mood thus fueled by the views of his distinguished advisers, Johnson launched in on a public defense of the war with an energy, vigor, and visibility that surpassed his effort of the spring. He would reiterate, for the Reverend Cotesworth Pinckney Lewis and all others who asked Why?, the progress that had been made in South Vietnam, the latitude of the San Antonio offer to North Vietnam, and the necessity of the American presence in Southeast Asia.

One forum for this spirited defense was a Friday afternoon reception for fifty CBS reporters and executives in Washington for a seminar on defense. The White House staff showed up in force to talk with the guests and then file reports on their conversations. Rostow, for example, discussed the situation in South Vietnam and the significance of the San Antonio formula; and Cater talked about media coverage, leading one executive to note that he was "appalled at the simplicity" of editorial coverage on the war by many stations. Yet Johnson's appearance before the group was the key; it struck those present as "a wholly new view" of the president. "Why," they asked, "can't he do that on television?"[131] His supporters had long lamented that he could not reach the public on the issue of Vietnam as he could individuals; as Lady Bird wrote, "I only wish he could reach two hundred million Americans with those simple, vivid pictures."[132]

In a televised press conference on November 17, 1967, he did so. The conversational man came across on camera. Using a lapel microphone and walking among the audience rather than remaining formally on the podium, Lyndon Johnson poured his heart into a defense of his policies in Vietnam in a way that startled and delighted his aides, impressed the media, and stunned his opposition. "People were affected," one speech writer savored. "He got across, really got across."[133] Kintner, who had struggled so with the Johnsonian style of televised delivery, glowed that it was "a masterpiece" that showed "the President as he is: persuasive, sincere, knowledgeable, and articulate."[134]

The other side of the political fence was equally impressed. Ray Price, an aide to Richard Nixon, assessed this new style as a real advantage for their competitor:

> What really brought it off so stunningly was that he was no longer trying to formulate sentences in a precise and guarded manner; he gave the impression of being no longer self-conscious about his *manner* of expression, but rather seemed to have his mind fixed on the thing he was talking *about*. It was this apparent unselfconsciousness that unleashed the power of the man.[135]

In unleashing that power, added Nixon adviser William Gavin, the press conference showed "the real LBJ rather than the pious hypocrite we've grown accustomed to."[136]

Johnson's conference included an impassioned acknowledgment of the difficulties he faced in gaining the public's understanding of the situation in Southeast Asia. "When we get in a contest of any kind— whether it is in a war, an election, a football game, or whatever it is," he observed, the American people "want it decided and decided quickly; get in or get out." He continued:

> They like that curve to rise like this [indicating a sharp rise] and they like the opposition to go down like this [indicating a sharply declining line].
>
> That is not the kind of war we are fighting in Vietnam. . . . It is a new kind of war for us. So it doesn't move that fast. . . .
>
> We are moving more like this [indicating gradual rise]. They are moving more like this [indicating decline], instead of straight up and straight down.[137]

"But overall," he assured his audience, "we are making progress"; the United States was keeping the commitments that had been made.

Having defended his approach to the war, despite the public impatience with his tactics, Johnson then clarified his view of dissenters, in an echo of the San Antonio address. He denied charges that he had declared protestors to be unpatriotic, contending that

> there is a great deal of difference . . . between criticism, indifference, and responsible dissent—all of which we insist on and all of which we protect—and storm trooper bullying, throwing yourself down in the road, smashing windows, rowdyism, and every time a person attempts to speak to try to drown him out.
>
> We believe very strongly in preserving the right to differ in this country, and the right to dissent. If I have done a good job of anything since I have been President, it is to insure that there are plenty of dissenters.
>
> I am amazed that the press in this country, who insist on the right to live by the first amendment, and to be protected by it, doesn't insist that these storm trooper tactics live by the first amendment, too, and that they be wiped out.

"Responsible dissent," Johnson contended, should not be confused with "some of the things that are taking place in this country which I consider to be extremely dangerous to our national interest, and I consider not very helpful to the men who are fighting the war for us." Never an enthusiast of mass demonstrations, whether the issue was civil rights or the war in Vietnam, Johnson felt that patriotic action and such political efforts as lobbying were the most appropriate and effective paths to follow; the media should not provide any encouragement for irresponsible protest.

That energetic news conference brought rave reviews from aides, congressional leaders, the public, and the press. Mail to the White House was almost unanimously favorable; the *Chicago Daily News* headlined "His Best Press Conference: Real LBJ Finally Cuts Loose"; and NBC scheduled a half-hour special on "the new Johnson" that same evening. The most picturesque response came from a former student of Goldstein's, who allowed that Johnson "came through as directly as if you were campaigning off a flat bed truck in Burleson County with Brazos mud oozing through your toes."[138]

Even such a vigorous and impressive performance proved short-lived in its effectiveness. By the end of the month two major events drew media attention to criticism of the war. First came the resignation of Robert McNamara as secretary of defense, as he left to serve as president of the World Bank. His departure, announced by the president on November 29, caught Washington by surprise and prompted a flurry of stories speculating about why he would step down then rather than waiting until the end of Johnson's term. Versions of the episode differ sharply: at one end of the spectrum McNamara reached his own decision to leave and had Johnson's every assistance in locating a new position, while at the other the boss notified all 107 World Bank representatives of the nomination before he informed the startled and embittered secretary.

In a story appearing the day after Johnson's announcement, Reston summarized the "two contradictory and fascinating explanations" that predominated in Washington:

> The first, which appeals to this conspiratorial town, especially in the poisonous mood of the moment, is that the President is "dumping" Mr. McNamara, who is less of a danger to him than the Pentagon and Saigon generals who have differed with Mr. McNamara in the past and could easily differ with him, with embarrassing political consequences, during the Presidential election campaign of 1968.
>
> The other goes to the underestimated side of Lyndon Johnson, which is intensely human, which rewards loyalty as the first rule of political life, which recognizes the human pressures on an intense Secretary of Defense who is trying to ride herd on the Pentagon and still deal with his rising company of Congressional opponents at the same time.[139]

As Reston observed, the former interpretation was by far the most popular; Kay Graham, for example, disdained the president's getting "rid of McNamara in that really terrible way."[140] Certainly McNamara had spent seven years in that pressure cooker of a post. Yet his disenchantment with the conduct of the war, well outlined in the Defense Department history that he commissioned, undoubtedly also entered into his departure. Johnson acknowledged in his memoirs that he had turned down McNamara's October 31 proposals to announce stabilization of the American combat forces, to cut back on bombardment of Hanoi, and to institute a major bombing halt before the end of the year. He also acknowledged that he took the rare step of outlining in a memorandum for the record his reasons for his opposition to McNamara's proposals, a step not taken until December 18, 1967, after the stories of dissension had broken. Yet he separated this discussion from the question of the secretary's departure by 350 pages.[141]

Despite Johnson's rejection of the story that McNamara was fired, contemporary press accounts viewed McNamara as the victim of internal politics and anticipated an increasingly hawkish stance concerning the war.

The media scarcely had time to broadcast the news of McNamara's departure before the second major event demanded coverage: on November 30, Senator Eugene McCarthy of Minnesota announced his intention to enter the upcoming presidential primaries. McCarthy's decision to challenge the incumbent of his own party, he declared, was predicated upon President Johnson's "evident intention to escalate and to intensify the war in Vietnam," coupled with "the absence of any positive indication or suggestion for a compromise or for a negotiated political settlement."[142]

The senator's prospects of winning the Democratic nomination appeared remote at best. Yet the significance of McCarthy's candidacy lay not in its chances of success but in its symbolic challenge to the incumbent's policies on Vietnam. The quixotic campaign underscored the intensity of the opposition to the war which Johnson had faced from Democrats since Morse and Gruening first raised their voices in protest; the president's house was publicly and indisputably divided.

In the face of these developments, Johnson continued his high-visibility defense of the war through the last month of 1967. He called another news conference for December 4, but it fell short of the November 17 performance. He refused to wear the lavalier mike again despite Christian's encouragement, returning to the security of the massive podium dubbed "Mother"; to make matters worse, he toyed distractedly with the podium's microphone. "This wasn't one of the better news conferences," the press secretary concluded, because "some of the reporters got the impression the President wasn't in much of a mood to answer questions."[143] Many answers were crisp and clipped; when one reporter requested information on the circumstances surrounding McNamara's departure, the response was this: "I think the best explanation of my viewpoint is in that statement [released on November 29]. I told just exactly what happened in that statement."[144]

Yet Johnson did not cease; he then took his case before the annual convention of the AFL-CIO on December 12. In nationally televised remarks, the president contrasted antiwar demonstrations with the efforts of those who had "left their homes to risk their lives for liberty and freedom in Vietnam":

> Oh, it is very easy to agonize over the television or to moralize or to pin your heart on your sleeve or a placard on your back—and think to yourself that you are helping somebody stop a war.
>
> But I only wish that those who bewail war would bring me just one workable solution to end the war.
>
> The peacemakers are out there in the field.[145]

"I am not going to be inflamed," Johnson warned the convention, "by a bunch of political, selfish men who want to advance their own interests. I am going to continue . . . doing my duty as I see it for the best of all my country, regardless of my polls or regardless of the election." The San Antonio rationale of American national security all but disappeared as Johnson enthusiastically returned to the more idealistic rationale of South Vietnamese liberty and an attack on dissenters, which attracted more attention than the rest of the address. While Johnson could see McPherson's point about the need for a more pragmatic approach for public understanding of the war when the aide had provided his carefully developed arguments in September, the president's more deeply engrained reactions favored the Rostow line, as became apparent in subsequent months. The change of justification, which seemed promising in the San Antonio address, never clearly emerged as the administration's primary argument because Johnson did not fully accept it as such himself.

Johnson's next step to defend his policies had been advocated by aides for almost four years: he agreed to a "Conversation with the President," using the same format as the well-received "Conversation" of March 16, 1964. While staff members from Cater to Kintner had urged Johnson to repeat his informal interview with representatives of the three networks, Jack Valenti presented the case that convinced him to do the program. The former special assistant ticked off four reasons why December demanded the show: the need for a boost in the polls, the success of the November 17 press conference, the opportunity to detract from McCarthy's announcement, and the loss of free broadcasts without equal time for Republicans in the rapidly approaching election year.[146] The president rose to the challenge, penning "Talk to George [Christian] & Frank [Stanton]—I'm ready," and the interview was taped on December 18.

In one segment of the program, Frank Reynolds of ABC explored the implication in Johnson's remarks of the evening and elsewhere that the media encouraged dissenters by providing them with coverage. The president contended that "a good part of every newscast you have will have some of these folks who are encouraging the dissent, appealing to them. They will be parading. They will have their signs." Asked by Reynolds if he was saying that the media gave "a disproportionate share of attention to this," Johnson denied such an interpretation, saying, "I think it is a matter for your judgment. I don't think it is up to the President to be making up your newscasts."

Despite this denial, Johnson frequently linked dissenters with the media, as he had in his press conference of November 17. In addition, staff members sometimes encouraged this interpretation, as when Fred Panzer advised Johnson that David Brinkley served as a "transmission belt" for the protestors' attempts to blame a demonstration that got out of hand on "an unruly minority."[147]

As the tape of "Conversation with the President" went on the air, Johnson himself had departed on the trip that capped his energetic advocacy of late 1967. What started as a trip to Australia for the memorial service for Prime Minister Harold Holt turned into what AP's Frank Cormier termed "the most bizarre presidential journey ever recorded."[148] Hopscotching around the world in four-and-a-half days, Johnson's itinerary included fast stops in Thailand, South Vietnam, Pakistan, and Rome as he stressed his objectives for Southeast Asia around the world.

The trip proved to be a particularly irritating one for the press. To begin with, Christian almost begged the president to inform the correspondents of his plans on the day before the trip. The press secretary pointed to the time required for immunizations, updated passports, and press charter arrangements; but more importantly he stressed that telling the network representatives of the trip in his "Conversation" while remaining silent before the White House corps would destroy "the trust and confidence of all our regulars, including Merriman Smith, Frank Cormier, and the others who have been

210

giving us the breaks for so many years.''[149] While the decision to travel was belated, Christian urged Johnson to minimize the negative reactions by providing as much advance notice as possible.

Even when news of the trip was released, most of the president's itinerary was kept secret. Security constituted one reason for the silence, especially concerning the visits to Thailand and South Vietnam; the complexity of the rushed arrangements was another. Yet the result angered reporters. The correspondents travelling with Johnson had difficulty learning of their location and destinations, often were unable to file copy, and sometimes discovered that they knew less about the trip than their stateside counterparts who made industrious use of leaks and imaginative readings of information. Adding to their annoyance were the long hours, unceasing travel, and rigors of jet lag. Carroll Kilpatrick of the *Washington Post* summarized the press corps' resentment during the trip:

> The President is driving staff and press unmercifully. There have been two heart attacks already because of the unrelenting pace. Press facilities have been sub-standard throughout; no advance notice; in some cases an obvious and deliberate attempt to mislead the press about destinations.[150]

As Tom Johnson observed when he sent the comments of Kilpatrick and others to the president, the reporters regarded the secrecy as a "personal and professional insult," and they were "reflecting in their stories their own personal fatigue, aggravation and dissatisfaction over the long hours and lack of sleep." The press office outlined the considerations of security, timing, and protocol as "points to explain to the press why this trip has been difficult and arduous"; at the president's request, the office also compiled a book of photographs from the trip for all media personnel who toured.[151] The correspondents, however, were not to be reconciled. Adding a special touch of irony to this episode of black comedy was the fact that the trip came on the heels of a memorandum from Christian to Johnson reviewing an article in the *Christian Science Monitor* that the press secretary felt had merit, especially with its discussion of "the irritations of travel, which remains our sorest spot with the White House regulars.''[152]

For the Johnson administration, the trip produced yet another black mark on the record of *Newsweek*. The magazine reported that Johnson's meeting with the pope in Rome had not gone well; according to the account, the pontiff resented the peremptory manner in which he was told that Johnson would be there, he disliked the late hour of 9:00 P.M., and he was not pleased with Johnson's effort to turn the visit to his own political advantage on the issue of Vietnam. Jack Valenti, who had returned to Johnson's service for the duration of the trip, called Katherine Graham and editor Osborn Elliott when the article appeared to complain heatedly that he had been there and *Newsweek*'s story simply was not true. "I was, as I think about it," Valenti later recalled, "neither charming nor diplomatic."

Johnson himself followed this call with a stinging telegram to the publisher, informing her that "for the sake of American relations abroad I cannot let go unanswered the completely false account" in her magazine, and that no amount of effort could "undo the damage" of those distorted reports. Graham later admitted that the magazine probably "went too hard on that story," considering that it was based on the report of their Vatican stringer and that their White House correspondent, despite the rigors of travel, disagreed with the assessment. At the time, however, the episode merely intensified the antagonism between Graham and Johnson.[153]

The pre-Christmas trip may have "proved little more than the speed of Air Force One" to some observers,[154] but the whirlwind of travel topped a determined, almost desperate effort by Lyndon Johnson to dramatize and justify his policies in Vietnam during the fall and winter of 1967. In his year-end report Westmoreland assured the president that "the friendly picture gives rise to optimism for increased success in 1968," and the invitations to the New Year's Eve party at the American embassy in Saigon beckoned people to "come see the light at the end of the tunnel."[155] For Johnson, however, there was the darkness of a disintegrated consensus. As Panzer had told him, people just didn't like the war.

8

Withdrawal from the Race, 1968–1969

In his memoirs Johnson declared 1968 to be "one of the most agonizing years any President has ever spent in the White House."[1] *Time*'s choice of him as "Man of the Year" presaged his agony, for the cover illustration depicted him as King Lear. Despite his staff's attempts to fortify him for the new year with a nine-page collection of compliments from the media since his first days in office, the next months would be wrenching for Lyndon Johnson.[2]

January began with an intensive examination of a question in the back of his mind for months now: to run or not to run for reelection, and if not, when to announce it? At the ranch for the holidays, he sat down for three hours one evening to talk through the issue with his wife and John and Nellie Connally. Taxes, riots, Vietnam: could he handle the burden for four more years? Did he want to? Lady Bird described the discussion as going "round and round on the same hot griddle, finding no cool oasis, no definite time for an acceptable exit."[3] That night Johnson considered announcing his decision not to be a candidate at the end of the 1968 State of the Union address, but he rejected that as a negation of all the proposals and exhortations in the message that would precede it.

Yet, ever one to keep his options open, Johnson remained undecided. On January 15, two days before the scheduled message to Congress, Horace Busby sent the president a draft of a statement that he would not be a candidate. Although Busby had left the White House staff in 1966, he had kept in touch, and Johnson trusted his former aide to find the words with which to announce his departure from the White House. Busby's comment on the resulting draft indicates that Johnson had had second thoughts about the conclusion he had reached at the ranch: "I agree, the forum and the occasion are the very best. Such a step, at this time, precludes any possibility that later events might be interpreted as the cause, as Truman's decision was partly attributed to Kefauver in New Hampshire."[4]

Johnson thus pursued the possibility of announcing his refusal to be a candidate during the State of the Union address. Contacted by telephone on the day of the speech, Governor Connally conceded that the message to Congress offered the best setting if Johnson felt he had to make such a statement, although the governor hoped that he would reconsider. On the same day, not only George Christian but also Mrs. Johnson tried their hand at drafting the announcement for the president.[5]

According to his memoirs, Johnson planned to deliver a version combining Christian's and Busby's drafts at the Capitol on that January 17, but discovered at the podium that he had not brought it with him. "Frankly," he conceded,

> I cannot say what I would have done that night if the paper had
> been in my pocket. But my best guess is that I would not have read
> it. Although the State of the Union occasion would have provided
> an excellent forum for my announcement, I sensed that the timing
> was not the best. I was asking the Congress that night for a heavy
> and demanding program. To couple such a request with a statement
> that I was not going to run for President might suggest to various
> people that I was not willing to fight for what I was asking.[6]

The "heavy and demanding program" for which Johnson was determined to fight centered on domestic legislation and the urgent need for a tax bill. In contrast to the top billing and extensive coverage devoted to Vietnam in the two preceding annual reports, the 1968 State of the Union relied on concise reiterations of his position, so frequently articulated at the end of the preceding year, which were then quickly subordinated to his other concerns. "Our country is being challenged," Johnson told the Congress, but "it is our will that is being tried, not our strength.'"[7] The situation in Vietnam showed signs of progress, he contended, and despite the enemy's hope that "America's will to persevere can be broken, . . . our patience and our perseverance will match our power. Aggression will never prevail." He thus suggested that the military war was under control, but the psychological battle was still being waged.

In the meantime, Johnson hoped, the San Antonio formula would provide "a basis for peace talks" so Americans could achieve their goal: "peace—peace at the earliest possible moment," with "a complete cessation of hostilities—a really true cease-fire." When hope for such a settlement appeared, Johnson assured his audience, he would inform the American people "at the earliest possible moment." Until that time, the United States would sustain its commitment of two decades "against the tyranny of want and ignorance in the world that threatens the peace." Johnson then turned to domestic affairs—from consumer concerns to jobs and housing—for the substantial remainder of his address. He did not, however, use the term "the Great Society."

The enthusiastic applause that had greeted the president led a grateful first lady to observe, "there was a different atmosphere from last year." In the afterglow, she mused that "there was an air of elation, good will, relief—a bright, short draught of the wine of success which we had tasted in 1964 and 1965."[8]

Kintner praised Johnson's 1968 State of the Union performance as well. To begin with, the timing was right, coinciding as it did with Kintner's suggestions: a 9:00 P.M. slot to attract a large number of viewers and to "assure good newspaper and radio coverage," filled by a speech that ran for forty-nine minutes. As the former network executive observed, this allowed time for the networks to seek congressional reactions (including those of Republicans, to lessen their claim to equal time) within the hour-long time period, which avoided "audience annoyance and network profit losses."[9]

In addition to the good timing, Kintner observed, the president appeared "comfortable, confident, conversational," and in "command of the camera" during his address, which was reflected in the large viewing audience. Earlier Kintner had concluded that the November 17 press conference and the December "Conversation" program had "solved the [president's] problem of acceptability and holding audiences" over television; the success of this latest effort seemed to him to underscore Johnson's new skill. Kintner liked the content as well as the delivery of the address, pointing out that Johnson's emphasis on informing the public about any reasonable potential for peace talks had drawn favorable attention:

> The importance of describing "exploration" of the Hanoi peace offensive is made very clear by the comment following the speech and by the comment in the [New York] Times and the [Washington] Post. I believe that it is essential to give the public as much information as is practical on what the feelers disclose.

One wonders whether Kintner fully appreciated his own oxymoron of a "peace offensive."

Despite Kintner's optimism, Mrs. Johnson felt her sense of elation swept away by "the press reports of the State of the Union Message—at least in the Eastern metropolitan papers"—which were "largely negative or unenthusiastic."[10] The congressional applause and the large television audience faded in the frustration at the media criticisms. The *New York Times* noted that Johnson had a good start on addressing serious domestic concerns, "but the money has drained into Vietnam that should have nurtured those beginnings and transformed them into sturdy accomplishments. And it is more than a diversion of money. It is a diversion of leadership, of human and material resources, of public excitement." *Newsweek* saw the State of the Union address as Johnson's "first campaign document of Presidential 1968," designed to depict the United States as "embattled but confident, divided but resilient, short on dollars but long on will—and safe in the hands of its incumbent management."[11]

Panzer's report on follow-up coverage of the State of the Union message showed little improvement. Signing himself "the Recording Angel of the *New York Times*," he reported that the paper buried Hanoi's rejection of Johnson's offer for talks in a ten-inch story five pages back, on a page "dominated by a Macy ad for 99 cent wine and a B. Altman ad for ladies' camel hair coats." In contrast, Panzer offered, the *Washington Post* ran a twenty-three-inch story on page one, bannering "LBJ Terms Dismissed by Hanoi."[12]

Other news reports in the wake of the annual address publicized a mock trial in Sweden that depicted the United States as a war criminal and a peculiar episode at the White House women's luncheon when actress Eartha Kitt exploded into a furious denunciation of the administration's war policy before Mrs. Johnson and her startled guests. During this same period, Mrs. Johnson encountered another problem which she termed "without a doubt, the most ridiculous international furor so far": when singer Robert Merrill announced that his program for the state dinner for British Prime Minister Harold Wilson would include "On the Road to Mandalay" and "Oh I Got Plenty o' Nuttin' " from *Porgy and Bess*, press accounts charged that the songs would insult the country that had just withdrawn its troops from the Suez and devalued the pound. The diplomatic prime minister insisted that the songs were among his favorites and should be retained.[13]

The president himself sought to counteract such coverage by ordering his staff members to distribute favorable information and stories. The White House received copies of letters from Paul Manheim to groups called "Publishers for Peace in Vietnam" and "Psychologists Committee on Vietnam" in which the New York man refuted their *New York Times* advertisements against the war and asked that each member of the group receive a copy of the refutation at Manheim's own expense. Johnson, upon reading them, asked Watson to "tell this fellow we are very grateful—get this printed by ad if they won't run it."[14]

Yet animosity between the media and the administration ran deep. The reporters who had been assigned to cover the Johnsons during their holiday in Texas discovered that on two occasions Johnson was in Austin while the press corps remained in San Antonio. That arrangement left the travelling press to rely on the good will of Austin reporters to keep them informed of the president's whereabouts. The White House Correspondents Association filed a formal letter of protest with the press office about the incidents, complaining that "if there had been any news developments" while the president was in Austin, "we would have looked pretty silly and our organizations' investments in our trip here would have been wasted." Christian sent the letter on to Johnson, reporting that "this is causing much resentment and confusion among reporters, including some who are generally our friends."[15]

The resentment and confusion among reporters only intensified the correspondents' lingering resentment over their whirlwind tour of the world with Johnson. The *Overseas Press Bulletin* headlined its story "LBJ Trip Tests Endurance of White House Press Corps," outlining the correspondents' complaints about the short notice of events, the deluge of statements and presentations, the difficulties in filing copy and developing pictures, the lack of sleep, and subsequent health problems. It was, according to the trade publication, a "nightmare trip."[16]

Yet Hugh Sidey's critical column for *Life* about the journey drew angry responses from his readers. He reported that they "gave me hell" about it; Sidey contended that "I have never had them eat me alive like this one." He told Loyd Hackler, who had worked on advanced planning for the trip, that he interpreted the reaction as a sign that people were starting to view Johnson more sympathetically.[17]

This reading coincided with a prediction from pollster Lou Harris: Johnson's ratings would experience an upturn, due in part to his good news conference in November and to a negative reaction to antiwar demonstrators. Furthermore, Harris reported that two of his recent polls showed that people were taking a harder line on the war in Vietnam; his findings showed that 63 percent opposed either a bombing halt or a deescalation of the fighting in order to work toward a negotiated peace. They also indicated that 45 percent felt that the United States' objective in Vietnam was "to stop Communist aggression once and for all in Southeast Asia," while 24 percent believed it to be "to force North Vietnam to withdraw from South Vietnam completely and eliminate all Communist influence." Harris did not ask whether the respondents agreed that those should be America's goals.[18]

Panzer told the president that these results were a clear indication of "the American people's determination to see this war out," and should be widely distributed to publicize this support of his policies. Panzer also reported that he seemed to be making progress in his efforts to "cultivate" Harris; the pollster was especially impressed with his gift copy of Johnson's book, *No Retreat from Tomorrow*.[19] In addition to the news about Harris, a Gallup survey also encouraged the president. Conducted at the first of the year, the poll indicated that 48 percent approved of the way in which he was handling his position, up from the gloomy low of 39 percent in August of 1967.

Johnson would look back longingly at Harris's assessments and Gallup's tally over the next several months. On January 23, the USS *Pueblo* and its crew were seized by the North Koreans. The incident not only increased international tensions but seemed to be yet another in a series in which small countries stymied America. Then, the war in Vietnam exploded with a particular fury into what would become known as the Tet offensive. The North Vietnamese and Viet Cong chose the wee hours of January 30, at the height of the Lunar New Year celebration of Tet, to launch a series of simultaneous attacks on major cities, bases, and towns throughout South Vietnam. The initial offensive was punctuated by an assault on the American embassy in which a Viet Cong suicide squad killed five American military men and held the supposedly impregnable compound for six hours before they were overcome. Heavy fighting followed throughout the South for another ten days, with battles raging even longer at two key sites: the U.S. Marine base at Khe Sanh, under seige by the North Vietnamese; and the beautiful holy city of Hue, occupied by the Viet Cong for almost four weeks.

The American people were stunned by the stories of Tet, in part because American correspondents were stunned by Tet. Before the new offensive reporters had to seek out skirmishes to cover, often on their own initiative; even then, journalists so rarely caught sight of the actual battles that the camera crews assigned most of their film to a category they entitled, "the wily VC got away again."[20] With Tet, however, the fighting was suddenly, inescapably, terrifyingly close to the Saigon-based news teams. The proximity of the battle guaranteed extensive coverage by media institutions: it was dramatic, it was easily accessible, and it was for many the first extended view of the enemy. The invasion of the American embassy and the house-to-house fighting in Saigon thus received especially heavy coverage.

On the night of January 31, for example, NBC's "Huntley-Brinkley Report" carried unedited embassy-battle footage as soon as it arrived in Tokyo. The chaos and destruction shown on the film were heightened by the fact that both the correspondent and the commentators were seeing the footage for the first time as it aired, along with an estimated audience of ten million homes. Both NBC and CBS then aired half-hour specials entitled "Vietcong Terror: A Guerrilla Offensive" and "Saigon Under Fire." The *New York Times*'s headlines paired Johnson's statements with news of the offensive, such as the February 3 banner: "Johnson Says Foe's Raids Are a Failure Militarily; Saigon, Hue Battles Go On." Inside, the *Times* editorialized that the Tet offensive, "which penetrated even into the United States Embassy in Saigon, offers further painful proof of the limitations of American power in Asia." Both *Time* and *Newsweek* devoted their covers and a dozen pages to the offensive, with color photographs of bloody Viet Cong bodies sprawled among the impeccable embassy landscaping and American dead piled on the back of an armored vehicle. In contrast to the few black and white long shots that had predominated the news magazines' coverage of the war, the vivid pictures focused graphically on the death and destruction, accompanied by headlines like "Hanoi Attacks—And Scores a Major Psychological Blow."[21]

Moreover, as the battles continued through February, the lack of familiarity with the Vietnamese language, culture, and countryside compounded the problem of a lack of mobility, which hampered both the ability and the inclination of many reporters to see the wider context of the offensive. As Peter Braestrup observes in his detailed analysis of Tet reporting, 90 percent of the media accounts focused on Saigon, Khe Sanh, and Hue, where bureaus were established; reports on the rest of the war, which entailed 85 percent of the American troop deployments and 80 percent of American casualties, were based largely on government information and the journalistic grapevine.[22]

The resulting news reports depicted an opponent not only willing to continue the battle but also capable of inflicting major losses on both South Vietnamese and American troops, contrary to the image of an enemy whose spirit and military machine were almost broken by bombing raids and American might. They encapsulated the corruption of the South Vietnamese government and military with the stomach-wrenching scene of General Loan, the national police chief, putting a bullet through the head of a captive, apparently in cold blood and without reason. They described Khe Sanh and Hue as microcosms of the entire war: the United States could move neither out of nor into areas that its troops should have been able to control. Thus Braestrup, who reported on the war for the *New York Times* and *Washington Post*, contended that "the collective emanations of the major media were producing a kind of continuous black fog of their own, a vague conventional 'disaster' image."[23] The "light at the end of the tunnel" became the conflagration around them, and the resulting black fog of despair enveloped the public as well.

The American people, emphasized correspondent Don Oberdorfer, were *"experiencing* the worst of the bloodshed through the new technology of television. The [government's] summaries were not believed. The projected experience was."[24] While the Gallup poll indicated that the percentage of self-described hawks had jumped to 61 percent in the wake of Tet, it also showed that the percentage approving of Johnson's handling of the war had shrunk to 35 percent. The initial aggressive reaction to the attacks was not coupled with support for the commander in chief.

In retrospect, Johnson would regret "not saying more about Vietnam in my State of the Union report. . . . If I had forecast the possibilities, the American people would have been better prepared for what was soon to come."[25] Both the military and the administration knew that the North Vietnamese were preparing for a major assault with what Westmoreland termed "a very unusual sense of urgency." Forewarning about these preparations might have lessened the severity of public shock. Yet Westmoreland himself later acknowledged that the extent, the timing, and the targets of the Tet offensive were unexpected:

> The extent of this offensive was not known to us, although we did feel it was going to be widespread. The timing was not known. I frankly did not think they would assume the psychological disadvantage of hitting at Tet itself, so I thought it would be before or after Tet. I did not anticipate that they would strike in the cities and make them their targets.[26]

Thus while a degree of public forewarning might have been possible, it could not have prepared the American people for the massive, coordinated strikes on the cities as well as the bases at the height of the Vietnamese Lunar New Year celebration, for Westmoreland and Johnson were not completely prepared themselves. What the general called a psychological disadvantage for the Viet Cong was in many respects a psychological and military advantage: a limited bombing halt had been announced for the holidays; a substantial proportion of the South Vietnamese forces had been granted leave; and American troops were expecting the attacks to begin after Tet since they had not come before.

The disparities between what was expected and what was reported startled not only correspondents and the public, but also members of government who contrasted the media's accounts of Tet with the official reports. McPherson, for example, recalled that Rostow's accounts of conditions in Southeast Asia "almost seemed hallucinatory" when compared with what he saw on the nightly newscasts. The speech writer recognized the significance of his reaction to the media:

> It is particularly interesting that people like me—people who had some responsibility for expressing the presidential point of view—could be so affected by the media as everyone else was, while downstairs, within fifty yards of my desk, was that enormous panoply of intelligence-gathering devices. . . . I assume the reason this is so, the reason I put aside my own interior access to confidential information and was more persuaded by what I saw on the tube and in the newspapers, was that like everyone else who had been deeply involved in explaining the policies of the war and trying to understand them and render some judgment, I was fed up with the "light at the end of the tunnel" stuff. I was fed up with the optimism that seemed to flow without stopping from Saigon.[27]

McPherson's account testifies to the far-reaching effects of media reports, within as well as outside of government. Townsend Hoopes, undersecretary of the United States Air Force at the time, provides further evidence with his report of reactions within the Pentagon to the disparity between news stories and official optimism.[28] The media's view of Tet galvanized concern about the progress of the war and the response of the American public.

Johnson moved immediately to counter the negativism of this Tet coverage. On the president's orders, General Wheeler told Westmoreland to "make a brief personal comment to the press at least once each day." The purpose of these statements, according to the message from the chairman of the Joint Chiefs of Staff, "should be to convey to the American public your confidence in our capability to blunt these enemy moves, and to reassure the public here that you have the situation under control."[29] Sent on January 31, as the extent of the initial offensive became known, this cable was joined by one from

Christian which underscored the vital purpose of news conferences by both Westmoreland and Bunker:

> We are facing, in these next few days, a critical phase in the American public's understanding and confidence toward our effort in Vietnam. . . . Nothing can more dramatically counter scenes of VC destructiveness than the confident professionalism of the Commanding General. Similarly, the dire prognostications of the commentators can best be put into perspective by the shared experience and wisdom of our Ambassador. . . . Appearances by you, in the immediate situation, will make a greater impact here at home than much of what we can say.[30]

To further emphasize the importance of both diplomatic and military dealings with the American media in Vietnam, Rostow instructed both Westmoreland and Bunker to give "authoritative" briefings daily, for without such guidance "the correspondents take over rather wildly, without poise and perspective and authority that only you two command."[31] The fact that Johnson's desire for daily briefings in Saigon was communicated not once but three times indicates the importance placed on countering negative news coverage by educating reporters about the significance of the Tet offensive. Rostow would later implicitly acknowledge the failure of these instructional efforts, as he pointed to Braestrup's work as a detailed confirmation of what the national security adviser had known at the time: that correspondents did not understand Third World countries, particularly those in turmoil, and thus filed confused and inaccurate stories.[32]

In the face of the Tet offensive, however, the persuasive efforts continued at home and abroad. Johnson himself held a news conference on February 2. He opened with a statement that informed his audience that "we have known for several months, now, that the Communists planned a massive winter-spring offensive," and he then assured them that "the stated purposes of the general uprising have failed."[33] In response to questions, Johnson warned that military victory constituted only one of the communists' objectives; the other was a "psychological victory." The president sought to encourage his listeners, saying that the enemy's attacks were no more catastrophic than familiar domestic problems: their offensive had "disrupted services," just as a power failure or a protest march or a riot might, but these raids were "anticipated, prepared for, and met," resulting in "the complete failure" of their military goals. As for the second objective, Johnson asserted that "when the American people know the facts . . . I do not believe that they [the communists] will achieve a psychological victory."

To insure that the American people knew those facts, the president took additional actions. He chastised a press pool aboard Air Force One for the media's failure to publicize the fact that Ho Chi Minh had violated the planned Tet truce—a "dastardly act" which was "something every schoolboy ought to know." Nor did they cover, Johnson complained, the tremendously high casualty rates inflicted upon the enemy troops or the fine performances of the South Vietnamese during the offensive.[34] Johnson then dispatched his advisers to spread the word: Rusk and McNamara to an hour-long special edition of NBC's "Meet the Press," Rostow to ABC's "Issues and Answers," and Katzenbach to CBS's "Face the Nation."

The State Department joined the effort by developing a "Briefing Book on Vietnam," designed "to provide a compilation of authoritative responses to basic questions raised about United States involvement in Vietnam." The book provided outlines for quick reference and extemporaneous speaking, a more detailed section with backup information, and a list of additional source material. The sections were organized to answer five questions, indicative of the administration's concerns:

1) Why are we fighting in Vietnam?
2) Why don't we negotiate to end the war right now?
3) So many people have told us we must stop bombing the North if we really want to talk. Why don't we?
4) Is the South Vietnamese army doing more fighting?
5) Why don't our allies give more help?[35]

That such an aid for officials speaking on the war should finally be developed in February of 1968 is a sign that the administration recognized the pressing need to publicly defend American involvement in Vietnam in the wake of Tet.

Johnson's staff contributed to the effort as well. Panzer was his usual busy self. First, he compared the "unfavorable" front-page, forty-eight-column-inch coverage that the *New York Times* gave to several clergymen's accusations of U.S. war crimes with the same story's "objective" sixteen column inches on page 22 of the *Washington Post*. He then turned to the Joseph Kraft column which contended that the Gallup and Harris polls demonstrated that "the country is not about to go out on a jag of fierce militancy." To public opinion analyst Panzer, Kraft's contentions were "palpable bunk based on the fuzziest wishful thinking" which should be discredited in Congress and the press. Finally, Johnson liked the aide's suggestion that a *New York Times* story on the poor intelligence-gathering system of the North Vietnamese, "if fleshed out with other similar examples, would make a good newspaper column." When no similar miscalculations could be uncovered, Panzer started a summary of the Viet Cong's atrocities and executions to "balance the criticism of our side's cruelty and help show Americans the nature of the enemy."[36]

In addition to Panzer's efforts, the "news patrol" which had been started by Benchley continued: staff member Bob Fleming sent the president regular reports on the balance and bias of nightly network newscasts, especially regarding Vietnam. Those reports frequently contained bad news; as Valenti observed from his post with the Motion Picture Association, "the networks are the most visible adversary of the administration," not only at home but also abroad. To help change the coverage, Valenti suggested that Johnson pursue NBC's Chet Huntley, who

> turns out to be a very vigorous supporter of the President. In private conversation he is committed to the President's course of action in Vietnam and approves of both his objectives and his tactics. Senator [Birch] Bayh [of Indiana] told me that Huntley was overjoyed at the unexpected meeting he had with the President at the White House—after the meeting he talked continually of how impressive the President was and how strong and wise he appeared to be.[37]

Valenti suggested to Bayh that Huntley should make his support public, especially in light of Brinkley's known opposition to the war. Despite his former aide's urging, however, Johnson did not meet with Huntley nor did he meet with Louis Heren of the London *Times*, even after Christian passed on the journalist's message that he "would like more ammunition" with which to defend the president.[38]

Johnson was reluctant to involve himself in these efforts to make members of the media understand his position, as he was assessing the military and political situation in Vietnam himself amid debate within the administration about the best ways of responding to the major offensive. In his news conference of February 2, the president had stressed that he had made certain that "every single thing that General Westmoreland believed that he needed at this time was available." When a correspondent asked whether the Tet strikes might lead to further deployment of American troops, Johnson's carefully handled answer revealed his awareness of the importance—and dangers—of media treatment: "I would not want to make predictions. Of course it is possible. . . . I wouldn't want your lead to say, though, 'Johnson predicts possibility of troops' because that is not anticipated. We see no evidence of that."[39] Johnson continued in this vein at some length, reiterating that "anything can happen on a moment's notice" in a situation like this, but that "there is nothing that is imminent at this moment." The next day, Johnson sought to discover more about Westmoreland's needs, instructing Wheeler to send a telegram: "The President asks me if there is any more reinforcement or help that we can give you." When the general had not replied by February 8, the chairman of the Joint Chiefs sent a second cable. This one did not mention the president, and it outlined specific additional divisions that were readily available. Beyond that, Wheeler pushed Westmoreland: "If you consider reinforcements imperative, you should not be bound by earlier agreements. . . . [The] United States Government is not prepared to accept defeat in Vietnam. In summary, if you need more troops, ask for them."[40]

Westmoreland responded to this invitation by requesting the immediately available divisions and then noting, "needless to say, I would welcome reinforcements at any time they can be made available." He granted that the additional troops would place him in a stronger position; he did not, however, argue that they were essential. Later, Westmoreland recalled: "It seemed to me that for political reasons or otherwise, the president and the Joint Chiefs of Staff were anxious to send me reinforcements. We did a little sparring back and forth. My first thought was not to ask for any, but the signals from Washington got stronger."[41] The extent of Johnson's involvement in the subsequent queries is open to question, since Wheeler did not mention the president.

Wheeler's insistent inquiries were consistent with the position of the Joint Chiefs of Staff on Tet. This military group pressured Johnson from early February on to assume an aggressive stance, including a much less restricted bombing area around Hanoi and the Haiphong harbor in order to limit "the enemy capability for waging war in the South." The president did not approve this request, undoubtedly aware of the certain protests that enemy military activity seemed undaunted by the major bombing efforts to date, as the Tet assaults demonstrated. Johnson also resisted the Joint Chiefs' recommendations for additional deployments along with a call-up of the reserves, which Wheeler's cables to Westmoreland supported, but he did not reject it out of hand. While he recognized that more troops might be necessary, he still disliked the emergency connotations of a reserve call-up, despite the military men's dire warnings of seriously inadequate troop strength in Vietnam and worldwide if both steps were not implemented quickly.

Johnson met with his advisers on February 12 and 13 to consider Westmoreland's cabled requests. Wheeler's urgings about the reserves were rejected, but Johnson approved an accelerated schedule for deploying the remaining 25,000 men of the 525,000 ceiling which he had already authorized before Tet. The president also approved an additional 10,500 troops above that initial ceiling for 1968, and then ordered study of the issue of reserves to continue.

In his news conference of February 16, then, Johnson displayed the same careful approach to the question of additional troops as he had two weeks earlier:

> We never know what forces will be required there. We have, tenta-
> tively, a goal. We would like to reach that goal as soon as we can.
> In light of the circumstances that existed when we set that goal, we
> hoped to reach it sometime this year. In light of the developments
> and the subsequent substantial increases in the enemy force,
> General Westmoreland asked that he receive approximately half of
> the remaining numbers under that goal during February or early
> March.[42]

Johnson did not clarify what those goals were, when they were established, in what ways they had changed, nor what would happen after early March.

The next day the president flew to Fort Bragg, South Carolina, and then on to the marine base in El Toro, California, and the battleship *Constellation* outside San Diego. In each case he bid farewell to men bound for Vietnam. Johnson acknowledged in his memoirs that his visits with these troops "were among the most personally painful meetings of my Presidency," as he shook the hands of soldiers headed to Southeast Asia for their second and third tours of duty. One who particularly touched him was the man whose first child, a boy, had been born just the morning before.[43] Johnson could not help but think of his treasured grandson and suffer from the knowledge that soon his two sons-in-law would be serving in Vietnam as well.

Upon his return from the bases, Johnson dispatched Wheeler to Vietnam to appraise the military and political situation there. The resulting report, cabled to Washington while its author was still en route home, emphasized major enemy advances despite heavy casualties. "In short," Wheeler warned, "it was a very near thing." In the general's view, however, the situation was "fraught with opportunities as well as dangers."[44] Wheeler's perspective paralleled that of

Westmoreland once the field commander had recognized the possibilities for further deployments in the face of Tet. To Westmoreland, the offensive signalled a change of enemy strategy which required a concommitant alteration of the American response:

> This has been a limited war with limited objectives, fought with limited means and programmed for the utilization of limited resources. This was a feasible proposition on the assumption that the enemy was to fight a protracted war. We are now in a new ball game where we face a determined, highly disciplined enemy, fully mobilized to achieve a quick victory. He is in the process of throwing in all his "military chips to go for broke." . . . I must stress equally that we face a situation of great opportunity as well as heightened risk.[45]

In order to take advantage of this opportunity, Wheeler outlined his recommendations, termed "force requirements," for 206,000 troops in a three-phase operation.

With Johnson at the ranch when Wheeler's report first arrived, the president's advisers met in Washington on February 26 and 27 to consider its recommendations. McNamara, in his last few days as secretary of defense, formulated three options for discussion: first, full compliance with the Wheeler-Westmoreland proposals for increasing military strength; second, a more limited increase joined by a specific new peace initiative; or third, the retention of current troop levels coupled with a redefined strategy of protecting only key military and civilian areas.[46] Clark Clifford, set to succeed as secretary of defense on March 1, noted a fourth alternative to put the others into perspective: a massive deployment of up to one million troops. Acknowledging Clifford's point, McNamara argued that the generals' requested levels were neither sufficient to launch a conclusive military campaign nor small enough to signal a reconceptualized military strategy. Indirectly, then, McNamara rejected the report's recommendations as simply more of the same policy of limited war, despite Westmoreland's argument that it constituted a new strategy.

As Johnson's advisers struggled with the ramifications of each alternative, the only firm conclusion they reached was that many questions needed answers before a decision could reasonably be reached. Included among the questions that Rostow cabled to Johnson was a familiar, nagging one: If the troop increase were approved, what would be "the rationale for public presentation in the U.S."? As Johnson phrased it, "How could such an increase be justified to the American people?"[47]

Arriving back in D.C. early on February 28, Johnson met with Wheeler and his top advisers to hear the general's warnings of failure without reinforcements and reserves, and his optimism about substantial gains with them. McNamara gave as his final official presentation a vigorous dissenting opinion, contending that the South Vietnamese should be given all responsibilities beyond those that could be handled by current troop levels revitalized by a small number of emergency reinforcements. Neither choice was an attractive one to Johnson: McNamara's plan seemed an implicit acknowledgment that America had been, and would continue to be, stymied in Southeast Asia; yet Wheeler's proposal entailed major military, political, and economic commitments during an election year that foreboded increasing disenchantment with the war. The president concluded that such a major decision needed further study, so he turned to the new secretary of defense to head a task force on the issue. Clifford "had not been living with Vietnam day in and day out as the others had," reasoned Johnson, "and I thought that a new pair of eyes and a fresh outlook should guide this study."[48]

Clark Clifford had worked in and with the White House in various capacities since he first served as special counsel for President Truman in 1945. Well liked and greatly respected by Johnson, the successful Washington lawyer had served on the Foreign Intelligence Advisory Board since 1961 and chaired it since 1964. This position provided access to sensitive information without removing him from the valuable perspective offered by the influential business and financial circles in which he moved. Clifford was among the "Wise Men" who in November had assured Johnson that he was on the right track concerning Vietnam. At the time the lawyer's major reservation about American involvement concerned the distinct lack of enthusiastic support from allies, which he detected in a tour of Southeast Asia with General Taylor that summer; but it remained a disquieting thought that did not dim his support for Johnson's policies. Clifford had thus been associated with but outside of the administration when he assumed McNamara's duties, along with the responsibility to chair the ad hoc task force on Vietnam.

Accounts of the president's original directive for the task force and Clifford's response to it vary. In his memoirs Johnson reported that he sent the group a detailed list of areas to explore. Drafted by Rostow, this memorandum touched on questions of the objectives of additional forces, budget problems, possibilities for negotiations, the role of the South Vietnamese, congressional actions and reactions, and, ever present among the considerations, problems with public opinion. Yet Clifford has insisted that he received no such directive and that his understanding of the group's purpose was "to determine how this new requirement could be met. We were not instructed to assess the need for substantial increases in men and material; we were to devise the means by which they could be provided." Schandler has concluded that a presidential directive did in fact go to both the Departments of State and of Defense, but that it was given relatively little attention by the task force.[49]

Under whatever instructions, it is clear that Clifford conducted a more broad-ranging review of America's involvement in Vietnam that Johnson had initially envisioned, for the discussions continually turned from the request for additional troops to the underlying question of the future course of action in Vietnam. The debate sparked by this fundamental issue was extensive and carefully attended to by Clifford. He spent his first official days on the job in a cross fire between those such as Rostow and Wheeler who argued that the requests had to be met and those like Paul Warnke, an assistant secretary of defense, who insisted that the United States should acknowledge negative public opinion, cut its losses, and seek negotiations rather than an impossible military victory.

Comparing a draft of the task force's report with the final version suggests the process by which the group's debate was translated into a formal statement. While the draft recommended approval of both the request for the initial 20,000 troops and a call-up of the reserves, it advocated further study of the plea for 185,000 more men, on the basis that Westmoreland's proposal provided "no assurance that this very substantial additional deployment would leave us a year from today in any different military position."[50] The draft then outlined the context in which the additional commitments should be examined, beginning with the premise that America's purpose in South Vietnam was "not an unlimited objective to be equated with that of preservation of the United States." Rather, policymakers must recognize realistic constraints on the pursuit of that objective:

—circumstances "under which it would become an unrealistic or even impossible objective," such as a demand for American withdrawal by the South Vietnamese government;
—the desire to avoid using certain means of warfare, "even if their use appeared essential to preserving our objective";
—limits on "the magnitude of forces and the time of deployment of those forces" which would not desirably be broached; and

—the existence of "other foreign policy, defense, and possibly economic objectives which are more important to the survival of the United States."

Given these already existing constraints, the draft implied, the administration could deny Westmoreland's request for massive reinforcements without denying the integrity of its commitment in Southeast Asia. In fact, "we will have failed in our purposes," noted the draft, if the war in Vietnam leads to "direct military confrontation with the USSR and/or China," if resources committed to Vietnam mean that "our other world-wide commitments . . . are no longer credible," or if "the attitudes of the American people towards 'more Vietnams' are such that our other commitments are brought into question as a matter of US will." The draft thus cast the argument in traditionally accepted foreign-policy terms—NATO, world esteem for America's word, and public support for other defense demands. It did not directly reject Westmoreland's additional request, but rather implied that it could not hold precedence over these other obligations.

Such was one attempt to reconcile the group's disparate views and to provide acceptable reasons for not approving the entire package requested. Yet in Hoopes's words, the "spare, terse, emotionless prose" of the memorandum that finally emerged from the task force "typified those papers that go to the President for action on issues of great heat and consequence."[51] Sent to Johnson on March 7, the draft presidential memorandum recommended meeting Westmoreland's request for the immediate deployment of 22,000 more troops, while tabling the request for the remaining 185,000 pending examination of the developments on a weekly basis. The document also approved of a major reserve call-up and urged greater pressure on the South Vietnamese to increase their participation; it reiterated the San Antonio formula but suggested no new peace initiatives. The memorandum acknowledged divisiveness only on the topic of bombing, where it noted that some members proposed "a substantial extension of targets" while others advocated only a "seasonal step-up through the spring." Even here, however, the option of a sharp curtailment of target areas was not mentioned, perhaps to avoid the fire it would certainly draw from the military and other hawkish elements within the administration.[52]

The drafting and submission of the memorandum did not stem the debate. When Clifford joined Johnson in the Oval Office on March 8

230

to discuss the task force's findings, he shared his growing misgivings about the effectiveness of the current policy. The adviser's doubts concerned Johnson, for as Clifford recollected: "He felt that when I came in, I was going to be a good, strong stalwart, a supporter of the status quo. As I changed it was disturbing to him. He was irritated with me. . . . The bloom was off our relationship."[53] Already feeling under siege, Johnson did not welcome this questioning within the ranks. He noted that the Clifford report had disappointed him, both because of "its totally negative approach to any possible negotiations" and because he "had begun to hope that some new approach might emerge from this study" given the dissenting views he knew existed within government.[54] George Christian recalled that initially the president was "mad" at Clifford for his disagreement, especially since he had been a "superhawk" before becoming secretary of defense.[55] Now Clifford's questions pushed for a new approach, although neither he nor the task force seemed to know what it would be. It was a frightening prospect. McPherson empathized with Johnson's distress:

> He did mind it—of course he did. I would have minded it. . . . The idea of opening this yawning issue, this chasm under your feet—imagine! Christ, you put five hundred and fifty thousand Americans out there; you've lost twenty-five thousand of them dead! What if it's wrong? What if we've made an error?[56]

The fundamental questions asked by this articulate, thoughtful, much-respected adviser opened the chasm beneath the president.

Although Clifford contrasted his own change of mind with Rusk's constancy, the secretary of defense had proffered the option not contained in the draft memorandum: a suspension of bombing above the nineteenth parallel. In a meeting with Johnson and his senior advisers on March 5, Rusk explained that the monsoon season would hamper air attacks during the next several months anyway, and he pointed out that bombing could be resumed at the first sign of major enemy activity. He argued against an elaborate diplomatic effort for negotiations during this period; his point was that a simply staged bombing halt should be considered. The president did give the proposal careful consideration, especially as it came from the cautious, constant Rusk.[57]

As Clifford questioned and Rusk queried, Westmoreland responded to the task force's proposals. He welcomed the 22,000 men as an initial reinforcement, but he insisted that the remainder of the

205,000-force package would be needed by the end of 1968.[58] The general's cable reached the White House as a civil rights debate on Capitol Hill erupted into a demand by such senators as Fulbright and Kennedy that Congress be consulted before any further troop increases were approved.

A *New York Times* story added further fuel to the fire when it presented an amazingly accurate account not only of the troop requests but also of the controversy it had engendered. The lead paragraph of the March 10 report stated that "General William C. Westmoreland has asked for 206,000 more American troops for Vietnam, but the request has touched off a divisive internal debate within high levels of the Johnson Administration." According to the article, the extent of this response reflected "the wrenching uncertainty and doubt in this capital about every facet of the war left by the enemy's dramatic wave of attacks at Tet." While Johnson angrily castigated the story as the attempt of a few unprincipled civilians within the Pentagon to pressure him on the troop decision through leaks and lies, authors Neil Sheehan and Hedrick Smith offer a fascinating view of a story pieced together from a variety of sources through the techniques of investigative reporting.[59] The *Times* account quickly garnered the attention not only of government but also of other media. Frank McGee ended a NBC special on Vietnam that same evening by referring to the reported request, and he concluded: "All that would be changed would be the capacity for destruction. . . . Laying aside all other arguments, the time is at hand when we must decide whether it is futile to destroy Vietnam in order to save it."[60]

McGee's gloomy assessment echoed the pessimistic report of another commentator a week-and-a-half earlier. Just returned from Vietnam, Walter Cronkite told the viewers of "CBS News" that the Tet offensive had resulted in a "split decision":

> It seems now more certain than ever that the bloody experience of Vietnam is to end in a stalemate. This summer's almost certain standoff will either end in real give-and-take negotiations or terrible escalation; and for every means we have to escalate, the enemy can match us. . . . And with each escalation, the world comes close to the brink of cosmic disaster.
>
> To say that we are closer to victory today is to believe, in the face of the evidence, the optimists who have been wrong in the past. To suggest we are on the edge of defeat is to yield to unreasonable pessimism. To say that we are mired in stalemate seems the only realistic, yet unsatisfactory, conclusion.[61]

As George Christian later acknowledged, "the shock waves rolled through the Government" when Cronkite delivered this somber assessment on his national newscast.[62] The most trusted man in America said that he did not trust the administration's optimism; paired with the grim news coverage provided by the media, Cronkite's conclusion seemed far more realistic than the official line.

It was against these escalating statements of public disenchantment and Clifford's careful survey of government disillusionment that Wheeler dispatched a discouraging word to Westmoreland, one that must have startled the field commander given their earlier exchanges. Rather than urging Westmoreland to ask for more troops if he could use them, Wheeler cautioned: "I was directed to keep you informed of the status of our forces in the US so that you will not in the future be placed in the position of asking for something that does not exist or is not available."[63]

The pessimistic media reports also affected Rusk's appearances before the Senate Foreign Relations Committee on March 11 and 12. Not only was the secretary questioned about the *Times* story, but his entire testimony was televised live. The eleven hours of questioning over two days constituted the most extensive cross-examination of a Cabinet member on record. Rusk acknowledged that the "entire situation is under consideration from A to Z." When asked about the *Times*'s account, he replied that

> certain units will be going out that had previously been scheduled under existing plans—the level of that 525,000 that the President talked about. But he has not made any fresh decisions or come to any new conclusions, and I think it would not be right for me to speculate about numbers or possibilities.[64]

Rusk thus walked a careful line between "requests" and "decisions," but he was clearly uncomfortable with the information the senators had obtained from the *New York Times*.

This kind of national news coverage concerned the president. In an interview with Walter Cronkite two years later, Johnson concluded that while the Viet Cong and North Vietnamese may have failed militarily with Tet, they did achieve the psychological victory they sought:

> Immediately the voices just came out of the holes in the wall and said, "Let's get out." And that's what Ho Chi Minh had been trying to do all the time— . . . to win in this country, in the homes of this country, what he could not win from the men out there that represented us.[65]

In his memoirs Johnson would blame this despair on the media's apparent competition to "provide the most lurid and depressing accounts" of the Tet offensive, leading to a "daily barrage of bleakness and near panic." Johnson contended that this negativism in the media, as well as in academia and in Congress, did not surprise him, but he admitted that he was astonished and disappointed to see the "dismal effect on various people inside government and others outside whom I had always regarded as staunch and unflappable." Although he listed no names, the description fits Clifford and McPherson perfectly. The unity for which Johnson had pleaded in San Antonio as a sign of America's determination to resist aggression seemed even more remote in the face of the media coverage of Tet and the resulting disillusionment, even within his administration. Instead the president heard the voices of dissent sending messages with which "Hanoi must have been delighted; it was exactly the reaction they sought."[66]

It was not at all the reaction Lyndon Johnson sought, especially not in an election year. Despite the 1964 campaign advice from Lady Bird to serve one term and no more, despite the fevered discussions of the fall and winter of 1967, despite the announcement for the end of the State of the Union address that somehow did not accompany him to the Hill, Lyndon Baines Johnson was still undecided about seeking reelection in 1968. As this man who prized keeping his options open confessed, "the firmest decisions can be altered at the last minute by a dramatic change in circumstances or by new, pertinent information."[67] Most of his staff, either not privy to the debate about his political future or unconvinced by his doubts, simply assumed "that it was going to happen, that the President would run again and that *the* thing you would be doing for several months would be working toward his re-election."[68]

The campaign machinery had thus been slowly gearing up for some time, and it accelerated in the early months of 1968. George Reedy returned to the White House to organize the effort along with veteran Democratic campaigner Charles Murphy, and Kintner offered his help even though he was returning to private business once his eye maladies healed.[69] After discussions with Johnson, columnist Robert Spivack developed key ideas for the campaign as well as methods for disseminating them, such as not allowing "any criticism by well-known persons to go unanswered for as long as 24 hours." Spivack's other suggestions, which had obviously gained a sympathetic ear from the president, included marshalling "a team of Administration representatives" to appear on newscasts and talk shows, who would attack "partisan critics" and "nit-pickers" while stressing responsi-

234

bility, national unity, and the "small sacrifices asked of those at home compared to what those in Vietnam are giving."[70]

Other staff members turned their attention to the charges of a credibility gap, which they knew would constitute an important campaign issue. The McGaffin and Knoll article from the preceding September had provided a sample of the problems yet to come, for the essay traced Johnson's loss of believability directly to his public handling of Vietnam:

> The Gap was opened, although no one knew it at the time, on August 11, 1964, when Lyndon Johnson, a candidate for election to the Presidency that he had inherited the previous November, addressed himself to the question of the American role in Vietnam. "Some others are eager to enlarge the conflict," he asserted. "They call upon us to take reckless action which might risk the lives of millions and engulf much of Asia, and certainly threaten the peace of the entire world. Moreover, such action would offer no solution at all to the real problem of Vietnam."[71]

The gap widened, the article asserted, when "on October 24, 1964, he told the American people, 'We are not about to send American boys nine or ten thousand miles to do what Asian boys ought to be doing for themselves.' " In his analysis of the article, Panzer told his fellow aides that it was a clear example of quoting Johnson out of context to fashion "an anti-Johnson 'credibility gap' garment that fits neither the facts nor the President"; but it was a technique that he acknowledged "will become more popular as the demand for whole cloth picks up in a campaign year."[72]

In both his November 17, 1967, news conference and his "Conversation" program, Johnson himself had faced questions contrasting his 1964 campaign statements with his subsequent actions. The president responded that such contrasts had "just been a part of the politicians' gambit of picking out one sentence before you get to the 'but' in it" and distorting his overall meaning: that the United States would supplement the South Vietnamese struggle against aggression without supplanting it, providing "whatever is necessary to keep the Communist conspiracy from gobbling up that nation."[73] To Johnson, these politically motivated charges obscured the proper patriotic perspective.

Despite this denial of any inconsistency by the president, however, Panzer found that early in 1968 "antiwar and anti-Johnson forces—an assortment of Republicans, Democrats, the old Left and the New Left—are focusing on the charge that LBJ lied to the American people in the 1964 campaign . . . in particular that he promised not to send American boys to fight an Asian war" (ellipses Panzer's). As evidence of "the need for rebuttal" of these charges, Panzer attached a column from the *Pittsburgh Press* captioned, "Own Words Haunt LBJ."[74] While Panzer, Christian, and Goldstein argued that the general idea of the credibility gap should be treated as a "mutual problem of press and government, . . . a communications gap," they contended that these specific charges needed to be countered as firmly and directly as possible. They offered the extensive refutation they had developed at the end of the previous year as a starting point, and they looked for opportunities to spread the word. For example, Panzer suggested Georgia Senator Richard B. Russell's acceptance of the annual VFW congressional award as a potential forum, for Panzer felt that it constituted "an ideal platform, an ideal speaker, [and] an ideal audience" for "an attack on the credibility gappers—mostly peaceniks."[75]

Johnson's staff thus proceeded on the assumption that the campaign would soon be in full swing. Republicans, like the staff they hoped to supplant, also assumed that Johnson would run that year, as did the political pundits. In Carl Rowan's assessment, the chances of the president not running for reelection "can't be better than a million to one."[76]

Yet the public dismay at the Tet offensive helped alter those odds, as did the racial disorders that had erupted into violence throughout the country, the nation's increasing economic problems, and the stagnation of Johnson's legislative program. In addition, as Reedy observed when he surveyed the task before him, there was the fact that "editorial criticism, not only of the President's policies but of his personality, . . . had swelled to a crescendo. The 'credibility gap' was no longer an issue but a factor taken for granted by most of the public."[77]

Underscoring the depth of what Kintner had identified as a profound sense of uneasiness across the nation was the surprisingly strong showing of Senator Eugene McCarthy in the New Hampshire primary on March 12. The candidate whose announcement in November had sparked some wonderment at his kamikaze political drive gained 42.2 percent of the vote three months later. While the president won with 49.4 percent, McCarthy came within 230 ballots of defeating him. Later analysis would reveal that McCarthy's votes included more from those who believed that Johnson's policy in Vietnam was too soft than from those seeking a withdrawal, by a margin of almost three to two.[78] Yet like Tet, at the time it was a psychological if not a technical victory. Although Johnson contended that he was prepared for the results because as an undeclared candidate his name was not on the ballot and thus had to be written in, Reedy remarked that prior to the New Hampshire primary only "a few people close to him [Johnson] had told him verbally that things were in very bad shape."[79]

Johnson's political problems were compounded when McCarthy's success spurred Robert Kennedy to declare his candidacy on March 16. According to one widely circulated account, Kennedy had proposed, through former JFK and LBJ aide Ted Sorensen, that the senator would stay out of the presidential race if the president would change his war policies. If not that, then Johnson should at least appoint Kennedy to be the head of a commission to investigate America's role in Vietnam. Although Kennedy may have considered it a reasonable political proposition, Johnson considered it blackmail and refused. Within four days of the New Hampshire primary, the senator from New York announced his intention to run, standing in the same Senate caucus room where his brother had started his campaign for the presidency eight years earlier. Kennedy based his candidacy on the contention that it was "unmistakably clear that we can change these disastrous divisive policies only by changing the men who are now making them."[80]

Kennedy's entry into the race marked a regeneration of the special rivalry between Johnson and his predecessor's younger brother. The president's grapevine had warned him, in confidential "read and tear up" memoranda, that Kennedy was scouting out his prospects for the highest office; now the rival had declared. Kearns's characterization of Robert Kennedy as "everything Lyndon Johnson hated in others (e.g., 'betrayal') and feared in himself (e.g., 'unmanliness')" seems an excess of psychohistorical analysis. Yet the heir to Camelot and the Irish Mafia's campaign organization posed a political threat worth noting, particularly to a Lyndon Johnson made nervous by the developments of early 1968.[81] Kintner, a friend of both families, had warned uneasily in December that he was "convinced that the bitterness and antagonism between supporters (reporters, political figures, etc.) of the President and of Senator Robert Kennedy will increase in intensity, and is now very marked in Washington and New York." His sense that many in the media favored Kennedy was echoed by others, including Cater, who cautioned in late March of 1968 that the image of Johnson as "an angry, embittered and isolated leader" as conveyed in the news compared badly with "Kennedy's emotional one."[82] "I felt," Johnson later told Kearns, that I was being chased on all sides by a giant stampede coming at me from all directions. On one side, the American people were stampeding me to do something about Vietnam. On another side, the inflationary economy was booming out of control. Up ahead were dozens of danger signs pointing to another summer of riots in the cities. I was being forced over the edge by rioting blacks, demonstrating students, marching welfare mothers, squawking professors, and hysterical reporters. And then the final straw. The thing I feared from the first day of my Presidency was actually coming true. Robert Kennedy had openly announced his intention to reclaim the throne in the memory of his brother. And the American people, swayed by the magic of the name, were dancing in the streets. The whole situation was unbearable for me. After thirty-seven years in public service, I deserved something more than being left alone in the middle of the plain, chased by stampedes on every side.[83]

Yet conflicting with this sense of despair and desperation was a determination to bring the country around to his point of view, defying critics and resisting aggression. At a VFW convention on the day of that first primary, Johnson suggested that New Hampshire was "the only place where a candidate can claim twenty per cent is a landslide, forty percent is a mandate, and sixty per cent is unanimous. . . . They're the only races where anybody can run—and everybody can win."[84]

Johnson's showing in the primary did not feel like a win to many of his staff members; Panzer, for example, cited poor organization as one reason why "we lost in New Hampshire." The veteran James Rowe found it "incredible" that the vote would be regarded as a "crushing defeat" for the president, but he acknowledged that the campaigners had to face some "dismal political facts":

I have said to you before that the *Tet* offensive by the Viet Cong is the cause of all this, including the popularity of McCarthy and the entry of Kennedy. It came as a great shock to the American people, including me, because we all believed (probably including you) the United States was doing very well militarily and not so well on some of the civil problems. Since then the middle group, in which I count the President, has dwindled alarmingly. There are more hawks and many more doves. The polls may show more hawks than doves but I insist . . . that none of us ever find more than one or two isolated hawks. Everyone has turned into a dove.[85]

238

Even Rowe, a self-described "old carrier man who believes in bomb-ing," had been stunned by the news of the offensive, and despite Panzer's claims and Gallup's tallies this political professional knew that Tet had changed the president's political fortunes. "We must find some way," Rowe counseled, "to communicate better with the people and with the young on Vietnam."[86]

That better way would be difficult to find, for reasons that Reedy outlined in a series of memoranda to the president. In his view, Johnson could not afford to engage in "the customary tactics of partisanship," for his responsibility as chief executive demanded that he "do everything possible to sustain the Nation's unity." The president thus faced the problem

> of holding to the middle ground and providing the nation with re-sponsible leadership during a trying period of its history. This is a posture difficult to sustain during a war period when people tend to take "either-or" positions—either surrender to the enemy or annihi-late him. It requires very careful and finely honed thought to avoid this type of polarization *but it must be done and it can be done.* (Emphasis Reedy's)[87]

Interestingly, Reedy urged restraint in terms of the president's re-sponsibilities, rather than using concepts of the political rewards to be reaped from acting presidential; yet he supported his recom-mendations with political assessments. In Reedy's estimation, Nixon was a hawk at heart who "will sooner or later blurt out some extreme statements"; McCarthy was a one-issue candidate who would find himself in the "peace-at-any-price" corner; and Kennedy "still looks like an opportunist who is trying to cash in on the guts of another man." As a consequence, all the administration needed to do was "to state its position clearly, . . . without any comment on the character of the opposition or its personalities." Johnson could win reelection, contended Reedy, but it was imperative that the president "remain aloof from the brawl."

Such detachment was difficult for a man of Johnson's tempera-ment. While he resisted Roche's urging to announce his candidacy, he liked the adviser's description of what would follow: "the air would be cleared, the drums would sound, and your millions of supporters would get a great injection of hope and vigor."[88] Johnson sought to gain that surge of support with two aggressive speeches in mid-March. Speaking to the National Alliance of Businessmen in Washington, Johnson admonished that "those who carry the burdens of public office must do their duty as they see it. . . . As your President,

I want to say this to you today: we must meet our commitments in the world and in Vietnam. We shall and we are going to win." In Minneapolis two days later, the National Farmers Union convention heard Johnson take an even harder line. Warning that the lessons of the *Lusitania* and Pearl Harbor should not be forgotten, he employed the folksy Johnsonian style typical of times of intensity:

> We soon learned that we must never permit an aggressor's appetite to go uncontrolled because the person he eats up today may make him more hungry for you tomorrow. . . . You may want peace with your neighbor, too, and you may be willing to go across the road and into his yard to try to talk him into it. But if he keeps his door barred and every time you call him the call goes unanswered, and he refuses to meet you halfway, your wanting peace with him won't get it for you.[89]

Johnson thus rejected "[the one] extreme that thinks that you can just have peace by talking for it, by wishing for it, by saying you want it, and all you need to do is to pull back to the cities," as well as "[the other] extreme that says, 'Let's go in with flags flying and get it over with quickly, regardless of the dangers involved.' " Johnson presented his policy as a prudent and measured one, but one that needed the understanding support of the public. "The time has come," he exhorted, "when we ought to unite, when we ought to stand up and be counted, when we ought to support our leaders, our Government, our men, and our allies until aggression is stopped, wherever it has occurred." The absence of this support would have dire consequences. Echoing his warning about the psychological victory of Tet, the president stressed, "we ought not let them win something in Washington that they can't win in Hue, in the I Corps, or in Khe Sanh. And we are not going to." Americans would not, vowed Johnson, "tuck our tail and violate our commitments."

The response was fast and furious. Rowe relied on his long friendship with Johnson to permit frank advice:

> The President must change his tactics on the hard line. I am shocked by the number of calls I have received today in protest against your Minneapolis speech. Our people on the firing line in Wisconsin said it hurt us badly. A number of "doves" called me to say they were against the President because of his Vietnam policy but were not resentful and bitter until the Minneapolis speech called them traitors. They said he should accept the fact and realize the country is divided over Vietnam and impugning their patrio-

> tism, as they say the speech did, merely infuriates them. Some people who support your Vietnam policy telephoned to say they thought the speech "hurt our side" a great deal.
>
> The Minneapolis speech said "win the war." . . . (The fact is hardly anyone today is interested in winning the war. Everyone wants to get out and the only question is how.)[90]

Johnson's aggressive demand for unity had boomeranged, antagonizing all sides. While Cater allowed that the speeches may have been effective with the immediate audiences, he noted that the news coverage conveyed that image of "an angry, embittered, and isolated leader" which the president should avoid. It was the same image that backfired in New Hampshire, when the Johnson ads cautioned that "Hanoi is listening" to McCarthy's campaign. The conception conveyed by such images underscored the problem identified by Humphrey: "people interpret our Vietnam position as fixed, hard, inflexible."[91] The same thundering calls for patriotism simply would not work any longer, especially in the wake of Tet.

So it was that those close to Johnson sought to break through the corrosive pall. Just as Clifford sought to redirect the administration's traditional military approach to Vietnam, Rowe and Reedy searched for a new public approach to the issue. Like Clifford, Rowe was uncertain about the specific path to be followed, but he knew that Johnson "must do something exciting and dramatic to recapture the peace issue." Reedy extended Rowe's idea by suggesting a way to utilize "one of the most important trump cards that a President has to play—his power of seizing the initiative."[92] Johnson should announce a thoroughgoing review of American policy in Vietnam, consulting with members of the Cabinet, Congress, the United Nations, and well-known hawks and doves, while making it clear that "the President reserves for himself, and for himself alone, the right of decision." Then Johnson would be able to deliver a major statement on Vietnam which, because of its broad basis in the consultations, could truly unify the country. According to Reedy, this course of action not only would enable the administration to establish the terms of the debate, but it also "presents the President as a man in control of events rather than as a beleaguered person with no option other than to reply to hostile critics." It would allow Johnson to display maximum flexibility without implications of weakness.

Johnson acknowledged the need for a major policy statement on Vietnam; in fact, the first draft of such an address in the White House files is dated February 3, shortly after the Tet offensive exploded. The politics involved in the evolution of what eventually became the March 31 speech are indicative of the value placed on major presidential statements as an articulation of policy, as various factions sought to have their versions accepted. In all, the files contain seven numbered drafts and innumerable revisions and alternatives, each attempting to place Tet in perspective and to announce the future course of America in Southeast Asia.[93]

Rostow fired off a quick critique of the first draft of that speech, saying that McPherson's version needed to point out the communists' two main targets: "the political life of South Viet Nam [and] the political life of the United States." The national security adviser followed this memorandum the next week with an outline for the president of "the kind of reporting and rallying speech you may wish to make." Rostow's schema reiterated familiar themes: assess Tet, explain where we are and where we are going, and vow to be ready for "the real thing" in negotiations while rejecting "phoney peace feelers and chicanery."[94]

In the storm of the major debates over deployments and policies that consumed February and March, the idea of a major statement surfaced occasionally but disappeared into the sea of contention over what exactly such a statement would say. McPherson produced a second major draft dated February 25, but not until almost a month later did the revisions begin in earnest. The writer circulated a new version on March 20; late that afternoon and again on March 22, Johnson met with a group including Rusk, Clifford, Abe Fortas, U.N. Ambassador Arthur Goldberg, and former National Security Adviser McGeorge Bundy to discuss the proposed statement. The exchange quickly focused on the question of a bombing halt, with a range of views being articulated. The secretary of state again advanced his proposal for a carefully staged limitation on bombing; while he did not anticipate that Hanoi would respond, he felt that it would help to reassure the public that the administration truly sought peace. Fortas opposed Rusk's plan on the grounds that any pause favored the North; Goldberg opposed it because it was not a total bombing halt; Clifford found it too open-ended, without the clear delineation of expectations he felt necessary to result in negotiations. Johnson then decided to separate the issue of peace initiatives from the rest of the statement, both to allow further study of the alternatives discussed and to lessen the risk of their premature disclosure. McPherson recollected that "at that time it seemed to me that the signal that was being given to all of us was that we are not going to do it. I never had any instructions to put a bombing pause in the speech, or to seriously consider it." In his memoirs, however, Johnson indicated that his reaction to the discussions included consideration of an option about which only Rusk knew: the president was "judging the possible impact of a peace move linked with an announcement of my decision to withdraw from politics at the end of my term. That consideration put things in another perspective."[95] For the moment, however, he remained silent on that option.

Although McPherson did not perceive a signal from Johnson to include a bombing pause in his draft, the aide did outline a sequence of negotiating steps in a short memorandum dated March 23. Depicting a "we say—they say" scenario that started with a cessation of bombing north of the twentieth parallel, McPherson implied that the exchange would end in a draw. Yet "the purpose of the exercise," he noted, was "to show the American people that we are willing to do every reasonable thing to bring about talks. Each step must be made in the open—not reported after the fact. We are genuinely seeking peace, and we made several offers and counter-offers." Johnson was intrigued, for he called for Rostow, Rusk, and Clifford to comment on the proposal.[96]

In the meantime Bundy, who was "proud to have been asked back [to the White House] at a tough moment," turned his attention to McPherson's draft after the meeting. Sharing his recommendations with only the president, Rostow, and McPherson the next day, the former adviser submitted to Johnson that his amendments to the draft grew "out of a deep sense that we haven't yet got what you need." In the attached memorandum, Bundy acknowledged that a dramatic move such as calling up the reserves might be the only way to break "the interlock between the bad turn in the war, the critical need for a tax increase, and the crisis of public confidence at home." Yet he stressed that the call-up posed many problems, especially for Lyndon Johnson:

> Why should *you* take the whole rap for calling reserves for Vietnam? No good military case for them exists, on anything I have seen, and to me what may make this call really necessary is simply that you may not be able to get the tax increase unless you can prove to some people that we need it for a war in which we are backing Westy [General Westmoreland] all the way. I have a feeling that the cost at home of sending more reserves will be very high and the real military return very low—specially because what people most want is to see the Vietnamese do more and us do less. I hate to see my President held ransom by military men, and their

Congressional friends, who really do not know what to do with the troops they are asking for.[97]

Bundy thus proffered an unusually blunt assessment of the political maneuverings of the Joint Chiefs. In doing so the former aide echoed the reservations penned by Clifford on the back of an envelope: "Check [with] Wheeler on 14,000 callup—they must be put to some kind of activity; . . . those to be called up must be made busy."[98] Given this assessment, Bundy suggested that the draft of the speech should justify the call-up "partly because if we do less we would be unfair both to our own Commander and to his troops," which would lessen the onus on Johnson. He also recommended that the move be cast as "both a limited and a secondary matter as against a new and stronger emphasis on efforts *for* the Vietnamese *by* the Vietnamese." Bundy held a pessimistic view of the "long-term odds" for Saigon's success with those efforts, which must have been disheartening to the president, but he based his advice on

> my belief that the sentiment in the country on the war has shifted very heavily since the Tet offensive. This is not because our people are quitters, and McCarthy and Kennedy did not create the shift, though they may benefit from it. What has happened is that a great many people—even very determined and loyal people—have begun to think that Vietnam really is a bottomless pit. . . . I think it is a miracle, in a way, that our people have stayed with the war as long as they have, but I do not see how we can carry them with us for very much longer if all we seem to offer is more of the same, with stalemate at a higher cost as the only prospect.

Bundy's argument countered the view of opponents to the war that was presented in Johnson's aggressive mid-March speeches; it echoed Cronkite's estimation of a costly stalemate; and it pointed to the concern shared by Rowe and McPherson: the home front, never especially united, had crumbled in the face of Tet, with potentially dangerous consequences.

Clearly Johnson was reevaluating his position in light of those consequences. At a news conference on March 22, the president announced that he was appointing Westmoreland to be chief of staff of the Army as of July 2. The announcement came in an offhanded manner, buried amidst announcements of a series of other appointments, and no successor to the post in Vietnam was named.[99] The effect was to minimize the move as a change in policy, casting it instead as a bureaucratic shuffle. While Johnson had staunchly supported the general, both publicly and privately, the change in military leadership clearly offered greater flexibility regarding Vietnam.

Then the president turned once again to the Wise Men for their counsel and advice. After extensive briefings and lengthy discussions on March 25, the group met with Johnson the next day. While several of the senior advisers, such as Taylor and Abe Fortas, argued that slow but steady progress could still be made with continued American support, most of the men reported deep misgivings about the war. Dean Acheson, secretary of state under President Truman, contended that the stakes simply were not worth the candle; and the majority of those gathered in the White House shared his misgivings. Puzzled by the changes of heart in these previously stalwart supporters, Johnson cross-examined the briefing officers "to find out whether they knew something I did not know" that could explain this major change from November. Yet as Rostow observed, the new view was based on a new perspective, for the Wise Men "were not focussing on Vietnam but on the political situation in the United States." Johnson conceded that all of the advisers were deeply concerned about the domestic divisiveness on the issue, and he traced both divisiveness and concern back to the media. The Wise Men, he submitted, were

> intelligent, experienced men. I had always regarded the majority of them as very steady and balanced. If they had been so deeply influenced by the reports of the Tet offensive, what must the average citizen in the country be thinking? . . . I remained convinced that the blow to morale was more of our own doing than anything the enemy had accomplished with its army. We were defeating ourselves.[100]

Again Johnson perceived his previously steady and loyal supporters to be deserting their posts due to the media's distortions. The president was deeply disturbed by what he learned.

Even as Johnson received the grim assessment of his informal panel of senior advisers, even with his thoughts of a withdrawal-for-peace statement, the campaign planning continued. The contradiction reflected Johnson's genuine indecision, as well as his devotion to open options that would remain most open in the absence of public speculation. The latter part of March thus was filled with strategy planning and political brainstorming, as aides and advisers worked to reelect the president. Rowe urged Johnson to gather a qualified trio of media consultants, headed by Kintner, and to get organized quickly in California. A group of staff members developed a list of eighteen "action images of the President at work," from a walking tour of a black neighborhood in Washington to photographs of grandson Lyn playing beside Johnson's desk as he worked, in order to alleviate that image of "an angry, embittered, and isolated leader" that Cater had identified.[101]

Often these campaign efforts earned the president's explicit approval. Johnson endorsed Panzer's idea that the Democratic National Committee organize a "Jaw Corps" to speak out on radio phone-in talk shows, which the aide dubbed "the modern forum for yesterday's stump speaker who operated on street corners and courthouse steps." The president asked for further consideration of Reedy's vision for reaching young voters: Johnson's supporters should organize "one of those electric guitar 'musical' groups to travel around to meetings. . . . They don't have to be very good musically to get by as long as they have rhythm and make enough noise." Johnson also concurred with Reedy's estimation of the upcoming Campaign Conference for Democratic Women as "the most perfect setup for trouble I have ever seen," enabling the McCarthy and Kennedy forces to create headlines from the divisiveness. In addition, the president ordered aides to find some way to distribute, "to all weeklies and dailies in the nation," Eisenhower's *Readers' Digest* article chastising critics of the war. Anticipating objections in an election year, however, he did not want either the White House or the Democratic National Committee to be the source.[102]

Even in the midst of these plans, however, people like Roche, Rowe, and Lou Harris pushed Johnson to declare his candidacy because "your troops need a standard to rally around," and his announcement would "clear the air and crystallize the situation." When Democratic leaders from Maryland asked whether Johnson was running, Rowe replied that "if he was not I was certainly wasting a lot of my time. The Attorney General remarked," Rowe reported, that "I was giving the same kind of assurance that Governor Agnew did about Rockefeller the day before he pulled out." His memorandum to the president on this exchange was dated March 28.[103]

On that same date five key advisers met to polish Johnson's address, now scheduled for nationally televised delivery in three days. Rusk, Clifford, Rostow, McPherson, and William Bundy gathered in Rusk's office that Thursday morning. Rather than suggesting minor emendations, however, Clifford called for an entirely new speech. "After these exhausting days" of meetings, the new secretary of defense had concluded that "the military course we were pursuing was not only endless, but hopeless. . . . Henceforth, . . . our primary goal should be to level off our involvement, and to work toward gradual disengagement." The current draft, contended Clifford, was completely unattuned to the deeply critical tenor of the country. As he later explained, "I said this was the wrong speech, that it was a speech about war. What the president needed was a speech about peace. For example, the first sentence read, 'I want to talk to you about the war in Vietnam.' I wanted that changed to 'I want to talk to you about peace in Vietnam.' "[104]

Although the president had not called for a new speech, his conversations with the Wise Men, with members of Congress, and with his staff had convinced him that a dramatic defense of American involvement had to be coupled with an equally dramatic move toward peace. Consequently, he had decided to adopt Rusk's proposal from early March, with the cessation of all bombing north of the twentieth parallel. The unilateral action would shed the stipulations of North Vietnamese withdrawal and signs of prompt, productive discussions that he had previously placed on pauses. Although Rusk and Rostow knew of this decision, Johnson did not announce it to the others, later attributing his silence to the "fear of another damaging press leak." Thus while Clifford's arguments on behalf of an end to the bombing were eloquent, the agreement that he gained from Rusk and Rostow as staunch supporters of the war was based on the fact that both already knew of Johnson's decision, as McPherson surmised and later interviews have borne out. The advisers' discussions thus led to work on a new version of the statement.[105]

On Saturday, March 30, that draft was scrutinized by Clifford, Rostow, Bundy, and McPherson, joined now by Johnson as well as Wheeler, Christian, and Rusk's deputy, Nicholas Katzenbach. The secretary of defense, with the eager assistance of McPherson, continually pushed to demilitarize the tone of the message and to emphasize conciliation and negotiation. Clifford knew of Johnson's key concern, as he noted during the meeting: "Can we stop bombing and call up troops at same time?"[106] McPherson worked to reconcile the two steps for the president. As one of the speech writer's assistants expressed it, they were "going for the jugular" of the problem, and so they strove to make the statement as clear and well refined as possible.[107]

By that evening, three key audiences had been notified that Johnson would announce the bombing halt: congressional leaders, Saigon, and American ambassadors in SEATO countries. The statement was essentially in place at that time, with the exception of the conclusion. At 9:30 P.M., McPherson sent a peroration to the president, explaining that "it does not light up the sky with rockets" because "if you come on with a strong 'we must resist aggression' line at the end of a peaceful initiative speech, people will say, 'ah—now here comes the *real* Johnson, Old Blood and Thunder'; and . . . the real purpose of the speech will be lost."[108]

The president, however, had a different peroration in mind. Calling on Horace Busby to redraft the announcement he had planned for January 17, and then comparing that draft with Harry Truman's remarks at the Jefferson-Jackson Day Dinner sixteen years earlier, Johnson decided to end his announcement of the peace initiative by announcing the end of his term as president. Busby therefore spent the day of the address in the Treaty Room, writing and revising the passage while well fortified with cigarettes and coffee.[109]

Firming Johnson's resolve to use such a closing were personal factors: at 7:00 A.M. that day, his daughter Lynda returned from her journey to the West Coast, where she had seen her husband off to Vietnam; met by her parents, exhausted and near tears, she asked why her husband had to risk his life "for people who did not even want to be protected." Lynda, who had voted absentee two days earlier with the announcement that "I'm putting on my button now and wearing it until November!," now echoed the question posed by the Episcopal minister just four-and-a-half months earlier: Why? Knowing that her daughter was suffering, yearning to comfort her husband, Lady Bird Johnson could only watch, seeing "such pain in his eyes as I had not seen since his mother died."[110]

The pain did not lessen when the president went to church later that day with Luci and her husband, for he knew that this son-in-law would soon join the other in Southeast Asia.

When he stepped before the television cameras at 9:00 P.M. on Sunday, March 31, 1968, Johnson had reached a watershed. He repeated his San Antonio formula and then presented his far-reaching proposal for the bombing halt, which made that formula obsolete. Then pausing only briefly, he said:

> With America's sons in the fields far away, with America's future under challenge right here at home, with our hopes and the world's hopes for peace in the balance every day, I do not believe that I should devote an hour or a day of my time to any personal partisan causes or to any duties other than the awesome duties of this office—the Presidency of your country.
>
> Accordingly, I shall not seek, and I will not accept, the nomination of my party for another term as your President.[111]

The president was ebullient. The audience was stunned. So, too, were the commentators, who searched for words of explanation for their viewers, and the White House correspondents, who pressed the president on his decision in a conference following the speech until he declared, "my statement speaks for itself. I don't see why we should have these high school discussions about it."[112]

The country first sat in shock and disbelief ("I knew it was March 31, and heard Johnson saying 'April Fool!,' " one listener recalled); then the president's popularity jumped from 36 percent to 49 percent. Almost 49,000 telegrams arrived at the White House within two days; of the 1,364 Watson had tallied, 752 were friendly and asked Johnson to reconsider his decision, 414 were friendly, and 77 were unfriendly. The remaining 121 were ambiguous, such as those that simply read, "Thank you." The White House would receive an estimated 30,000 letters in all after the March 31 speech.[113]

On April 3, 1968, the White House would also receive a message from Hanoi: North Vietnam was ready to talk.

"Lyndon Johnson did not like to be compared with a crippled waterfowl," observed George Christian, "and he should not be." A lover of politics to his very marrow, even after the March 31 speech he could more accurately be called a "screaming eagle" than a "lame duck," as ABC's Frank Reynolds commented one evening.[114] The month of April was consumed with following up the nebulous diplomatic opening with which Hanoi had provided him on April 3, including lengthy discussions with South Vietnamese leaders and another conference in Hawaii. Finally, on May 3, 1968, Johnson was able to announce that talks would begin in Paris on May 10. The dramatic announcement of March 31 and vigorous diplomatic follow-up seemed to be working.[115]

Spicing these efforts was a flurry of interviews and talks with correspondents as they sought to discover what had led to the president's decision to withdraw, how he assessed the upcoming convention and elections now that he was out of the race, what future he foresaw for Vietnam, and how he would evaluate his presidency. These interviews stressed the general public image he wanted to convey: that Lyndon Johnson "is going to be President until the day he walks out of here," which did not allow any ebb in the administration's activity eight or nine months before that day.[116] The effort was not always successful; *Time* printed a piece entitled "The Administration—Winding Down," and reporters from the *Wall Street Journal* and elsewhere talked of a lack of "zip" and a listlessness in Johnson's

White House. Although Christian found the *Time* story to be "relatively mild," he "had a long discussion" with correspondents to dissuade them from this image of ennui; he cautioned the staff against giving the impression "that we were already packing up to go home"; and he took heart at a proposed *Newsweek* essay on the dedication of remaining staff and Cabinet members which would help offset that feeling.[117]

Johnson himself had lost none of his spark, as one staff member who remained would discover just six weeks before the man left office. When Joseph Califano informed the president that he had talked with columnist Joseph Kraft, Johnson responded: "May I *again—again* ask you and all your *associates* to please meet with press members during your association with my adm[inistration] upon request of Press Secretary Christian only—This request has been made before and will not be made again."[118] Media coverage always concerned Johnson. So did the economic development of Southeast Asia, a project on which he continued to work throughout 1968. Despite Eugene Black's missions and meetings, however, Congress would not pass further funding for the Asian Development Bank until 1970, under the next administration. The timing must have galled Lyndon Johnson.

Even with this continued activity, however, Mrs. Johnson noticed that the president became more relaxed, more detached, and more philosophical as he worked to preserve his record and savored the prospect of personal peace that lay ahead. Johnson retained the commitment to be president to the end; but the departure of a number of staff and Cabinet members added poignancy, especially when one party mushroomed into a farewell salute to four people.[119]

The press's attitudes toward Johnson also relaxed to a degree after his March 31 announcement. It was not only that the attention was now diffused among the viable political candidates, contended Christian, the last and longest lasting of Johnson's press secretaries. The correspondents also felt, he postulated, "sort of a nostalgia that here this boisterous, active, newsworthy Administration was going to come to a close." They may have rankled at his secrecy and raved at his travel habits, but the correspondents recognized that there was "hardly a dull day in the Johnson Administration." Lyndon Johnson was "fascinating," James Reston recalled; when he left office, "everyone in Washington had a personal story to tell. When Nixon left, nobody had any stories."[120]

The months following Johnson's withdrawal from the campaign thus saw a number of supportive columns and letters, and a Gallup

250

poll declaring him to be "the most popular living figure on college campuses today." The aide sending the latter information to the president added that "a certain young candidate with a youthful haircut was not mentioned at all."[121] Johnson's staff members urged him to capitalize on that support by re-emphasizing domestic affairs "to erase the 'war President' image," especially in light of the Paris peace talks. They also reminded themselves, in preparing reports and speeches, that "the President deserves a product that will *not* raise the specter of a credibility gap."[122]

The summer and fall of 1968 were far from carefree, however. On April 4, Martin Luther King was assassinated in Memphis, a death that touched off rioting and provided a grimness one week later to Johnson's signing of his third civil rights bill as president. On June 5 the horror was repeated when Robert Kennedy, jubilantly celebrating his primary victory in California, was gunned down in a Los Angeles hotel. The tension and despair of November 1963 returned.

At the tumultuous August convention in Chicago, Hubert Humphrey gained the Democratic nomination for president. Johnson watched the proceedings on television at the ranch, declining to attend. The combination of presidential candidate and vice-presidential incumbent roles was not easy for Humphrey; faced with an unpopular war but still part of the administration, he found himself attempting a delicate balancing act in which he tried to reconcile his political obligations with his political aspirations. Johnson, in turn, tried to avoid showing Humphrey an excess of favoritism by, for example, informing him of developments concerning Vietnam by way of conference calls with the other candidates rather than notifying the vice-president first. The situation was conducive to hurt feelings, stories of a rift, and pressure to learn more of Johnson's intentions. A somewhat exasperated McPherson finally suggested that the best answer to the question "What is the President going to do for the Vice President?" was to say that Johnson's "strongest contribution . . . [is] devoting himself to meeting the foreign and domestic problems our country faces today."[123]

Not even after the convention did Johnson's presidential pace slacken. He spent the month of October working on a settlement with the North Vietnamese, which would allow the complete cessation of bombing without unduly endangering American forces in the South. Balancing the still disparate factions within his administration, wrestling with the South Vietnamese leaders for their cooperation, and struggling to prevent press speculation from undercutting his efforts added an almost intoxicating tension to the latter months of his presidency. In a televised address on Thursday, October 31, Johnson informed the American people that

> I have now ordered that all air, naval, and artillery bombardment of North Vietnam cease as of eight A.M. Washington time, Friday morning. I have reached this decision . . . in the belief that this action can lead to progress towards a peaceful settlement of the Vietnam war. . . . What we now expect . . . are prompt, productive, serious, and intensive negotiations in an atmosphere that is conducive to progress.[124]

Christian later revealed that public speculation over this new peace effort had been diverted, much to the administration's relief, when the news broke that Jacqueline Kennedy would marry Aristotle Onassis. This development for the former first lady brought relief of another kind as well, as Mrs. Johnson mused:

> One of the oddest things is that as the result of the wedding which will happen tomorrow on a Greek island, I feel strangely freer. No shadow walks beside me down the hall of the White House or here at Camp David . . . I wonder what it would have been like if we had entered this life unaccompanied by that shadow? (Ellipses hers)[125]

Similarly, Lady Bird would ponder whether her husband's job would have been easier had he placed more of his own people in strategic positions following the 1964 election. Others shared her thought as they traced part of the credibility gap to the difficulties posed by a double-layered staff.

By October of 1968, however, such speculations were idle. Even Johnson's announcement of an end to all bombing was viewed by many as a politically expedient move timed to gain votes for the vice-president. More than two-thirds of the telegrams to reach the White House after the speech were critical.[126] Five days later, Humphrey lost to the Republican candidate—the man of whom Johnson had said four years earlier, "I knew in my heart that it was not right for Dick Nixon to ever be President of this country."[127]

The day after Lyndon Johnson announced his decision not to run for reelection, he spoke to the National Association of Broadcasters; three days before leaving office, he appeared before the National Press Club. In these two sets of remarks, both made at critical times during the end of his presidency, Johnson addressed the issue of presidential-press relations.

On April 1, 1968, Johnson told the NAB members that "the very deep and very emotional division in this land that we love today" stemmed in part from the problems of "informing the people":

> I think I can speak with some authority about the problem of communication. I understand, far better than some of my severe and perhaps intolerant critics would admit, my own shortcomings as a communicator.
>
> How does a public leader find just the right word or the right way to say no more and no less than he means to say—bearing in mind that anything he says may topple governments and may involve the lives of innocent men?
>
> How does that leader speak the right phrase, in the right way, under the right conditions, to suit the accuracies and contingencies of the moment when he is discussing questions of policy, so that he does not stir a thousand misinterpretations and leave the wrong connotation or impression?
>
> How does he reach the immediate audience and how does he communicate with the millions of others who are out there listening from afar?
>
> The President, who must call his people and summon them to meet their responsibilities as citizens in a hard and an enduring war, often ponders these questions and searches for the right course.[128]

Lyndon Johnson did ponder those questions. He was particularly uncertain of the appropriate responses in an age in which informing the people depended to such a large extent on media—channels with which he was uncomfortable and interpreters with whom he often did not agree.

At the end of his presidency, then, Johnson would joke with the members of the National Press Club about the ancestor who "was in a fight at the Alamo—that is, the Alamo Hotel in Eagle Pass, Texas." He would also tell of showing his gallbladder scar only after reporter Sarah McClendon asked, "Mr. President, you have been in office for two years and what do you have to show for it?" Putting aside such lightheartedness, however, Johnson suggested that the

> relationship between the President and the press has always had the nature . . . of a lover's quarrel. I'm not sure it is ever going to be much different. And that doesn't bother me as long as both sides concern themselves with the basic fundamentals, and as long as Presidents and each member of the press base their acts upon the

respect for each other's purposes. . . . I would be less than candid if I failed to say that I am troubled by the difficulties of communicating with and through the press.[129]

Once out of office, he would express his discomfort with that relationship in terms that turned the lover's quarrel into a shotgun wedding, with Johnson as the reluctant groom.[130]

Lyndon Baines Johnson "regretted more than anyone could possibly know that I was leaving the White House without having achieved a just, an honorable, and a lasting peace in Vietnam."[131] He lamented "the difficulties of communicating with and through the press" as well as his inability to quiet the dissenters who had, he was convinced, such a disastrous effect on the course of America's involvement in Vietnam. To Johnson, one problem caused the other, for he remained convinced that the lack of public support for his policies and ultimately his inability to achieve that just, honorable, and lasting peace was due to the ability of the media

> to create a climate of dissent and opposition in Washington and New York and the academic community that was a tremendous distortion of the way the country felt. But this had its effect. . . . The overall effect, I think, was to weaken the effectiveness of America's action [and] to diminish the chances for a successful negotiation of a peace settlement.[132]

On January 20, 1969, Lyndon Johnson left the home he had made in the capital to return to the Hill Country of Texas. His direct responsibility for the war was over, as was his daily relationship with the press; but both would bother him until the day he died—January 22, 1973.

Epilogue

The primary significance of this study is its account of media influence on Lyndon Baines Johnson's Vietnam war rhetoric. It is a story of tragic dimensions, with a protagonist who envisioned himself as the quintessential national leader becoming increasingly mired down in a nasty, brutish war that was thousands of miles from home, which despite his best efforts he was unable to sufficiently justify to either the press or the American public. As a story of communication failure, its implications for contemporary American life are profound.

Lyndon Johnson had come to the presidency believing that he was the right man in the right place at the right time to lead America forward. Eric Goldman has concluded that he was "the tragic figure of an extraordinarily gifted President who was the wrong man from the wrong place at the wrong time under the wrong circumstances."[1] Yet given the constraints of the rhetoric of a limited war and presidential-press relations, no one could be right.

Notes

Unless otherwise noted, the archival materials cited below are from the Lyndon B. Johnson Library in Austin, Texas (see Bibliography, pp. 321ff.).

Chapter 1. Introduction

1. In his memoirs, Johnson posited that "three separate conditions were required before social change could take root and flourish in our national life—a recognition of need, a willingness to act, and someone to lead the effort. In 1963 I saw those three conditions coming together in historic harmony." See Lyndon B. Johnson, *The Vantage Point: Perspectives of the Presidency, 1963–1969* (New York: Holt, Rinehart and Winston, 1971), 70.

2. Scott Nearing, *War or Peace?* (New York: Island Press, 1946), 12; A. A. DeWeerd, "Civilian and Military Elements in Modern War," in *War as a Social Institution*, ed. J. D. Clarkson and T. C. Cochran (New York: Columbia University Press, 1941), 111. I am indebted to David M. Berg for his generosity in sharing the concept of the rhetoric of limited war.

3. Michael J. Arlen, *Living-Room War* (New York: Viking Press, 1969), 6. For discussions of the difficulties faced by correspondents, see for example Bernard C. Cohen, *The Press and Foreign Policy* (Princeton: Princeton University Press, 1963), 95; Malcolm W. Browne, "Viet Nam Reporting: Three Years of Crisis," *Columbia Journalism Review* 3 (Fall 1964): 4–9.

4. Johnson, *Vantage Point*, 149; Leslie H. Gelb, "The Essential Domino: American Politics and Vietnam," *Foreign Affairs* 50 (April 1972): 459–75.

5. David Halberstam, *The Best and the Brightest* (Greenwich, Conn.: Fawcett Publications, 1969), 778.

6. Cited by Bernard Fall, "Master of the Red Jab," *Saturday Evening Post*, November 24, 1962, 20.

7. William C. Westmoreland, interview with George Esper, "3 Years Later, Viet Memories Haunt Many," Lafayette, Indiana, *Journal and Courier*, April 30, 1978, A-7.

8. George C. Herring, "The War in Vietnam," in *Exploring the Johnson Years*, ed. Robert A. Divine (Austin: University of Texas Press, 1981), 42 and 55.

9. See Philip E. Converse, Warren E. Miller, Jerold G. Rusk, and Arthur C. Wolfe, "Continuity and Change in American Politics: Parties and Issues in

256

the 1968 Election," *American Political Science Review* 63 (December 1969): 1083–105.

10. Michael Baruch Grossman and Frances E. Rourke, "The Media and the Presidency: An Exchange Analysis," *Political Science Quarterly* 91 (Fall 1976): 455. Following the practice of the White House press corps and the White House Press Office, the term "press" refers to both print and broadcast media throughout this study.

11. Ibid., 456.

12. Ibid., 456–57.

13. Ibid., 457.

14. Cited in "Mr. President . . . Mr. President . . . ," *Inside Story*, transcript of program aired November 1981 on PBS.

15. Cable, Johnson to Westmoreland, February 14, 1967, Ex PR 18, box 359.

16. Elmer E. Cornwell, Jr., "The Johnson Press Relations Style," *Journalism Quarterly* 43 (Spring 1966): 8.

17. Delmer D. Dunn, *Public Officials and the Press* (Reading, Mass.: Addison-Wesley, 1969), 169.

18. Bill D. Moyers, "The Press and Government: Who's Telling the Truth?" *Mass Media in a Free Society*, ed. Warren K. Agee (Lawrence: University Press of Kansas, 1969), 19.

19. Ibid.

20. Oral history interview transcript no. 2, March 10, 1969, 15–16 and 18.

21. Dunn, *Public Officials*, 169.

22. Liz Carpenter, *Ruffles and Flourishes* (New York: Doubleday, 1970), 98.

23. Cited in Doris Kearns, *Lyndon Johnson and the American Dream* (New York: Harper & Row, 1976), 313–14.

24. Cited in Theodore H. White, *The Making of the President, 1968* (New York: Atheneum Publishers, 1969), 101.

25. David L. Paletz and Robert M. Entman, *Media Power Politics* (New York: Free Press, 1981), 54.

Chapter 2. The Prepresidential Years

A wealth of materials on Lyndon Johnson's prepresidential years is available. The most exhaustive account yet published is Robert A. Caro's *The Path to Power*. The first of a proposed trilogy of Johnson's life and times, *Path* begins with the settlement of the Texas Hill Country and concludes with Johnson's unsuccessful bid for the Senate in 1941. Caro's extensive research (including a wide range of oral histories) and well-drawn portraits of the

historical contexts are constrained by his contention that Lyndon Johnson's
complexities may be simply explained: the man was completely amoral and
possessed by a raw passion for power.

Doris Kearns provides a more concise yet still detailed account of Johnson's youth from a psychohistorical perspective in *Lyndon Johnson and the
American Dream*. Like Caro's work, Kearns's analysis is marred by the
simplicity of her explanations (his mother fostered his idealism and the drive
to succeed, his father the interest in politics and power). Also like Caro,
Kearns's perspective is both fascinating and informative.

The cultural-historical perspective of Ronnie Dugger's volume, *The Politician*, serves as a good complement to Kearns's work. Although most of the
biographical material is available elsewhere, the Texan's explanations of
Johnson's attitudes as encapsulations of frontier values and myths are
thoughtful and provocative.

Most biased but still useful are the earliest books on Johnson. Glowing
accounts include Pool, Craddock, and Conrad's *Lyndon Baines Johnson: The
Formative Years*, written by three historians at San Marcos. The campaign
biographies of 1964 by Mooney, Provence, and White offer similarly golden
views of the man. In contrast, Haley provides a bitter account from the right
in *A Texan Looks at Lyndon: A Study in Illegitimate Power*. A more carefully
researched view is offered by Alfred Steinberg in *Sam Johnson's Boy*.

One of the more enjoyable accounts of Johnson's family background is *My
Brother Lyndon*, by younger sibling Sam Houston Johnson. Sam Houston's
irreverence and storyteller's touch provide a vividly human view of Lyndon.
More research-oriented but still highly readable is Merle Miller's *Lyndon: An
Oral Biography*, based on oral histories. The oral histories at the Johnson
Library offer another rich resource.

The best account of Johnson's years in the Senate is Evans and Novak's
Lyndon B. Johnson: The Exercise of Power. It is concise, detailed, well
researched, and well written. In a different vein, George Reedy's *Lyndon B.
Johnson: A Memoir* provides an intimate view of the man from one who
worked for him from the Capitol to the White House.

1. Merle Miller, *Lyndon: An Oral Biography* (New York: G. P. Putnam's
Sons, 1980), 26.

2. Interview with Tom Nichols, secretary to the president, San Marcos,
March 31, 1965, in William C. Pool, Emmie Craddock, and David E. Conrad,
Lyndon Baines Johnson: The Formative Years (San Marcos: Southwest Texas
State College Press, 1965), 99. Harry Provence relates that years later, Dr.
Evans, the president of San Marcos during this period, would tease his former
assistant: "Lyndon, I declare you hadn't been in my office a month before I
could hardly tell who was president of the school—you or me." See Harry

258

Provence, *Lyndon B. Johnson: A Biography* (New York: Fleet Publishing Corp., 1964), 30.

3. Cited in Pool, Craddock, and Conrad, *Formative Years*, 110.

4. Robert A. Caro, *The Years of Lyndon Johnson: The Path to Power* (New York: Alfred A. Knopf, 1982), 194; 160. Caro relies especially on the assessments of two of the original founders of the White Stars, who felt that Johnson slipped control of their organization away from them. Caro includes the contention that Johnson stole elections at San Marcos; see pp. 178–80.

5. Miller, *Lyndon*, 30.

6. Quoted by Caro, *Path*, 203.

7. Miller, *Lyndon*, 41.

8. Caro, *Path*, 225; chap. 13.

9. Arthur Perry, cited by Booth Mooney, *The Lyndon Johnson Story*, rev. ed. (New York: Farrar, Straus, 1964), 18.

10. Jones as quoted by Ronnie Dugger, *The Politician* (New York: W. W. Norton, 1982), 190.

11. Ava Johnson Cox, quoted by Caro, *Path*, 442; see chap. 21.

12. Caro, 436–37, 501.

13. Ibid., chap. 27, provides a compelling description of life in the Texas Hill Country without electricity as well as the changes that power brought.

14. In ibid., chaps. 20, 23, and 24, Caro details these entanglements. Briefly, the questions involved the dam's purpose (the publicly approved flood control and irrigation or the politically charged production of power), the construction of a federal dam on state-owned property, and reimbursement for extensive construction already undertaken by Brown and Root without the clarification of such legalities. Caro contends that the solution Johnson set forth was filled with "violations of law and logic . . . but law and logic could not stand on Capitol Hill against raw power—and Johnson had power on his side" (p. 467). Brown's token of gratitude, according to Caro, consisted of unlimited and unrestricted funding for Johnson's political ambitions. In chap. 35, Caro describes the investigation of these contributions by the Internal Revenue Service, an investigation that Caro argues would have ended Johnson's political career had it not been halted by President Roosevelt himself. Identifying less nefarious motivations behind Johnson's maneuvering for the dam, Dugger points instead to Johnson's desire to bring cheap public electricity to the country while engendering a minimum of antagonism from the power industry (pp. 209–15).

15. Dugger, *Politician*, 215.

16. Johnson as quoted in ibid., 309; see also chaps. 2 and 27.

17. Quoted by Miller, *Lyndon*, 76.

18. Caro, *Paths*, chap. 32, especially p. 659.

19. The election of 1948 has continued to be controversial. In 1977, a former Texas election judge declared that he knew at the time that Johnson had stolen the election. A former FBI agent and Stevenson supporter who investigated the charges of fraud contended that the official certainly was aware of the stolen votes, because "he's the guy that did the actual vote stealing. . . . The 202 votes are in his handwriting." Moreover, the supporter argued, Johnson did not need to make any arrangements for the ballots, for the boss of the machine in the contested county would have delivered them against Coke Stevenson no matter who his opponent was. See Miller, *Lyndon*, 124–37.

20. Rowland Evans and Robert Novak, *Lyndon B. Johnson: The Exercise of Power* (New York: New American Library, 1966), 36.

21. Ibid., 42.

22. Hubert H. Humphrey, oral history interview transcript (OH), August 17, 1971, 4.

23. Evans and Novak in *Exercise of Power* observe that "no record was kept and the exact number—[Hubert] Humphrey remembers just three votes—is now lost forever" (p. 68). Like the editing of the *Congressional Record*, the obliterated vote is an example of the ways in which Congress's consideration for its own members makes the historian's job more difficult. The election was recorded as unanimous.

24. George E. Reedy, *The Twilight of the Presidency* (New York: World Publishing, 1970), 56.

25. Cited in Mooney, *Johnson Story*, 93–94.

26. Cited in Doris Kearns, *Lyndon Johnson and the American Dream* (New York: Harper & Row, 1976), 141.

27. Humphrey, OH, 16.

28. Cited, for example, in Evans and Novak, *Exercise of Power*, 61.

29. Ibid., 115–16. In *American Dream*, Kearns offers a similar description of the Treatment, pp. 123–24; almost any book on Johnson's political career will refer to his powerful personality.

30. Evans and Novak, *Exercise of Power*, 95.

31. Cited by Kearns, *American Dream*, 136. In a strongly anti-Johnson campaign biography, James Haley's criticism is harsher: "Johnson had destroyed the purpose and function for which the Congress was created. By destroying its deliberative nature, he had destroyed Congress itself." See James Evetts Haley, *A Texan Looks at Lyndon: A Study in Illegitimate Power* (Canyon, Tex.: Palo Duro Press, 1964), 184.

32. Cited in William L. Rivers, *The Opinionmakers: The Washington Press Corps* (Boston: Beacon Press, 1967), 23.

33. Willie Day Taylor, oral history interview transcript no. 1, November 29, 1968, 29.

260

34. Stewart Alsop, "Lyndon Johnson: How Does He Do It?," *Saturday Evening Post*, January 24, 1959, 13–14.

35. Recounted in Provence, *Biography*, 75.

36. Two or three hours before Johnson's heart attack, he had become enraged at a reporter for what he perceived to be badgering—a psycho-physiological condition which might have been part precursor, part cause of the heart attack.

37. Alsop, "Lyndon Johnson: How Does He Do It?," 14.

38. Cited by Provence, *Biography*, 88.

39. Evans and Novak, *Exercise of Power*, chap. 12; George Reedy, *Lyndon B. Johnson: A Memoir* (New York: Andrews and McMeel, 1982), 127–28.

40. Kearns, *American Dream*, 160; Lippmann as cited by Philip Geyelin, *Lyndon B. Johnson and the World* (New York: F. A. Praeger, 1966), 16.

41. Robert S. Allen, oral history interview transcript, May 30, 1969, 21.

42. Geyelin, *Johnson and the World*, 36. In *American Dream*, Kearns offers an acid estimation of Johnson's behavior, declaring that on his vice-presidential trips Johnson was "once again the spoiled, demanding, and exuberant child" (p. 167).

43. See, for example, George E. Reedy, oral history interview transcript no. 3, December 19, 1968, 8. Elsewhere, Reedy contends that Johnson performed well while visiting Third World countries because they reminded him of his youth in Texas, but that he grew defensive when facing more advanced countries. See Reedy, *Memoir*, 24.

44. Evans and Novak, *Exercise of Power*, 348.

45. Memorandum, Johnson to Kennedy, May 23, 1964, "Mission to Southeast Asia, India, and Pakistan," Vice-Presidential Security File, Vice-Presidential Travel, Vice President's Visit to Southeast Asia, May 9–24, 1961 (1). The copy at the Johnson Library has been sanitized; the excised passage can be found in the *Pentagon Papers* version.

Chapter 3. Transition to the Presidency, November 1963 to Spring 1964

1. Johnson, *Vantage Point*, 93.

2. Memorandum, Liz Carpenter to Johnson, November 23, 1963, Diary Backup for November 23, 1963. The Diary Backup also indicated that Mrs. Johnson called Mrs. Graham that day. Philip and Katherine Graham, publishers of the *Washington Post* and *Newsweek*, had visited the LBJ ranch during Johnson's tenure as Senate majority leader, around 1956 or 1957; moreover, Evans and Novak note that Ted Sorensen and John Kenneth Galbraith wrote the first draft of Johnson's initial message to Congress and the nation at the Graham home. Philip Graham committed suicide in August

of 1963, leaving Katherine in charge of the publications taken over from her parents. See Katherine Graham, oral history interview transcript, March 13, 1969, 36, Johnson Library; Agnes Meyer papers, subject file 1910–72, White House correspondence, Johnson administration, box 71, Library of Congress; Evans and Novak, *Exercise of Power*, 368.

3. Address Before a Joint Session of the Congress, November 27, 1963, *Public Papers*, 8.

4. "LBJ Takes Command," *Newsweek*, December 9, 1963, 20.

5. Cited by Eric Goldman, *The Tragedy of Lyndon Johnson* (New York: Alfred A. Knopf, 1969), 96.

6. Louis Heren, *No Hail, No Farewell* (New York: Harper & Row, 1970), 24–25. Lincoln, Kinch, and Timmons, all journalists, observed that the press corps' fondness for Kennedy created difficulties for Johnson. See Gould Lincoln, oral history interview transcript, September 28, 1968, 10; Sam E. Kinch, Sr., oral history interview transcript, June 3, 1970, 17; Bascom Nolly Timmons, oral history interview transcript, March 6, 1969, 21.

7. Geyelin, *Johnson and the World*, 7.

8. Johnson, *Vantage Point*, 95.

9. James B. Reston, interview with the author, May 17, 1980, Notre Dame, Indiana.

10. Memorandum, Nancy H. D. [Handman Dickerson] to Johnson, November 25, 1963, Diary Backup, November 25, 1963, box 1.

11. For letters of thanks see, for example, Johnson to John S. Haye, President, Post-Newsweek Stations, January 15, 1964 (Ex PR 18, box 355), thanking him for a WTOP editorial; Johnson to Ted Lewis, *New York Daily News* Washington Bureau Chief, February 4, 1964 (Ex PR 18, box 355), thanking him for "the really outstanding piece of photographic work." For letters of welcome, see, for example, Johnson to Everett D. Collier, *Houston Chronicle*, February 5, 1964, Ex PR 18, box 355. For requests, see letter, William K. Goolrick, *Saturday Evening Post*, December 13, 1963, requesting a story on the Johnson ranch and its history, with an attached memorandum from Reedy to Johnson, December 14, 1963, recommending cooperation; letter, Charles Roberts, *Newsweek*, February 5, 1964, requesting photographs of Johnson with staff members, with attached memorandum from Reedy to Johnson which the president marked "disapprove," all in Ex PR 18, box 355.

12. Daily Diary, November 27, 1963. The entry indicates that Alsop assured Johnson that his speech before Congress was a "triumphant success."

13. Frank Cormier, *LBJ: The Way He Was* (Garden City, N.Y.: Doubleday, 1977), 4–5. While Cormier indicates such passages as direct quotations from Johnson and others throughout his book, he never indicates whether these passages were tape-recorded, taken down in shorthand, or reconstructed from

262

notes and/or memory. For similar versions of this story, see Hugh Sidey, *A Very Personal Presidency: Lyndon Johnson in the White House* (New York: Atheneum, 1968), 172; and Theodore H. White, *The Making of the President, 1964* (New York: Atheneum, 1965), 72–73.

14. Dan Rather, CBS News correspondent, the transcript of a symposium at the Johnson Library: in *The Presidency and the Press*, ed. Hoyt Purvis (Austin: Lyndon B. Johnson School of Public Affairs, University of Texas at Austin, 1976), 29.

15. Cormier, *LBJ*, 5; Reedy, *Memoir*, 60.

16. Sidey, *Very Personal Presidency*, 171–72.

17. Rivers, *Opinionmakers*, 170–71.

18. Chester R. Huntley, oral history interview transcript, May 12, 1969, 8.

19. This account is drawn primarily from Goldman, *Tragedy of Lyndon Johnson*, especially chapter 7. According to a memorandum to the president from Dick Nelson, a meeting he held with Goldman, Abe Fortas, Horace Busby, George Reedy, and Bill Moyers recommended "that no formal group should be organized; that Professor Goldman should be given status as a member of the President's staff on whatever basis is appropriate, [and] that this appointment should be made public so that Professor Goldman will have sufficient status to deal effectively with those people with whom he will be expected to deal." Obviously not all of their recommendations were taken. The memorandum, dated December 12, 1963, is in CF SP 2-4, box 88.

20. Evans and Novak, *Exercise of Power*, 422.

21. Remarks on the Third Anniversary of the Alliance for Progress, March 16, 1964, *Public Papers*, 384.

22. Lady Bird Johnson, *A White House Diary* (New York: Holt, Rinehart and Winston, 1970), 338–39; Evans and Novak, *Exercise of Power*, 405.

23. Cited in Geyelin, *Johnson and the World*, 183.

24. President's News Conference of April 7, 1954, *Public Papers*, Dwight D. Eisenhower, 383.

25. Cited in Geyelin, *Johnson and the World*, 192.

26. President's News Conference of May 5, 1961, *Public Papers*, John F. Kennedy, 354.

27. Statistics from the Office of the Assistant Secretary of Defense (Comptroller), cited in Guenter Lewy, *America in Vietnam* (New York: Oxford University Press, 1978), 24.

28. Heren, *No Hail*, 40.

29. Halberstam, *Best and Brightest*, 349.

30. Transcript of Broadcast on NBC's "Huntley-Brinkley Report," September 9, 1963, *Public Papers*, JFK, 658–61.

31. Memorandum, Johnson to Kennedy, May 23, 1961, Vice-Presidential

Security File, Vice-Presidential Travel, Vice-President's Visit to Southeast Asia, May 9–24, 1961 (1).

32. William S. White, oral history interview transcript no. 1, March 5, 1969, 20.

33. Johnson, *Vantage Point*, 42; Address Before a Joint Session of the Congress, November 27, 1963, *Public Papers*, 8.

34. Memorandum, Mansfield to Johnson, December 7, 1963, National Security File (NSF): Vietnam (VN), box 2, no. 119a. Halberstam contends that Kennedy rejected Mansfield's document of disenchantment (*Best and Brightest*, 256–57).

35. Memorandum, McNamara to Johnson, December 21, 1963, NSF:VN, box 1, no. 130. This memorandum has been sanitized both by the Department of Defense and by donor stipulations.

36. Memorandum, McCone to Johnson, December 23, 1963, NSF:VN, box 1, no. 142.

37. Memorandum, McNamara to Johnson, December 21, 1963, NSF:VN, box 1, no. 130.

38. See the President's News Conference of February 29, 1964, *Public Papers*, 324, a statement that brought a handwritten note from Lodge to Johnson, thanking the president for his "expression of confidence" (March 1, 1964, NSF:VN, box 2, no. 82). See Johnson, *Vantage Point*, 44, for a list of the posts to which new people were assigned; see the memorandum for the record by Michael V. Forrestal, Department of Defense, February 20, 1964, NSF:VN, box 2, no. 99. A memorandum from Forrestal to Bundy on March 9, 1964, indicating the rapid handling of a Lodge request, implied that Lodge had complained of poor treatment again (NSF:VN, box 2, no. 50).

39. Memoranda, Mike Mansfield to Johnson, January 6, 1964, with a copy of his commencement address at Michigan State University on June 10, 1962, NSF:VN, box 1, nos. 118–19; Bundy to Rusk and McNamara, January 6, 1964, NSF:VN, box 1, no. 120c; and [Rusk, January 6 or 7, 1964], "U.S. Policy on Vietnam," NSF:VN, box 1, no. 120a. McNamara's memorandum of refutation (NSF:VN, box 1, no. 120b) has been withdrawn due to security classifications.

40. Heren, *No Hail*, 24–25. Heren observed that even what the press regarded as such a manipulative request did not heavily impair the respect and warm feelings that media members had for the smooth young President Kennedy. Halberstam, *Best and Brightest*, 257, contends that Kennedy warned his aides against close association with journalists during their tours of Vietnam.

41. Memorandum, Forrestal to Johnson, January 31, 1964, NSF:VN, box 1, no. 103.

264

42. Memorandum, Forrestal to Bundy, April 20, 1964, NSF:VN, box 3.

43. Memorandum, Forrestal to Bundy, March 18, 1964, NSF:VN, box 2, no. 59.

44. Cable, Rusk/State Department to the American embassy in Saigon, March 20, 1964, NSF:VN, box 3, no. 36. The *New York Herald Tribune* and the *Washington Star* were also mentioned.

45. Cable, Henry Cabot Lodge to Murrow, January 10, 1964, NSF:VN, box 1, no. 66.

46. Browne, *Columbia Journalism Review* 3 (Fall 1964): 6.

47. Cable, Lodge to W. Averell Harriman, Undersecretary of State, March 3, 1964, NSF:VN, box 2, no. 42.

48. Memorandum, Bundy to Johnson, March 13, 1964, NSF:VN, box 2, no. 55.

49. Memorandum, W. W. Rostow to Rusk, May 6, 1964, NSF:VN, box 3, no. 123.

50. Johnson, *Vantage Point*, 66.

51. Letter, Johnson to the Speaker of the House of Representatives, May 18, 1964, NSF:VN, box 4, no. 41b.

52. Drew Pearson, December 1, 1963, in an item cited by the organization syndicating Pearson's column in its letter encouraging editors to renew their subscriptions—a copy of which is in the Johnson files. See mimeographed letter from John Osenenko, Bell-McClure Syndicate to editors, n.d., Ex PR 18, box 355.

53. Memorandum, Horace Busby to Johnson, January 23, 1964, Ex FG 1, box 9.

54. Carpenter, *Ruffles and Flourishes*, 251.

55. For discussions of accessibility, see Chalmers Roberts (*Washington Post*), oral history interview transcript, April 23, 1969, 12–13; Arthur Krock, oral history interview transcript, November 21, 1968, 23; and Timmons, OH, 21. A memorandum from Chris Camp in the White House Press Office to Ken O'Donnell, Liz Carpenter, Sanford Fox, and Major Stover on December 13, 1963, lists dinner guests for December 16 (Ex PR 18, box 355). Finally, Lady Bird Johnson, *White House Diary*, 29–30, and Reston in his interviews with the author, May 17, 1980, mentioned the Restons' visit to the ranch.

56. Letter, Charles W. Bailey to Johnson, February 26, 1964, Ex PR 18, box 355.

57. President's News Conference of January 25, 1964, *Public Papers*, 230; see also 232–33.

58. Mimeographed report, "From Edward R. Murrow and the News—American Broadcasting Corporation," February 24, 1964, in Ex PR 18, box 355.

59. Appearing on "Meet the Press" after he left the White House, Salinger

criticized Johnson's Latin American policy for containing "the seeds of destruction" for United States and Latin American relations. See the transcript of "Meet the Press," May 24, 1964, in the Lawrence Spivak papers, A-43, Library of Congress. In a memorandum to Johnson dated February 4, 1964, Salinger objected that the transfer of White House photographer Yoichi Okamoto ("Okie") was both unfair and unwise. Current articles mentioning the man were not based on interviews with him, Salinger contended; moreover, his work would be especially helpful during the campaign. Although Johnson merely wrote "not approved" at the bottom of Salinger's protest, Okamoto returned later to take a sizeable portion of the official White House photographs, including many that appear in the Johnsons' memoirs. Salinger's memorandum is contained in CF PR 18, box 83.

60. Reedy, interview with the author, May 19, 1978; and OH no. 3, 28.

61. Eugene Patterson, oral history interview transcript, March 11, 1969, 8–15. This account serves as an example of the potential usefulness of oral history interviews. The story is related by a number of authors, but attributed only to "a journalist"; the oral history interview fills in many of the details. Although it includes quotations, it is doubtful that Patterson would claim exact authenticity for the citations; rather, this style suited the manner of his oral history interview.

62. Letter, James Rowe to Johnson, April 9, 1964, Ex PR 18, box 356.

63. Cabell Phillips, "White House Aides Seek to Impugn Baker Witness; Attempt to Use Secret U.S. Documents to Cast Doubt in Press on Reynolds, Who Testified on Gift to Johnson," New York Times, February 8, 1964, 1-A.

64. Transcript of Television and Radio Interview Conducted by Representatives of Major Broadcast Services, March 15, 1964, Public Papers, 365. At his February 29 press conference, Johnson had brushed off a question about Baker being under investigation by the Senate (Public Papers, 323). Perhaps this helps explain why Baker depicts Johnson as a "coward who never stood up for his friends."

65. President's News Conference of April 4, 1964, Public Papers, 437.

66. Cormier, LBJ, 85.

67. " 'Mr. President, You're Fun,' " Time, April 10, 1964, 23.

68. George E. Reedy, interview with the author, May 19, 1978, Milwaukee, Wisconsin.

69. Ibid.

70. William S. White, oral history interview transcript no. 2, March 10, 1969, 8–9.

71. Memorandum, Jack Valenti to Bill Moyers and Horace Busby, April 6, 1964, Ex PR 18, box 356. The ten newspapers listed by Valenti are the Washington Star, the Washington Daily News, the New York Post, the New York Daily News, the New York Times, the Baltimore Sun, the Philadelphia

266

Inquirer, the Washington Post, the New York Herald Tribune, and the New York Journal American. Other newspapers fell in the province of Wayne Phillips. Throughout the White House Central Files are memoranda reporting to Johnson the placement of especially noteworthy pieces, as well as commending the insertion efforts of various loyal congressmen.

72. Evans and Novak, Exercise of Power, 438.

73. Goldman, Tragedy of Lyndon Johnson, 118.

74. Reedy, OH no. 3, 35.

75. Evans and Novak, Exercise of Power, 444.

76. Draft of a memorandum, ABC, CBS, and NBC to Johnson, January [ ], 1964 (date left blank), proposing the facilities (Gen WH 3-3, box 5); draft of letter, Johnson to the networks, April 30, 1964, thanking them for their generosity in "financing the design, construction, and maintenance of these modern facilities" (Ex WH, box 5). The former proposal almost reads as if it had been drafted by the White House staff.

77. The bureau chiefs' meeting was proposed in a letter from Paul Martin of Gannett Newspapers to Jack Valenti on May 13, 1964 (Ex PR 18, box 356). On May 19, Reedy compiled a list of bureau chiefs and correspondents (Ex PR 18, box 356), and the meetings were instituted. One such gathering was held August 12 at 6:30 P.M.; see memorandum to Cater, August 3, 1964, Ex PR 18, box 356.

78. List and memorandum, Reedy to Valenti, May 13, 1964; revised list and memorandum, May 19, 1965, both Ex PR 18, box 356.

Chapter 4. Increasing Complications,
Spring 1964 to Winter 1964–65

1. According to Sidey, Very Personal Presidency, 48. See also Lady Bird Johnson, White House Diary, 107–8.

2. Lady Bird Johnson, White House Diary, 117.

3. Sidey, Very Personal Presidency, 48.

4. Memorandum, McNamara to Johnson, December 21, 1963, NSF:VN, box 1, no. 130.

5. Lady Bird Johnson, White House Diary, 158.

6. Halberstam, Best and Brightest, 144.

7. Cited in Neil Sheehan et al., The Pentagon Papers as Published by the "New York Times" (New York: Bantam Books, 1971), 247–49.

8. For example, in a memorandum to Johnson dated June 24, 1964 (NSF:VN, box 15), McGeorge Bundy reports that "John McCone [director of the CIA] has been telling everybody in Government that you can easily get a Congressional Resolution if you want one. . . . I have told him that he should

convert Morse first." See also Cater's memorandum to William Bundy, June 12, 1964, Cater files, box 13, Memos to the White House Staff, May–November, 1964.

9. Johnson, *Vantage Point*, 115.

10. Memorandum, Rostow to Rusk, May 6, 1964, NSF:VN, box 3, no. 123, Vietnam Memos, vol. III, 5/64.

11. Memorandum, Cater to Johnson, June 23, 1964, Cater files, box 13, Memos to the President, May–August, 1964. At the bottom of Cater's several suggestions, Johnson's handwritten note says, "Doug—This good—Carefully comb Humphrey for all ideas and then forward to appropriate officials."

12. Memorandum, Bundy to Johnson, June 24, 1964, along with draft, Douglass Cater, dated June 22, 1964 (NSF:VN, box 15, Vietnam/Southeast Asia—Draft Statements, Speeches, etc.).

13. This notation is in Johnson's handwriting at the bottom of Bundy's memorandum to Johnson, June 24, 1964, NSF:VN, box 15.

14. Remarks at the Annual Swedish Day Picnic, Minnehaha Park, Minneapolis, June 28, 1964, *Public Papers*, 830.

15. Memorandum, Cater to Johnson, with Johnson's handwritten response, June 29, 1964, Cater files, box 13.

16. Johnson, *Vantage Point*, 70.

17. Lady Bird's entries for May 14, June 14, and July 11, 1964, all explicitly link Johnson's indecision regarding the 1964 campaign to his concern over the situation in Vietnam (pp. 137–40, 166–67, and 176).

18. See, for example, Horace Busby's memorandum of public relations ideas, sent to Johnson January 23, 1964 (Ex FG 1, box 9), which included suggestions for combatting stories of his ill health (discussed in greater detail in chapter 3). Compare with Johnson, *Vantage Point*, 92–101.

19. Johnson, *Vantage Point*, 93–94, cited the memorandum in full, while Lady Bird Johnson, *White House Diary*, 137–40, paraphrased it. Stated in terms of the negatives presented by each course of action, the memorandum's primary criterion is pain: which would be the least painful course? All citations in these two paragraphs are from *Vantage Point*.

20. Lady Bird Johnson, *White House Diary*, 166–67. Lady Bird's diary is peppered with references to Johnson's indecision. In addition to the entries referring to Vietnam (see note 17), see also the passages on pp. 165–66, 175, and 192.

21. Cormier, *LBJ*, 67.

22. Ibid., 91.

23. Johnson, *Vantage Point*, 96.

24. Ibid., 88, 95.

25. Columnist Drew Pearson, generally supportive of Johnson, ac-

knowledged this role of "shop talk" in the columnists' work in a letter to Bill Moyers, July 9, 1965, Ex PR 18, box 357. See also memorandum, Perry Barber to Jack Valenti, December 9, 1964, Ex PR 18, box 356.

26. Elmer Cornwell, "The Truman Presidency," in *The Truman Period as a Research Field*, ed. Richard S. Kirkendall (Columbia: University of Missouri Press, 1967), 145. According to William S. White, Johnson "never liked the huge press conference because he always had kind of a feeling there was something phony about it, particularly under television." See White, OH no. 2, 15.

27. M. L. Stein, *When Presidents Meet the Press* (New York: Julian Messner, 1969), 154; see also Cormier, *LBJ*, 59, and James B. Reston, "The Press, the President, and Foreign Policy," *Foreign Affairs* 44 (July 1966): 563.

28. George Reedy, OH no. 3, 39.

29. White, OH no. 2, p. 15, characterizing Johnson's attitude; Reedy, OH no. 3, p. 39.

30. Reedy, OH no. 3, p. 34.

31. Goldman, *Tragedy of Lyndon Johnson*, 202.

32. Sidey, *Very Personal Presidency*, 46.

33. Related in Cormier, *LBJ*, 63.

34. Geyelin, *Johnson and the World*, 143; Sidey, *Very Personal Presidency*, 117. According to Sidey, "a rather normal week's White House output of words, by mouth and on paper, was more than twenty thousand. His private background sessions for reporters rarely lasted less than an hour. Three hours was not unusual. One Saturday meeting . . . went for seven hours." Reston also mentions this lavish attention in his *Foreign Affairs* essay, "Press, President, and Foreign Policy," 563–64. Chalmers Roberts notes that such talkative meetings were particularly popular with Johnson during the 1964 campaign (OH, 13–14). George Reedy claims that Johnson was so horrified of long, dull weekends that he would call up newsmen and carry on for several hours about his overwork. See Reedy, 26.

35. Reedy, OH no. 3, p. 37.

36. Ibid., 38. Reedy admitted that his use of statistics was flawed, since combining the audiences for all media does not take into account the duplications there.

37. Ibid., 35.

38. Ibid., 38.

39. Arthur L. Edson as cited by Cormier, *LBJ*, 62. See also Lady Bird Johnson, *White House Diary*, 132–33.

40. Reedy, OH no. 3, p. 38.

41. According to Cormier, *LBJ*, 63.

42. Heren, *No Hail*, 36.

43. Cormier, *LBJ*, 71. See, for example, Lady Bird Johnson, *White House Diary*, 174 and 182.

44. Cormier, *LBJ*, 28. William L. Rivers describes the flurry of activity and the difficulties of tracking Johnson during these ranch visits in *Opinionmakers*, 23. Charles Roberts of *Newsweek* told the garbage-truck saga in an address at the University of Minnesota, October 13, 1966, entitled "The President and the Press." Kinch observed that when the press was moved from Austin to San Antonio, they charged that Johnson wanted to remove them from the feud between Johnson's friend John Connally and Ralph Yarborough. Instead, Kinch asserts, the press corps was "getting a little tired of Austin," and Johnson wanted to be able to visit his Austin office without always being trailed by the media (OH, 15–17). Reedy contended that the reporters would have been closer to the feud in San Antonio than in Austin, in his interview with the author, May 19, 1978. Johnson's desire to work in Austin without the press corps along would later lead to a formal protest by the White House Correspondents Association, as chapter 8 details.

45. Reedy, OH no. 3, p. 33. Johnson's last press secretary, George Christian, offers elaboration on Johnson's views of travel plans in *The President Steps Down: A Personal Memoir of the Transfer of Power* (New York: Macmillan, 1970), 19–20.

46. Jack Valenti, *A Very Human President* (New York: Pocket Books, 1976), 212.

47. Ibid., 212, 209–13. White concurs even more strongly with this interpretation, attributing the credibility gap to "reportorial pique" over Johnson's insistence on keeping his options open (White, OH no. 2, p. 5).

48. Sheehan et al., *Pentagon Papers*, 260.

49. In a memorandum to George Reedy on August 7, 1964, clarifying the chronology of events, McGeorge Bundy stressed that the National Security Council's discussion of Johnson's proposed course of action "was marked by thoroughness, clarity, and an absence of significant disagreement" (NSF:VN, box 15).

50. Johnson, *Vantage Point*, 115.

51. Arthur M. Schlesinger, Jr., *The Imperial Presidency* (New York: Popular Library, 1974), 177.

52. See Johnson's discussion of this conference, in *Vantage Point*, 115–17. Apparently Halleck later raised objections, for Bundy sent a memorandum to Walter Jenkins on August 24, 1964, thanking him for his summary of the leadership meeting: it "gives me everything I need, and it bears out the recollection of others present. I am sure that on this basis we can deal with Halleck sharply as and when we need to." The memorandum is contained in NSF:VN, box 16, 3A (2).

270

53. McPherson relates a scene in the Senate when the aide encouraged the majority leader to support the repeal of the loyalty oath. Johnson "wheeled on me, and leaning over until we were nose to nose, said, 'No, sir. I'm not going to do it. You liberals want me to get the Democratic party into a national debate: "Resolved: That the Communist Party is good for America," with the Democrats taking the affirmative, and I'm not going to do it.'" See Harry McPherson, *A Political Education* (Boston: Little, Brown, 1972), 108.

54. Box 1497 of Reedy's files contains a folder entitled What Goldwater Said, 1953–1964, including such items as Goldwater's April 7, 1964, speech in Oregon; his interview in the May 20, 1964, issue of *Newsweek*; his appearance on "Issues and Answers" on May 24, 1964; and his "Remarks at Tucson, Arizona" on June 25, 1964.

55. Radio and Television Report to the American People Following Renewed Aggression in the Gulf of Tonkin, August 4, 1964, *Public Papers*, 927.

56. Public Law 88-408, August 10, 1965, *United States Statutes at Large*, vol. 78, 88th Cong., 2d sess., 1964, 384.

57. Sheehan et al., *Pentagon Papers*, 259–60.

58. Johnson, *Vantage Point*, 113.

59. Ibid., 117–18. The term "Southeast Asia" implies a broader obligation than "Gulf of Tonkin" does—both in the sense of geography and in the sense of time. The official designation of Public Law 88-408 is as a joint resolution "to promote the maintenance of international peace and security in Southeast Asia."

60. Goldman, *Tragedy of Lyndon Johnson*, 180.

61. Reedy, *Twilight*, 40.

62. Lewy, *America in Vietnam*, 35.

63. Memorandum, James L. Greenfield to Rusk, August 6, 1964, NSF:VN, box 6, no. 127.

64. Jules Witcover, "Where Washington Reporting Failed," *Columbia Journalism Review* 9 (Winter 1970–71): 10.

65. James Aronson, *The Press and the Cold War* (Indianapolis: Bobbs-Merrill, 1970), 219.

66. Sheehan et al., *Pentagon Papers*, 270.

67. Johnson, *Vantage Point*, 98.

68. Ibid., 99.

69. Philip Graham detailed his version in Theodore H. White, *Making of the President, 1964*, 407–15. O'Donnell and Powers's account is in their book, *"Johnny, We Hardly Knew Ye"* (Boston: Little, Brown, 1970), 193–97.

70. Booth Mooney reports this incident in his oral history interview, April 8, 1969, 33.

71. Johnson, *Vantage Point*, 2.

72. As cited by Kearns, *American Dream*, 199–200. As with other quotations of Johnson by Kearns, no exact date or context for these remarks is given.

73. Charles McDowell, Jr., *Campaign Fever: The National Folk Festival from New Hampshire to November 1964* (New York: William Morrow, 1965), 29.

74. Johnson, *Vantage Point*, 100. The memorandum is reprinted on pp. 576–77; all citations are drawn from this. The available files at the Johnson Library shed little light on this episode; for instance, fourteen memoranda have been withdrawn from Marvin Watson's file on Robert Kennedy in accordance with donor stipulations, leaving only newspaper punditry concerning the attorney general's potential candidacy.

75. While Johnson says in his memoirs that he told Kennedy of this exclusion by virtue of his Cabinet position, the memorandum does not mention this reason, focusing instead on the lack of necessary political strength that Kennedy could offer to the party's ticket (Johnson, *Vantage Point*, 99–100, 576–77).

76. McDowell, *Campaign Fever*, 143.

77. Cormier, *LBJ*, 95.

78. Evans and Novak, *Exercise of Power*, 470n. Actually it was not the last report; Johnson mentioned groups for Rusk, Freeman, and McNamara in *Vantage Point*, 99.

79. White, *Making of the President, 1964*, 264.

80. Memorandum, Bundy to Johnson, August 20, 1964, NSF:VN, box 16, no. 185a.

81. Cited in Goldman, *Tragedy of Lyndon Johnson*, 210, and Cormier, *LBJ*, 98.

82. See Cormier, *LBJ*, 98, and Goldman, *Tragedy of Lyndon Johnson*, 211. In his memoirs, Johnson wrote that he asked both Humphrey and Dodd to come because "I had told Dodd earlier that I would advise him of my decision before I announced it publicly"; he did not explain why he did so in person rather than by telephone (*Vantage Point*, 101).

83. Evans and Novak, *Exercise of Power*, 485.

84. Cormier, *LBJ*, 96–99.

85. Chester R. Huntley, OH, 19.

86. President's News Conference of August 18, 1964, *Public Papers*, 978.

87. News Conference No. 391, August 25, 1964, Press Secretary's News Conferences, box 4.

88. Johnson, *Vantage Point*, 96–98; Lady Bird Johnson, *White House Diary*, 192–93. In the first of a series of five postpresidential interviews conducted by Walter Cronkite, Johnson echoed his concern at that late date in

1964 about "a general inability to stimulate, inspire, and unite all the people of the country." The transcript for the interview, "Why I Chose Not to Run," aired on December 27, 1969, is in the oral history file of the Johnson Library.

89. Lady Bird Johnson, *White House Diary*, 192; Johnson, *Vantage Point*, 98. Johnson noted that *Time* "just that week had run a highly critical article about Lady Bird." Apparently he was referring to "The Multimillionaire," an article on the Johnsons' business interests that appeared in the August 21, 1964, issue, pp. 15–16.

90. President's News Conference Before Departing for Atlantic City for the National Convention, August 26, 1964, *Public Papers*, 1007.

91. Johnson, *Vantage Point*, 110. Even with the Great Society posters, two huge pictures of Johnson and Kennedy flanked the speakers' stand, underscoring the relationship between the two men.

92. Kearns posits Johnson's fear of losing as a major theme in *American Dream*, tying his illnesses to his insecurity: appendicitis before his election to Congress, kidney stones before his election to the Senate, and the 1955 heart attack during a tense period as Senate majority leader. From the perspective of cognitive dissonance, Johnson's doubts about accepting the nomination in 1964 would have pressured him all the more to want a large victory once he did decide to run.

93. Johnson, *Vantage Point*, 103.

94. Memorandum, Reedy to Johnson, August 18, 1964, Ex PR 18, box 356.

95. Remarks in Atlantic City at the Convention of the United Steelworkers of America, September 22, 1964, *Public Papers*, 1106.

96. Cormier, *LBJ*, 109; see also Goldman, *Tragedy of Lyndon Johnson*, 209, and James Deakin, *Lyndon Johnson's Credibility Gap* (Washington, D.C.: Public Affairs Press, 1968), 13.

97. Remarks in Manchester to the Members of the New Hampshire Weekly Newspaper Editors Association, September 28, 1964, *Public Papers*, 1163.

98. Ibid.; see also Remarks in Memorial Hall, Akron University, October 21, 1964, *Public Papers*, 1391. When Humphrey appeared on "Meet the Press" on September 20, 1964, Lawrence Spivak asked him why the Democrats continually implied that Goldwater would use nuclear weapons in Southeast Asia when he had stated he would not. Humphrey responded that Goldwater was a "shifting target," making it difficult at times to know exactly what his proposals were, and that the Republican *had* said he would "defoliate" the jungles of Vietnam. The transcript is contained in the Spivak papers, A-44, Library of Congress.

99. Remarks at a Barbeque in Stonewall, Texas, August 29, 1964, 1022; see also Remarks in New York City Before the American Bar Association, August 12, 1964, 1311; Remarks in Manchester, September 28, 1964, 1164; and

Remarks in Memorial Hall, Akron University, October 21, 1964, 1391, all in *Public Papers*.

100. Johnson, *Vantage Point*, 68.

101. Ibid. Four years later, Rostow would assure the president that his statements had been reasonable: "As I read it now, the question on your mind must have been the possibility of triggering a war with Communists with all that involved" (memorandum, October 3, 1968, NSF:VN, box 17). As discussed in chapter 8, staff members anticipating the 1968 election prepared themselves to refute charges of inconsistency.

102. Johnson, *Vantage Point*, 68.

103. Goldman, *Tragedy of Lyndon Johnson*, 229. Johnson himself devoted six pages to campaign trips, savoring the recollection of realizing "what a landslide was in the making" (*Vantage Point*, 105–10).

104. Columnist Mary McGrory suspected this campaign style to be "a program of self-revelation" intended to counter his image as a manipulative politician (cited in McDowell, *Campaign Fever*, 199); a more plausible explanation lies in Johnson's sheer exuberance at being unleashed among his constituency. Aides encouraging a greater informality of style included W. I. Jorden, a *New York Times* reporter who moved to the State Department. Jorden sent a memorandum to Douglass Cater on September 18, 1964, to complain that "a distinctive Johnson style of presentation has failed thus far to emerge in the campaign." Passed on to the president, the memorandum urged that he drop the "Kennedy or pseudo-Kennedy tone in prepared remarks" to better "convey a clear impression of his strengths or his unique approach to problems and to people" (Gen PR 3/J, box 11). Once Johnson adopted this approach, however, Max Freedman and other journalists would complain of a lack of substance in Johnson's campaign speeches (memorandum, Cater to Johnson, October 16, 1964, Ex FG 1, box 10).

105. Cormier, *LBJ*, 114–15. Cormier notes that he had not made any such claims in his stories, and speculates that he may have been simply a representative of the culprit group who happened to be handy. See also Goldman, *Tragedy of Lyndon Johnson*, 238, who relates a similar story about Johnson's October trip to Louisville; Evans and Novak, *Exercise of Power*, 499; White, *Making of the President, 1964*, 265.

106. President's News Conference of October 3, 1964, *Public Papers*, 1195–96.

107. See memorandum, Cater to Johnson, October 1, 1964, regarding the praise of a professor at the University of Maryland for Johnson's book, *My Hope for America*, with Johnson's handwritten notation at the bottom: "Doug—leak this—L" (Cater files, box 13, Memos to the President, September–November 1964). Ex PR 18, box 356 and Ex FG 1, box 10 contain a number of letters and telegrams in September, October, and November 1964,

274

thanking editors, publishers, and journalists for their support. In addition, Johnson invited Kay Graham to the ranch for the last weekend in August, and an effusive note of thanks from Sylvia Porter Collins on November 4, 1964, brought instructions from the president to invite her to the ranch some time as well (Ex PR 18, box 356). One notable example of soliciting media reactions came on October 18, 1964, when Moyers sent telegrams to thirty-four editors and publishers asking for their opinions of Johnson's speech of that evening on recent events in Russia, China, and Great Britain (Ex PR 18, box 356). Finally, in Ex PR 18, box 356, several memoranda from September refer to a request from the National Newspaper Publishers Association for a conference with Johnson. When Johnson approved it, he asked, "Who are they?"; Reedy responded, "These are Negro newspaper publishers and we should set something up fast."

108. According to Melvyn H. Bloom, the Republican National Headquarters contacted pro-Goldwater papers in the Midwest, promising to hold a press conference on the suppressed story if it did not appear. The editors in turn pressured the news services in Washington, who would no longer keep the story off the wires. See Bloom, *Public Relations and Presidential Campaigns* (N.Y.: Thomas Y. Crowell, 1973), 167–68. Both Kearns (*American Dream*, 207–8) and Goldman (*Tragedy of Lyndon Johnson*, 250) say Johnson attributed the entire affair to a Republican conspiracy which framed Jenkins, but Johnson makes no reference to the incident in *Vantage Point*.

109. Kearns, *American Dream*, 208.

110. Cited by Goldman, *Tragedy of Lyndon Johnson*, 250. When she said goodbye to the Jenkins family as they left Washington to return to Texas, Lady Bird Johnson recorded in her diary that "Walter is as much a casualty of the incredible hours and burdens he has carried in government service as a soldier in action" (*White House Diary*, 204).

111. Statement by the President on Walter Jenkins, October 15, 1964, *Public Papers*, 1354–55.

112. George Reedy, oral history interview transcript no. 4, December 20, 1968, 3. Reedy explained it as an attempt to put the situation into perspective—unnecessary at that point because the press already had it in perspective and undesirable because Johnson was "tired and . . . overstimulated by an extremely successful day of campaigning," so he did not do it well.

113. Reedy, OH no. 4, p. 3, and Cormier, *LBJ*, 129. Reedy did not specify who the "certain members of the press" were.

114. Cited by Goldman, *Tragedy of Lyndon Johnson*, 253.

115. Cited by Kearns, *American Dream*, 209.

116. Cited by Kearns, *American Dream*, 291. In *Vantage Point*, Johnson says that the vote might not have represented "a mandate for unity," but he knew it was "a mandate for action" (p. 110).

117. Memoranda and letters on various facets of the planning of the facility extend from December 29, 1964, to April 23, 1965, when Valenti informed Johnson that the White House Television Theatre was ready, in Ex WH, box 5. See also CF WH, box 98, from which a memorandum from Gordon Chase to Valenti dated January 21, 1965, is withdrawn because it discusses security aspects of the facility.

118. Memorandum, Cater to Johnson, November 28, 1964, Ex PR 18, box 356.

119. At the top of Cater's November 28 memorandum is written: "For George Reedy—Your view? JV." On November 30, Reedy sent his reaction to Valenti (Ex PR 18, box 356).

120. Memorandum, Perry Barber to Valenti, December 9, 1964, Ex PR 18, box 356.

121. Letter, Philip Potter to Johnson, December 5, 1964, Ex PR 18, box 356. The three-page letter is filled with typographical errors (corrected here), which may indicate the comfortable relationship between the two men, or may indicate either a time bind or Potter's lack of typing skills.

122. Letters, Hoyt to Johnson, February 10, 12, and 13, 1965, all attached to memorandum, Valenti to Johnson, February 13, 1965; and letter, Valenti to Hoyt, February 13, 1965 (Ex PR 18-2, file 1/1/65–4/9/65).

123. Memorandum, Dave Waters and Simone Poulain to Johnson, December 15, 1964, Ex PR 18, box 356.

124. Memorandum, Liz Carpenter to Johnson, December 4, 1964, Ex PR 18, box 356. Carpenter had also advised Valenti, prior to a holiday trip to the ranch, that "women help to get pictures on page 1, so get some" (memorandum, November 19, 1964, Ex PR 18, box 356).

125. Liz Carpenter, interview with the author, July 20, 1979, Austin, Texas.

126. Memorandum, Cater to Johnson, December 26, 1964, Ex PR 18, box 356.

127. Reedy, *Twilight*, 22.

128. Johnson had continued the meetings with the bureau chiefs begun earlier that year, meeting with groups on December 14 and 16, 1964 (memoranda, Willie Day Taylor to Johnson, December 14 and 15, 1964, Ex PR 18, box 356). In addition, when White House radio and television correspondents requested a background session similar to that given for the print media, Johnson granted it. See memoranda in Ex PR 18, box 356, on December 17 and 26, 1964, and January 19, 1965.

129. Memorandum, Valenti to Cater, January 4, 1965, Ex PR 18, box 356. Valenti requested reactions from Reedy, Moyers, Busby, Carpenter, Goodwin, and Goldman. The only responses to his request in the White House Central Files are a memorandum from Liz Carpenter to Johnson, January 5,

276

1965, and a memorandum from McGeorge Bundy to Johnson, January 7, 1965 (both in Ex PR 18, box 356).

130. Memorandum, Tom Johnson to Moyers, January 17, 1965, Ex PR 18, box 356.

131. Interview with the author, May 19, 1978, Milwaukee, Wisconsin; and Reedy, OH no. 3, p. 33.

132. Cormier, *LBJ*, 90.

133. Johnson had banished Okamoto to the USIA early in 1964 when stories broke that he was the President's "personal photographer"—a move that annoyed then press secretary Pierre Salinger. See Salinger's memorandum to Johnson, February 4, 1964, CF PR 18, box 83.

134. Memorandum, Al Spivak to Jack Valenti, January 21, 1965, Ex PR 18, box 356.

135. President's News Conference of February 4, 1965, *Public Papers*, 133–34.

136. Memorandum, Cater to Johnson, February 4, 1965, Cater files, box 13; memorandum, Palmer to Johnson, February 10, 1965, Ex PR 18-2, file 1/1/65–4/9/65.

137. According to Lady Bird's entry for February 9, 1965, Humphrey came to dinner, "his usual exuberant self," telling of this explanation for his absence (*White House Diary*, 240). Mrs. Johnson's account stresses Johnson's illness and her hope that "he doesn't let the speculation of the columnists and his own sense of rising to duty cause him to go to Churchill's funeral" despite his health (p. 232).

138. Evans and Novak, *Exercise of Power*, 526.

139. Reedy, OH no. 3, p. 31.

140. See Goldman's account of the event and its press coverage, *Tragedy of Lyndon Johnson*, 277–79.

141. Letter, Moyers to Alsop, January 18, 1965; letter, Alsop to Moyers, January 21, 1965; and letter, Moyers to Alsop, January 22, 1965 (all in Ex FG 1, box 11).

142. Memorandum, Connie to George Reedy, February 9, 1965, with request from Valenti for information for White, Ex PR 18, box 356.

143. Memorandum, Angier Biddle Duke to Jack Valenti, January 26, 1965, Ex PR 3, box 10.

144. Written on a memorandum from Reedy to Johnson, February 19, 1965, which encouraged Johnson to grant the request in Gemmell's letter of February 18 (Ex PR 18, box 357).

145. Johnson's handwritten note on memorandum, Rather to Reedy, n.d., Ex PR 18, box 356.

146. Cormier, *LBJ*, 147–48.

147. Lady Bird Johnson, *White House Diary*, 199.

148. Johnson, *Vantage Point*, 120.

149. President's News Conference at the LBJ Ranch, November 28, 1964, *Public Papers*, 1615.

150. Joseph Alsop, "Matter of Fact: Accepting Defeat," *Washington Post*, December 23, 1964, A21.

151. Evans and Novak, *Exercise of Power*, 555.

152. Memorandum, Johnson to Bundy, December 29, 1964, NSF:VN, box 10, no. 139. The enclosures were Cousins's December 12 editorial in the *Saturday Review*, E. Palmer Hoyt's letter to Johnson of December 19 with a *Denver Post* editorial; and a memorandum to Hoyt from Bill Hosokawa, a *Post* editor.

153. Memorandum, Johnson to McNamara, January 7, 1965 (NSF:VN, box 10, no. 129), with the enclosed *U.S. News* article dated January 11, 1965. Johnson's missive echoes Bundy's memorandum to the president dated January 4, 1965 (NSC History, box 40, vol. I, tab. 2).

154. Memorandum, Bundy to Johnson, January 27, 1965, cited by Johnson, *Vantage Point*, 122. The memorandum has not been declassified at the time of this writing.

Chapter 5. The Evolution of the Johns Hopkins Address, April 7, 1965

1. Johnson, *Vantage Point*, 125. Johnson does not indicate whether such quotations are drawn from memory, notes, or transcripts. Ronnie Dugger develops a fascinating argument about the influence of Texas frontier mythology on Johnson's presidential perspective in parts 1 and 5 of *Politician*.

2. Telegram, Taylor to Johnson, January 27, 1965, NSC History, July 1965 Troop Decision, box 40, tab 11. John McNaughton drafted a telegram to Ambassador Taylor on January 25, 1965, sending a copy to Bundy with the note that "this follows Bob's suggested line (he is out of town). Cy [Vance] approves" (NSC History, July 1965 Troop Decision, box 40, vol. I, tab 9, no. 20). Rusk responded to Taylor's cable on January 27, 1965, asking for recommendations on a public rationale for the evacuation; he requested that General Khanh of the South Vietnamese government issue a strong statement of support because the "press here [is] already starting to play Khanh-Buddhist link and possible trend toward negotiation" (NSC History, July 1965 Troop Decision, box 40, tab 12).

3. Memorandum, Bundy to Johnson, February 7, 1965, NSC History, July 1965 Troop Decision, box 40, vol. I, tab 22, no. 45).

4. Halberstam, *Best and Brightest*, 631.

5. Cited in Kearns, *American Dream*, 263.

6. Transcript, background briefing with George Reedy and McGeorge Bundy, February 8, 1965, NSC History, July 1965 Troop Decision, box 40, tab 30.

7. Memorandum, Busby to Bundy, February 9, 1965, in Busby files, box 19 (1301), Memos for McGeorge Bundy.

8. Telegram, McNaughton to Westmoreland, February 8, 1965, NSC History, July 1965 Troop Decision, box 40, vol. I, tab 29, no. 59.

9. Memorandum, Greenfield to Rusk, February 16, 1965, NSC History, July 1965 Troop Decision, box 40, vol. I, tab 59, no. 122a.

10. Telegram, Taylor to McNamara, [February] 22, 1965, NSC History, July 1965 Troop Decision, box 40, vol. II, tab 74, no. 14a.

11. Lewy, *America in Vietnam*, 42.

12. Memorandum, James C. Thomson, Jr. to McGeorge Bundy, February 15, 1965, NSF:VN, box 12, no. 187. There is no indication, such as a note saying "for the President's night reading," that Johnson saw this memorandum.

13. Cited in "We Will Be Far Better Off Facing the Issue," *Time*, February 26, 1965, 19–21.

14. Goldman, *Tragedy of Lyndon Johnson*, 402–3.

15. Joseph Alsop, "'We Can' or 'We Can't,'" *Washington Post*, February 8, 1965, A-17.

16. James B. Reston, "What Are Our Aims in Vietnam?," *New York Times*, February 12, 1965, 28.

17. Letter, James Rowe to Johnson, April 9, 1964, Ex PR 18, box 356. Obviously Johnson was taken with Rowe's analogy, for in Kearns's account he used it verbatim to explain why the columnists had turned against him on Vietnam (Kearns, *American Dream*, 313–14).

18. Rivers, *Opinionmakers*, 55.

19. Walter Lippmann, "The Viet-Nam Debate," *Washington Post*, February 18, 1965, A-21.

20. See, for example, letter, Johnson to E. Palmer Hoyt, March 4, 1965, NSF:VN, box 12, no. 200b; letter, George W. Ball to Drew Pearson, February 26, 1965, NSF:VN, box 12, no. 149; and letter, Pearson to Ball, March 6, 1965, Moyers files, box 72, Pearson.

21. Memorandum, Rowan to Johnson, February 26, 1965, regarding a February 21 article by John Cowles, Jr. (NSF:VN, box 12, no. 148).

22. Memorandum, Cater to Johnson, March 12, 1965, Cater files, box 13, Memos to the President.

23. Letter, Hoyt to Valenti, March 24, 1965, Ex PR 18-2, 1/1/65–4/9/65.

24. According to "Mr. Valenti's notes on the Johns Hopkins speech" (Statements, box 127, April 7, 1965 Remarks), the "President gave orders to prepare such a speech two weeks before" it was delivered on April 7, 1965,

which would have been around March 24; Bundy's first outline is dated March 26, verifying Valenti's recollections (memorandum, Bundy to Rusk, March 26, 1965, NSF:VN, box 12, no. 164). The two pages of notes by Valenti, undated and typed up in very rough form, follow the evolution of the speech from Johnson's original call for a draft to shortly before its delivery. For the remainder of this chapter, this document will be referred to as "Valenti's notes."

25. Busby's files contain three compilations of previous policy statements on Vietnam, apparently prepared in early March of 1965. See the Busby files, box 31, (1305), Vietnam (1 of 2).

26. Memorandum, Bundy to Rusk, March 26, 1965, NSF:VN, box 12, no. 164.

27. Memorandum, Bundy to Johnson, March 28, 1965, NSF:VN, box 12, no. 160.

28. Cater's files (box 13) contain several memoranda with references to the Mekong River project. Busby found Johnson's vice-presidential statements on the region's development, relating them in a memorandum of April 1, 1965; in Busby files, box 51 (1313), Memos to the President. After Johnson had delivered the Johns Hopkins speech, he ordered the circulation of a letter from Arthur Goldschmidt outlining the potential for the Mekong River, sent just before the vice-president's trip to Southeast Asia. The letter, dated May 4, 1961, is attached to a memorandum, Juanita Roberts to Busby, April 10, 1965, in Busby files, box 31 (1305), Vietnam (2 of 2).

29. Draft, 4/5/65-3, Statements, box 126, Baltimore, Maryland. The final speech referred to "Viet Nam's steaming soil" anyway.

30. Memorandum, Goodwin to Johnson, n.d., Statements, box 126, Baltimore, Maryland.

31. Draft, 4/5/65-3, Statements, box 126, Baltimore, Maryland.

32. The seventeen nations were Afghanistan, Algeria, Ceylon, Cyprus, Ethiopia, Ghana, Guinea, India, Iraq, Kenya, Nepal, Syria, Tunisia, Uganda, the United Arab Republic, Yugoslavia, and Zambia.

33. Telegram, Rusk to Taylor, March 22, 1965; telegram, Taylor to Rusk, March 23, 1965; telegram, Rusk to Taylor, March 23, 1965; and telegram, Taylor to Rusk, March 24, 1965; all in NSC History, July 1965 Troop Decision, box 40, vol. II, tabs 114–21.

34. Memorandum, McCone to Johnson, April 1965, NSC History, July 1965 Troop Decision, box 40, vol. II, no. 74c; and memorandum, McCone to Rusk, McNamara, Bundy, and Taylor, April 2, 1965, NSF:VN, files 74, 76, 77; file VN 2E, 5/65–7/65, 1965 Troop Decision.

35. Memorandum, [McNaughton to McNamara], March 24, 1965, NSC History, July 1965 Troop Decision, box 40, vol. II, tab 120.

36. See National Security Action Memorandum 328, April 6, 1965, from Bundy to McNamara, Rusk, and McCone, reporting on Johnson's decisions of

April 1. The memorandum is reprinted in Sheehan et al., *Pentagon Papers,* no. 98, pp. 442–43. See also pp. 328–407. Johnson discussed this memorandum in *Vantage Point,* 39–41; yet the ordering of his discussion and the vagueness of dating gives the impression that these discussions came about after the Johns Hopkins speech rather than before.

37. Lewy, *America in Vietnam,* 46.

38. President's News Conference of April 1, 1965, *Public Papers,* 364.

39. Memoranda, Cater to Johnson and Cater to Bundy, both dated March 30, 1965, with Kraft column on "The Whims of LBJ" from *Le Nouvel Observateur,* March 11, 1965 (Cater files, box 13, Memos to the President).

40. Sidey, *Very Personal Presidency,* 78. The April 4, 1965, headlines focused on Johnson's anger: the *New York Times* bannered "Pres Is Cool to Pearson Plan," while the *Washington Post* echoed "LBJ Cool to Proposal by Pearson That U.S. Suspend Viet Air Raids."

41. Press Secretary's News Conference No. 676, 11:35 A.M., April 5, 1965, in Press Secretary's News Conferences, box 6.

42. Draft, 4/5/67, Statements, box 126, Baltimore, Maryland. One difficulty in working with speech drafts in the Johnson files is that there are numerous copies of various drafts, but few if any contain any indication of date, speech writer, or whose annotations are contained there. A researcher must play detective to trace the evolution of a speech, matching drafts to memoranda and comparing changes with the samples contained in the Johnson Library's handwriting file.

43. Unindicated draft, Statements, box 126, Baltimore, Maryland.

44. This passage is attached to a memorandum, Nell Yates to Dorothy Territo, April 8, 1965, Statements, box 126, Baltimore, Maryland; compare with the passage as it appears in the Address at Johns Hopkins University, "Peace Without Conquest," April 7, 1965, *Public Papers,* 395.

45. Valenti's notes.

46. Diary Backup, April 6, 1965; see also Ronald Steel, *Walter Lippmann and the American Century* (Boston: Little, Brown, 1980), chap. 43.

47. Memorandum, Bundy to Johnson, April 6, 1965 (Diary Backup, April 6, 1965).

48. Reedy's interview with the author, May 19, 1978, Milwaukee, Wisconsin; Sidey, *Very Personal Presidency,* 85–86; Evans and Novak, *Exercise of Power,* 567; and Steel, *Walter Lippmann,* 562–63.

49. Valenti's notes; compare with the Johns Hopkins address, April 7, 1965, *Public Papers,* 398.

50. Valenti's notes. Valenti comments that "State did not react well to the bold proposals of the Pres.," but he does not indicate who in the State Department objected, nor does he indicate which "bold proposals" posed problems—the Mekong River development, the billion dollar figure, the offer of unconditional discussions, or some other aspect.

51. Ibid.

52. Ibid.

53. Sidey, *Very Personal Presidency*, 129.

54. In a memorandum to Johnson, April 7, 1965 (CF SP 3, box 89), George Ball told him that he would receive the ambassadors of Yugoslavia, Ghana, Afghanistan, and Ethiopia at the State Department the next day "as a follow-up of your speech," with Ball giving them the American response to the plea for peace negotiations. Johnson's handwritten note at the bottom reads: "Jack—we want to release at WH."

55. All references to this speech are taken from the text in *Public Papers* for 1965, 394–99. Johnson had bound copies of this address sent to all members of Congress on May 3, 1965, including those who had protested his policies (Ex SP 3-72).

56. It is at this point that the two paragraphs composed by Potter, refuting the argument of China's destined dominance and paralleling American responsibility in Asia and in Europe, appear.

57. It was in this passage that the word "purpose" was substituted for "policy" to "avoid nitpicks from the [military] commanders" (draft, 4/5/65-3, Statements, box 126, Baltimore, Maryland).

58. "'A Path for Reasonable Men,'" *Newsweek*, April 19, 1965, 25. The Ex ND 19/CO 312 files (box 215) contain a number of letters from Johnson to editors thanking them for their support.

59. "The President Opens the Door," editorial, *New York Times*, April 8, 1965, 38; "Sword and Olive Branch," editorial, *Washington Post*, April 8, 1965, A-24.

60. Joseph Alsop, "Matter of Fact: A Great Speech," *Washington Post*, April 9, 1965, A-25.

61. Memorandum for the record from CLC [Chester L. Cooper], April 13, 1965, NSF:VN, box 13, no. 243.

62. Bundy cites these reactions from the *Congressional Record* in a memorandum to Johnson, April 10, 1965, Statements, box 126, Baltimore, Maryland.

63. Memorandum, Cater to Johnson, April 7, 1965, Cater files, box 13, Memos to the President.

64. Cited in "Democrats Hail Johnson's Talk; G.O.P. Sees Move to Buy Peace," *New York Times*, April 8, 1965, 17.

65. Cited in memorandum, Bundy to Johnson, April 10, 1965, Statements, box 126, Baltimore, Maryland.

66. Cited in "Reaction Is Mixed on Viet Speech," *Washington Post*, April 8, 1965, 11, and "Democrats Hail Johnson's Talk; G.O.P. Sees Move to Buy Peace," *New York Times*, April 8, 1965, 17. Although congressional reaction to Johnson's speech was mostly supportive, both headlines imply a substantial negative component.

282

67. Cited by *Newsweek* in "'A Path for Reasonable Men,'" April 19, 1965, 25. Bundy's memorandum to Johnson summarizing congressional reaction does not mention Dirksen's reservations. Perhaps they did not appear in the *Congressional Record*; perhaps Bundy decided not to mention them.

68. "Vietnam's 'Wider War,'" editorial, *New York Times*, April 6, 1965, A-38. The title refutes the administration's continual insistence that "we seek no wider war."

69. The main news story was written by Charles Mohr; see "President Makes Offer to Start Vietnam Talks Unconditionally: Proposes $1 Billion Aid for Asia," *New York Times*, April 8, 1965, A-1 and A-16.

70. Ibid.

71. Murray Marder, "President's Use of 'Unconditional' in Speech Viewed As Significant," *Washington Post*, April 8, 1965, 1.

72. Walter Lippmann, "The Baltimore Address and After," *Washington Post*, April 13, 1965, A-13.

73. Walter Lippmann, "Is Uncertainty Necessary?," *Washington Post*, April 6, 1965, A-17; idem, "The Falling Dominoes," *Washington Post*, April 23, 1965, A-21; and cited in Steel, *Walter Lippmann*, 572. By August of 1966, Lippmann endorsed a peace candidate for senator from Massachusetts as a man who "not only tells the truth, but . . . tells it without weasling and hedging and fudging" (see *New York Times* advertisement in Watson files, Vietnam I, August 18, 1966).

74. Cited in Sidey, *Very Personal Presidency*, 85–86.

75. For an example of continued administrative efforts to convince the columnist, see letter, Bundy to Lippmann, April 20, 1965; letter, Lippmann to Bundy, April 23, 1965, and letter, Bundy to Lippmann, April 28, 1965 (all in Ex ND 19/CO 312, box 214). The last letter rebukes Lippmann for the tone of his April 23 column on "the things which the President's advisers should stick in their pipes and smoke." For evidence of later bitterness, see memorandum, Panzer to Moyers, March 17, 1966, an eleven-page memorandum with thirty-four footnotes on Lippmann's inconsistencies (filed with March 31, 1967, memorandum to Johnson on the credibility gap, Ex FG 1, box 14); and memorandum, Robert Kintner to Johnson, August 12, 1966, on a book on Lippmann's views over the years (Ex PR 18, box 358). In addition, a memorandum from Rostow to Johnson, May 9, 1966, outlining Lippmann's position over the preceding twenty years has been withdrawn from CF PR 18, box 83, by security classifications.

76. Lady Bird Johnson, *White House Diary*, 256.

Chapter 6. Growing Discontent, 1965–1966

1. Memorandum, Robert McNamara to Johnson, April 26, 1965, NSF:VN, box 13, VN Memos XXXIII.

2. Memorandum, Dick Goodwin to Johnson, April 27, 1965, Ex SP "Open," SP 3-72.

3. Telegram, W. Tapley Bennett to Johnson, April 28, 1965, NSC History, Dominican Crisis 1965, Incoming State Cables, 4/24–4/4/65, no. 118.

4. George Reedy, interview with the author, May 19, 1978, Milwaukee, Wisconsin.

5. Cormier, *LBJ*, 188.

6. Statement by the President on the Situation in the Dominican Republic, April 30, 1965, *Public Papers*, 465–66.

7. Radio and Television Report to the American People on the Situation in the Dominican Republic, May 2, 1965, *Public Papers*, 469–74.

8. Memorandum, Busby to Bundy, May 11, 1965, in Busby files, box 19, (1301), Memos for McGeorge Bundy.

9. Chart and chronology, "Press Contacts—April 28–May 9, 1965," Ex PR 18, box 357.

10. Memoranda on Reston, Cater to Johnson, May 4 and May 26, 1965, Cater files, box 13, Memos to the President; and memorandum on Krock, Busby to Johnson, May 7, 1965, in Busby files, box 51 (1313), Memos for the President.

11. Memorandum, Cater to Johnson, May 22, 1965, Cater files, box 13, Memos to the President.

12. See chart, "The President and the Press," April 26, 1965 (Ex PR 18, box 357), comparing on-record press conferences for the first 519 days of Johnson's and Kennedy's presidencies and noting the myriad of Johnson's other press contacts, which included twelve walks.

13. Memorandum, Busby to Johnson, April 6, 1965, in Busby files, box 51 (1313), Memos to the President; and memorandum, Busby to Bundy, May 11, 1965, in Busby files, box 19 (1301), Memos for McGeorge Bundy. For a discussion of news emerging from a Cabinet meeting, see memorandum, Joe Laitin to Busby, April 29, 1965, in Busby files, box 51 (1313), Memos for the President.

14. Memorandum, Busby to Johnson, April 28, 1965, in Busby files, box 51 (1313), Memos to the President (see also a memorandum dated April 30, 1965, in the same file); and memoranda, Busby to Reedy, May 13, and June 18, 1965, in Busby files, box 20 (1301), Memos for George Reedy.

15. Memorandum, Okamoto to Moyers, August 10, 1965, Ex PR 18, box 357.

16. Memorandum, Marvin Watson to Johnson, May 14, 1965, regarding the president's instructions of April 12 (Ex PR 18, box 357); see also memorandum, Cater to Johnson, June 10, 1965, Cater files, box 13, Memos to the President.

17. Handwritten at the bottom of a memorandum from Cater to Johnson, September 13, 1965, Cater files, box 14, Memos to the President. See also the

284

letter regarding syndication from Dick Berlin of the Hearst Corporation to Jack Valenti, September 22, 1965 (Ex PR 18, box 357), as well as the extensive Diary Cards for Means.

18. Memoranda, Busby to Johnson, May 10 and 12, 1965, in Busby file, box 51 (1313), Memos to the President.

19. Memorandum, Moyers to Busby, Valenti, and Cater, April 9, 1965, Ex PR 18, box 357.

20. Memorandum, Busby to Moyers, April 21, 1965, Ex PR 18, box 357.

21. Memorandum, Valenti to Johnson, May 3, 1965, regarding L. L. L. Golden's piece in the *Saturday Review* of May 8, 1965 (Ex PR 18, box 357); and memorandum, Valenti to Johnson, November 15, 1965, on Leo Rosten's "Two Hours with LBJ," *Look*, Novermber 16, 1965 (Ex FG 1, box 12).

22. Letter, Chuck Roberts to Moyers, July 30, 1965, Ex PR 18, box 357.

23. "Various Editorials from the Press on President Kennedy's Press Conferences," filed April 9, 1965, Ex PR 18-2, 1/1/65–4/9/65.

24. Letter, Johnson to Jean Franklin, May 18, 1965, Ex PR 18, box 357.

25. Memorandum, Watson to Johnson, April 27, 1965, Ex PR 18, box 357.

26. Letter, Kermit Gordon to Moyers, July 28, 1965, Ex PR 18, box 357.

27. Letter, Gene Latimer to Johnson, July 12, 1965, Ex PR, box 357. Contrast this view with that provided in Caro, as discussed in chapter 2.

28. DeVier Pierson, oral history transcript no. 2, March 20, 1969, 23; Reedy, *Memoir*, 158.

29. The passages from the speech are selected from Valenti, *Human President*, 73; Goldman, *Tragedy of Lyndon Johnson*, 337; Evans and Novak, *Exercise of Power*, 532. Valenti's reaction to the furor is on pp. 71–72 of his book. Later, Mrs. Johnson would describe a foreign minister's toast to the president as so favorable that "I almost thought he was quoting from Jack Valenti" (Lady Bird, *White House Diary*, 640).

30. Cited by Goldman, *Tragedy of Lyndon Johnson*, 279.

31. Telephone interview with Henry Trewhitt by the author, November 21, 1983; Goldman, *Tragedy of Lyndon Johnson*, 409.

32. George Reedy, interview with the author, May 19, 1978, Milwaukee, Wisconsin; Reedy, OH no. 3, 30, and OH no. 4, 10–11.

33. Reedy interview, May 19, 1978. Unfortunately, Reedy could not recall what Johnson's plans had been.

34. Memorandum, Moyers to Busby, Valenti, and Cater, April 19, 1965, Ex PR 18, box 357; and memorandum, Liz Carpenter to Johnson, January 5, 1965, Ex PR 18, box 356.

35. William S. White, OH no. 2, 7; and letter, Pearson to Moyers, July 9, 1965, Ex PR 18, box 357. Pearson told Moyers he "would like to pass on to you some ideas I expressed rather ineffectually to the President the other day on his press relations."

36. Evans and Novak, *Exercise of Power*, 533.

37. Memorandum, Moyers to Johnson, October 7, 1965, Ex PR 18, box 357.

38. Cormier, *LBJ*, 197.

39. Memorandum, Moyers to Johnson, October 7, 1965, Ex PR 18, box 357.

40. "Hurting Good," *Time*, October 29, 1965, 23. Cormier recalled that he regarded the episode as "a typically Johnsonian gesture and did not refer to it until well down in my account. I realized my error of news judgment after photos of the impromptu exhibition caused a national stir" (*LBJ*, 201–2).

41. Memorandum, Valenti to Johnson, May 12, 1965 (Ex PR 18, box 357, relating a discussion with *Time*'s John Steele. See also "On Two Fronts," *Time*, May 7, 1965, 23–24.

42. Booth Mooney, oral history interview transcript, April 8, 1969, 45. See Goldman, *Tragedy of Lyndon Johnson*, 419-30 and 445–75, for details on the festival. Given his description of his encounters with the first lady over the festival, Goldman no doubt found Mrs. Johnson's diary entry for the day after the festival ironic: "Poor Dr. Goldman. He had worked so hard. And yet the total result must have been a towering headache, if not heartbreak" (*White House Diary*, 287).

43. Cited by Goldman, *Tragedy of Lyndon Johnson*, 474.

44. Lady Bird Johnson, *White House Diary*, 286. Mrs. Johnson described the day as "Black Tuesday."

45. Goldman, *Tragedy of Lyndon Johnson*, 450–51.

46. Telegram, Johnson to Taylor, May 10, 1965, NSF:NSC History, Deployment of Major U.S. Forces to Vietnam, July 1965, vol. 4, no. 6a.

47. Telegram, Sharp to Westmoreland, June 13, 1965, NSC History, July 1965 Troop Decision, box 42, tab 295.

48. Memorandum, Katzenbach to Johnson, June 10, 1965, NSC History, July 1965 Troop Decision, box 42, tab 281; and Memorandum of Law, n.d., in the same files, tab 286.

49. Johnson's guns-and-butter balancing act is the thesis of Larry Berman's book, *Planning a Tragedy* (New York: W. W. Norton, 1982), e.g., chap. 5.

50. Memorandum, Greeenfield to Rusk, June 17, 1965, NSC History, July 1965 Troop Decision, box 42, vol.V, tab 305, no. 27a.

51. Telegram, Taylor to Rusk, June 15, 1965, NSC History, July 1965 Troop Decision, box 42, vol. V, tab 299, no. 19a.

52. Cited by John W. Finney, "U.S. Denies Shift on Troop Policy in Vietnam War," *New York Times*, June 10, 1965, 1.

53. Memorandum on the friendly representative, Cater to Johnson, June 22, 1965, Cater files, box 13, Memos to the President; Morse's opposition, discussed in a Memorandum for the President on United States Politics in Vietnam, n.d., attached to memorandum, Bundy to Johnson, June 21, 1965, and letter, Johnson to Morse, n.d. (NSC History, July 1965 Troop Decision, box 42, vol. V, tab 322, no. 53a).

286

54. Memorandum, Bundy to Johnson, June 19, 1965, NSC History, July 1965 Troop Decision, box 42, vol. V, tab 319, no. 50a.

55. "Outline of Public Justification for Increased US Military Support in Vietnam," n.d., NSC History, July 1965 Troop Decision, box 42, vol. V, tab 326, no. 57a.

56. Memorandum, William Bundy [to McGeorge Bundy], June 23, 1965, NSF:VN, box 14, VN Memos, C-XXXV, 6/16–30/65, no. 332.

57. Memorandum, Valenti to Johnson and Moyers, July 14, 1965, Ex FG 1, box 11.

58. Memoranda, Cater to Johnson, July 10, 15, and 20, 1965, Cater files, box 13, Memos to the President.

59. Memorandum, McNamara to Johnson, July 20, 1965, NSF:NSC History, Deployment of Major U.S. Forces to Vietnam, July, 1965, vol. 6, no. 56a.

60. Memorandum, Bundy to Johnson, July 19, 1965, NSF:VN, box 15, no. 45.

61. Memorandum for the record, meetings on Vietnam, July 21, 1965, CLC [Chester L. Cooper], July 22, 1965, NSF:VN, file 74, 76, 77, VN 2E, 5/65–7/65: 1965 Troop Decision. Six pages of this nine-page memorandum are sanitized.

62. Memorandum, Possible Items for Discussion, July 22, 1965, 2:30 P.M., NSF:VN, file 74,76,77, VN 2E, 5/65–7/65: 1965 Troop Decision.

63. Johnson, *Vantage Point*, 149.

64. Memorandum, Bundy to Johnson, July 21, 1965, NSF:VN, box 15, 1965 Troop Decision.

65. President's News Conference of July 28, 1965, *Public Papers*, 794–803.

66. Cited by Goldman, *Tragedy of Lyndon Johnson*, 415.

67. Lady Bird Johnson, *White House Diary*, 260.

68. Pamphlet, "Toward Peace with Honor: Statement of the President at his Press Conference, The White House," July 28, 1965, Ex PR 18-2, 6/19/65–10/12/65; and pamphlet, "Why Vietnam?" August 20, 1965, in McPherson files, box 28 (1752), Vietnam-1965.

69. Diary Backup for July 28,1965, lists an off-the-record meeting with Fulbright at 5:00 P.M.—after the press conference.

70. Handwritten note by Johnson on memorandum, McNamara to Johnson, July 28, 1965, commenting on letter, Mansfield to Johnson, July 27, 1965 (NSC History, July 1965 Troop Decision, box 40, vol. I, tab 60, no. 129); and handwritten note by Johnson on memorandum, Cater to Johnson, July 22, 1965, Cater files, box 13, Memos to the President.

71. Memorandum, Watson to Johnson, August 9, 1965 (Diary Backup, August 19, 1965); a memorandum on Black's report of his meeting with Fulbright is withdrawn due to donor stipulations (Jones to Watson, August 21, 1965; Diary Backup, August 20, 1965). CF IT 80, box 59, contains some

correspondence on the Asian Development Bank, but most memoranda are withdrawn in accordance with national security restrictions.

72. Letter, E. Palmer Hoyt to McNamara, June 23, 1965, CF PR 18, box 83.

73. Unindicated memorandum to Johnson, December 10, 1965 (CF PR 18, box 83), reporting the comments of John Secondari after two weeks in Vietnam; and memorandum, Cater to Johnson, August 5, 1965 (Ex PR 18, box 357), reporting his conversation with Barry Zorthian, USIA officer in Saigon.

74. Unindicated memorandum to Johnson, December 10, 1965 (CF PR 18, box 83), on Secondari's comments.

75. Memorandum, McPherson to Johnson, September 22, 1965, in McPherson files, box 28 (1752), Vietnam-1965; and memorandum, Bundy to Johnson, October 4, 1965, Ex PR 18, box 357.

76. Handwritten note by Johnson on a memorandum, Cater to Johnson, July 26, 1965, Cater files, box 13, Memos to the President.

77. Ex ND 19/CO 312, box 216, contains a memorandum from Joe Califano to Johnson dated August 19, 1965, in which Califano urged the president to "make it available to the press"; Johnson's handwritten response asked Califano to "send me any clippings or columns you get from leaking this."

78. The Ex ND 19/CO 312 files contain a memorandum from Reedy to Johnson, June 30, 1965, concerning a ninety-minute ABC special entitled "A Primer on Vietnam" (box 216), and an undated, unindicated note to Juanita Roberts asking her to remind Johnson of the four CBS special news reports broadcast between August 9 and September 6, 1965 (box 217).

79. Remarks to the Delegates to the White House Conference on Education, July 21, 1965, *Public Papers,* 771.

80. Memorandum, Goldman to Johnson, October 1,1965; and memorandum, Califano to Johnson, October 14, 1965 (both in Ex ND 19/CO 312, box 217).

81. Letter, Ep Hoyt to Valenti, October 18, 1965, Ex ND 19/CO 312, box 217.

82. Memorandum, Cater to Johnson, December 28, 1965, Ex PR 18, box 357.

83. Memorandum, McNamara to Johnson, November 30, 1965, as reprinted in Sheehan et al., *Pentagon Papers,* 489. This document has not yet been officially declassified so it is not available from the Johnson Library. See also cable, Rusk to Lodge, cited in Herbert Y. Schandler, *The Unmaking of the President* (Princeton: Princeton University Press, 1977), 38.

84. Michael Davie, *LBJ: A Foreign Observer's Viewpoint* (New York: Ballantine Books, 1966), 122–23.

85. Cited in Lady Bird's entry for January 5, 1966, *White House Diary,* 347.

86. Rostow had recommended as early as November of 1965 that the State of the Union for 1966 "give heavier emphasis to foreign affairs" (see memo-

288

randum, Jack Valenti to Johnson, November 8, 1965, Statements, box 32), and Johnson's speech writers had proceeded on that basis (memorandum, Will Sparks and Bob Hardesty to Jack Valenti, November 30, 1965, Statements, box 31; and "Outline," undated, Statements, box 32, in State of the Union 1966 brown file no. 7). See Annual Message to the Congress on the State of the Union, January 12, 1966, *Public Papers,* 9–10.

87. Lady Bird Johnson, *White House Diary,* 351–52.

88. Johnson's concern is quoted in ibid., 355; Leslie H. Gelb and Richard K. Betts's description is in *The Irony of Vietnam* (Washington, D.C.: Brookings Institution, 1979), 274.

89. "The Hawaii Conference," *Time,* February 11, 1966, 20.

90. See Reston's columns in the *New York Times,* especially "Johnson's Most Effective Enemy," April 24, 1966, sec. 4, p. 10; and "Count Ten Before You Hurt," July 3, 1966, sec. 4, p. 6. The parallel between Vietnam and the Alamo in Johnson's mind, suggested here by Reston, is more fully explored by Ronnie Dugger in chapter 2 of *Politician.*

91. Johnson, *Vantage Point,* 48; memorandum, McPherson to Moyers, March 5, 1966, in McPherson files, box 28 (1752), Vietnam-1966.

92. Memorandum, "C" to Bundy, February 3, 1966, NSF:VN, box 16, file 3A (2).

93. J. William Fulbright, "Introduction," in *The Vietnam Hearings* (New York: Random House, 1966), ix–x.

94. Memorandum, Reedy to Johnson, March 22, 1966, Ex PR 18, box 358.

95. Memorandum, Valenti to Johnson, March 12, 1966, and memorandum, Valenti to Rusk, March 14, 1966, both in Ex ND 19/CO 312, box 220. Bundy appeared on "Meet the Press" on February 20, 1966, and Humphrey on March 13, 1966 (see transcripts in the Lawrence Spivak papers, A-46, Library of Congress).

96. Memorandum, McPherson to Moyers, March 3, 1966, in McPherson files, box 28 (1752), Vietnam-1966. The same file contains a series of correspondence on this topic from February to July of 1966.

97. Lady Bird Johnson, *White House Diary,* 362.

98. Memorandum, Kintner to Johnson, July 6, 1966, and memorandum, Kintner to Moyers, April 30, 1966 (CF PR 18, box 83).

99. Memoranda, Kintner to Johnson, June 24, 1966, CF PR 18, box 83, and August 18, 1966, Ex PR 18, box 358.

100. Memoranda, Kintner to Johnson, May 26, and June 4, 1966, CF PR 18, box 83.

101. Memoranda, Kintner to Johnson, May 10, 1966, EX FG 1, box 12, and May 4 and June 4, 1966, CF PR 18, box 83. Another presidential meeting with Alsop set up at Kintner's instigation is discussed in a memorandum, Kintner

to Califano, July 13, 1966, attached to a memorandum, Califano to Johnson, July 25, 1966, in Califano files, box 57 (1728), Press Contacts.

102. Memorandum, Kintner to Johnson, July 28, 1966, CF FG 1, box 16. See also the memoranda from Kintner to Marvin Watson, July 29, 1966, and to Johnson, August 3, 1966, in the same file.

103. Katherine Graham, oral history interview transcript, March 13, 1969, 26. This version is confirmed by Kintner's draft of a letter from Johnson to Graham, May 19, 1966, CF PR 18, box 83.

104. Letter, Katherine Graham to Johnson, May 16, 1966, CF PR 18, box 83. Philip Graham, her husband and publisher of the *Post*, had committed suicide in August of 1963.

105. Draft of a letter by Kintner, from Johnson to Graham, May 19, 1966, with marginal notations in Johnson's handwriting (CF PR 18, box 83). The identity of the ghostwriter is indicated on the carbon copy, between Johnson's initials and those of the secretary (such as "LBJ:Kintner:mf" or "LBJ:GER:mf").

106. Draft of a letter by Moyers from Johnson to Graham, May 23, 1966, with marginal notations in Johnson's handwriting (CF PR 18, box 83).

107. Memorandum, John W. Macy, Jr., to Johnson, September 21, 1966, Ex FG 1, box 13; and memorandum, Kintner to Johnson, May 6, 1966, CF WH 10, box 99.

108. Memorandum, Fred Panzer to E. Hayes Redmon, April 12, 1966, Ex FG 1, box 12, a ten-page response to Deakin's article which Moyers placed in the president's night reading on April 20; and a seven-page chart, "Analysis of Charges in NET 'The President and the News,'" April 19,·1966 (Ex PR 18, box 358), answering the criticism of Ben Bagdikian, Douglas Kiker, Al Otten (the *Wall Street Journal* correspondent whom Johnson earlier declared to be unfair), and Philip Potter—Johnson's independent friend from the *Baltimore Sun*.

109. Memorandum, Kintner to Johnson, September 21, 1966, with Johnson's handwritten notations (CF SP, box 86).

110. Memorandum for the file from P. Siemien, Eric Goldman's office, May 17, 1966, Ex PR 18, box 358. The president ordered six journalists removed from the guest list for the Presidential Scholars reception and eleven others added. Katherine Graham was among those added, on the day after she wrote her letter seeking reconciliation.

111. The refutations are in a memorandum, Ernest K. Lindley to Rusk, January 10, 1966, Panzer files, box 377, Lippmann, Walter. The withdrawn documents, all from the same file, are a memorandum, Lindley to Rusk, on "More Regarding Lippmann," January 28, 1966; letter, Alec France to Lindley

290

on "Review of Lippmann Positions," February 14, 1966; and memorandum, Rostow to Johnson, on "Lippmann Positions," May 9, 1966. The Walter Lippmann project, dated August 1966, is contained in CF Oversize Attachments, box 19.

112. Memorandum, Kintner to Johnson, June 23, 1966, CF PR 18, box 83; and memoranda, Charles Maguire to Kintner, June 27, 1966, and Kintner to Johnson, June 28, 1966 (Ex FG 1, box 12).

113. Memorandum, Kintner to Johnson, June 3, 1966, and memorandum, Kintner to Moyers, April 30, 1966 (CF PR 18, box 83).

114. Lady Bird Johnson, *White House Diary*, 183; see also 396 and 428.

115. Letter, Ed Plaut to Douglass Cater, July 25, 1965. Moyers forwarded this seven-page letter to Johnson's night reading on August 3, 1965. On June 27, 1966, eleven months later, Plaut sent a six-page letter echoing the earlier one to Cater; when Cater sent it on to Moyers, he termed it "interesting, if not altogether conclusive" (July 25, 1966). All documents are filed together in Ex FG 1, box 12, file 6/18/66–8/7/66.

116. As reported in a memorandum, Kintner to Johnson, June 17, 1966, Ex PR 18, box 358.

117. Memorandum, Will Sparks to Kintner, August 26, 1966, CF SP, box 86; and analysis by Ervin Duggan attached to memorandum, Cater to Johnson, May 11, 1966, Cater files, box 14, Memos to the President.

118. E. Hayes Redmon told Moyers of Gallup's view (memorandum, July 19, 1966, Ex FG 1, box 12); the popularity of the concept might be measured by its rapid circulation to Johnson and seven other staff members. Memoranda urging Johnson to be active, tough, and aggressive rather than "another sweet, tender man" include Hal Pachios to Moyers, August 10, 1966, Ex PR 18-1, box 358; Tom Johnson to Moyers, August 10, 1966, Ex PR 18, box 358; Komer to Kintner, October 6, 1966, Ex FG 1, box 13; and Kintner to Johnson, September 15, 1966, CF PR 18, box 83.

119. Memorandum, Valenti to Johnson, August 29, 1966, Ex PR 18, box 358. Attached to the Valenti memorandum is a typed note saying "I agree. Send it to Bill Moyers. LBJ:mf, 8-29-66."

120. Letter, Daniel J. Dwyer to Moyers, June 20, 1966, Ex PR 18, box 355.

121. Heren, *No Hail*, 257.

122. Memorandum, Moyers to Johnson, July 14, 1966, Ex PR 18, box 358. See also Hal Pachios's memorandum to Moyers, June 23, 1966, bringing the letter from Dwyer to Moyers's attention (Ex PR 18, box 358). Dwyer and his editor, Howard MacDonald, wrote glowing letters of appreciation to both Johnson and Moyers on August 12, 1966 (Ex PR 18, box 358).

123. Memorandum, McPherson to Moyers, August 4, 1966, in McPherson files, box 28 (1752), Vietnam-1966.

124. Memorandum, Valenti to Johnson, August 23, 1966, Ex PR 18, box 358. On October 1, 1966, Valenti forwarded a copy to Kintner, noting that "I still think it is valid."

125. Letter, Horace Busby to Johnson, May 23, 1966, Ex FG 1, box 12. Busby observed that "the past eight months have taught me anew that the glass in the White House goldfish bowl is opaque, both ways."

126. Cited in "Talking Points with Senator Hill," July 16, 1966, attached to memoranda, Cater to Johnson, July 11 and 14, 1966, Cater files, box 15, Memos to the President.

127. Memoranda, Cater to Johnson, February 22 and March 10, 1966, Cater files, box 14, Memos to the President.

128. Memorandum, Cater to Johnson, August 4, 1966, Cater files box 15, Memos to the President.

129. McPherson's handwritten notation is at the bottom of a letter, Heller to McPherson, July 15, 1966, attached to Heller's letter to Johnson of July 12, 1966; the documents are in the McPherson files, box 28 (1752), Vietnam-1966. For other materials on Heller's proposal, see Califano files, box 57 (1758), Post-Vietnam Planning, including letter, Heller to Johnson, July 12, 1966, with Johnson's handwritten notation to Califano at the bottom; memorandum, Califano to Ackley, July 16, 1966; and memoranda, Ackley to Califano, August 1 and November 28, 1966.

130. Johnson, *Vantage Point*, 249. This echoes a memorandum from Cater to Johnson on "some headlines I would like to see coming out of the Manila conference" October 4, 1966 (Cater files, box 15, Memos to the President.)

131. Memoranda, Kintner to Johnson, October 16, 1966, and Moyers to George Christian, October 6, 1966 (Ex PR 18, box 358); and memoranda, Kintner to Christian, October 14 and 15, 1966, Ex TR 100, Manila Conference, box 28, file 11/23/63–10/16/66.

132. Memorandum, Kintner to Johnson, October 27, 1966, CF CO 312, box 13. See cables in CF PR 18, box 83: from Hayes Redmon to Moyers, October 18, 1966; from Califano to Johnson, October 18–November 2, 1966; and from Kintner to Jake Jacobsen, November 5, 1966. See also Kintner's memorandum to Johnson, October 17, 1966, CF CO 312, box 12.

133. Memorandum for the record from Moyers's accounts, typed by Marie Fehmer, October 20, 1966, Diary Backup, box 48, October 17–November 2, 1966 Asian Trip.

134. President's News Conference of November 4, 1966, *Public Papers*, 1320. A year later reporters were still fuming over this episode. In a memorandum to Johnson on October 25, 1967, Cater reported a conversation with Martin Nolan of *Reporter* magazine, who objected on a television show to the fact that Johnson "taunted" correspondents by publicly claiming that their stories on the campaign swing were products of their "imagination," when "everyone knew that the advance men had worked on the trip and that Bill Moyers had given background information on it" (Ex FG 1, box 15).

135. Pierson, OH no. 2, 29–30; Tom Johnson, in Purvis, *Presidency and Press*, 33.

136. Cited in Cormier, *LBJ*, 231.

137. The files for Ex PR 18, box 358, contain memoranda from Tom Johnson to six members of the Administration, assigning charges needing refutation (December 13, 1966); see follow-up memorandum in the same file, Kintner to Johnson, December 14, 1966. In her oral history interview, Graham said she went back to White House functions "two or three times" after her letter to Johnson, but then "something happened" and she was ousted again (p. 27).

138. Memorandum, Johnson's orders to Cater as typed by Marie Fehmer, December 4, 1966, Ex FG 1, box 13.

139. Memorandum, Kintner to Johnson, November 28, 1966, with Johnson's handwritten notations, Ex PR 18, box 358.

140. Attached to a memorandum from Charles Maguire to Kintner, November 7, 1966, is a twenty-seven page report of Johnson's November 3 meeting with Kintner, Cater, McPherson, Sparks, Hardesty, Panzer, McNulty, Schoen, Coyne, Wattenberg, Duggan, and Maguire.

141. Valenti, *Human President*, 120; letter, Drew Pearson to Johnson, December 5, 1966, Ex PR 18, box 358; and two memoranda, Tom Johnson to Johnson, both December 9, 1966, Ex PR 18, box 358.

142. Lady Bird Johnson, *White House Diary*, 462, 464.

Chapter 7. Intensified Opposition, 1967

1. Lady Bird Johnson, *White House Diary*, 469.

2. Ibid.

3. Annual Message to the Congress on the State of the Union, January 10, 1967, *Public Papers*, 2.

4. Transcript, "Dan Rather's Spot on CBS, Saturday, January 7, 1967," Ex FG 1, box 13.

5. Lady Bird Johnson, *White House Diary*, 472.

6. Ex PR 18, box 359 contains memoranda to Johnson from Kintner, Rostow, and Cater, January 11, 1967, reporting on responses. The same file contains a list of people contacted by Joseph Califano that day; at the bottom Johnson wrote, "This is of no value—what did they say?" See also memorandum, Kintner to Christian, January 16, 1967, Ex SP, State of the Union 1967, box 25.

7. See text of letters exchanged and discussion of the episode in Johnson, *Vantage Point*, 252–55, 592–95.

8. "The Other War," *Newsweek*, February 20, 1967, 32.

9. Peter Benchley, a writer and associate editor for *Newsweek* who came to the White House as a speech writer in February of 1967, recalled that at the time of his initial interview with the president, Johnson was "quite upset" about the "Periscope" department. Benchley told Johnson that *Newsweek*'s

proud boast of 80 percent accuracy "was some claim when you were claiming that one out of every five items was an out-right lie." The president asked Benchley "to try to give an honesty to the relationship between the Administration and *Newsweek*" by encouraging the magazine to check out the rumors with the White House—an effort that Benchley reported did not work out (oral history interview transcript, November 20, 1968, 3–4). A year earlier Johnson had instructed Kintner to discover how the "Periscope" items were submitted and selected (memoranda, Kintner to Johnson, January 14, 1966, and Kintner to Christian, January 16, 1966, in CF PR 18, box 83).

10. "The Other War," 31. In "Bobby Abroad," *Newsweek* concluded the discussion of Kennedy's handling of the "peace feeler" by citing officials in the State Department: " 'If he didn't know what he was talking about,' said one, 'then he was acting irresponsibly. But if he did know what he was talking about then he was also acting irresponsibly' " (February 13, 1967, 35).

11. The report is found in "The Other War," 32. In her oral history interview (p. 22), Katherine Graham recalled that she was "called up into Rostow's office and was told that there hadn't been an argument, that we got the story wrong, and naturally he wanted us to take the story back.... We just decided—and I think it has been borne out since—that there was a hell of a row in the office."

12. Memorandum, Kintner to Johnson, February 8, 1967 (Ex FG 1, box 13), referring especially to the *Newsweek* accounts. Regarding the Andy Glass story in the *Washington Post*, see memorandum, Christian to Johnson, March 8, 1967, Christian files, box 3, Press Contact Report; and also letter, Bundy to Robert F. Kennedy, February 21, 1967, letter, Bundy to David Ginsburg, March 13, 1967, and memorandum, Horace Busby to Marvin Watson, n.d., all of which are attached to letter, David Ginsburg to Johnson, March 14, 1967, in CF FG 1, box 16. Busby's memorandum refers to the "sensitivity" of the correspondence. In addition, Rostow told Johnson that when Hugh Sidey came to see him, "I hit him hard on the *Time* piece on the February 6 interview with Senator RFK. I gave him the facts. He agreed they were badly off-base; apologized; and promised to inform the high brass of *Time*" (memorandum, March 16, 1967, in Christian files, Press Contacts I).

13. See Salisbury's account of his trip in *Behind the Lines—Hanoi, December 23–January 7* (New York: Harper & Row, 1967). For examples of both positive and negative reactions of journalists, see James Boylan, "A Salisbury Chronicle," *Columbia Journalism Review* 5 (Winter 1966–67): 12–15; "Passing Comment," *Columbia Journalism Review* 5 (Winter 1966–67): 2; and James Aronson, *The Press and the Cold War* (Indianapolis: Bobbs-Merrill, 1970), 253–61. Lippmann's remark is taken from a letter to the Pulitzer Prize board, January 30, 1967, cited in Steel, *Walter Lippmann*, 576. Lewy argues that "Salisbury, in effect, had given the authority of his byline to unverified

communist propaganda and that the *New York Times* had printed this information as though Salisbury had established it himself with his own on-the-scene reporting." See Lewy, *America in Vietnam*, 400.

14.. W. Phillips Davison, "Making Sense of Viet Nam News," *Columbia Journalism Review* 5 (Winter 1966–67): 7. See also "Are We Getting Through?" *Columbia Journalism Review* 5 (Fall 1966): 41–44; and Jules Witcover, "Where Washington Reporting Failed," *Columbia Journalism Review* 9 (Winter 1970–71): 7–12.

15. White, press release and transcript, May 23, 1966, Ex ND 19/CO 312, box 220; and Salisbury, cited by Boylan, "Salisbury Chronicle," 14.

16. In his interview with the author, May 19, 1978, George Reedy asked not to talk about his opinion of Moyers. In Reedy's book, *Lyndon B. Johnson: A Memoir*, Moyers's name is conspicuously absent, although the alert reader can detect throughout the text several veiled references that are less than complimentary. Christian's view is contained in his interview with the author, July 18, 1979, Austin, Texas, and in his oral history interview no. 3, p. 1.

17. Valenti, *Human President*, 54.

18. White pointed to Moyers as the source of stories about ill-treated staff in OH no. 2, 11–13. See also Willie Day Taylor, OH no. 1, 38; and Goldstein, oral history interview transcript no. 4, December 19, 1968, 8.

19. Mooney compared *Time*'s coverage of the two men and noted that Johnson was "absolutely blind to it for so long but he finally became quite bitter about Bill." Mooney also contended that Moyers maneuvered Reedy out of the White House press secretary's post, and that Johnson "treated Reedy badly in that connection"—a view that Reedy shares. See Mooney, oral history interview transcript, April 8, 1969, 41–42. In a memorandum to the president on February 21, 1967, Panzer sent a chart of his popularity by months and press secretaries, prefaced as "the background information you asked for today" (Ex FG 1, box 14).

20. Letter, John P. Roche to Christian, December 4, 1968, Ex PR 18, box 362. Noting Moyers's popularity elsewhere, Roche continued, "when Himself takes a sideswipe at Billy, most people miss the point—and those who get it can sock it back with interest. Why give them ammunition?"

21. Charles Bartlett, "President Johnson and His Pettiness," *Los Angeles Times*, January 24, 1967. Bartlett was especially critical of Johnson's brusque treatment of Moyers. Tom Johnson sent a copy of the piece to Johnson that day, terming it "rather critical" (Ex FG 1, box 13). See also memorandum, Kintner to Johnson, February 9, 1967 (CF PR 18, box 83), with handwritten response by Johnson.

22. Memorandum and table, Tom Johnson to Johnson, January 20, 1967, Ex PR 18, box 359. Those listed were primarily secretaries (including Willie

Day Taylor, Juanita Roberts, and Marie Fehmer) or worked for Mrs. Johnson (such as Bess Abell and Liz Carpenter).

23. See memoranda to Johnson from Califano, January 5, 1967, Wattenberg, January 17, 1967, and Tom Johnson, January 26, 1967 (Ex PR 18, box 359).

24. Memorandum, Cater to Watson, January 11, 1967, Ex PR 18, box 359; when Watson asked Johnson if he should see Reston, the president responded, "see me."

25. In a letter to Christian on March 14, 1967, the president of Gannett Newspapers, Paul Miller, reported that his staff told him "you already have the 'complete confidence' of the reporters assigned to the White House. . . . This is the highest kind of testimonial, and I congratulate you" (Christian files, Press Contacts I). For examples of journalists holding Christian in high esteem, see the oral histories of White, no. 2, p. 13; Allen, 22–24; Drew Pearson, April 10, 1969, 20; and Timmons, 21–22; see also Dan Rather in Purvis, *Presidency and Press*, 28.

26. Letter, Reedy to Johnson, January 3, 1967, Ex PR 18, box 359.

27. Tom Johnson, assistant press secretary, informed staff members of the reinstatement of this practice in a memorandum on January 13, 1967 (CF PR 18, box 83). Christian's files contain a form for Tom Johnson to attach to the daily press contact reports, checking off each of the thirty-five staff members who submitted reports (Christian files, box 3, Press Contact Report; around February 1967).

28. Christian, OH no. 1, 6.

29. Memorandum, Kintner to Johnson, January 27, 1967, reporting on meeting with Rostow, McPherson, Cater, Christian, and Califano (Ex PR 18, box 359).

30. Twenty-page memorandum by Fred Panzer for Johnson, January 21, 1967, and one-page attachment, January 23, 1967, both in Ex FG 1, box 13. In a memorandum to Kintner on February 6, 1967, Panzer enclosed a letter to the editor entitled "On Credibility"; not until the final paragraph does one realize it is a description of Woodrow Wilson, not Lyndon Johnson (Ex FG 1, box 13).

31. Philip Potter, "Johnson's Credibility Gap: Public Relations and Disputed Questions of National Survival," *Baltimore Sun*, January 16, 1967, 1A, 9A.

32. Kintner discussed these charges in a memorandum to Johnson, February 8, 1967, Ex FG 1, box 13.

33. See "The Credibility Gap—I," *Washington Post*, March 28, 1967, A-17, and "Credibility Gap—II," *Washington Post*, March 30, 1967, A-21.

34. Walter Lippmann, speech upon receiving the first annual Federal City Club Award, reprinted in "A Sort of Farewell to Washington," *Washington*

296

Post, March 19, 1967, E-1. A copy is included in the collection on Lippmann in the Panzer files, box 377.

35. The Panzer files, box 340 (9), for example, include the category of "Credibility Gap"; one file, labeled "Credibility File," includes among other pieces Lippmann's series; a speech by Eric Sevareid delivered to the Massachusetts legislature on January 24, 1967; a *Boston Herald* editorial by George Minot on "The Widening Gap Called Credibility" dated April 30, 1967; the McGaffin and Knoll essay in the September 1967 *Progressive,* discussed later in this chapter; and two ads from newspapers in November. Watson's files also contain a variety of memoranda, letters, and clippings, some of which have been withdrawn from each file due to donor restriction.

36. Memorandum, James R. Jones to Marvin Watson, February 15, 1967, reporting a conversation with Ted Knapp of Scripps-Howard (Christian files, box 3, Press Contact Report). Knapp had told Jones that the president was now "very frank about the situation in Vietnam," whereas there had been "Administration embellishment of facts, and figures, in the past." In a February 22, 1967, memorandum, Bob Fleming reported to Christian that Merriman Smith of the UPI had complained about the slow news beat (Christian files, box 3, Press Contacts I).

37. President's News Conference of February 27, 1967, *Public Papers,* 219–23. In a memorandum to Christian, Tom Johnson reported that six correspondents had said they were pleased with the press conference and the president's performance, including Chuck Bailey of Cowles, who crowed, "This is the kind we like. TV can go to hell, as far as I'm concerned." Al Spivak of the UPI said, "This is one of the busiest days for news in a long time. I'm glad to see it pick up after last week" (February 27, 1967, in Christian files, box 3, Press Contact Report).

38. Lady Bird Johnson, *White House Diary,* 493. See President's News Conference, March 9, 1967, *Public Papers,* 303–12.

39. Address on U.S. Policy in Vietnam, Delivered Before a Joint Session of the Tennessee State Legislature, March 15, 1967, *Public Papers,* 353. This passage is also cited in a compilation of past presidential statements on Vietnam, covering February 1967 to September 1968, contained in NSF:VN, box 17, file 7C (1), Past Presidential Statements, 1953–67.

40. Joint Statement Following the Meeting in Guam with Chairman Thieu and Prime Minister Ky, and the President's News Conference in Guam following the conference, both March 21, 1967, *Public Papers,* 381–37. Johnson discusses the Guam conference in *Vantage Point,* 259–61.

41. Memorandum, Kintner to Johnson, February 17, 1967, Ex FG 1, box 14.

42. Memorandum, Reedy to Johnson, January 3, 1967, Ex PR 18, box 359.

43. Eric Sevareid, "Politics and the Press," message to a joint session of the

Massachusetts state legislature in Boston, January 24, 1967, 5, 16. Christian sent a copy of the speech to Johnson's night reading on February 25, 1967, Ex FG 1, box 14.

44. Willard Deason sent a Smith article from the *Washington Post* with the first charge as a headline to Johnson on December 19, 1966 (Ex FG 1, box 13); John P. Roche referred to Smith's column in a memorandum to the president, April 17, 1967 (Ex FG 1, box 14); and Cater reported Smith's disenchantment and writing plans to Johnson in a memorandum dated March 22, 1967, with handwritten notations by Johnson (Cater files, box 16, Memos to the President).

45. "LBJ and the 'Credibility Gap,' " *Report*, March 1967, sent to Johnson on March 10 by Panzer (Ex FG 1, box 14); and "Credibility and the Press," *Washington Star*, January 5, 1967, with a set of clippings defending Johnson filed in Ex PR 18, box 359.

46. Panzer summarized comments from the March 12–14 seminar, reported in the March 25, 1967, edition of *Editor and Publisher*, in a memorandum on March 31, 1967 (Ex FG 1, box 14). While most of the panelists cited were foreign, Panzer concluded that it was proof "that Lippmann's view of the 'Credibility Gap' is not shared by others."

47. From the transcript of Smith's speech, April 24, 1967, in CF FG 1, box 16, attached to a memorandum from Watson to Johnson on May 25, 1967. Smith had responded to Johnson's letter of condolence upon his son's death by assuring the president of his continued support for the administration's policies. Smith's letter, written on February 19, 1966, is on display in the museum section of the Johnson Library.

48. Memorandum, Rosemary D. McBride to Tom Johnson, February 28, 1967, reporting on her lunch with Chuck Roberts of *Newsweek*, Bob Pierpont of CBS, and Al Spivak of UPI (Christian files, box 3, Press Contact Reports). In addition to McBride's report, Christian's file contains several other memoranda noting the new sense of optimism: Cater to Christian, February 23, 1967, saying Mel Elfin of *Newsweek* detected "a significant swing in the press's attitude toward the President"; Tom Johnson to Christian summarizing six correspondents' praise for Johnson's press conference, February 27, 1967; and Hal Pachios, telling Christian of the preceding day's lunch with Roberts, Pierpont, and Ray Scherer (March 2, 1967).

49. Memorandum, Reedy to Johnson, January 3, 1967, Ex PR 18, box 359.

50. "Eyes only" memorandum from Kintner to Johnson, March 2, 1967, CF PR 18, box 83.

51. Lady Bird Johnson, *White House Diary*, 508.

52. Memorandum, Kintner to Christian, April 20, 1967, Christian file, Press Contacts I. On January 18, 1967, Kintner had reported to the president

298

on the first "weekly meeting to develop items for columnists," which Cali-fano, McPherson, Cater, Rostow, and Christian would attend (memorandum, Ex PR 18, box 359).

53. Speech to the White House Correspondents Association Dinner, April 28, 1967, Statements, box 224. Perhaps because the decision to speak was last-minute, Johnson's remarks are not contained in *Public Papers*.

54. Cormier, *LBJ*, 242. For example, Cormier says Johnson was "poking fun at both himself and the press corps," not that he was taking cheap shots at the correspondents.

55. Letter, Merriman Smith to Jack Valenti, May 22, 1967, in CF FG 1, box 16, with memorandum from Marvin Watson to Johnson, May 25, 1967, and other documents. Valenti sent the letter to Watson, who forwarded it to the president, along with a copy of Smith's speech—for which the UPI, Smith reported, had received several thousand requests. Smith mentions other problems he faced, including suits against him for his investigation of the Garrison case in New Orleans, tied to Kennedy's assassination.

56. Remarks at the Reception for the 1966–67 White House Fellows, May 1, 1967, *Public Papers*, 490. Cater had told Johnson that "the most news-worthy item comes on page 3 [of the drafted speech] when you speak of the right not only to criticize but also to answer criticism," a passage that followed the paragraph on Osler (memorandum, May 1, 1967, in Cater files, box 16, Memos to the President, May 1967; also attached to draft of speech in Statements, 5-1-67, box 224).

57. Christian, OH no. 3, 22. Christian discussed Johnson's indecision on pp. 19–22; he described Prime Minister Pearson as "kind of a pink cloud fellow" on foreign relations (p. 20). Johnson's concerns about the Mideast were shared by Rostow as cited in William C. Spragens and Carole Ann Terwoord, *From Spokesman to Press Secretary: White House Media Operations* (Washington, D.C.: University Press of America, 1981), 155–56.

58. Letter, Max Frankel to George Christian, May 26, 1967, Ex PR 18, box 359. Christian forwarded Frankel's letter to Johnson on May 31, 1967. The Daily Diary cards for Frankel list lunch with Johnson and Christian on May 22, 1967, four days before Frankel wrote this memorandum, and an off-the-record meeting with the president in the Oval Office on September 15, 1967, almost four months afterwards. Perhaps Christian rather than the president met with Frankel.

59. Interview with Barbara Klaw, "Lady Bird Remembers," *American Heritage* 31 (December 1980): 17; see also Johnson, *Vantage Point*, 368; and Ball and McPherson as cited by Miller, *Lyndon*, 488.

60. Notes on Johnson's discussion with Wheeler and Westmoreland, April 27, 1967, taken by John T. McNaughton, document no. 125 as contained in

Sheehan et al., *Pentagon Papers*, 567–68. These notes are not available from the Johnson Library at the time of this writing.

61. Memorandum, "Future Actions in Vietnam," McNamara to Johnson, May 19, 1967, document no. 129 in Sheehan et al., *Pentagon Papers*, 577–85. This memorandum is not available from the Johnson Library at the time of this writing.

62. "Memorandum on Vietnam Policy," Bundy to Johnson, received May 4, 1967, document no. 126 in Sheehan et al., *Pentagon Papers*, 569–72. This memorandum is not available from the Johnson Library at the time of this writing.

63. When Walt Rostow appeared on "Meet the Press" on July 9, 1967, Spivak asked if this were true, and Rostow denied it. See transcript in the Lawrence Spivak papers, box 18, Library of Congress; and Johnson's discussion of McNamara's trip in *Vantage Point*, 262–63 and 370.

64. Johnson, *Vantage Point*, 360–70.

65. Cited by Lady Bird Johnson, *White House Diary*, 558. Patrick Lyndon Nugent was born to daughter Luci and her husband on June 21, 1967.

66. Taken from Michael Davie, *LBJ: A Foreign Observer's Viewpoint* (New York: Ballantine, 1966), 36–37. Doris Kearns provides an example of meetings transformed in *American Dream*, 3–4.

67. Notes on the meeting with legislators in memorandum, Ed Hamilton to Johnson, September 11, 1967 (Diary Backup, box 75, September 12, 1967). See "Special Message to the Congress Proposing a U.S. Contribution to the 'Special Funds' of the Asian Development Bank," September 26, 1967, *Public Papers*, 860–64. For extensive memoranda on this legislation see Diary Backup, boxes 74 and 75, August 18 and September 11 and 12, 1967; and CF IT 80, box 59, Asian Development Bank.

68. Cited by Kearns, *American Dream*, 326.

69. J. William Fulbright, "The Price of Empire," speech delivered before the American Bar Association Convention in Honolulu, August 9, 1967, reprinted in the *Congressional Record*, 90th Cong., 1st sess., August 9, 1967, 11265–8.

70. Memorandum, Panzer to Johnson, September 16, 1967, Watson files, box 28 (1375B), Panzer memos.

71. Lady Bird Johnson, *White House Diary*, 556; see also Johnson, *Vantage Point*, 83–85.

72. Remarks in Baltimore to Delegates to the National Convention of the United States Jaycees, June 27, 1967, *Public Papers*, 659. The president's rejection of the original speech is recounted by Benchley in his oral history, 10–11.

73. Boyd's change of position was reported to Johnson in a memorandum

from Christian, August 7, 1967, Christian files, Press Contacts I. Christian reported on his conversation with *U.S. News* correspondent Jack Sutherland in a memorandum to Johnson, August 9, 1967, Christian files, Press Contacts II. Harry C. McPherson told Christian of the "devastating" segment aired on the Huntley-Brinkley broadcast in a memorandum, July 18, 1967 (Ex PR 18, box 360); Marvin Watson sent the memorandum to McNamara on July 20.

74. Memorandum, Kintner to Johnson, May 9, 1967, Ex PR 18, box 359.

75. The two *Newsweek* accounts are "The First Team," July 17, 1967, 23–24, and "The President in Trouble," September 4, 1967, 17–21. In memoranda to Johnson, Christian reported that he had "chastised" Chuck Roberts of *Newsweek* for "cutting up Walt Rostow," and that Roberts not only denied such intent in the story but returned the following day to say he felt Christian was misinterpreting the account (July 19 and 20, 1967, in Christian files, Press Contacts II). In classic debate style, aide and speech writer Will Sparks refuted *Newsweek*'s assessment of Johnson by first arguing "that Vietnam is not a major war and that there is no rebellion at home, major or otherwise," and then by listing domestic turbulence during the War of 1812, World War I, and World War II to argue that Johnson was not the first to face both. See memorandum, Sparks to Tom Johnson, August 28, 1967, Ex FG 1, box 15. An analysis of twenty-seven passages in the cover story on Johnson is contained in CF Oversize Attachments, box 35, 11/29/67. In the attached memorandum, dated November 28, 1967, Tom Johnson informed the president that five of the passages were incorrect; "in short the article is about 19% inaccurate."

76. James Deakin, "The Dark Side of LBJ," *Esquire* 68 (August 1967): 45.

77. Richard H. Rovere, "Letter from Washington," *New Yorker*, September 23, 1967, 157–60, 164–68.

78. Christian, *President Steps Down*, 212–15. Unfortunately Dan Rather does not mention the episode in his book, *The Camera Never Blinks* (New York: Ballantine Books, 1977). Pertinent documents from the WHCF include memorandum, Christian to Johnson, August 30, 1967 (Christian files, Press Contacts II), in which Christian lists his two-sentence assessment in a matter-of-fact way; memorandum, Tom Johnson to Christian, September 21, 1967, and letter, Christian to Richard Rovere, November 24, 1967 (both in Ex FG 1, box 16, file for 11/23/67–11/30/67). Tom Johnson assured Christian, evidently startled by the Rovere story, that obviously "no deception was intended in any way."

79. Earlier Tom Johnson had sent a memorandum to the president warning that "in both meetings with the Democratic Congressmen today and Tuesday, the President has said: 'the bombing has reduced infiltration by half.' If this gets to the press, we may have difficulty supporting the statement" (August 9, 1967, Ex PR 18, box 360). The staff was not insensitive to

charges of deception. Not everyone was convinced, however: in his oral history interview Benchley said Christian was "guilty of relaying to the press the misinformation," and referred to Rovere's story (Benchley, OH, 48–49).

80. Patterson, OH, 12–14. According to this interview, Patterson supported the war at the time and agreed to serve as an observer only if another journalist who did not support the war was also selected—in this case, Knight. Johnson's first choice was not Patterson but Russ Wiggins, executive editor of the *Washington Post*, who declined because of the paper's policy and the need to "preserve the appearance of independence" in order to best "speak out for the Administration." See memoranda, McPherson to Johnson, August 21 and 22, 1967, in McPherson files, box 29 (1752), Vietnam—1967 (Part II).

81. Johnson, *Vantage Point*, 265.

82. Transcript, Eric Sevareid, CBS News with Walter Cronkite, October 2, 1967, in McPherson files, box 29 (1752), Vietnam—1967 (Part II).

83. Memorandum, Tom Johnson to Christian, August 15, 1967, CF PR 18, box 83; this view is echoed in a memorandum from Kintner to Johnson, August 1, 1967, CF FG 1, box 16.

84. Memorandum, Kintner to Watson, August 9, 1969, CF FG 1, box 16.

85. Benchley's report is contained in a memorandum from Christian to Johnson, August 14, 1967, Ex PR 18, box 360. Benchley did not concentrate on ABC because Christian had told him he felt "they are doing a reasonably objective job . . . [and] the other two [networks] . . . tend to offend."

86. Memorandum, Cater to Johnson, September 1, 1967, citing Ted Etherington, president of Wesleyan University and former president of the American Stock Exchange (Cater files, box 16, Memos to the President, September 1967).

87. Tydings's views are contained in a memorandum, McPherson to Johnson, August 25, 1967, in McPherson files, box 29 (1752), Vietnam, Vietnam—1967 (Part II).

88. Sheehan et al., *Pentagon Papers*, 540.

89. Letter, McPherson to Fischer, August 8, 1967. In a letter dated August 2, 1967, Fischer had asked McPherson to comment, "in confidence and strictly for my guidance in revision," on the galleys for an article on Johnson. McPherson sought reactions from Rostow and Roche, which led Fischer to make what he termed "fairly extensive revisions" in the piece (letter, Fischer to McPherson, August 14, 1967). All correspondence and memoranda are contained in McPherson files, box 29 (1752), Vietnam—1967 (Part II).

90. Memorandum, John P. Roche to Johnson, September 7, 1967, Ex PR 3, box 10. Secretary Nell Yates attached a note to the letter, telling Juanita Roberts, "Mr. Watson thinks the President will want copies of this. We have a supply too." According to Goldman, the person who succeeded him "felt

302

called upon to open his tenure with hairy-chested press statements bran-
dishing phrases like 'the artsy-craftsy set' and 'high-class illiterates' who live
in 'jackal bins,' and describing himself as an 'unabashed veteran cold
warrior' " (*Tragedy of Lyndon Johnson*, 478).

91. Memorandum, Rowe to Johnson, January 6, 1967, Watson files, box 30
(1375C), Jim Rowe.

92. Memorandum, McPherson to Johnson, August 25, 1967, with typed
message from Johnson via Jim Jones at bottom, McPherson files, box 29
(1752), Vietnam—1967 (Part II).

93. Memorandum, Rostow to Johnson, September 21, 1967, Statements,
box 237, September 29, 1967: San Antonio; and memorandum, Rostow to
Johnson, September 15, 1967, NSF:VN, box 17, 7C (1), Past Presidential
Statements 1953–67.

94. Memorandum, McPherson to Johnson, September 28, 1967,
10:20 A.M., Statements, box 237, September 29, 1967: San Antonio.

95. Memorandum, McPherson to Johnson, September 28, 1967, Statements, box 237, September 29, 1967: San Antonio. This memorandum is not
the same as that with the time, cited above. This two-page memorandum
discusses the "Rostow-Katzenbach-Nitze-Busby" revision of McPherson's
draft. "Beginning with standard definitions of the war" as the Rostow-
Katzenbach-Nitze-Busby revision did, McPherson argued, "is calculated to
put your audience asleep. It has all been heard so many times before."

96. Memorandum, McPherson to Johnson, September 28, 1967,
10:20 A.M., Statements, box 237, September 29, 1967: San Antonio.

97. Lady Bird Johnson, *White House Diary*, 571. While she apparently
agreed with the need for the public to understand, she noted that "we keep on
hoping for a suggestion that somebody *else* can do."

98. Address on Vietnam before the National Legislative Conference, San
Antonio, Texas, September 29, 1967, *Public Papers*, 876–81.

99. Ibid.

100. Johnson, *Vantage Point*, 267.

101. Letter, Busby to Rostow, October 4, 1967, Ex SP, box 177. Busby
worked on the San Antonio speech with Rostow.

102. Memorandum, Goldstein to Johnson, October 4, 1967, Ex SP, box
177.

103. President's News Conference at the LBJ Ranch, September 30, 1967,
Public Papers, 884.

104. "Thunder from a Distant Hill," *Time*, October 6, 1967, 25. Marvin
Watson kept track of newspaper articles on the speech, pencilling a note to
himself to "get answers to bad ones—get good ones in [the Congressional]
Record" (Watson files, Vietnam I).

105. See memorandum on McHugh, with column attached, Watson to Johnson, November 21, 1967; and memorandum, Jim Jones to Bess Abell, the White House social secretary, November 27, 1967 (both in Ex SP, box 77). See also letter, Johnson to *Star* editor Newbold Noyes, November 22, 1967, with Johnson's handwritten note at the bottom (Ex PR 18-2, box 376).

106. William H. Brubeck wrote McPherson that the American embassy in London had "made a lot of effective use" of the San Antonio speech; McPherson responded that "the San Antonio speech was a pretty good apologia, I thought" (letters dated October 13 and 19, 1967, both in Statements, box 237, September 29, 1967, San Antonio). See also memorandum summarizing telegrams, Jim Jones to Johnson, October 1, 1967, Statements, box 237, September 29, 1967: San Antonio. Jones reported that of 170 total telegrams, 116 were favorable and 54 were not.

107. Contained in a collection of telegrams following the San Antonio speech, September 29, 1967, Ex SP, box 177.

108. Richard Goodwin had already written a book-length critique of American involvement in Vietnam, entitled *Triumph or Tragedy* (New York: Random House, 1966). Douglass Cater, when asked about a *New York Times* story on Goodwin's opposition, responded, "it didn't surprise me. . . . I have known Goodwin a long time before coming to the White House, and nothing he might do would surprise me" (memorandum, Cater to Johnson, October 16, 1967, Ex PR 18, box 360).

109. Memorandum, Tom Johnson to Johnson, October 12, 1967 (Ex PR 18, box 360), with speech by Luce on September 22, 1966.

110. Lady Bird Johnson, *White House Diary*, 578, 575–82. While such confrontations were not new—her attendance at a concert in New York had been picketed in May, for example (pp. 515–17)—they intensified in October of 1967. Lunch with Lynda at the Jockey Club, for instance, brought people who approached the pair about the war. In May of 1968, she praised students of the Moravian Seminary as "darling girls. . . . I couldn't imagine one of them walking in a picket line or throwing rocks at their Dean" (p. 670). In addition to the demonstrations Mrs. Johnson faced, she was the object of a bomb scare on a New York to Washington flight, and daughter Luci and her husband tried to travel quietly to avoid publicizing the times they would be on airplanes (pp. 551–52).

111. Ibid., 589. Mrs. Johnson commented that when she heard the minister speak on Vietnam, she "turned to stone outside and boiled on the inside," especially upset that this should happen in an Episcopal church and at a time when daughter Lynda's fiancé—scheduled to go to Vietnam as a marine—was present.

112. See memoranda, Rowe to Johnson, January 6, 1967, Watson files, box

304

30 (1375C); and Roche to Johnson, September 8, 1967, and Roche to Califano, McPherson, O'Brien, and Watson, July 5, 1967, both in Watson files, box 29 (1375B), Roche, John—memos.

113. Memorandum, Kintner to Johnson, August 9, 1967, CF FG 1, box 16. On February 21, 1967, Kintner had warned Christian that stories of Wells as the "image maker" for the president were still circulating, in part because someone at the agency had given "the type of answer that makes reporters think there is something to a story" (memorandum, Christian files, box 3, Press Contact Report). Kintner had told Jack Sutherland of *U.S. News* that Wells was an acquaintance of Johnson's and Kintner's, not an adviser.

114. Lady Bird Johnson, *White House Diary*, 595.

115. Ibid., 583.

116. William McGaffin and Erwin Knoll, "The White House Lies," *Progressive*, September 1967, 13–18, attached to a memorandum from Cater to Watson, October 4, 1967, noting, "here is the article the President asked about" (Watson files, Credibility Gap). Christian's file on the credibility gap (box 2) includes Morrie Ryskind, "The Widening Gap," *Los Angeles Herald Examiner*, November 8, 1967; Lyle Denniston and Robert Walters, "The Johnson Presidency," *Washington Star*, November 19, 1967; and a copy of *Newsweek*, November 27, 1967. An advertisement for the credibility-gap game is attached to memorandum, Panzer to Watson, November 29, 1967 (Watson files, Credibility Gap); Panzer's files also contain a *New York Times* article from November 26, 1967, entitled " 'Credibility Gap' Fun for Skeptics," in box 340 (9), Credibility Gap.

117. Memorandum, Rostow to Johnson, October 16, 1967, Ex PR 18, box 360. According to Rostow, he told Childs that no such prediction was made and that the only tension in the meeting with Kennedy revolved around "where the leak on the conversation in the French Foreign Office occurred." Childs, who said he had received his information from the senator, told Rostow, "I guess Senator Kennedy is trying to hot it up again."

118. From transcript, "Face to Face," November 26, 1967, Christian files, box 2, Face to Face. Moyers, who appeared on the same program, contended that "some more imaginative proposals out of some of the departments" might not have been followed up, but that he knew of no proposals that came to the White House that were ignored. Kintner's memorandum of November 20, 1967, had warned Johnson that the Evans and Novak series "could be very anti-Administration" (CF FG 1, box 16).

119. The undated draft, "The Incredible 'Credibility Gap,' " is contained in Ex FG 1, box 16, 1/1/68–1/8/68. See especially memoranda, Goldstein to Watson, October 26, 1967, and Goldstein to Johnson, November 4, 1967, Panzer files, box 340 (9), Credibility Gap.

120. Memoranda, Sparks to Panzer, December 8, 1967, Panzer files, box 340 (9), Credibility Gap; and Roche to Johnson, October 20, 1967, Ex FG 1, box 15.

121. Goldstein sent Watson a critical review of Evans and Novak's book from the October 26 London *Times Literary Supplement* (memorandum, October 31, 1967, Watson files, Credibility Gap). See also memorandum, McPherson to Johnson, November 2, 1967 (Ex PR 18, box 360), in which he cited the passage from a book by William Shannon entitled *The Heir Apparent—Robert Kennedy and the Struggle for Power*.

122. Memorandum, Goldstein to Christian, October 23, 1967, Ex SP 3-162, box 38. The source of the proposal to delete the comment is unclear.

123. Komer advised Christian that Alsop had been "badgering me and my staff. He asked for documents on Viet Cong difficulties mentioned to him by Cy Vance. We'll feed him discreetly" (memorandum, April 19, 1967, Christian file, Press Contact Report). The seven Alsop columns from October 1967 are contained in NSF:VN, box 15.

124. Memorandum, A. O. [Arthur Olson, State Department] to Rostow, October 10, 1967, in NSF:VN, box 15.

125. Letter, Harold Kaplan to Rostow and Christian, October 16, 1967, on the program sponsored by the Ford Foundation's Public Broadcasting Laboratories (NSF:VN, box 13); and memoranda, McPherson to Johnson, October 10, 1967, and McPherson to Christian, November 1, 1967, both in McPherson files, box 29 (1752), Vietnam—1967 (Part II).

126. Memoranda, Panzer to Johnson, October 7, October 18, November 3, and November 9, 1967, all in Watson files, box 28 (1365B), Panzer, Fred—memos.

127. Document sent to Johnson, October 10, 1967, NSF:VN, box 16, 3A (1).

128. Correspondence of October 19, 24, and 27, 1967, NSF:VN, box 13.

129. Lady Bird Johnson, *White House Diary*, 595.

130. Panzer's proposal was contained in a memorandum to Johnson on October 21, 1967; a memorandum of the same day indicates that the president responded, "Tell Barefoot Sanders to talk to me about it." Sanders was on the congressional liaison staff for the White House.

131. Various memoranda to Johnson, November 3, 4, and 5, 1967, Diary Backup, box 81.

132. Lady Bird Johnson, *White House Diary*, 587.

133. Whitney Shoemaker, oral history interview transcript, November 25, 1968, 23.

134. Memorandum, Kintner to Johnson, November 20, 1967, CF FG 1, box 16. Kintner encouraged Johnson to continue that format.

135. Memorandum, Ray Price to Richard M. Nixon, November 27, 1967,

306

reprinted in Joe McGinniss, *The Selling of the President, 1968* (New York: Pocket Books, 1968), 207.

136. "We've got to do the same," Gavin continued. "We've got to do better." Memorandum, William Gavin to Nixon, n.d., reprinted in McGinniss, *Selling of the President*, 222–23.

137. President's News Conference, November 17, 1967, *Public Papers*, 1048. The bracketed notations on Johnson's gestures are included in this text of the speech.

138. The files for Ex PR 18-2, box 376, are filled with praise for the conference from a variety of sources, including the memorandum on mail and telegrams from Shoemaker to Christian, November 20, 1967; the *Chicago Daily News* article of November 18, 1967; a memorandum on the NBC special, Tom Johnson to Johnson, November 17, 1967; and memorandum, Goldstein to Johnson, November 17, 1967.

139. James Reston, "McNamara's Departure: Washington Still Puzzled," *New York Times*, November 30, 1967, 1.

140. Graham, OH, 38–39.

141. See Johnson, *Vantage Point*, 20, 373–78, 600–601.

142. As cited by the *New York Times*, December 1, 1967, 40.

143. Two memoranda, Christian to Johnson, December 4, 1967, Ex PR 18-2, box 376. In his interview with the author (July 18, 1979, in Austin, Texas), Christian said of the November 17 conference that "everyone claims to be the father of that son." Yet he noted that Johnson preferred "Mother," never again using the lavalier microphone despite its success. Given the Johnsons' metaphors of war for press conferences, the president undoubtedly felt more comfortable behind a barrier.

144. President's News Conference, December 4, 1967, *Public Papers*, 1088–94.

145. Remarks to Delegates to the National Convention, AFL-CIO, December 12, 1967, *Public Papers*, 1129.

146. Memorandum, Valenti to Johnson, n.d., attached to a memorandum from Christian to Watson with suggested advertising copy, December 18, 1967 (Diary Backup, box 87, December 18, 1967). Valenti's memorandum has Johnson's handwritten note at the top and a notation on the side: "12-5-67— Jones told JV." Bob Fleming of the press office breakfasted with correspondents Ray Scherer, Dan Rather, and Frank Reynolds to develop areas of questions, reported in a memorandum, Christian to Johnson, December 15, 1967 (Diary Backup, box 87, December 18, 1967). The transcript of the program is contained in "A Conversation with the President," Joint Interview for Use by the Television Networks, December 19, 1967, *Public Papers*, 1158–73. Taped on December 18, the program was aired the following day.

147. Memorandum, Panzer to Johnson, October 16, 1967, Watson files, Vietnam I. The same files contain a memorandum from Ernest Goldstein to

Johnson, October 25, 1967, reporting that his Sunday flight to Boston was "filled with affluent demonstrators returning to their classes." Taking a quick poll, Goldstein found that "if the Republicans nominate Romney, Reagan, or Nixon, the majority of those who marched will vote for you."

148. Cormier, *LBJ*, 246. Mrs. Johnson's description was similar but kinder: "the fastest, longest, hardest trip any President of the United States has ever taken" (Lady Bird Johnson, *White House Diary*, 605). Holt had disappeared while swimming in shark-infested water off the Australian coasts; it was a special loss for Johnson, for Holt had supported the American effort in Vietnam.

149. Memorandum, Christian to Johnson, December 18, 1967, Ex TR, box 42, TR 136.

150. Memorandum, "Statement Taken from Tom Johnson on Press Corps Attitudes," Maguire to Johnson, n.d., 11:00 A.M., Diary Backup, box 87, December 22–23, 1967, Khorat, Thailand, Royal Thailand AFB. According to the *Overseas Press Bulletin* of January 13, 1968, Charles Franks, a CBS sound technician, suffered a mild heart attack on the way to Thailand, and Cyril Renni of RCA had a lung collapse in Canberra, Australia. Franks blamed lengthy assignments and the numerous inoculations before the journey. The article is contained in Ex TR, box 42, TR 136.

151. Undated, unindicated memorandum, "Points to Explain to the Press," Diary Backup, box 87, December 19, 1967, Honolulu International Airport, Honolulu, Hawaii; memoranda, Tom Johnson to Jones, December 7, 1967, and Tom Johnson to Juanita Roberts, December 26, 1967, both in Ex TR, box 42, TR 136, Australia; and memorandum, Tom Johnson to Jim Jones, December 26, 1967, Diary Backup, box 87, 12/19/67 Honolulu International Airport, Honolulu.

152. Memorandum, Christian to Johnson, December 7, 1967, Ex FG 1, box 16. Christian summarized an article by Saville Davis entitled "LBJ Shucks Protective Shell."

153. "LBJ and the Pope," *Newsweek*, January 8, 1968, 40; Valenti, *Human President*, 232–37; telegram, Johnson to Graham, January 2, 1968, Ex TR, box 42, TR 136); and Graham, OH, 23–24.

154. McPherson, *Political Education*, 322.

155. As cited by Lewy, *America in Vietnam*, 71; and Halberstam, *Best and Brightest*, 787.

Chapter 8. Withdrawal from the Race, 1968–1969

1. Johnson, *Vantage Point*, 532.

2. Memorandum, Cater to Johnson, December 29, 1967, Cater files, box 16, Memos to the President, December 1967. In presenting the compilation, Cater observed that "it goes a little way toward restoring faith in mankind."

308

3. Lady Bird Johnson, *White House Diary*, 612. Lady Bird mentions meetings on this topic from May of 1967 through January of 1968. Johnson, in what Kearns describes as "a section of his memoirs that reads as if it were a defense attorney's brief," discussed his debate in *Vantage Point*, 425–37. See Kearns, *American Dream*, 342–43. In his oral history interview, Christian indicated that Johnson first gave serious thought to not running in 1968 during the late summer of 1967 (no. 1, p. 11)—a view echoing a memorandum for the record of a conversation between Christian and Dorothy Territo, the Johnson archivist, on March 19, 1969 (Statements, box 266, March 31, 1968). According to the memorandum, Johnson told Connally in August of 1967 he would not run again, asked Connally and Christian to help draft a statement in October, asked Busby to draft one in December, and asked Christian to do another in January. At the end of March, Busby outlined the draft used in the March 31, 1968, speech.

4. Memorandum, Horace Busby to Johnson, January 15, 1968, Statements, box 266, March 31, 1968. Lady Bird's diary entry for that day notes that when she chastised her husband for his late lunch hour of 3:30 P.M., he gave the "rather plaintive" response that he always seemed to be behind—a mood exacerbated by his indecision (*White House Diary*, 615).

5. Lady Bird Johnson, *White House Diary*, 616–18. Connally's views were reported in a memorandum for the record of conversation between Territo and Christian, March 19, 1969, Statements, box 266, March 31, 1968.

6. Johnson, *Vantage Point*, 430. Kearns (*American Dream*, 343) finds Johnson's account of his forgetfulness to be an explanation "not entirely convincing from this man of meticulous detail."

7. Annual Message to the Congress on the State of the Union, January 17, 1968, *Public Papers*, 25–33.

8. Lady Bird Johnson, *White House Diary*, 618–20.

9. Memoranda, Kintner to Johnson and Kintner to Watson, both December 29, 1967, attached to letter, Watson to Kintner, January 2, 1968, CF FG 1, box 16; memorandum with Kintner's suggestions, Watson to Johnson, January 5, 1968, CF SP 2–4/1968, box 88, State of the Union 1968); and memorandum via telephone, Kintner to Johnson, January 18, 1968, CF SP 2–4/1968, box 88, State of the Union 1968. Kintner had suggested that the speech be no longer than forty-five minutes; given Johnson's propensity for long speeches, he did well.

10. Lady Bird Johnson, *White House Diary*, 620. Mrs. Johnson's initial reactions had not been totally positive; she mentioned "the first maggots of doubt" when no legislators expressed the sense of commitment she felt was necessary after the speech.

11. Editorial, "The State of the Union," *New York Times,* January 18, 1968, 38; and "The State of LBJ," *Newsweek*, January 29, 1968, 16–17.

12. Memorandum, Panzer to Christian, January 22, 1968, Ex FG 1, box 17.

13. Lady Bird Johnson, *White House Diary*, 641; 620–24; and 629–31.

14. Manheim's letters of December 26, 1967, are attached to a memorandum to Watson, over the typed initials LBJ:JRJ:dbm, 1/8/68. "JRJ" is Jim Jones. All correspondence is in Watson files, Vietnam 2. The "they" to whom the memorandum refers may be the media generally or the *New York Times* specifically; Johnson's referent is unclear.

15. Letter, Carroll Kilpatrick, Garnett D. Horner, and Peter Lisagor of the White House Correspondents Association to Christian, included in a telegram from Christian to Johnson through Jim Jones, January 4, 1968; and telegram, Christian to Johnson, January 4, 1968 (both in CF PR 18, box 83).

16. "LBJ Trip Test Endurance of White House Press Corps," *Overseas Press Bulletin*, January 13, 1968, 55 (Ex TR, box 42).

17. Reported in memorandum, Hackler to Christian, January 17, 1968, Ex FG 1, box 17. See Hugh Sidey, "Around the World with Lyndon B. Magellan," *Life*, January 5, 1968, 24B–24D.

18. Harris's prediction, conveyed in a confidential telephone call, is reported in a memorandum, Panzer to Jim Jones, December 29, 1967, CF PR 2, box 83. Harris's surveys were reported in the *Washington Post* of December 23 and 30, 1967.

19. Memorandum, Panzer to Johnson, January 4, 1968, Watson files, box 28 (1375B), Panzer, Fred—memos.

20. Halberstam, *Best and Brightest*, 787.

21. Don Oberdorfer discussed television coverage of the offensive in *Tet!* (Garden City, N.Y.: Doubleday, 1971), 36–37 and 158–71. The *New York Times* editorial, "Bloody Path to Peace?," is in the February 1, 1968, issue on p. 36. The Tet offensive was the cover story for *Newsweek* on February 12 and 19 and for *Time* on February 9, 1968.

22. Peter Braestrup, *The Big Story: How the American Press and Television Reported and Interpreted the Crisis of Tet 1968 in Vietnam and Washington*, 2 vols. (Boulder, Colo.: Westview Press, 1977). See especially chap. 8 in vol. 1.

23. Braestrup, *Big Story* 1:706. For an account of the reporting, editing, and distribution of the Loan story, see George A. Bailey and Lawrence W. Lichty, "Rough Justice on a Saigon Street: A Gatekeeper Study of NBC's Tet Execution Film," *Journalism Quarterly* 49 (Summer 1972): 221–29.

24. Oberdorfer, *Tet!* 159.

25. Johnson, *Vantage Point*, 380.

26. Interview with Westmoreland cited by Schandler, *Unmaking of a President*, 75. Westmoreland's estimation of the enemy's preparation is cited in Miller, *Lyndon*, 500; according to the Johnson Library, this document is

still classified. See also Westmoreland's book, *Report on the War in Vietnam: Section 2, Report on Operations in South Vietnam, January 1964–June 1968* (Washington, D.C.: Government Printing Office, 1969), 157; and W. W. Rostow, *The Diffusion of Power* (New York: Macmillan, 1972), esp. 502–3.

27. Interview with McPherson cited in Schandler, *Unmaking of a President*, 81–82. A sense of McPherson's frustration at the time is conveyed by his unfinished poem, contained in Statements, box 362, March 31 speech:

While we talked & dreamed of
peace sent emissaries throughout the world
answered with a cannon shot
hit provincial centers—killed 1000s of civilians
at this hour shelling Saigon
led by men never elected to anything
trying to take over SVN by the only means they know—brute force
they . . .

28. Townsend Hoopes, *The Limits of Intervention* (New York: David McKay Co., 1969), 145.

29. Cable, Wheeler to Westmoreland, January 31, 1968, cited by Schandler, *Unmaking of a President*, 83.

30. Cable, Christian to Bunker and Westmoreland, January 31, 1968, cited by Schandler, *Unmaking of a President*, 83.

31. Cable, Rostow to Bunker and Westmoreland, February 3, 1968, cited by Schandler, *Unmaking of a President*, 84.

32. Rostow, interview with the author, December 22, 1977, Austin, Texas; see also Rostow, *Diffusion of Power*, 492.

33. President's News Conference of February 2, 1968, *Public Papers*, 155–63. See also Johnson, *Vantage Point*, 383.

34. According to Frank Cormier, *LBJ*, 264; and Johnson, *Vantage Point*, 383, 384, and 414.

35. The briefing book is contained in NSF:VN, box 15. Panzer suggested that similar briefing books should be developed on other topics for the administration's supporters, in a memorandum to Johnson, March 13, 1968, Watson files, box 28 (137B), Panzer, Fred—memos.

36. See memoranda from Panzer to Christian, February 6, 1968, and from Panzer to Johnson, February 15 and 21, 1968, Watson files, box 28 (1975B) Panzer, Fred—memos; and memorandum, Panzer to Johnson, February 9, 1968, with Johnson's handwritten notations, Watson files, Vietnam 2.

37. Memoranda, Valenti to Watson, February 28 and 29, 1968, Watson files, box 31 (1375C), Jack Valenti files. See Ex PR 18, box 361, for examples of Fleming's memoranda.

38. Memorandum, Christian to Watson, February 16, 1968 (Diary Backup, box 92, February 20, 1968), with Johnson's approval of an appointment for Heren at the bottom. According to the Diary Cards, however, Johnson did not meet with Heren until May 6, almost three months later.

39. President's News Conference of February 2, 1968, *Public Papers*, 155–63. See also Benchley's account of the difficulties of writing a speech for the presentation of a military award during the Tet siege of Khe Sanh, as "Rostow wanted to make a very strong commitment without saying we were going to hold it" (Peter Benchley, oral history interview transcript, November 20, 1968, 10).

40. Cables, Wheeler to Westmoreland, February 3 and 8, cited in Sheehan et al., *Pentagon Papers*, 594–95; also in Marvin Kalb and Elie Abel, *The Roots of Involvement* (New York: W. W. Norton, 1971), 209–10. According to the Johnson Library, these cables are still security classified.

41. Cables, Westmoreland to Wheeler, February 8 and 9, 1968, cited above; and Westmoreland's interview with Schandler, *Unmaking of a President*, 97. Westmoreland's cable of February 9 is available in NSF, NSC History of the March 31 Speech, box 47.

42. President's News Conference of February 16, 1968, *Public Papers*, 238.

43. Johnson, *Vantage Point*, 397–98.

44. Memorandum, "Report of Chairman, J.C.S., on Situation in Vietnam and MAVC Requirements," Wheeler to Johnson, February 27, 1968, in Sheehan et al., *Pentagon Papers*, 615–21. This document is still classified in the Johnson Library.

45. Cable, Westmoreland to Wheeler, February 12, 1968, NSF, NSC History of March 31 speech, box 47.

46. Johnson, *Vantage Point*, 389–90.

47. Cable, Rostow to Johnson, February 27, 1968, NSF, NSC History of the March 31 Speech, box 47; and Johnson *Vantage Point*, 390.

48. Johnson, *Vantage Point*, 392–93.

49. Ibid., 392–94; Clark M. Clifford, "A Viet Nam Reappraisal: The Personal History of One Man's View and How It Evolved," *Foreign Affairs* 47 (July 1969): 609; and Schandler, *Unmaking of a President*, 133–38.

50. Draft, "Memorandum for the President," March 4, 1968, NSF, NSC History of March 31 Speech, box 49.

51. Hoopes, *Limits of Intervention*, 178.

52. See Johnson, *Vantage Point*, 397; and Sheehan et al., *Pentagon Papers*, 603.

53. Interview with Clifford cited by Schandler, *Unmaking of a President*, 245.

54. Johnson, *Vantage Point*, 398.

312

55. George Christian, interview with the author, July 18, 1979, Austin, Texas.

56. Cited in Miller, *Lyndon*, 503.

57. See Johnson, *Vantage Point*, 399–400; and "Comments on the Attached Draft," Rusk to Johnson, March 5, 1968, Declassified Documents from Unprocessed Files, box 2.

58. Cable, Westmoreland to Johnson, March 8, 1968, cited in Sheehan et al., *Pentagon Papers*, 604; not available in the Johnson Library.

59. Neil Sheehan and Hedrick Smith, "Westmoreland Requests 206,000 More Men, Stirring Debate in Administration," *New York Times*, March 10, 1968, 1; see also Johnson, *Vantage Point*, 402–3, and Schandler, *Unmaking of a President*, 199–205.

60. Frank McGee, "Sunday Report," March 10, 1968, cited by Oberdorfer, *Tet!* 273.

61. Transcript in Braestrup, *Big Story* 2: 188–89.

62. Cited in William T. Small, *To Kill a Messenger* (New York: Hasting House, 1970), 123.

63. Cable, Wheeler to Westmoreland, March 11, 1968, cited in Schandler, *Unmaking of a President*, 230; not available in the Johnson Library.

64. Senate Committee on Foreign Relations, *Hearings, Foreign Assistance Act of 1968, Part I—Vietnam*, 1. Lady Bird, seeing Rusk the day before he started his testimony, commented that "even he looks weary" (*White House Diary*, 637).

65. Johnson in an interview for CBS with Walter Cronkite, "LBJ: The Decision to Halt the Bombing," aired February 6, 1970. The transcript for this interview and for the other four in the series are in the oral history files at the Johnson Library.

66. Johnson, *Vantage Point*, 383–84.

67. Ibid., 366.

68. Pierson, OH no. 3, 3.

69. See, for example, Reedy, interview with the author, May 19, 1978; George Reedy, OH no. 4, 14, 16–18; and memoranda, Kintner to Johnson and Kintner to Watson, December 29, 1967, including Kintner's offers to aid in the campaign (attached to letter, Watson to Kintner, January 2, 1968, CF FG 1, box 16). On March 14, 1968, Horace Busby sent a delightfully peculiar letter to the former press secretary about his return to the White House: "Dear Reedy: I don't know what you are doing or why—your press is unaccustomedly opaque—but I am glad that you are there to do it" (Reedy files, box 16, George Reedy/A–Z).

70. Memorandum, "The 1968 Campaign," February 6, 1968, with attached note: "Marv—Enclosed is for the President; came up in our talk on night of Jan. 22—Bob," in Watson files, box 31 (1375C), Robert Spivack file.

71. William McGaffin and Erwin Knoll, "The White House Lies," *Progressive,* September 1967, cited in Panzer draft, "The Incredible 'Credibility Gap,'" n.d., Ex FG 1, box 16, 1/1/86–1/8/68. See chapter 4 for a discussion of these 1964 campaign statements.

72. Panzer draft, "The Incredible 'Credibility Gap'" n.d., Ex FG 1, box 16, 1/1/68–1/8/68.

73. "A Conversation with the President," Joint Interview for Use by the Television Networks, December 19, 1967, *Public Papers,* 1161. In March Johnson called for a copy of the speech most frequently quoting his "American boys in Asia" statement; in a memorandum of March 11, 1968, Panzer sent the president a highlighted set of his remarks made in Akron, Ohio on October 21, 1964. See Panzer, box 340 (9), Credibility Gap.

74. Memorandum, Panzer to Goldstein, Christian, and Watson, February 21, 1968, CF FG 1, box 16. Attached is Clayton Fritchey, "War is Asian Boys' Task: Own Words Haunt LBJ," *Pittsburgh Press,* February 14, 1968 (CF FG 1, box 16).

75. Memorandum, Goldstein to Johnson, January 20, 1968, in Panzer, box 340 (9), Credibility Gap; memorandum, Panzer to Goldstein, Christian, and Watson, February 21, 1968, CF FG 1, box 16; and memorandum, Panzer to Christian, Goldstein, and Watson, March 7, 1968, PR 18, box 361. Panzer contended that "for strategic reasons, the best place to hit the extreme left is in the South, or through a southern spokesman who would insure wide coverage in the South—the most Hawkish section of the U.S." See the discussion of refuting the credibility gap in chapter 7, including the forty-two-page undated draft that countered the charges, contained in Ex FG 1, box 16, file 1/1/68–1/8/68.

76. Carl Rowan, *Chicago Daily News,* February 17, 1968, cited by Johnson, *Vantage Point,* 433. See also the memoranda of the Nixon primaries effort, reprinted in Joe McGinniss, *Selling of the President, 1968,* e.g., 228.

77. Reedy, *Twilight,* 68.

78. Converse et al., *American Political Science Review* 63 (December 1969): 1092.

79. Memorandum, Kintner to Johnson, December 29, 1967 (attached to letter, Watson to Kintner, January 2, 1968, CF FG 1, box 16); Johnson, *Vantage Point,* 537–38; and Reedy, *Twilight,* 68–69. Miller observes that the New Hampshire ballot was not typical for write-in candidates, for it included a portion, forwarded to the White House, which "entitled the voter to a picture of Lady Bird and Lyndon by return mail" (*Lyndon,* 608).

80. Cited in the *New York Times,* March 17, 1968, 68, under headline, "Kennedy's Statement and Excerpts." When Kennedy appeared on "Meet the Press" on August 6, 1967, he made his disagreement with Johnson's foreign and domestic policies clear without directly attacking Johnson. See tran-

314

script, in the Lawrence Spivak papers, box 19, Library of Congress. For stories of the proposed bargain, see for example Theodore H. White, *The Making of the President, 1968* (New York: Atheneum, 1969), 162; Miller, *Lyndon*, 507; or Sidey, *Very Personal Presidency,* 293–95.

81. Memoranda, C. R. Smith to Warren Woodward, January 15, 1968, and Woodward to Watson, January 16, 1968, both in Watson files, box 25 (1375A), Kennedy, Robert; see also Kearns, *American Dream*, 259.

82. Memorandum, Kintner to Johnson, December 29, 1967 (attached to letter, Watson to Kintner, January 2, 1968, CF FG 1, box 16); and memorandum, Cater to Johnson, March 28, 1968, Ex FG 1, box 18. See also Huntley, OH, 14; Pearson, OH, 22.

83. Quoted by Kearns, *American Dream*, 343.

84. Remarks at a Dinner of the Veterans of Foreign Wars, March 12, 1968, *Public Papers,* 381. Johnson also joked about McCarthy's impending candidacy at his November 17, 1967, press conference. When asked if he agreed with the senator's statement that he was running because "he believes it would be a healthy thing to debate Vietnam in the primaries," the president responded, "I don't know how I am going to be, after all this opposition develops, so far as my state of health is concerned. But I am very healthy today. I don't know whether this criticism has contributed to my good health or not" (*Public Papers,* 1050–51).

85. Memorandum, Rowe to Johnson, March 19, 1968, Watson files, box 30 (1375B and C), Jim Rowe. Panzer's assessments, which were based on conversations with polltakers Harris and Scammons, were sent to the president in a memorandum of March 13, 1968 (Watson files, box 28 (1375B), Panzer, Fred—memos). Had McCarthy's candidacy not been viewed as a kamikaze effort, Johnson's majority would not have been perceived as a defeat. As Donald R. Matthews points out, Ronald Reagan attracted a larger share of the voters in the New Hampshire primary of 1976 than McCarthy had in 1968, yet he was not declared the "winner" because the incumbent Ford's draw was so much better than expected. See Matthews, "'Winnowing': The News Media and the 1976 Presidential Nominations," in *Race for the Presidency: The Media and the Nominating Process,* ed. James David Barber (Englewood Cliffs, N.J.: Prentice-Hall, 1978), 63.

86. Memorandum, Rowe to Johnson, March 15, 1968, Watson files, box 29 (1375B), Roche memos.

87. See memoranda, Reedy to Johnson, one dated March 14 and two dated March 16, 1968, all in Watson files, box 28 (1375B), George Reedy memos. Reedy's identification of Kennedy's ruthless image found support in a joke that circulated through Washington after the senator from New York announced his candidacy: Democrats could now choose a hawk, a dove, or a vulture (see Heren, *No Hail,* 196).

88. Memorandum, Roche to Johnson, March 14, 1968, Watson files, box 29 (1375B), Roche memos.

89. Remarks at a Meeting of the National Alliance of Businessmen, March 16, 1968, and Remarks to Delegates to the National Farmers Union Convention in Minneapolis, March 18, 1968, both in *Public Papers*, 402–5 and 406–13. The NAB address was based on an outline provided by Abe Fortas.

90. Memorandum, Rowe to Johnson, March 19, 1968, Watson files, box 30 (1375B and C), Jim Rowe. The parenthetical comment is Rowe's.

91. Memorandum, Cater to Johnson, March 20, 1968, in Ex FG 1, box 18; memorandum, Humphrey to Johnson, March 20, 1968, Watson files, box 28 (1375B), Panzer memos. Panzer reported Harris's observation that the "Hanoi is listening" slogan cost the Johnson campaign, for it was "too personal," while Reedy contended that it "came dangerously close to giving him [McCarthy] a 'character assassination' issue." See memorandum, Reedy to Johnson, March 14, 1968, Watson files, box 28 (1375B), George Reedy memos.

92. Memorandum, Rowe to Johnson, March 19, 1968, Watson files, box 30 (1375B and C), Jim Rowe; and memorandum, Reedy to Johnson, March 20, 1968, Watson files, box 28 (1375B), George Reedy memos.

93. See Statements for March 31, 1968, boxes 261–66, which contain approximately twenty-seven inches of drafts, revisions, and memoranda on the address. In addition, a report entitled "Problems We Can Anticipate in U.S. Public Opinion" has been withdrawn under national security restrictions.

94. Draft, sent to McPherson by Larry Levinson, February 3, 1968, Statements, box 261, March 31, 1968; and memoranda, Rostow to Johnson, February 5 and 11, 1968, Statements, boxes 261 and 262, March 31, 1968. On a draft of February 5, 1968, Clark Clifford scratched, "Is there a policy to avoid referring to Divine Providence?" (Statements, box 261, March 31, 1968).

95. See Johnson's discussion of the meeting in *Vantage Point*, 411–13; and interview with McPherson cited in Schandler, *Unmaking of a President*, 252.

96. Memorandum, McPherson to Johnson, March 23, 1968 (Declassified Documents from Unprocessed Files, box 2), with Johnson's handwritten notations at top.

97. Memorandum, Bundy to Johnson, March 21, 1968, Statements, box 266, March 31, 1968. Bundy referred to McPherson's draft of March 20, 1968.

98. Notes by Clifford on the back of an envelope, n.d., Statements, box 266, March 31, 1968.

99. President's News Conference of March 22, 1968, *Public Papers*, 429–36. Johnson had defended Westmoreland in his previous news conference of February 16.

100. See Johnson's discussion of these meetings, *Vantage Point*, 415–18; and Rostow's interview with Schandler, *Unmaking of a President*, 262.

316

101. Memorandum, Rowe to Johnson, March 15, 1968, Watson files, box 30 (1375B and C), Jim Rowe; and memorandum, Cater to Johnson, March 28, 1968, Ex FG 1, box 18.

102. Memorandum, Panzer to Johnson, March 14, 1968, with Johnson's handwritten notation to "ask [the DNC] to get busy," Watson files, box 28 (1375B), Panzer memos; memorandum, Reedy to Johnson, March 29, 1968, with Johnson's handwritten notation to Watson that "this may deserve attention," in Watson files, box 28 (1375B), Reedy memos; memorandum, Reedy to Johnson, March 29, 1968, with typed notation of Johnson's reaction attached, Watson files, box 28, (1375B), George Reedy memos; and memorandum, Jim Jones to Watson, March 28, 1968, Watson files, Vietnam 2, relaying Johnson's instructions on Eisenhower's essay. "His first choice," Jones noted, "is Palmer Hoyt, if he will do it." The same files contain a galley of the article, which appeared in the April 1968 issue of *Reader's Digest.*

103. Memorandum, Roche to Johnson, March 14, 1968, Watson files, box 29 (1375B), Roche memos; memorandum, Panzer to Johnson, March 30, 1968, Watson files, box 28 (1375B), Panzer memos; and memorandum, Rowe to Johnson, March 28, 1968, Watson files, box 30 (1375C), Jim Rowe.

104. Clifford, "Vietnam Reappraisal," 613; and interview with Clifford cited by Schandler, *Unmaking of a President,* 473.

105. See McPherson, *Political Education,* 436–37; Johnson, *Vantage Point,* 420; and Schandler, *Unmaking of a President,* 274–75.

106. Handwritten notes by Clifford from meeting of March 30, 1968, Statements, box 266.

107. Memorandum, Don Furtado to McPherson, March 30, 1968, Statements, box 266, March 31, 1968.

108. Memorandum, McPherson to Johnson, March 30, 1968, 9:30 P.M., Statements, box 266, March 31, 1968. McPherson cited Clifford's emphatic endorsement of this conclusion, rather than a more aggressive ending.

109. According to memoranda and notes in the Statements files, Busby had his first draft to be typed at 2:06 P.M., March 31; Johnson requested Truman's statement that he would not run for reelection (3/29/52) at 3:47 P.M., and Busby had another draft for Johnson's revision at 6:30 P.M. Statements, box 266, contains an undated, unindicated chronology for March 31, 1968, and a memorandum for the record from Juanita Roberts about Johnson's request for Truman's remarks. In addition, the Diary Backup for March 31, 1968, file II, contains secretary Marie Fehmer's notes on the day, transcribed from shorthand on August 30, 1968. The undated, unindicated chronology in Statements, box 266, commented that "the Treaty Room table looked as if Busby had been there for some time. There was a coffee urn on a tray with just one cup, and an ash tray filled with cigarette remains."

110. See Johnson, *Vantage Point,* 431–32; Lady Bird Johnson, *White House*

Diary, 642; memorandum, Liz Carpenter to Johnson, March 29, 1968 (Diary Backup, March 30, 1968); and Marie Fehmer's notes in Diary Backup, March 31, 1968, file II.

111. President's Address to the Nation Announcing Steps to Limit the War in Vietnam and Reporting His Decision Not to Seek Reelection, March 31, 1968, *Public Papers,* 476. Descriptions of the pause before this passage offer a case study in differing perceptions. Kearns, who felt Johnson "spoke gravely, gently," and without the "sarcasm" and "piety" that had flawed other presentations, characterized it as "an inexpressible moment, which must have compressed the stormy inward clashes of a lifetime" (*American Dream,* 348). In contrast, Goldman, who found Johnson to be "a lecturish, querulous schoolmaster" that night, felt the pause showed that "he had not lost his pleasure in surprises" (*Tragedy of Lyndon Johnson,* 512). The two perceptions of the pause are not necessarily irreconcilable.

112. President's News Conference of March 31, 1968, *Public Papers,* 478. Huntley commented in his oral history interview on his surprise (Huntley, OH, 22), and Marvin Barrett wryly noted "When LBJ Stunned the Experts," *Columbia Journalism Review,* 7 (Summer 1968): 10. See also Sidey, *Very Personal Presidency,* 296–97. In *Vantage Point,* 433, Johnson commented, "I believed that because of the 'informed guidance' the press had given the people, all the nation—except a dozen or so individuals—would be shocked and surprised" by his announcement that he would not be a candidate.

113. Memorandum, Juanita Roberts to Johnson, April 2, 1968, Statements, box 266, March 31, 1968; and Shoemaker, OH, 12.

114. Christian, *President Steps Down,* 1–2.

115. See Johnson, *Vantage Point,* 493–504. Johnson traveled to Honolulu on April 17 and again on July 18, 1968 (ibid., 510–11).

116. Memorandum, Christian to Jim Jones, June 27, 1968, Ex FG 1, box 19. See also memorandum, Bob Fleming to Jim Jones, April 10, 1968, on Howard K. Smith's off-the-record interview with Johnson, and memorandum, Christian to Johnson, April 30, 1968, on Sidey's request for an interview to discover "the type of world the President would like to leave to his grandchildren" (both in Ex FG 1, box 18); memorandum, Christian to Jones, June 27, 1968, on an interview with Saul Pett of the AP, and memoranda, Christian to Johnson and Rostow to Johnson, September 5, 1968, on questions from Peter Lisagor of the *Chicago Daily News* (Diary Backup, box 110, September 5, 1968, and Ex FG 1, box 19); memorandum, Loyd Hackler to Jones, October 8, 1968, on an interview with Ray Scherer of NBC (Ex FG 1, box 20); and memorandum, Christian to Jones, November 26, 1968, on Chuck Bailey's request for an interview (Ex FG 1, box 21).

117. Memorandum, Christian to Johnson, May 4, 1968, Ex FG 1, box 18.

118. Memorandum, Califano to Johnson, December 6, 1968, with John-

318

son's handwritten notation, Ex PR 18, box 362. Califano had caught Johnson at a time when his feelings were especially bitter about Bill Moyers's handling of the press office, as indicated in memorandum, Reedy to Johnson, December 3, 1968, Ex FG 1, box 21, and letter, John Roche to Christian, December 4, 1968, Ex PR 18, box 362.

119. Lady Bird Johnson, *White House Diary*, 662–64; 669;692. On May 29, 1968, Reedy sent Goldstein, Cater, Wayne Crover, and Joe Frantz a chronology of Johnson's life and career, with notes on resources and people to interview (Ex FG 1, box 18). Goldman, noting Johnson's "fierce concern with posterity," discusses the president's request for departmental histories to be placed in the Johnson Library (*Tragedy of Lyndon Johnson*, 513–14). The farewell party for McNamara was also for three other departing members of the administration.

120. Christian, OH, no. 2, pp. 14–17; and Reston, interview with the author, May 17, 1980, Notre Dame, Indiana. Christian mentioned the sharp barbs of Art Buchwald which retreated into a nostalgic column at the end. Christian served as press secretary for almost twenty-five months, as compared with Salinger's four, Reedy's sixteen, and Moyers's eighteen.

121. Memorandum, William H. Crook, Director of VISTA, to Johnson, May 31, 1968, Ex FG 1, box 18. Also see article by Max Kempelman, "When Press Bites Man," *Columbia Journalism Review*, Spring 1968, placed in Johnson's night reading May 7, 1968 (Ex PR 18, box 361); letter from Johnson to Richard Wilson, May 9, 1968, Ex FG 1, box 18; letter, Drew Pearson to Christian, May 15, 1968, Ex FG 1, box 18; memorandum, Panzer to Johnson on Robert Spivak column, August 20, 1968, Ex FG 1, box 19; memorandum, Hackler to Johnson on Pearson's defense of Johnson on the "Mike Wallace Show," September 26, 1968, Ex FG 1, box 20; letter, Palmer Hoyt to Johnson, October 25, 1968, Ex FG 1, box 20; memoranda, Charles Maguire to Johnson on two *New Yorker* staff sending complimentary letters, November 18, 1968, Ex FG 1, box 21; and letter, Thomas Corcoran to Johnson, November 25, 1968, Ex FG 1, box 21.

122. See memorandum, on domestic affairs, Tom Johnson to Johnson, May 8, 1968, Ex FG 1, box 18; Liz Carpenter echoed this viewpoint in a memorandum to the president and the first lady after Robert Kennedy's assassination, June 9, 1968, Ex FG 1, box 18. See memorandum on credibility, Panzer to Charles Maguire, May 15, 1968, Ex FG 1, box 18; see also memorandum, Joseph Califano to McPherson, March 8, 1968, Ex FG 1, box 17.

123. McPherson's recommendation came in a memorandum to Christian, October 4, 1968 (Ex FG 1, box 20). See also Christian's file entitled "Nasty Stories" and Goldman, *Tragedy of Lyndon Johnson*, 263–64. According to Christian, Humphrey was hurt by Johnson's approach. When Evans and Novak published a column claiming that Humphrey was repudiating the

president, however, the vice-president called to assure him that he was "heartbroken" and "especially disturbed" by such charges (memorandum, Jim Jones to Johnson, July 18, 1968, Ex FG 1, box 19). This echoed an earlier memorandum in which Humphrey denounced columns by Pearson and by Evans and Novak as being "phony as a $3 bill" (memorandum, Humphrey to Johnson, March 9, 1967, Ex PR 18, box 359).

124. President's Address to the Nation upon Announcing His Decision to Halt the Bombing of North Vietnam, October 31, 1968, *Public Papers,* 1099–103. For discussions of the October efforts, see Johnson, *Vantage Point,* 514–29; Christian, *President Steps Down* (throughout the entire book); and Schandler, *Unmaking of a President,* 319.

125. Lady Bird Johnson, *White House Diary,* 725, as well as 694–95 and 734; see also Christian, *President Steps Down,* 65.

126. Memorandum, Rostow to Johnson, November 1, 1968, Ex SP, box "Open—Misc.," SP 3-274, Bombing Halt in Vietnam, 10/31/68.

127. Remarks at the Civic Center Arena in Pittsburgh, October 27, 1964, *Public Papers,* 1477.

128. Remarks in Chicago Before the National Association of Broadcasters, April 1, 1968, *Public Papers,* 482–83.

129. President's News Conference at the National Press Club, January 17, 1969, *Public Papers,* 51.

130. In the first book Johnson published after leaving the presidency, he classified his section on the fourth estate as "the musings of a man who has seen the press in recent years only from the open end of the gun barrel—an angle from which the press rarely has occasion to see itself." See Lyndon Baines Johnson, *The Choices We Face* (New York: Bantam Books, 1969), 140.

131. Johnson, *Vantage Point,* 529.

132. Lyndon B. Johnson, oral history interview with Elspeth Rostow, transcript no. 2, September 28, 1970, 1.

Epilogue

1. Goldman, *Tragedy of Lyndon Johnson,* 531.

Bibliography

Sources used in this investigation included both published and unpublished materials. Published sources may be broadly divided, as the bibliography indicates, into works by Johnson; works about Johnson; works on the presidency, the press, and public opinion; works on Vietnam and American foreign policy; general contemporary histories; contemporary press accounts; and contemporary historiographies. In keeping with the perceptions of government and media people alike, the "prestige press" predominate the category of contemporary press accounts.

Integral to the investigation were unpublished materials, primarily the holdings of the Lyndon B. Johnson Library in Austin, Texas. The heart of the presidential documents, of major importance to this study, is contained in the White House Central Files, maintained in the Johnson Library essentially as they were established during the Johnson administration. Based on an elaborate system of classification, cross-referencing, and reproduction, the White House Central Files provided the working file system for the White House staff.

The White House Central Files by Subject constituted a primary resource for this study. These files contain memoranda to the president, frequently with Johnson's handwritten notations; memoranda among his staff members; letters to administration members and their responses; drafts and final copies of speeches; and copies of articles and materials sent to Johnson. The collection has two major divisions, each using the same sixty-two categories: the central files consist of parallel collections, General (primarily routine inquiries from the general public) and Executive (more exclusive and therefore more useful for this study); while the Confidential Files, indicated in notations by "CF" preceding the White House file-manual code, contain sensitive information that was most useful to the study. The categories with the richest store of information for this investigation are the PR 18 files called "Publicity," which include material on Johnson's relationship with the press, his coverage by the press, and his televised appearances; the FG 1 files entitled "Federal Government—Organizations—The President," which address the problem of the credibility gap and related issues; and the

322

"National Security-Defense" files on Vietnam, with material on both military and publicity decisions.

A major supplement to the White House Central Files by Subject are the White House Central Files by Name of Aide. Although technically part of the White House Central Files, these papers were kept by the office staffs of the aides themselves and transferred only intermittently to the Central Files Office. They therefore vary not only in content but also in manner and degree of organization; some aides failed to leave any files at all. Although much of the materials contained in these files is duplicated in the subject files, these collections do occasionally yield papers not found elsewhere, such as the George Christian files on credibility and "Nasty Stories."

Another collection of significance for this study is "Country File: Vietnam" in the National Security Files. Separate from the White House Central Files, the National Security Files include memoranda and reports from the National Security Council, the Central Intelligence Agency, and such administration officials as Special Assistants for National Security Affairs McGeorge Bundy and Walt W. Rostow. The files have two major limitations for use by researchers: processing and restrictions. Less than 5 percent of the almost ninety-five feet of material in the country file for Vietnam has been processed by the library staff, and security classifications severely restrict the use of even that which has been reviewed. The available papers, however, were useful.

An important supplement to the White House Central Files category of "Speeches" is the collection entitled "Statements of Lyndon B. Johnson, 1937–1968." Compiled by Dorothy Territo, the Johnson family archivist, the "Statements" files contain those drafts, memoranda, letters, and final copies of Johnson's addresses not placed in the subject files.

Two administrative tools that provided information about the details of president-press contacts are the Daily Diary and the Diary Backup. The president's Daily Diary, kept by Johnson's secretaries, chronicles Johnson's official and personal activities from the time he awakened to the time he retired. The diary lists appointments, speeches, telephone calls, meetings, and ceremonies, with names and exact times included. The subject of conversations and meetings, the president's reactions, and paraphrases of conversations as remembered by White House secretaries may be noted here, although detailed recountings and verbatim transcripts are not available. (While Johnson did tape record some meetings and conversations, the eight boxes of tapes now in storage at the library indicate that it was a relatively infrequent practice. Johnson stipulated that the cartons remain sealed for fifty years.)

The President's Appointment File, more generally known as the Diary Backup, contains background information, correspondence, memoranda, and notes pertaining to each day's schedule, appointments, and appearances. A day's files might therefore contain a memorandum from an aide regarding an interview with a journalist scheduled that day, with comments on the journalist's stated intention for seeking the interview and on past coverage of Johnson by both the journalist and the organization represented.

In addition, the Johnson Library has an extensive oral history collection, most of which was gathered under the auspices of the University of Texas Oral History Project. The tapes themselves are unavailable to researchers, and the transcriptions, which must be approved by the interviewee before they are deeded to the library, occasionally contain blank spaces labeled only "restricted by donor." Certain interviews are closed for a period of years or require the written permission of the donor for access. Unfortunately, the transcriptions often contain misspellings, inconsistencies, and nonsensical passages, thus requiring careful use. Yet the interviews offer a wealth of anecdotes and observations about all phases of Johnson's life, career, and personality. The interviews with George Christian, George Reedy, Drew Pearson, William S. White, Chet Huntley, and Arthur Krock were especially relevant to this study.

The above materials constituted the primary resources for the study. In addition, several collections from the Manuscripts Division of the Library of Congress were also examined, such as the papers of Agnes Meyer, writer and mother of Katherine Graham, the publisher of *Newsweek* and the *Washington Post*. Because the predominant source of materials was the Johnson Library, the Library of Congress materials are so designated in the Notes; all other file references are to the holdings of the Johnson Library.

Unpublished Sources

I. *Holdings of the Lyndon B. Johnson Library, Austin, Texas*

   A. Papers of Lyndon B. Johnson
      White House Central Files—By Subject, 1963–1969

Ex PR 18	Publicity (2' 4¼")
CF PR 18	Publicity (3")
CF PR 18-2	Press Conferences (5")
Ex PR 3	Administration Complaints—Criticisms (5")
Ex SP	Speeches to the Nation and to Groups (2' 4")
CF SP 3	Speeches to the Nation and to Groups (1' 2")
Ex ND 19/CO 312	National Security-Defense/Vietnam (2' 7½")
CF CO 312	Countries: Vietnam (2")
Ex FG	Federal Government (4½")

324

CF FG 1	Federal Government—Organizations—The President (4' 6")
Ex FG/RS/PR 18	Federal Government/Reports and Statistics/Publicity (4½")
CF FG/RS/PR 18	Federal Government/Reports and Statistics/Publicity (3")
CF FG 1-1 to FG 11-2-1	Federal Government—Organizations (6")
CF FG 600	Task Force on Asian Development (2")
CF WH 1 to WH 13	White House Administration (9")
Gen WH 3-2-2	White House Administration (4½")
Ex TR	Trips (2' 5½")
CF IT	International Organizations (¼")

Daily Diary, 1963–69
President's Appointment File, 1963–69 (Diary Backup)
Statements of Lyndon B. Johnson, 1963–69 (6' 2")
CF Oversized Attachments
Press Secretary's News Conferences
Vice-Presidential Security File, Vice-Presidential Travel

B. National Security Files

Country File: Vietnam (7')
Speech File (½")
National Security Council History: Deployment of Major U.S. Forces to Vietnam, July 1965 (9")
National Security Council History: March 31, 1968, Speech (2")
National Security Council History: Dominican Crisis, 1965 (−¼")

C. White House Central Files—By Name of Aide

Horace Busby, speech writer; longtime associate of Johnson's (7")
Joseph Califano, special assistant (1")
Douglass Cater, special assistant (1½')
George Christian, press secretary, January 1, 1967–January 19, 1969 (4")
Ernest Goldstein, special assistant, (1")
Richard Goodwin, speech writer (1")
Harry McPherson, special assistant; speech writer (9")
Bill D. Moyers, press secretary, July 9, 1965–January 1, 1967; speech writer; special assistant (2½")
Frederick Panzer, assistant press secretary (2' 3½")

George Reedy, press secretary, March 19, 1964–July 9, 1965 (1')
W. Marvin Watson, special assistant; appointments secretary (1' 4")

D. Oral History Interviews

Robert S. Allen, Washington columnist; former partner of Drew Pearson; May 30, 1969.

Peter B. Benchley, speech writer; White House staff assistant; November 20, 1968.

Lloyd Bentsen, U.S. senator, Texas; June 18, 1975.

Hale Boggs, U.S. congressman, Louisiana; no. 1, March 13, 1969; no. 2, March 27, 1969.

Joseph H. Carter, speech writer; December 3, 1968.

Douglass Cater, special assistant; no. 1, April 29, 1969; no. 2, May 8, 1969.

George Christian, press secretary; special assistant; no. 1, November 11, 1968; no. 2, December 4, 1969; no. 3, February 27, 1970; no. 4, June 30, 1970; no. 5, July 1, 1971.

Ernest Goldstein, special assistant; no. 1, December 9, 1968; no. 2, December 10, 1968; no. 3, December 19, 1968; no. 4, December 19, 1968.

Katherine Graham, publisher, *Washington Post*, March 13, 1969.

W. Averell Harriman, ambassador at large, 1965–68; undersecretary of state for political affairs; chief negotiator at the Paris Peace Talks concerning Vietnam, 1968–69; June 16, 1969.

Hubert H. Humphrey, vice-president of the United States, 1964–69; U.S. senator, Minnesota; August 17, 1971.

Chester R. Huntley, NBC News commentator; May 12, 1969.

Lyndon B. Johnson, interviewed by Walter Cronkite, CBS News: no. 1, December 27, 1969; no. 2, February 6, 1970; no. 3, May 2, 1970; no. 4, January 27, 1972; no. 5, February 1, 1973.

———, interviewed by Elspeth Rostow; September 28, 1970.

———, interviewed by Raymond Henle, director, Hoover Library, January 8, 1971.

———, interviewed by Robert C. McKay, chairman, National Education Association, May 21, 1965.

Sam E. Kinch, Sr., newspaperman; June 3, 1970.

Arthur Krock, newspaperman; author; November 21, 1968.

Gould Lincoln, newspaperman with the *Washington Evening Star*, 1909–67; September 28, 1968.

———, interviewed by Jerry N. Hess, Harry S. Truman Library; August 10, 1967.

326

John McCormack, Speaker of the House of Representatives; September 23, 1968.

Booth Mooney, biographer; journalist; April 8, 1969.

Richard Elliot Neustadt, special consultant; n.d. (approximately 1968–69).

Eugene Patterson, editor of the *Atlanta Constitution*, 1960–68; March 11, 1969.

Drew Pearson, newspaper columnist; April 10, 1969.

W. DeVier Pierson, special counsel; no. 1, March 19, 1969; no. 2, March 20, 1969; no. 3, March 27, 1969.

George Reedy, special assistant to the vice-president, 1961–63; press secretary; no. 1, December 12, 1968; no. 2, December 12, 1968; no. 3, December 19, 1968; no. 4, December 20, 1968; no. 5, February 14, 1972.

Chalmers Roberts, reporter, *Washington Post*, 1949–71; April 23, 1969.

Arthur M. Schlesinger, Jr., historian; author; presidential adviser to President Kennedy; November 4, 1971.

Whitney Shoemaker, special assistant; November 25, 1968.

Willie Day Taylor, secretary; no. 1, November 29, 1968; no. 2, November 29, 1968.

Bascom Nolly Timmons, newspaperman; March 6, 1969.

Edwin L. Weisl, Sr., lawyer; national Democratic committeeman; chief counsel, U.S. Senate Preparedness Committee; counsel, Committee on Space and Astronautics; May 13, 1969.

William S. White, biographer; journalist; columnist; no. 1, March 5, 1969; no. 2, March 10, 1969.

II. *Interviews by the author*

Liz Carpenter, July 20, 1979, Austin, Texas.
George Christian, July 18, 1979, Austin, Texas.
Bob Hardesty, July 20, 1979, Austin, Texas.
George E. Reedy, May 19, 1978, Milwaukee, Wisconsin.
James B. Reston, May 17, 1980, Notre Dame, Indiana
Walt W. Rostow, December 22, 1977, Austin, Texas.

III. *Holdings of the Library of Congress*

Papers of Agnes Meyer, writer and mother of Katherine Graham. Subject File: White House Correspondence, Johnson Administration.

Papers of Helen Rogers Reid, of the *New York Herald Tribune* publishing family. General Correspondence: Lyndon B. Johnson correspondence, 1959.

Papers of Eric Sevareid, CBS commentator. Book, Article, and Speech File: draft of *Candidates: 1960.*

Papers of Lawrence Spivak, creator and director of "Meet the Press." Selected transcripts of "Meet the Press," 1960–69.

IV. *Theses and Dissertations*

Bradley, George L. "A Critical Analysis of Lyndon Johnson's 'Peace' Rhetoric, 1963–1969." Ph.D. dissertation, University of Kansas, 1974.

Dill, Karen Dawn. "The Four-Step Flow of Communication: The Role of Government and the Mass Media in Influencing Public Opinion." M.A. thesis, University of Kansas, 1970.

Latimer, Harry David. "The Press Secretaries of Lyndon Johnson." Ph.D. dissertation, Brown University, 1973.

Pardue, Eugenia. "The President and the Press: A Case Study of Lyndon Johnson and the Washington Press Corps." M.A. thesis, Texas Christian University, 1969.

Published Sources

I. *Works by Johnson*

Johnson, Lyndon Baines. *The Vantage Point: Perspectives of the Presidency, 1963–1969.* New York: Holt, Rinehart and Winston, 1971.
———. *The Choices We Face.* New York: Bantam Books, 1969.
———. *This America.* New York: Random House, 1966.
———. *The Weekly Compilation of Presidential Papers.* Washington, D.C.: Office of the Federal Register, August 1965–January 1969.
———. *My Hope for America.* New York: Random House, 1964.
———. *A Time for Action: A Selection from the Speeches and Writings of Lyndon B. Johnson, 1953–1964.* New York: Atheneum, 1964.
———. *Public Papers of the Presidents of the United States: Lyndon B. Johnson.* 10 volumes. Washington, D.C.: Office of the Federal Register, National Archives and Records Service, 1963–69.
———. "Introduction." In *Essays on Radicalism in Contemporary*

America, ed. Leon Bordon Blair. Austin: University of Texas Press, 1972.

————. "In Quest of Peace." *Reader's Digest* 94 (February 1969): 221ff.

II. *Works About Johnson*

A. Books

Baker, Leonard, *The Johnson Eclipse: A President's Vice-Presidency.* New York: MacMillan, 1966.

Barton, Thomas F. *Lyndon B. Johnson: Young Texan.* Indianapolis: Bobbs-Merrill, 1973.

Bell, Jack. *The Johnson Treatment: How Lyndon B. Johnson Took Over the Presidency and Made It His Own.* New York: Harper & Row, 1965.

Berman, Larry. *Planning a Tragedy.* New York: W. W. Norton, 1982.

Burns, James McGregor, ed. *To Heal and to Build: The Programs of Lyndon B. Johnson.* New York: McGraw-Hill, 1968.

Caidin, Martin, and Edward Hymoff. *The Mission.* Philadelphia: J. B. Lippincott, 1964.

Caro, Robert A., *The Years of Lyndon Johnson: The Path to Power.* New York: Alfred A. Knopf, 1982.

Carpenter, Liz. *Ruffles and Flourishes.* New York: Doubleday, 1970.

Christian, George. *The President Steps Down: A Personal Memoir of the Transfer of Power.* New York: Macmillan, 1970.

Cormier, Frank. *LBJ: The Way He Was.* Garden City, N.Y.: Doubleday, 1977.

Davie, Michael. *LBJ: A Foreign Observer's Viewpoint.* New York: Ballantine Books, 1966.

Deakin, James. *Lyndon B. Johnson's Credibility Gap.* Washington, D.C.: Public Affairs Press, 1968.

Divine, Robert A., ed. *Exploring the Johnson Years.* Austin: University of Texas Press, 1981.

Dugger, Ronnie. *The Politician: The Life and Times of Lyndon Johnson—The Drive for Power, from the Frontier to Master of the Senate.* New York: W. W. Norton, 1982.

Evans, Rowland, and Robert Novak. *Lyndon B. Johnson: The Exercise of Power—A Political Biography.* New York: New American Library, 1966.

Faber, Harold, ed. *The Road to the White House: The Story of the 1964 Election by the Staff of The New York Times.* New York: McGraw-Hill, 1965.

Frantz, Joe B. *LBJ: Thirty-Seven Years of Public Life.* Shoal Creek Pub., 1974.

Geyelin, Philip L. *Lyndon B. Johnson and the World.* New York: F. A. Praeger, 1966.

Goldman, Eric F. *The Tragedy of Lyndon Johnson.* New York: Alfred A. Knopf, 1969.

Graff, Henry. *The Tuesday Cabinet: Deliberation and Decision on Peace and War under Lyndon B. Johnson.* Englewood Cliffs, N.J.: Prentice-Hall, 1970.

Haley, James Evetts. *A Texan Looks at Lyndon: A Study in Illegitimate Power.* Canyon, Tex.: Palo Duro Press, 1964.

Harvey, James C. *Black Civil Rights during the Johnson Administration.* Jackson: University and College Press of Mississippi, 1973.

Harwood, Richard, and Haynes Johnson. *Lyndon.* New York: *Washington Post* Book, Praeger, 1973.

Heath, Jim F. *Decade of Disillusionment: The Kennedy-Johnson Years.* Bloomington: Indiana University Press, 1975.

Heren, Louis. *No Hail, No Farewell.* New York: Harper & Row, 1970.

Hoopes, Townsend. *The Limits of Intervention: An Inside Account of How the Johnson Policy of Escalation Was Reversed.* New York: McKay, 1969.

Johnson, Lady Bird. *A White House Diary.* New York: Holt, Rinehart and Winston, 1970.

Johnson, Sam Houston. *My Brother Lyndon.* New York: Cowles, 1969.

Kearns, Doris. *Lyndon Johnson and the American Dream.* New York: Harper & Row, 1976.

Kluckhorn, Frank L. *Lyndon's Legacy: A Candid Look at the President's Policymakers.* New York: Devin-Adair, 1964.

LBJ: Images of A Vibrant Life. Austin: Friends of the LBJ Library, 1973.

Ladd, Bruce. *Crisis in Credibility.* New York: New American Library, 1968.

Lichtenstein, Nelson, ed. *Political Profiles: Johnson Years.* New York: Facts on File, Inc., 1976.

Lincoln, Evelyn, *Kennedy and Johnson.* New York: Holt, Rinehart and Winston, 1968.

Maguire, Jack R. *Talk of Texas.* Shoal Creek Pub., 1973.

McGaffin, William, and Erwin Knoll. *Anything But the Truth: The Credibility Gap—How the News is Managed in Washington.* New York: G. P. Putnam's Sons, 1968.

McDowell, Charles, Jr. *Campaign Fever: The National Folk Festival from New Hampshire to November 1964.* New York: William Morrow, 1965.

McPherson, Harry. *A Political Education*. Boston: Little, Brown, 1972.

Miller, Merle. *Lyndon: An Oral Biography*. New York: G. P. Putnam's Sons, 1980.

Mooney, Booth. *LBJ: An Irreverent Chronicle*. New York: T. Y. Crowell, 1976.

————. *The Lyndon Johnson Story*. Rev. ed. New York: Farrar, Straus, 1964.

Newlon, Clarke. *L.B.J.: The Man from Johnson City*. New York: Dodd, Mead, 1964.

Petit, Don R., ed. *Inaugural 1965: Threshold of Tomorrow—The Great Society*. Washington, D.C.: 1965 Presidential Inaugural Committee, 1965.

Pool, William C., Emmie Craddock, and David S. Conrad. *Lyndon Baines Johnson: The Formative Years*. San Marcos: Southwest Texas State College Press, 1965.

Provence, Harry. *Lyndon B. Johnson: A Biography*. New York: Fleet Pub., 1964.

Reedy, George. *Lyndon B. Johnson: A Memoir*. New York: Andrews and McMeel, Inc., 1982.

Roberts, Charles. *LBJ's Inner Circle*. New York: Delacorte Press, 1965.

Rowen, Hobart. *The Free Enterprisers: Kennedy, Johnson, and the Business Establishment*. New York: G. P. Putnam's Sons, 1964.

Schandler, Herbert Y. *The Unmaking of the President*. Princeton: Princeton University Press, 1977.

Sherrill, Robert. *The Accidental President*. New York: Pyramid Books, 1968.

Sidey, Hugh. *A Very Personal Presidency: Lyndon Johnson in the White House*. New York: Atheneum, 1968.

Steinberg, Alfred. *Sam Johnson's Boy: A Close-up of the President from Texas*. New York: Macmillan, 1968.

Valenti, Jack. *A Very Human President*. New York: Pocket Books, 1976.

White, Theodore H. *The Making of the President, 1968*. New York: Atheneum, 1969.

————. *The Making of the President, 1964*. New York: Atheneum, 1965.

————. *The Making of the President, 1960*. New York: Atheneum, 1961.

White, William S. *The Professional: Lyndon B. Johnson*. Boston: Houghton Mifflin, 1964.

Wicker, Tom. *JFK and LBJ: The Influence of Personality Upon Politics*. New York: William Morrow, 1968.

Ziegler, Henry O. *Lyndon B. Johnson: Man and President*. New York: Popular Library, 1963.

B. Articles and Chapters

Alsop, Stewart. "Lyndon Johnson: How Does He Do It?" *Saturday Evening Post*. January 24, 1959, 213–14.

Andrews, James R. "The Rhetoric of Alliance." *Today's Speech* 16 (February 1968): 20–24.

Bagdikian, Ben H. "Press Agent—But Still President." *Columbia Journalism Review* 4 (Summer 1965): 10–13.

———. "JFK to LBJ: Paradoxes of Change." *Columbia Journalism Review* 2 (Winter 1964): 32–36.

Barrett, Marvin. "When LBJ Stunned the Experts." *Columbia Journalism Review* 7 (Summer 1968): 10.

Benchley, Peter. "Rose Garden Rubbish and Other Glorious Compositions." *Life*, May 23, 1969, 60B–60D.

Brooks, William D. "A Field Study of the Johnson and Goldwater Campaign Speeches in Pittsburgh." *Southern Speech Journal* 32 (Summer 1967): 273–81.

Bunge, Walter, Robert V. Hudson, and Chung Woo Suh. "Johnson's Information Strategy for Vietnam: An Evaluation." *Journalism Quarterly* 45 (Autumn 1968): 419–25.

Conkin, Paul K. "The Johnson Years: An Essay Review." *Wisconsin Magazine of History* 56 (Autumn 1972): 59–64.

Connelly, F. Marlin. "Some Questions Concerning Lyndon Johnson's Rhetoric in the 1964 Presidential Campaign." *Southern Speech Communication Journal* 37 (Fall 1971): 11–20.

Cornwell, Elmer E., Jr. "The Johnson Press Relations Style." *Journalism Quarterly* 43 (Spring): 3–9.

Deakin, James. "The Dark Side of LBJ." *Esquire* 68 (August 1967): 45–48, 134–35.

Dovring, Karin. "New Deal for the World." *Frontiers of Communication: The Americas in Search of Political Culture*, 57–64. Boston: Christopher Publishing Co., 1975.

Gordon, William, and Robert Bunker. "The Sentimental Side of Mr. Johnson." *Southern Speech Journal* 52 (Fall 1966): 58–66.

Hall, Robert N. "Lyndon Johnson's Speech Preparation." *Quarterly Journal of Speech* 51 (April 1965): 409–14.

332

———. "Lyndon B. Johnson's Speaking in the 1941 Senate Campaign." *Southern Speech Journal* 30 (Fall 1964): 15–23.

Harding, H. F. "Democratic Nominee: Lyndon B. Johnson." *Quarterly Journal of Speech* 50 (December 1964): 409–14.

Hendrix, J. A. "The Shivercrat Rebellion: A Case Study in Campaign Speaking Strategies." *Southern Speech Journal* 33 (Summer 1968): 289–95.

Huitt, Ralph K. "Democratic Party Leadership in the Senate." *American Political Science Review* 55 (June 1961): 333–44.

Ivie, Robert L. "Presidential Motives for War." *Quarterly Journal of Speech* 60 (October 1974): 337–45.

Kearns, Doris. "Lyndon Johnson's Political Personality." *Political Science Quarterly* 91 (Fall 1976): 385–410.

Klaw, Barbara. "Lady Bird Johnson Remembers." *American Heritage* 31 (December 1980): 4–17.

McCroskey, James C., and Samuel V. O. Prichard. "Selective Exposure and Lyndon B. Johnson's 1966 'State of the Union' Address." *Journal of Broadcasting* 11 (Fall 1967): 331–37.

McGaffin, William, and Erwin Knoll. "The White House Lies." *Progressive*, September 1967, 13–18.

Moyers, Bill D. "The Press and Government: Who's Telling the Truth." In *Mass Media in a Free Society*, ed. Warren K. Agee, 16–37. Lawrence: University Press of Kansas, 1969.

Patton, John H. "An End and a Beginning: Lyndon B. Johnson's Decisive Speech of March 31, 1968." *Today's Speech* 21 (Summer 1973): 33–41.

Phelps, Waldo, and Andrea Beck. "Lyndon Johnson's Address at the U.C.L.A. Charter Day Ceremony." *Western Speech* 29 (Summer 1965): 162–71.

Pratt, James W. "An Analysis of Three Crisis Speeches." *Western Speech* 34 (Summer 1970): 194–203.

Rovere, Richard H. "Letter from Washington." *New Yorker*, September 1967, 157–60 and 164–68.

Sellen, Robert W. "Old Assumptions versus New Realities: Lyndon Johnson and Foreign Policy." *International Journal* 28 (Spring 1973): 205–29.

Sidey, Hugh. "Around the World with Lyndon B. Magellan." *Life,* January 5, 1969, 24B–24D.

Smith, F. Michael. "Rhetorical Implications of the 'Aggression' Thesis in the Johnson Administration's Vietnam Argumentation." *Central States Speech Journal* 23 (Winter 1972): 217–24.

Turner, Kathleen J. "Press Influence on Presidential Rhetoric: Lyndon Johnson at Johns Hopkins University, April 7, 1965." *Central States Speech Journal* 33 (Fall 1982): 425–36.

Weiss, Harold, and Haddon Robinson. "Lyndon B. Johnson." *Quarterly Journal of Speech* 46 (October 1960): 241.

Williams, T. Harry. "Huey, Lyndon, and Southern Radicalism." *Journal of American History* 60 (September 1973): 267–93.

Wise, David. "Those White House Tranquilizers." *Columbia Journalism Review* 4 (Winter 1966): 17–20.

III. *The Presidency, the Press, and Public Opinion*

A. Books

Aronson, James. *The Press and the Cold War.* Indianapolis: Bobbs-Merrill, 1970.

Barber, James David, ed. *Race for the Presidency: The Media and the Nominating Process.* Englewood Cliffs, N.J.: Prentice-Hall, 1978.

Barber, James David. *The Presidential Character.* Englewood Cliffs, N.J.: Prentice-Hall, 1972.

Bartley, Robert L., Irving Kristol, Rowland Evans, Douglass Cater, and Paul H. Weaver. *Press, Politics, and Popular Government.* Ed. George F. Will. Washington, D.C.: American Enterprise Institute for Public Policy Research, 1972.

Bloom, Melvyn H. *Public Relations and Presidential Campaigns.* New York: Thomas Y. Crowell, 1973.

Boorstin, Daniel J. *The Image: A Guide to Pseudo-Events in America.* New York: Harper & Row, 1961.

Braestrup, Peter. *Big Story: How the American Press and Television Reported and Interpreted the Crisis of Tet 1968 in Vietnam and Washington.* 2 vols. Boulder, Colo.: Westview Press, 1977.

Broder, David S. *Changing of the Guard: Power and Leadership in America.* New York: Simon and Schuster, 1980.

Brown, Charlene J., Trevor R. Brown, and William L. Rivers. *The Media and the People.* New York: Holt, Rinehart and Winston, 1978.

Cater, Douglass. *Power in Washington: A Critical Look at Today's Struggle to Govern in the Nation's Capital.* New York: Random House, 1964.

———. *The Fourth Branch of Government.* New York: Random House, Vintage Books, 1959.

334

Cirino, Robert. *Power to Persuade: Mass Media and the News.* New York: Bantam, 1974.

Chase, Harold W., and Allen H. Lerman, eds. *Kennedy and the Press: The News Conferences.* New York: Thomas Y. Crowell Co., 1965.

Clarkson, Jesse D., and Thomas C. Cochran, eds. *War as a Social Institution: The Historian's Perspective.* New York: Columbia University Press, 1941.

Cohen, Bernard C. *The Press and Foreign Policy.* Princeton: Princeton University Press, 1963.

Cornwell, Elmer E., Jr. *Presidential Leadership of Public Opinion.* Bloomington: Indiana University Press, 1965.

Crouse, Timothy. *The Boys on the Bus.* New York: Ballantine Books, 1972.

Dickerson, Nancy. *Among Those Present.* New York: Random House, 1976.

Dunn, Delmer D. *Public Officials and the Press.* Reading, Mass.: Addison-Wesley Pub., 1969.

Edelman, Murray. *The Symbolic Uses of Politics.* Urbana: University of Illinois Press, 1964.

Gallup, George H. *The Gallup Poll—Public Opinion, 1935–1971.* Vol. 3, *1959–1971.* New York: Random House, 1972.

Geyelin, Philip L., and Douglass Cater. *American Media: Adequate or Not?* Washington: American Enterprise Institute for Public Policy Research, 1970.

Graber, Doris A. *Verbal Behavior and Politics.* Urbana: University of Illinois Press, 1976.

Grossman, Michael Baruch, and Martha Joynt Kumar. *Portraying the President: The White House and the News Media..* Baltimore: Johns Hopkins University Press, 1981.

Hargrove, Erwin C. *The Power of the Modern Presidency.* Philadelphia: Temple University Press, 1974.

———. *Presidential Leadership: Personality and Political Style.* New York: Macmillan, 1966.

Koenig, Louis. *The Chief Executive.* New York: Harcourt, Brace & World, 1968.

———. *The Invisible Presidency.* New York: Rinehart, 1960.

Kraft, Joseph. *Profiles in Power: A Washington Insight.* New York: New American Library, 1966.

Krock, Arthur. *Memoirs: Sixty Years on the Firing Line.* New York: Funk and Wagnalls, 1968.

———. *In the Nation: 1932–1966.* New York: McGraw-Hill, 1966.

MacDougall, A. Kent. *The Press: A Critical Look from the Inside.* Princeton, N.J.: Dow Jones Books, 1972.

MacNeil, Robert. *The People Machine: The Influence of Television on American Politics.* New York: Harper & Row, 1968.

McGinniss, Joe. *The Selling of the President, 1968.* New York: Pocket Books, 1968.

Minow, Newton N., John Bartlow Martin, and Lew M. Mitchell. *Presidential Television.* Twentieth Century Fund Report. New York: Basic Books, 1973.

"Mr. President . . . Mr. President . . . ?" Transcript of "Inside Story," aired on PBS, November 1981.

Mueller, John F. *War, Presidents, and Public Opinion.* New York: Wiley, 1973.

Nearing, Scott. *War or Peace?* New York: Island Press, 1946.

Neustadt, Richard. *Presidential Power: The Politics of Leadership.* New York: Wiley, 1960.

O'Donnell, Kenneth P., and David F. Powers. *"Johnny, We Hardly Knew Ye": Memories of John Fitzgerald Kennedy.* Boston: Little, Brown, 1970.

Paletz, David L., and Robert M. Entman. *Media Power Politics.* New York: Free Press, 1981.

Pollard, James. *The Presidents and the Press.* New York: Macmillan, 1947.

Purvis, Hoyt, ed. *The Presidency and the Press.* Austin: Lyndon B. Johnson School of Public Affairs, University of Texas at Austin, 1976.

Rather, Dan, with Mickey Herskowitz. *The Camera Never Blinks: The Adventures of a TV Journalist.* New York: Ballantine Books, 1977.

Reedy, George E. *The Presidency in Flux.* New York: Columbia University Press, 1973.

———. *The Twilight of the Presidency.* New York: World Publishing, 1970.

Reston, James. *The Artillery of the Press: Its Influence on American Foreign Policy.* New York: Harper & Row, 1966.

Rivers, William L. *The Adversaries: Politics and the Press.* Boston: Beacon Press, 1970.

———. *The Opinionmakers: The Washington Press Corps.* Boston: Beacon Press, 1965, 1967.

Roberts, Charles W. *The President and the Press.* Newspaper Guild Lecture. Minneapolis: University of Minnesota, 1966.

336

Rosenau, James N. *Public Opinion and Foreign Policy: An Operational Formulation.* New York: Random House, 1961.

Roshko, Bernard. *Newsmaking.* Chicago: University of Chicago Press, 1975.

Schlesinger, Arthur M., Jr., and Alfred de Grazia. *Congress and the Presidency: Their Role in Modern Times.* Washington, D.C.: American Enterprise Institute for Public Policy Research, 1967.

Schlesinger, Arthur M., Jr. *The Imperial Presidency.* New York: Popular Library, 1973.

Small, William T. *To Kill a Messenger.* New York: Hastings House, 1970.

Smith, A. Merriman. *Merriman Smith's Book of Presidents: A White House Memoir.* Ed. Timothy G. Smith. New York: Norton, 1972.

———. *Thank You, Mr. President.* New York: Harper & Row, 1946.

Smith, Howard K., Osborn Elliott, and Merriman Smith. *The News Media—A Service and a Force.* Ed. Festus Justin Viser. Memphis, Tenn.: Memphis State University Press, 1970.

Sorensen, Theodore C. *Watchmen in the Night: Presidential Accountability after Watergate.* Cambridge: MIT Press, 1975.

Spragens, William C., and Carole Ann Terwoord. *From Spokesman to Press Secretary: White House Media Operations.* Washington, D.C.: University Press of America, 1981.

Steel, Ronald. *Walter Lippmann and the American Century.* Boston: Little, Brown, 1980.

Stein, M. L. *When Presidents Meet the Press.* New York: Julian Messner, 1969.

West, J. B. *Upstairs at the White House.* New York: Warner Books, 1973.

Wyckoff, Gene. *The Image Candidates: American Politics in the Age of Television.* New York: Macmillan, 1968.

B. Articles

Bagdikian, Ben H. "The Way It Was and the Way I Call Them: An Appraisal of the Accuracy of Public Affairs Columnists." *Columbia Journalism Review* 5 (Fall 1966): 5–10.

———. "How Editors Pick Columnists." *Columbia Journalism Review* 5 (Spring 1966): 40–45.

———. "The President Nonspeaks." *Columbia Journalism Review* 2 (Spring 1963): 42–46.

Balutis, Alan P. "Congress, the President and the Press." *Journalism Quarterly* 53 (Autumn 1976): 509–15.

Berg, David M. "Communicating with the People: The Relationship between Government and the Press." *Quarterly Journal of Speech* 57 (October 1971): 349–57.

Converse, Philip E., Warren E. Miller, Jerold G. Rusk, and Arthur C. Wolfe. "Continuity and Change in American Politics: Parties and Issues in the 1968 Election." *American Political Science Review* 63 (December 1969): 1083–105.

Cornwell, Elmer E., Jr. "Presidential News: The Expanding Public Image." *Journalism Quarterly* 36 (Summer 1959): 275–83.

DeWeerd, A. A. "Civilian and Military Elements in Modern War." In *War as a Social Institution*, ed. J. D. Clarkson and T. C. Cochran, 95–112. New York: Columbia University Press, 1941.

Goodman, Sandy. "Can *Newsweek* Really Separate Fact from Opinion?" *Columbia Journalism Review* 7 (Summer 1968): 26–29.

Grossman, Michael B., and Francis E. Rourke. "The Media and the Presidency: An Exchange Analysis." *Political Science Quarterly* 91 (Fall 1976): 455–70.

Lippmann, Walter. "On Understanding Society." *Columbia Journalism Review* 8 (Fall 1969): 5–9.

Peabody, Robert L., Norman J. Ornstein, and David W. Rohde. "The United States Senate as a Presidential Incubator: Many Are Called but Few Are Chosen." *Political Science Quarterly* 91 (Summer 1976): 237–58.

Pious, Richard M. "Is Presidential Power 'Poison'?" *Political Science Quarterly* 89 (Fall 1974): 627–43.

"Report on Simultaneous Television Network Coverage of Presidential Addresses to the Nation." *Congressional Record.* January 20, 1976, H 105–9.

Reston, James. "The Press, the President and Foreign Policy." *Foreign Affairs* 44 (July 1966): 553–73.

———. "The President and Public Opinion." In *Theory and Practice of American Foreign Policy*, ed. Morton Gordon and Kenneth N. Vines, 194–204. New York: T. Y. Crowell, 1955.

Steinberg, Charles S. "The Olympian: Walter Lippmann's Career as a Philosopher-Journalist," *Columbia Journalism Review* 7 (Fall 1968): 26–30.

Stern, Laurence, and Erwin Knoll. "Washington: Outsiders' Expose." *Columbia Journalism Review* 3 (Spring 1964): 18–23.

Wicker, Tom. "The Greening of the Press." *Columbia Journalism Review* 10 (May/June 1971): 7–12.

Witcover, Jules. "How Well Does the White House Press Perform?" *Columbia Journalism Review* 12 (Nov./Dec. 1973): 39–43.

338

———. "Salvaging the Presidential Press Conference." *Columbia Journalism Review* 9 (Fall 1970): 27–34.

IV. *Vietnam and American Foreign Policy*

A. Books

Arlen, Michael J. *Living-Room War.* New York: Viking Press, 1969.

Bacciocco, Edward J., Jr. *The New Left in America: Reform to Revolution, 1956 to 1970.* Stanford: Hoover Institution Press, Stanford University, 1974.

Berman, Larry. *Planning a Tragedy: The Americanization of the War in Vietnam.* New York: W. W. Norton, 1982.

Cooper, Chester. *The Lost Crusade: America in Vietnam.* New York: Dodd, Mead, 1970.

Draper, Theodore. *The Abuse of Power.* New York: Viking, 1966.

Fifield, Russell H. *Americans in Southeast Asia: The Roots of Commitment.* New York: T. Y. Crowell, 1973.

Gelb, Leslie H., and Richard K. Betts, *The Irony of Vietnam: The System Worked.* Washington, D.C.: Brookings Institution, 1979.

Gettleman, Marvin E., ed. *Viet Nam: History, Documents, and Opinions on a Major World Crisis.* Greenwich, Conn.: Fawcett Publications, 1965.

Goodwin, Richard. *Triumph or Tragedy?* New York: Random House, 1966.

Griffin, Clifford S. *Their Brother's Keeper: Moral Stewardship in the United States, 1800–1865.* New Brunswick, N.J.: Rutgers University Press, 1960.

Halberstam, David. *The Best and the Brightest.* Greenwich, Conn.: Fawcett Publications, 1969.

———. *The Making of a Quagmire.* New York: Random House, 1964.

Kahin, George, and John Lewis. *The U.S. in Vietnam.* New York: Delta, 1967.

Kalb, Marvin, and Elie Abel. *The Roots of Involvement.* New York: W. W. Norton, 1971.

Kendrick, Alexander. *The Wound Within: America in the Vietnam Years, 1945–74.* Boston: Little, Brown, 1974.

Lewy, Guenter. *America in Vietnam.* New York: Oxford University Press, 1978.

Lifton, Robert Jay. *Home from the War.* New York: Simon and Schuster, 1973.

Oberdorfer, Don. *Tet!* Garden City, N. Y.: Doubleday, 1971.

Poole, Peter A. *The United States and Indochina, from FDR to Nixon.* Hinsdale, Ill.: Dryden Press, 1973.

Reedy, George E. *Who Will Do Our Fighting For Us?* New York: World Pub., 1969.

Rostow, W. W. *The Diffusion of Power.* New York: Macmillan, 1972.

Rovere, Richard. *Waist Deep in the Big Muddy.* Boston: Little, Brown, 1968.

Salisbury, Harrison. *Behind the Lines—Hanoi: December 23–January 7.* New York: Harper & Row, 1967.

Schlesinger, Arthur M., Jr. *The Bitter Heritage: Vietnam and American Democracy, 1941–1966.* Greenwich, Conn.: Fawcett Publications, 1967.

Schoenbrun, David. *Vietnam: How We Got In, How to Get Out.* New York: Atheneum, 1968.

Sheehan, Neil, Hedrick Smith, E. W. Kenworthy, and Fox Butterfield, eds. *The Pentagon Papers as Published by the New York Times.* New York: Bantam Books, 1971.

Vogelsang, Sandy. *The Long Dark Night of the Soul: The American Intellectual Left and the Vietnam War.* New York: Harper & Row, 1974.

Westmoreland, William C. *A Soldier Reports.* New York: Doubleday, 1976.

White, Ralph K. *Nobody Wanted War: Misperceptions in Vietnam and Other Wars.* Garden City, N.Y.: Doubleday, 1968.

Zacharias, Donald W., ed. *In Pursuit of Peace: Speeches of the Sixties.* New York: Random House, 1970.

B. Articles and Chapters

Arbatov, G. A. "American Foreign Policy on the Threshold of the 1970's." *Orbis* 15 (Spring 1971): 134–53.

"Are We Getting Through?" *Columbia Journalism Review* 5 (Fall 1966): 41–44.

Bailey, George. "Interpretive Reporting of the Vietnam War by Anchormen." *Journalism Quarterly* 53 (Summer 1976): 319–24.

———. "Television War: Trends in Network Coverage of Vietnam, 1965–1970." *Journal of Broadcasting* 20 (Spring 1976): 147–58.

Bailey, George, and Lawrence W. Lichty. "Rough Justice on a Saigon Street: A Gatekeeper Study of NBC's Tet Execution Film." *Journalism Quarterly* 49 (Summer 1972): 221–29.

340

"Behind the Vietnam Story." *Columbia Journalism Review* 3 (Winter 1965): 14–18.

Blumberg, Nathan. "Misreporting the Peace Movement." *Columbia Journalism Review* 9 (Winter 1970–71): 28–32.

Boylan, James. "A Salisbury Chronicle." *Columbia Journalism Review* 5 (Winter 1966–67): 10–14.

Browne, Malcolm W. "Viet Nam Reporting: Three Years of Crisis." *Columbia Journalism Review* 3 (Fall 1964): 4–9.

Clifford, Clark M. "A Viet Nam Reappraisal: The Personal History of One Man's View and How It Evolved." *Foreign Affairs* 47 (July 1969): 601–22.

Davison, W. Phillips. "Making Sense of Viet Nam News." *Columbia Journalism Review* 5 (Winter 1966–67): 5–9.

Diamond, Edwin. "Who is 'The Enemy'?" *Columbia Journalism Review* 9 (Winter 1970–71): 38–39.

Draper, Theodore. "The Dominican Intervention Reconsidered." *Political Science Quarterly* 86 (March 1971): 1–36.

Fall, Bernard. "Master of the Red Jab." *Saturday Evening Post*, November 24, 1962, 18–21.

Friendly, Fred W. "TV at the Turning Point." *Columbia Journalism Review* 9 (Winter 1970–71): 13–20.

Fulbright, J. William. "Introduction." In *The Vietnam Hearings*, i–v. New York: Random House, 1966.

Gelb, Leslie H. "The Essential Domino: American Politics and Vietnam." *Foreign Affairs* 50 (April 1972): 459–75.

Gibson, Scott L. "'Radical' Trends in American Historiography: The New Left and the Vietnam War." *Michigan Academician* 5 (Spring 1973): 457–63.

Goodman, Allan E. "Ending the Viet Nam Conflict: Expectations in Hanoi and Saigon." *Orbis* 16 (Fall 1972): 632–45.

Gregg, Richard B. "The 1966 Senate Foreign Relations Committee Hearings on Vietnam Policy: A Phenomenological Analysis." In *Explorations in Rhetorical Criticism*, ed. G. P. Mohrmann, Charles J. Stewart, and Donovan Ochs, 223–43. University Park, Pa.: Pennsylvania State University Press, 1973.

Johnstone, William C. "The Political Commitment." *Current History* 54 (January 1968): 1–6.

McCartney, James. "Can the Media Cover Guerrilla Wars?" *Columbia Journalism Review* 7 (Winter 1970–71): 33–37.

MacDonald, Charles B. "Official History and the War in Vietnam." *Military Affairs* 32 (Spring 1968): 2–11.

McGovern, George, and John P. Roche. "The Pentagon Papers: A Discussion." *Political Science Quarterly* 87 (June 1972): 173–91.

McNulty, Thomas M. "Vietnam Specials: Policy and Content." *Journal of Communication* 25 (Autumn 1975): 173–80.

"Media and Vietnam: An Appraisal." *Columbia Journalism Review* 9 (Winter 1970–71): 26–27.

"Passing Comments: Views of the Editors." *Columbia Journalism Review* 5 (Winter 1966–67): 2.

"Passing Comments: Views of the Editors—Viet Nam, Viet Nam." *Columbia Journal Review* 7 (Spring 1968): 2.

Porter, D. Gareth. "Vietnam: Politics of the Paris Agreement." *Current History* 65 (December 1973): 247–51, 272.

Roskin, Michael. "From Pearl Harbor to Vietnam: Shifting Generational Paradigms and Foreign Policy." *Political Science Quarterly* 89 (Fall 1974): 563–88.

Schoenbrun, David. "My Peace Feeler." *Columbia Journalism Review* 4 (Winter 1966): 26–27.

Shaplen, Robert. "The Challenge Ahead." *Columbia Journalism Review* 9 (Winter 1970–71): 40–46.

Showalter, Stuart W. "American Magazine Coverage of Objectors to the Vietnam War." *Journalism Quarterly* 53 (Winter 1976): 648–52, 688.

Stillman, Don. "Tonkin: What Should Have Been Asked." *Columbia Journalism Review* 9 (Winter 1970–71): 21–25.

Van Alstyne, Richard W. "The Vietnam War in Historical Perspective." *Current History* 65 (December 1973): 241–46, 273–74.

"Vietnam Register." *Columbia Journalism Review* 6 (Winter 1967–68): 4–13.

Witcover, Jules. "Where Washington Reporting Failed." *Columbia Journalism Review* 9 (Winter 1970–71): 7–12.

Wright, James D. "*Life, Time,* and the Fortunes of War." *Transaction* 9 (January 1972): 42–52.

V. *General Contemporary Histories*

Druks, Herbert. *From Truman through Johnson: A Documentary History.* 2 vols. New York: Robert Speller & Sons, 1971.

Gardner, Lloyd C., Arthur M. Schlesinger, Jr., and Hans J. Morgenthau. *The Origins of the Cold War.* Waltham, Mass.: Ginn-Blaisdell, 1970.

342

Kirkendall, Richard S. *The Global Power: The United States Since 1941*. Boston: Allyn and Bacon, 1973.

Schlesinger, Arthur M., Jr., ed. *The Dynamics of World Power: A Documentary History of United States Foreign Policy, 1945–1973*. Vol. 4, *The Far East*, R. Buhite. New York: Chelsea House Publishers, 1973.

———. *The Crisis of Confidence: Ideas, Power, and Violence in America*. Boston: Houghton Mifflin, 1969.

———. *A Thousand Days: John F. Kennedy in the White House*. Boston: Houghton Mifflin, 1965.

Sorensen, Theodore C., *Kennedy*. New York: Harper & Row, 1965.

———. *Decision-Making in the White House: The Olive Branch or the Arrows*. New York: Columbia University Press, 1964.

Steinbeck, John. *America and Americans*. New York: Viking Press, 1966; Bantam Books, 1968.

Sundquist, James L. *Politics and Policy: The Eisenhower, Kennedy, and Johnson Years*. Washington, D.C.: Brookings Institution, 1968.

VI. *Contemporary Press Accounts*

New York Times, 1963–69.

Newsweek, 1963–69.

Time, 1963–69.

U.S. News and World Report, 1963–69.

Washington Post, 1963–69.

VII. *Contemporary Historical Methodology*

A. Books

Barraclough, Geoffrey. *An Introduction to Contemporary History*. New York: Basic Books, 1964.

Brooks, Philip C. *Research in Archives: The Use of Unpublished Primary Sources*. Chicago: University of Chicago Press, 1969.

Clark, G. Kitson. *The Critical Historian*. New York: Basic Books, Inc., 1967.

Hexter, J. H. *The History Primer*. New York: Basic Books, 1971.

———. *Reappraisals in History*. Evanston: Northwestern University Press, 1962.

Kirkendall, Richard S., ed. *The Truman Period as a Research Field: A Reappraisal, 1972*. Columbia: University of Missouri Press, 1974.

———. *The Truman Period as a Research Field.* Columbia: University of Missouri Press, 1967.

Loewenheim, Francis L., ed. *The Historian and the Diplomat: The Role of History and Historians in American Foreign Policy.* New York: Harper & Row, 1967.

Perman, Dagmar Horna, ed. *Bibliography and the Historian.* Santa Barbara, Calif.: Clio, 1968.

Saveth, Edward N., ed. *American History and the Social Sciences.* New York: Free Press of Glencoe, 1964.

Small, Melvin, ed. *Public Opinion and History: Interdisciplinary Perspectives.* Detroit: Wayne State University Press, 1970.

Smith, Page. *The Historian and History.* New York: Alfred A. Knopf, 1966.

Stephens, Lester D., ed. and comp. *Historiography: A Bibliography.* Metuchen, N.J.: Scarecrow Press, 1975.

Winks, Robin W., ed. *The Historian as Detective: Essays on Evidence.* New York: Harper & Row, 1968.

B. Articles

Bogue, Alan G. "U.S.A.: The 'New' Political History." *Journal of Contemporary History* 3 (January 1968): 5–27.

Kirkendall, Richard S. "A Second Look at Presidential Libraries." *American Archivist* 29 (July 1966): 371–86.

———. "Presidential Libraries—One Researcher's Point of View." *American Archivist* 25 (October 1962): 441–48.

Luthy, Herbert. "What's the Point of History?" *Journal of Contemporary History* 3 (April 1968): 3–22.

Mazlish, Bruce. "Group Psychology and Problems of Contemporary History." *Journal of Contemporary History* 3 (April 1968): 163–77.

Medlicott, W. N. "Contemporary History in Biography." *Journal of Contemporary History* 7 (Jan./April 1972): 71–106.

Mousnier, Roland, and Rene Pillorget. "Contemporary History and Historians of the Sixteenth and Seventeenth Centuries." *Journal of Contemporary History* 3 (April 1967): 93–109.

Schlesinger, Arthur M., Jr. "On the Writing of Contemporary History." *Atlantic Monthly* 219 (April 1967): 69–74.

Thomson, David. "The Writing of Contemporary History." *Journal of Contemporary History* 2 (January 1967): 25–34.

Tugwell, Rexford G. "The President and His Helpers: A Review-Article." *Political Science Quarterly* 82 (June 1967): 253–67.

Woodward, C. Vann. "History and the Third Culture." *Journal of Contemporary History* 3 (April 1968): 23–35.

Index

350